FAMILY VALUES AND THE NEW SOCIETY

FAMILY VALUES AND THE NEW SOCIETY

Dilemmas of the 21st Century

GEORGE P. SMITH II

Westport, Connecticut
London

Library of Congress Cataloging-in-Publication Data

Smith, George Patrick, 1939–
    Family values and the new society : dilemmas of the 21st century /
George P. Smith II.
        p.   cm.
    Includes bibliographical references and index.
    ISBN 0–275–96221–0 (alk. paper)
    1. Family.   2. Family—Moral and ethical aspects.   3. Social
values.   I. Title.
HQ518.S634 1998
306.85—dc21   97–43942

British Library Cataloguing in Publication Data is available.

Library of Congress Catalog Card Number: 97–43942
ISBN: 0–275–96221–0

First published in 1998

Praeger Publishers, 88 Post Road West, Westport, CT 06881
An imprint of Greenwood Publishing Group, Inc.

Printed in the United States of America

The paper used in this book complies with the
Permanent Paper Standard issued by the National
Information Standards Organization (Z39.48–1984).

10 9 8 7 6 5 4 3 2

To Charles and Jana Britton, Patrick and Patricia Clendenen, Robert and Joan Everitt, Allan and Linda Kaulbach, Douglas and Carol Kmiec, Raymond and Julia Marcin, Giovanna and Kenneth Nunnenkamp, Kent and Suzann Owen, James and Allison Prenetta, as well as George and Rosalind Winterton, whose lives validate the integrity of the family as an institution and whose wonderful friendships have fortified and renewed my faith over the years.

Contents

Preface

The chapters presented in this book focus on a number of situations where old and new moral and ethical values, together with political and social forces, are, depending on one's view, combining to either challenge or enhance the traditional notion of family. Moral and religious convictions, as well as levels of cultural tolerance or intolerance, inevitably shape beliefs about the family, and these in turn will vary, often dramatically, from community to community and from state to state. Beliefs are all too often tested and sustained by emotional feeling rather than objective analysis.

Under five major headings, I have sought to present an objective analysis of complex normative value systems as they are tested within the family unit. Originally, I had planned to have an opening chapter in this book devoted to religious principles and views on the family and to show how they have structured traditional thinking here. I decided against this approach because as I researched the specific chapter areas within the headings, I found a pervasiveness of religious, ethical, and moral values throughout all of the areas of concern. Consequently, these values, principles, and concerns have been presented—and indeed integrated—into the considerations in well over half of the chapters.

The centrality of motherhood—its reproductive rights and responsibilities, together with the limits of its societal recognition for single, unmarried women, and the state's efforts to regulate its development—is examined within different social contexts and degrees of integration simply because its conventional recognition in the state of marriage is the foundation for what has become recognized as the traditional family. While a generalist overview of feminism is undertaken in Chapter 2, within Chapters 3, 4, 5, 6, and 7 are found an in-depth exploration of the themes raised originally in Chapter 2 itself. The reason for this is that the concerns of feminist philosophy for reproductive autonomy and equality in marital relationships are basic to any understanding of the discontinuities or, indeed, dilemmas which are presented to the "new" family as it prepares for the 21st century. The ability to accommodate or even resolve these concerns can only be acquired if the reasoning and the policies behind them are first understood.

Without question, then, the achievement of enhanced reproductive independence is seen through use of the rather startling advances of the new assisted biological technologies. Chapter 5 treats extensively as a unit, rather than three separate facets, the principal procedures used to achieve this new procreative freedom—artificial insemination, surrogation, and *in vitro* fertilization. Of practical necessity, then, this chapter is the most comprehensive in the whole book.

The central purpose of this book is to present a framework for analysis of these various competing interests and value systems. By studying the etiology of their development and use, ways by which they can be implemented or, as the case may be, discarded, a full and informed discourse can be initiated and new, reasonable policies developed as the notion of family and its stasis is both reconsidered and redesigned in the new millennium.

Institutions, in the final analysis, can only survive if they can be demonstrated to have a function within the contemporary social structure. Indeed, no political institution survives if it is not flexible in the face of change. Equally, no institution—political, religious, or social—can flourish if it has no practical function to pursue and, furthermore, if the conditions in which it flourished have altered so fundamentally that it has nothing to sustain it.

The ineluctable conclusion to be reached is that perhaps traditional values will have to be reshaped for them to have any sustained relevance in a society that is slowly, but surely, rethinking its definition of marriage and of family as well as the whole value system used to support both institutions. The goal of any new social, ethical, moral, legal, and religious realignment or construct, however, should be to find a reasonable balancing point which seeks to accommodate the Judaeo-Christian values so important to the vast majority of Americans yet, at the same time, assures a level of some responsiveness for the growing number of marginalized who choose to view marriage as but a secular matter of contract, with no religious significance whatsoever. This accommodation must arise, however, through political debate and resolution and not be made preemptively by a judicial system devoid of responsiveness and accountability to the political will of the majority. In simple utilitarian terms, then, the greatest social good for the greatest number of citizens should be sought and maintained here.

Acknowledgments

In June, 1994, as a visiting scholar at the Poynter Center for the Study of Ethics and American Institutions at Indiana University in Bloomington, Indiana, I began plotting the organizational development and preparing the bibliography for this present book. To Professor David H. Smith, the director of the center, I express my sincere thanks for the generous assistance that he provided me during my visit.

In the spring of 1995 I continued my work on this book as a visiting scholar in the Program in Law, Medicine and Ethics at the Boston University Schools of Medicine and Public Health where I had the pleasure of being associated with its director, Professor George J. Annas. To him, I record my lifetime debt of personal gratitude for his professional encouragement, inspiration and loyalty.

In July and August 1995 I was a visiting scholar at the Center for Law and Health at the Indiana University School of Law, Indianapolis, Indiana, and commenced the actual writing of this book. To Dean Norman Lefstein and Professor Eleanor D. Kinney, director of the center, and to Professor James F. Bailey, III, the director of the law library and his outstanding reference librarians, Bruce L. Kleinschmidt and Minde C. Browning, I acknowledge a very large debt of gratitude to them for their simply outstanding assistance and support.

In May 1996 I continued writing the first draft of this book while serving as a visiting fellow at the Center for Bioethics at the University of Pennsylvania School of Medicine, Philadelphia, Pennsylvania, where its director, Professor Arthur L. Caplin, was—as always—a most genial host and source of strength for me in my work.

In June 1996 I was a visiting fellow at the Institute for the Study of Applied and Professional Ethics at Dartmouth College in Hanover, New Hampshire, where I continued my writing and research. To Professor Ronald M. Green, the director of the institute, and to his most capable assistant, Julie S.Wright, I record my very sincere appreciation for their assistance and very generous support and encouragement.

In July and August 1996 I moved on to Wolfson College at Cambridge University, England, where I renewed my Fellowship at Wolfson College and began the final phase of writing this book. I also held the rank of visiting fellow at the Research Centre for International Law. To Professor James A. Crawford, the Whewell Professor of International Law and codirector of the center, and to Professor Sir David G. T. Williams, then Vice Chancellor of the University and his wife, Lady Sally, I express my enduring appreciation for their steadfast loyalty, friendship, and encouragement over the years

Finally, in July and August 1997 I returned to alma mater where I was a visiting professor at Indiana University's School of Law, Bloomington, and at the School of Medicine in Indianapolis, where I completed the book's editing. At the law school, special thanks are owing to Dean Alfred C. Aman, Jr., and Assistant Dean Angela Lieurance and Dr. Gregory Gramelspacker at the medical school for their encouragement and support of this project.

Over the course of time this book was being researched, the following students provided assistance and I express to them my sincere appreciation for their work: Lisa P. Connelly, Ralph C. Conte and John E. Durkin. Special thanks are also owing to Tal S. Grinblat for his loyal friendship and to A. Laurie Fraser for her superb computer skills in preparing this book.

Although parts of some of the essays in this book have appeared elsewhere, in their format and context here, however, they have been edited extensively, updated with substantial additions and reorganized.

Chapter 4 is adapted from *Procreational Autonomy v. State Intervention: Opportunity or Crisis for a Brave New World?*, 2 NOTRE DAME JOURNAL OF LAW, ETHICS AND PUBLIC POLICY 635 (1986) and *Sexuality, Privacy and the New Biology*, 67 MARQUETTE LAW REVIEW 263 (1984).

Chapter 5 draws from *Toward an International Standard of Scientific Inquiry*, 2 HEALTH LAW MATRIX, JOURNAL OF LAW-MEDICINE 167 (1992); *The Baby M Decision: Love's Labor Lost*, 16 LAW, MEDICINE AND HEALTH CARE 121 (1990); *The Razor's Edge of Human Bonding: Artificial Fathers and Surrogate Mothers*, 5 WESTERN NEW ENGLAND LAW REVIEW 639 (1983); *The Perils and Peregrinations of Surrogate Mothers*, 1 INTERNATIONAL JOURNAL OF MEDICINE AND LAW 325 (1982); and *Through a Test Tube Darkly: Artificial Insemination and the Law*, 67 MICHIGAN LAW REVIEW 127 (1968).

Chapter 6 is adapted from *Incest and Intrafamilial Child Abuse: Fatal Attractions or Forced and Dangerous Liaisons?* 23 JOURNAL OF FAMILY LAW 833 (1991).

Chapter 7 is adapted from *Nudity, Obscenity and Pornography: The Streetcars Named Lust and Desire*, 4 JOURNAL OF CONTEMPORARY HEALTH LAW AND POLICY 155 (1988).

Chapter 8 has evolved from various views on the subject of death that I have presented in: *Restructuring The Principle of Medical Futility*, 11 JOURNAL OF PALLIATIVE CARE 9 (1995); *Reviving the Swan, Extending the Curse of Methuselah or Adhering to the Kevorkian Ethic?*, 2 CAMBRIDGE QUARTERLY OF HEALTHCARE ETHICS 49 (1993); *Re-thinking Euthanasia and Death with Dignity: A Transnational Challenge*, 12 ADELAIDE LAW JOURNAL 480 (1990); *All's Well That Ends Well: Toward a Policy of Assisted Rational Suicide or Merely Enlightened Self-Determination?*, 22 UNIVERSITY OF CALIFORNIA-DAVIS LAW REVIEW 275 (1989).

Chapter 9 is adapted from *Market and Non Market Mechanisms for Procuring Human and Cadaveric Organs: When the Price Is Right*, 1 MEDICAL LAW INTERNATIONAL 17 (1993) and *The Frankenstein Myth and Contemporary Human Experimentation: Spectre, Legacy, Curse or Imperative* 2 BIO LAW S463 (1990).

Chapter 1

Familial Challenges, Conflicts, or Dilemmas in the New Millennium

In his State of the Union Address in 1996, President William J. Clinton acknowledged that the Nation's primary challenge was to "strengthen the American Family" and observed that since families are the very foundation of American life if stronger families are built, America itself will be stronger.[1] Indeed, the basic source of human progress is said to be—rightfully—the traditional nuclear heterosexual family which provides for the survival of the larger social community, for it is from this social unit that a bond of faithfulness and trust is forged which allows for the creation of children as a testament to its steadiness.[2] While recognizing family, and parenthood, are linked, ideally, to form "the good life,"[3] it remains a vexatious conundrum to find agreement on the content of these terms as they evolve in contemporary society.

CHANGING LIFESTYLES

A decade ago, a child in a single-parent home was much more likely to be living with a divorced parent than a parent who has never married. As out-of-wedlock births have risen, that has changed. Accordingly, today 37 percent of children in single-parent homes live with a divorced parent, only slightly higher than the 35.8 percent living with a never married parent.[4]

After the year 2000, as those individuals born after 1970 emerge, the United States will find itself a nation divided into two groupings—coupled or decoupled by patrimony more than race, religion, class, education, or gender. One group will, consequently, grow up in the presence and provision of fathers, the other grouping will consist of those who do not.[5] Sadly, in 1986, for the first time in contemporary history, a majority of all poor families in America had absent fathers.[6] And, with this absence comes the most acute manifestation of paternal disinvestment: juvenile violence[7] and single mother births.[8]

Even more startling than these statistics is the growing American opinion that it is proper morally for an unmarried woman to have a child without the benefit of being married.[9] The statistics go far to support this opinion when it is realized that every year approximately 350,000 teenage girls have babies out of wedlock. Presently, more than half of teenage boys and girls have indulged in sex by the time they have reached their eighteenth birthday and 15 percent of the girls who become teenage mothers come from a middle-class background.[10] And, only 20 percent of these mothers who never marry receive formal child support.[11]

According to reports from the National Center for Health Statistics in 1993, California's out-of-wedlock births were 35 percent of all births reported in that year. This was the ninth highest rate in the country. Interestingly, the nation's capital reported 67.8 percent of its newborns were to unwed mothers—with the national average being 31 percent.[12] In 1996, however, the Centers for Disease Control and Prevention reported a 4 percent drop in the out-of-wedlock national birth rate.[13] Even with this drop, teenage pregnancies and out of wedlock births are helping maintain America's infant mortality rate above that of other industrialized nations.[14]

The United States has the highest teen pregnancy rates of any of the developed countries, with 6.1 percent of all mothers in the United States being found within the fifteen to nineteen age range.[15] It is thought that these mortality rates could be lowered if out-of-wedlock births were to decrease; for these actual teen pregnancies numbering 500,000 a year are often compounded by risk factors of poverty, substance abuse, and poor education.[16]

Cohabitation has become a common stage of life in contemporary society. The U.S. Census Bureau reported in December 1996 that nearly 3.7 million American households are made up of unmarried couples[17] Among graduates of college, more than a quarter have lived with someone prior to marriage.[18] In 1970, while there was just one "cohabiting" couple for every one hundred married-couple households, by 1995 that ratio had increased to six unmarried couples for every one hundred married households.[19]

In Europe, while presently single-parent homes account for one in eight families, some sociologists are predicting that if present growth rates continue, this could well become the dominant social unit in Europe easily within thirty years.[20] Presently, in France, 36 percent of all births take place out of wedlock to 2.2 million unmarried couples which is more than seven times the number in 1968.[21] While, as elsewhere, having a child without the benefit of marriage becomes a visible way to assert one's identity and find someone to love in an increasingly lonely society, in France a desire to reap economic benefits of upward to $800 a month in support for each such child born of a single parent is seen as an added inducement to single parenting. Sadly, for two million children living in single-parent homes in France, however, it has been found that there are higher rates of delinquency, school dropouts, and eventual joblessness than for children raised in two-parent households.[22]

NEW MODELS OF PARENTING

The ideal of an androgynous fatherhood, or fatherhood without masculinity, has emerged as the animating principle of the contemporary "New Father Model."[23] Consistent with this comes a program by gays and lesbians to challenge the right of the biological family to define what constitutes a family unit and, instead, advocates advancement of a subjective notion which allows everyone to decide what a family is under various sets of circumstances according to *individual* standards.[24] In attempting to "redefine" family according to same-gender preferences, one California entrepreneur has opened the only sperm bank in North America which matches specifically gay males with lesbians—thereby allowing same-gender opportunities for reproductive autonomy to individuals of this disposition.[25]

Hard Questions

Grappling with the need to either reshape or revitalize modern family law demands hard questions be raised and answers sought. The first and foremost concern is the problem of whether to confer legal protection of same-gender "marriages" and families based on an expanded recognition of a private freedom to define one's life.[26] Should family like behaviors be allowed to take a priority over recognized forms? Should sexual relations between "blended" family members continue to be held illicit?[27] While marriage law has been a primary source for setting sexual norms, a recognizable trend has been seen which seeks to discard traditional barriers to marriage on the basis that they violate the rights of individual choice without any real sense of purpose.[28] Finally, society must decide whether it wishes to continue to marginalize a relatively small, yet vocal, community of people who, at one level or other, conduct themselves as members of a family unit and exhibit some of those values seen in true heterosexual marriages. The benefits of expanded recognition here, must of course, be weighed against the social, political, economic, and ethical costs involved in such a move.[29]

Deregulating Family Law

What has been termed "the constitutionalization of family law" in America tends to reenforce deregulation of this very body of law itself. Thus, the traditional defenses of marriage and of sexual prohibitions are made quite difficult as a consequence of judicial demands for rational explanations and proof that any such prohibition tested is wise or reasonable and effective. Rather than viewing challenges to family law as but challenges to broad rules prescribing norms of family conduct, more and more courts are tending to confront issues of this nature on a case-by-base basis as disputes involving individual protected liberties.[30]

RESPONSIBLE REPRODUCTION

In the farcical movie *Junior*, Arnold Schwarzenegger gives birth to a baby conceived in the union of his sperm and a frozen ovum, and then nurtured in his abdomen with female hormones and the drug "Expectane." Schwarzenegger proclaims: "My body, my choice!"[31] While abdominal pregnancies, or those outside the womb, are indeed rare— happening approximately once within every ten thousand pregnancies (and seldom resulting in live births)—a few do in fact succeed.[32] Although no scientific record exists validating male pregnancies,[33] the comedic license taken in *Junior* nonetheless belies the real pathos of those who are incapable of fecundation and the lengths to which society may be thought to pressure women to reproduce—either artificially, *in vitro*, or through surrogation.[34] Indeed, those four words by Schwarzenegger, "My body, my choice," effectively frame the central issues of procreational autonomy (or self-determination) versus social responsibility and control.[35]

Compelled by aspirations to minimize human suffering and improve the genetic and psychic well-being of its citizens,[36] the federal government has—over the years—encouraged expansion of the legal, ethical, and medical research perimeters of fecundity. It thereby combats not only infertility, but birth defects and other disorders.[37]

The U.S. Congress considered the extent to which research on laboratory human fertilization should be federally funded in August 1978.[38] Unable to stir itself from a vacuous lethargy and resolve this vexatious issue, sixteen years later the Congress relied on the Human Embryo Research Panel of the National Institute of Health for definitive action. Accordingly, on September 27, 1994, the panel recommended a series of guidelines allowing for funding of a wide range of research on human embryos (developed from test-tube fertilization) with less than fourteen days of developmental age.[39] Yet, on December 3, 1994, President Clinton stated that no federal monies would be expended for research on human embryos.[40] Acknowledging that complex ethical and moral questions were at issue, however, the President's order did not bar support for studies using surplus fertilized eggs from fertility clinics.[41]

In a 1994 book titled, CHILDREN OF CHOICE: FREEDOM AND THE NEW REPRODUCTIVE TECHNOLOGY, Professor John Robertson of the University of Texas Law School, analyzes conflicts of values generated by the new reproductive technologies of *in vitro* fertilization, artificial insemination, Norplant, surrogation, and so on. He seeks "to show the importance of procreative liberty—the freedom to decide whether or not to have off-spring" —in devising a framework for resolving the inherent controversies which the reproductive technologies create.[42]

For Robertson, the "framework" for problem solving is tied to the development, promotion and recognition of policies which guarantee procreation as a "basic right" and "dominant value" in contemporary society. Curtailments of this right, he urges, "invariable have to rely on information, education, counseling, subsidies and incentives so that the freedom of choice in matters of reproduction is protected."[43] For neoconservatives, this framework is not at all balanced, but is skewed to the left.[44]

While recognizing that procreative rights are not absolute[45] and that reproduction can be "irresponsible"[46] when moral obligations "to reproduce responsibly" are not met,[47] Robertson is loathe to recommend or even to find reasons that justify the use of reversible reproductive technologies, such as Norplant, to limit reproduction.[48] Rather, education, counseling, incentives (which, to my way of thinking are little more than bribes), and subsidies are advanced as components of the only just and redeeming social policy to follow.[49]

Robertson offers his analytical "framework" or, more correctly, his premise of procreative liberty, as but a "template to guide inquiry and evaluation, and to assure that moral inquiry and public policy do not ignore the importance of personal choice in these matters."[50] This template is deficient because it does not truly recognize individual *responsibility*. Rather, it emphasizes only self-indulged, irresponsible acts of so-called procreative self-determination.

Be it either under a Rawlsian theory of primary social good achieved through attainment of a sense of one's own worth or self-respect,[51] or a theory of social contract espoused by the Founding Fathers that seeks a balance between the government's right to manage and control and the individual need or right to be free and autonomous, each citizen must accept moral responsibility for choices that often bring negative consequences or failures.[52] Taking responsibility is a sign of maturity.[53] Thus, mature people who have not only taken charge of themselves but of their conduct are regarded as responsible persons and citizens.[54] Simply put, responsible citizens "*own* their actions and *own* up to them."[55]

When a citizen cannot fulfill the obligations of the social contract, society (e.g., the government) assumes those obligations[56] and must extract a consideration of some type for its actions. In situations where equal procreational liberties cannot be fully enjoyed, "it is not ultimately repugnant to the priority of liberty to allow severe or unequal restrictions of liberty *now*, if these measures are found necessary to boost productivity to the point where full and equal liberty can be truly realized *later*."[57]

To Professor Robertson, the meaning of procreative liberty is placed within an unyielding argument for "presumptive moral and legal protection for reproductive technologies that expand procreative options."[58] Again, for him, procreative decisions are always to be left to those "whose procreative *desires* are most directly involved."[59] Sadly, he fails to appreciate the fact that so many members of modern American society have neither the will nor the intelligence to care about the consequences of their ill-conceived actions, nor an ability and will to become educated.[60] They are the societal "dropouts" who have no willingness to understand that for every right government grants, there is a commensurate responsibility that right be exercised *reasonably* or rationally. For these individuals, the government must act, justly and humanely, to direct or reshape their lives and, when necessary, to safeguard their best interests (and those of society), even to the extent of infringing upon the "sanctity" of their personal procreative "freedoms." Obviously, this position is odious to all who reflexively embrace the *absolute* principle of civil liberty, for it requires them to view presently harsh and unpleasant situations *as they are* and not as they ideally *ought* to be. Hope may spring eternal,[61] but as Professor Frank Michelman has cautioned, a right too distended causes injustice[62] and compromises individual self-respect.[63]

The Quayle Thesis

Some will remember Vice President Dan Quayle's "controversial" remarks before the Commonwealth Club of California in San Francisco on May 19, 1992, when he concluded," marriage is a moral issue that requires cultural consensus, and the use of social sanctions. Bearing babies irresponsibly is simply wrong. Failing to support children one has fathered is wrong. We must be unequivocal about this. It does not help matters when prime time TV has Murphy Brown—a character who supposedly epitomizes today's intelligent, highly paid, professional women—mocking the importance of fathers, by bearing a child alone, and calling it just another "life style choice." The popular press had a field day reporting these remarks were nothing more than an out-and-out attack on single mothers and working men.[64]

As a private citizen, Dan Quayle, Esquire, returned to the Commonwealth Club on September 8, 1994, and in a thoughtful speech revisited the issue of a valueless society—this after having been previously vindicated by the April 1993 issue of the *Atlantic Monthly* which headlined, "Dan Quayle Was Right," and then in various articles within the issue which detailed the harmful effects of divorce on children and the decline of the family as a social unit.[65]

Family disruption is best understood not as a single event but as a string of disruptive events: separation, divorce, life in a single-parent family, life with a parent and a live-in lover, the remarriage of one or both parents, life in one stepparent family combined with visits to another stepparent family; the break up of one or both stepparent families and so on.[66] Those who suggest these events and, indeed, trends, pose not only a serious threat to children and to the nation are dismissed as pessimists and unable to accept the new *facts of life*. The preferred or popular view is that the changes in family structure are, on balance, positive. The expansion of the boundaries of freedom and choice mean all too often men leave wives for younger women and teenage girls get pregnant "accidentally" on a regular basis.[67]

A Religious Focus?

Another major challenge facing contemporary society is to confront the problem of whether it is wiser to keep the nation "on course" in its maintenance of Judaeo-Christian morality or to chart a midcourse change which seeks to replace this traditional morality with radical moral relativism. Although Justice Antonin Scalia of the U.S. Supreme Court has reminded that it is foolhardy to both deny the relevance of moral perceptions to law and to also acknowledge society's moral beliefs have not effect on its constitutional perceptions in general,[68] the Pew Research Center found, from a survey of 1,975 adults, that religious teaching has little effect in shaping common attitudes on broad social issues such as welfare and the role of women in the workplace.[69] Individual rationality is, however, said to be a function of social norms which, as such, either operate as taxes or subsidies, depending on the particular context of the social action being evaluated.[70] Nonetheless, it is maintained steadfastly, that the "bedrock of moral order is religion."[71] And, further, that religion is indeed a guide[72] in building and maintaining common values—values that provide a basis for tolerable human life and which include "the obligations of love and friendship, the duties of benevolence, or at least restraints against harm and destruction of life."[73]

STABILIZING MORAL VALUES

At the heart of how people relate to one another are moral values—for these values are but a true reflection of what individuals think of themselves.[74] Having a core of shared moral values allows for and promotes social progress.[75] But, what are moral values? They are the obligations, responsibilities, freedoms, and rights which arise from the social contract all individuals have with their government.[76] Laws are taken, properly, then, as but the moral codes of the body politic or as "the officially sanctioned moral dictates of the state."[77]

Because the dominant force in contemporary society has been changed,[78] common-sense values are forever being tested, retested, and even changed as the situation dictates. Yet, the underlying hope is that truth will always triumph;[79] but, of course, it does not. While a link has been found between religion and morality—with the decline in the popular culture coinciding with the decline in the influence of religion—it is "not conceded universally that morality flows from religion."[80] Sadly, today, the unconstrained self is celebrated by popular culture and those who would seek to question it or redirect it are savaged.[81]

A New Self-Discipline

Instead of acceding to the ever insistent demand for decadence[82] and allowing the positive forces of evil within history to run free, and to corrupt and infect,[83] mankind needs to live within the bounds of a new self-discipline or reasonable moral order—one that acknowledges that a veil of ignorance and restraint is preferred to a life of unfettered hedonism.[84] While the inner voice of conscience perhaps is the best gauge for reestablishing what was known as traditional morality,[85] the search for conscience through the centrality of life values is complicated when there are severe weaknesses within family structures and other institutions which have served, over the ages, as the teaching units and repositories for these values.

With the decline of the public school systems, a strong contributing factor is seen in the erosion of moral standards, for, sadly, more and more students and teachers, alike, have little respect for one another.[86] By definition, however, any attempt to instill stronger societal value must commence with the children; since it is with children that morals may be instilled in early life and have a greater chance for continuation. All children have within them the capacity for good and bad acts, and their capacity for good must be nurtured.[87]

Since the traditional family structure is weakened, if not lost, renewed positive efforts must be undertaken to teach moral values in the schools and religious institutions. Schools, in particular, "are charged with bestowing upon students the knowledge and skills required for successful life."[88] Such lives, then, should surely include universally recognized values which can be taught initially in the primary schools and carried forward in a "practical" setting within the junior high and high school environments.[89] Yet, the only obligation teachers have is to teach those who *want* to learn. Ultimately, true educational stimulation must come from parents who in turn must also oversee and encourage their children's' education.[90] And, when the parental unit is dysfunctional or dissolved, other institutional support must be made available to assist in the learning process; otherwise, students grow up expecting to fail and to accept failure in "small digestible packages."[91] As important, is the whole fabric of democratic self-rule which is jeopardized when the family fails in its task to teach the lessons of independence, self-restraint, responsibility, and right conduct. These values are undeniably the essential core of a free, democratic society.[92]

The State Responsibility

What is the role of the state in relation to children? The basic assumption to be made, and which may be accepted as valid, is that the state always seeks to maximize the aggregate welfare of not only children, but of all of its citizens. For children, in particular, to achieve a high level of utility over their lifetimes, a considerable investment of not only parental time but also market inputs (food, clothing, tuition, etc.) must be made. In a particular child, then, the optimal level of investments is that which is expected to maximize the combined welfare of the child, his parents, and other family members.[93] Depending, rather obviously, upon such factors as the child's aptitudes and the parents' wealth, the necessary level of optimality will vary. This level will also vary with the degree to which the parents love the child; for, the "more they love it, the higher will be the optimal investment, because the costs of the investment will be felt very lightly, even not at all, by the parents."[94]

MEDIATING STRUCTURES FOR RENEWAL

In 1977 Peter L. Berger and Richard John Neuhaus suggested fruitful public policy approaches lie *not* in pursuing the lines of attack long cherished by liberals and conservatives alike. Rather, they promoted the principle of "mediating structures"—such as family, church, neighborhood, and voluntary association—as the linchpin to maintaining a healthy civil society with a foundation of values to support its effective operation.[95]

The working definition of mediating structures embraced those institutions that stand between the private world of individuals and the large, impersonal structures of modern society. They "mediate" by constituting a vehicle by which personal beliefs and values could be transmitted into megainstitutions. The importance of intermediate institutions has been affirmed by many authors in modern political thought, going at least as far back as Edmund Burke's defense of the "small platoons" against the geometric abstract of the French revolutionaries.[96]

The most important large institution in the ordering of modern society is the modern state itself. Additionally, there are large economic conglomerates of capitalist enterprise, big labor, and the growing bureaucracies that administer wide sectors of the society, such as in education and the organized professions. These institutions are termed properly megastructures. The central purpose of revitalizing mediating structure is *not* to attack megastructures, but to find better ways in which they can relate to the "little platoons" in everyday life. This goal is achieved, then, through the exercise of empowerment.[97]

Actualizing empowerment through mediating structures is the noble goal of a new, federal legislative initiative. Indeed, Indiana's Senator Dan Coats has formulated a creative and visionary effort that he terms *The Project for American Renewal*, which is designed to encourage and indeed sustain value shaping institutions in American society. An ambitious legislative package of eighteen recommendations buttressed by planned congressional hearings to probe three essential themes of national concern—compassion and voluntarism, community empowerment, and the family—this truly outstanding project will serve as both a primer and a blueprint to initiate a national dialogue on how to confront America's cultural decay after relimitations of government are first achieved.[98]

It is widely accepted social fact that America's cultural breakdown will continue and worsen without the recovery of civil society—families, neighborhoods, churches and synagogues, schools and voluntary associations (from neighborhood watches to the PTA). In nearly every community, these institutions once created an atmosphere in which most problems—a teenage girl "in trouble," rowdy neighborhood kids, the start of a drug problem at the local high school—could be confronted *before* their repetition threatened the existence of the community itself.[99]

The decline of these institutions which instill values without public coercion has resulted in terrible human carnage, afflicting every strata of society, but especially the inner cities. Without the restraining influence of healthy families, churches, synagogues, and neighborhoods—influences that are literally "civilizing" a society, at worst, fall into chaos.[100]

If the renewal of civil society is a viable next step for Americans to take, two immediate challenges are presented. First, the realization must be understood that even if government directly undermines civil society, it cannot directly reconstruct it. The civil society is organic and not mechanical. It can be coaxed and nurtured, not engineered. Second, ways by which society can nurture itself must be found. Even with the dismantling of the Great Society, three major questions must be answered: How can the civil society be encouraged and, at the same time, have degrees of social dislocation minimized? How can social institutions be revived? And, how can the type of individual and civic atrophy which has occurred during the last thirty years be reversed?[101]

The key answer to concerns and challenges is to be found in the devolution of power through both state governments and private and religious institutions. It must be recognized, accordingly, that the distribution of power within government is finally less important than the redistribution of power *beyond* government.[102]

This, then, is the synthesizing principle of *The Project for American Renewal.* Instead of proposing legislative enactments designed to "rebuild" civil society, the project attempts to take the side of people and institutions who are rebuilding their own communities, and who often feel isolated and poorly equipped. Its components direct attention and support to community development corporations, religious charities, private schools for inner-city students, neighborhood watches, and communities trying to restore the importance of marriage and family. The goal, in that margin where it is possible, is to apply *private resources to public problems*, expanding the society while limiting the state.[103]

A founding principle of the modern, liberal state is that society must change if there is to be hope for individuals to change. The realist recognizes, however, that this principle is precisely backwards. Thus, *individuals* must change if there is ever to be a positive change in the course of modern society.[104] Matters of behavior and character have assumed a central place in America's debate on social policy—the value men and women place on life and property, the commitment they show to marriage, the sacrifices they make for their children. Sadly, centralized bureaucratic antipoverty programs have failed, and that failure has had great human costs measured in broken homes and violent streets.[105]

CONCLUSIONS

A 1996 NEWSWEEK poll revealed an interesting attitude toward promiscuous sex. Seventy percent surveyed expressed their opinion that having an affair is always harmful to a marriage, while 22 percent said adultery could be good for a marriage. Only 50 percent held the view that adultery is wrong because of its immoral nature.[106] The poll found that instead of finding an adherence to morality within a marriage, those interviewed were most interested in not getting caught in indiscretions![107]

Homosexuality and lesbianism will never be seen as a normal variant of human sexuality and be accepted in the personal and private sphere of family members, friends, neighbors, and colleagues. No widespread, imminent acceptance of this lifestyle is seen by mainstream society. Because of the core or traditional "values" of same-gender preference advocates is different from heterosexuals and, indeed, is seen as threatening to the very moral fabric of America, contemporary society is far from accepting those "values." Political correctness simply will not carry the day.

The real test over the immediate future is whether legislatures can act responsibly in shaping new policies or amending present ones to deal with new social units where more than two parents are seen or where two parents of the same gender assert the status of a family.[108] More and more "constructed families" are being developed where relationships between adults, as well as between adults and children, are arranged on an *ad hoc* basis or by agreement.[109] Before law can act, society must determine first, descriptively, the role new family structures will play today within modern times and, second, the role they *ought* to play in the future.[110]

If a "collective reconsideration of the continued vitality of the old normative system"[111] must be undertaken because of the new fluidity of reconstituted family structures,[112] judicial authoritarianism must not be allowed to stand in place of shaping policy through representative institutions. Rather, each state legislature must enact laws responsive to these issues.[113] Reasonable and sensible lawmaking, together with the use and implementation of mediating social structures, will go far in finding a reasonable and acceptable balance between social stability and morality and individual opportunity for reasonable change.[114]

The new opportunities for reproductive autonomy must be measured always by recognition of a coordinate responsibility that these opportunities be made available within a framework of reasonable use. *Enhanced* fecundity is not a constitutional right nor is there a national guarantee that the single and unmarried, as well as married individuals, have a right to design a family according to their personal dictates at all costs.

Whether the New Society will accept a revised code of morality which condones unfettered experimentation in family structures remains to be seen. The succeeding chapters in this book will consider whether these new and often vexatious issues are merely challenges to a time-honored institution long considered the very bulwark of society which can be met or whether they have escalated to conflicts or dilemmas that threaten and transform the very foundation of the traditional heterosexual nuclear family.

In the final analysis, perhaps what will be seen is that moral perceptions do change with time and become more situational than *a priori*. Depending upon individual viewpoints, these new forms of contemporary life and morality may *not* be challenges, conflicts or dilemmas. Rather, they may be viewed as compatible extensions of autonomy and pluralism which, in turn, give vibrancy to the principle of inclusiveness.   Truly, then, these matters will be viewed or colored by sociopolitical standards, ethical and religious values, and the cultural perspective of the day—together with the particular individual or advocate's preferences.[115]

NOTES

1. *State of the Union Address*, WASH. POST, Jan. 23, 1996, at A3.

2. S.W. ITZKOFF, THE DECLINE OF INTELLIGENCE IN AMERICA: A STRATEGY FOR NATIONAL RENEWAL 127 (1994).

3. Michael H. v. Gerald D., 491 U.S. 110, 141 (1989) (Brennan, J. dissenting). *See The 90's Family, Gone to Pot*, WASH. POST, Nov. 9, 1993, at D1.

4. CENSUS BUREAU REPORT, MARITAL STATES AND LIVING ARRANGEMENTS (Mar. 1996) (compiled on the basis of a 1994 survey).

See Vobjeda, *Americans Delay Trip to Altar: Single-Parent Home Is as Often Result of No Marriage as Broken One*, WASH. POST, Mar. 13, 1996, at A3.

TIME Magazine reports one-fourth of all American households consist of a single person. Wright, *The Evolution of Despair*, TIME Mag., Aug. 28, 1995, at 50.

5. D. BLANKENHORN, FATHERLESS AMERICA: CONFRONTING OUR MOST URGENT SOCIAL PROBLEM 1 (1995).

6. *Id.* at 43.

See Fox-Genovese, *The Legal Status of Families as Institutions*, 77 CORNELL L. REV. 992, 995 (1992) (suggesting that perhaps marriage partners ought not to be allowed to assume responsibility for new families until the children of a first marriage are self-sufficient).

7. BLANKENHORN, *supra* note 5 at 45.

See Wilson & Jaffee, *Adolescent Medicine* 273 J.A.M.A. 1657 (June 7, 1995) (surveying children and adolescents who have experienced assault or abuse); Vobjeda, *HHS Study Finds Sharp Rise in Child Abuse*, WASH. POST, Sept. 19, 1996, at A8.

8. BLANKENHORN, *supra* note 5 at 45.

9. *Id.* at 76.

See W. FARRELL, THE MYTH OF MALE POWER: WHY MEN ARE THE DISPOSABLE SEX (1993).

10. Chazin, *Teen Pregnancy: Let's Get Real*, READERS DIGEST 49 (Sept. 1996). *See* Raspberry, *Motherhood Too Soon*, WASH. POST, Oct. 4, 1996, at A23.

11. *Id.*

See Stevens-Simon, et al., *The Effect of Monetary Incentives and Peer Support Groups on Repeat Adolescent Pregnancies: A Randomized Trial of the Dollar-a-Day Program*, 277 J.A.M.A. 977 (1997).

12. Bancroft, *California's Unwed Birth Rate May Be Less Than Epidemic*, PHILADELPHIA INQUIRER, May 4, 1996, at A1.

13. Havemann, *Birth Rate for Unwed Women Falls*, WASH. POST, Oct. 5, 1996, at 1.

14. Singh, *Infant Mortality in the United States: Trends, Differentials, and Projections, 1950 through 2010*, 85 AM. J. PUB. HEALTH 957 (1995).

15. *Id.*

16. *Id.*

See generally Goodman, *Sex Without Consequences*, WASH. POST, Feb. 18, 1995, at A21.

17. Vobjeda, *Cohabitation of 85 Pct. Over Decade*, WASH. POST, Dec. 5, 1996, at A15.

18. *Id.*

19. *Id.*

20. Drozdiak, *In a Singularly Family Way: Out-of-Wedlock Births Are Losing Their Stigma in France*, WASH. POST, May 16, 1996, at 1.

21. *Id.*

22. *Id.*

23. BLANKENHORN, *supra* note 5 at 117.

See Nelson, *Patriarchy or Equality: Family Values or Individuality*, 70 ST. JOHN'S L. REV. 435 (1996).

24. *See* K. WESTON, FAMILIES WE CHOOSE (1991).

25. Brinkley, *In Oakland, New Sperm Bank Is Helping to Redefine Family*, WASH. BLADE, Feb. 2, 1996, at 12.

26. Woodhouse, *Towards A Revitalization of Family Law*, 69 TEX. L. REV. 245, 288 (1990).

27. *Id.*

28. *Id.* at 286.

29. *Id.* at 286-88.

30. *Id.* at 287.

31. Kempley, *Junior: Schwarzenegger's Fetal Attraction*, WASH. POST, Nov. 23, 1994, at D-1.

32. Teresi, *How to Get a Man Pregnant*, N.Y. TIMES Mag., Nov. 27, 1994, at 54.

33. *Id.*

34. G.P. SMITH, II, BIOETHICS AND THE LAW: MEDICAL, SOCIO-LEGAL AND PHILOSOPHICAL DIRECTIONS FOR A BRAVE NEW WORLD, Chs. 5 & 8 (1993).

See D.G. WNEK, BARREN IN THE PROMISED LAND: CHILDLRESS AMERICANS AND THE PURSUIT OF HAPPINESS (1995); Shacochis, *Missing Children: One Couple's Anguished Attempt to Conceive*, HARPER'S Mag., 55 (Oct. 1996).

35. J.A. ROBERTSON, CHILDREN OF CHOICE: FREEDOM AND THE NEW REPRODUCTIVE TECHNOLOGY (1994).

36. G.P. SMITH, II, GENETICS, ETHICS AND THE LAW (1982). *See* Fletcher, *Where in the World Are We Going with the New Genetics*, 5 J. CONTEMP. HEALTH L. & POL'Y 33 (1989).

37. *See generally* G.J. ANNAS, STANDARD OF CARE: THE LAW OF AMERICAN BIOETHICS (1993).

38. Sullivan, *Renewed Research on Human Fertilization in Labs Urged*, N.Y. TIMES, Aug. 5, 1978, at 24.

39. Schwarz, *Panel Backs Funding of Embryo Research*, WASH. POST, Sept. 28, 1994, at A-1. *See* Green, *Research Embryos: A Step Forward for Medicine*, WASH. POST, Oct. 16, 1994, at C-7.

40. Leary, *Clinton Rules out Federal Money for Research on Human Embryos Created for that Purpose*, N.Y. TIMES, Dec. 3, 1994, at 8.

41. *Id. See* G.P. Smith, II, THE NEW BIOLOGY: LAW, ETHICS AND BIOTECHNOLOGY, Ch. 11 (1989). *See also* P. LAURITZEN, PURSUING PARENTHOOD: ETHICAL ISSUES IN ASSISTED REPRODUCTION (1993).

42. Robertson, *supra* note 35.

See also Jones, *Reproductive Autonomy and Evolutionary Biology: A Regulatory Framework for Trait Selection Technologies*, 19 AM. J. L. & MED. 187 (1993); Posner, *The Ethics and Economics of Enforcing Contracts of Surrogate Mothers*, 5 J. CONTEMP. HEALTH L. & POL'Y 21 (1959).

43. Robertson, *supra* note 35 at 80.

44. *See* Smith, *Procreational Autonomy v. State Intervention: Opportunity or Crisis for a Brave New World?*, 2 NOTRE DAME J. L. ETHICS & POL'Y 635 (1986).

45. Robertson, *supra* note 35 at 93.

46. *Id.* at 72.

47. *Id.* at 93.

48. *Id.*

49. *Id.* at 80.

50. *Id.* at 221.

51. JOHN RAWLS, A THEORY OF JUSTICE (1971).

52. Cinelli & Nunnenkamp, *Sterilization Technology and Decisionmaking: Rethinking the Incompetent's Rights*, 2 J. CONTEMP. HEALTH L. & POL'Y 275, 280-3 (1986).

53. THE BOOK OF VIRTUES 185 (W.J. Bennett, ed. 1993).

54. *Id.* at 186.

55. *Id.*

56. *Supra* note 52.

57. Michelman, *In Pursuit of Constitutional Welfare Rights: One Vision of Rawls' Theory of Justice*, 121 U. PA. L. REV. 962, 1000 (1973).

58. Robertson, *supra* note 35 at 220.

59. *Id.* at 235.

60. R.J. HERNSTEIN & C. MURRAY, THE BELL CURVE: INTELLIGENCE AND CLASS STRUCTURE IN AMERICAN LIFE, Chs. 13-6 (1994).

61. Alexander Pope, *An Essay on Man*, Epistle I, line 95 (E. Merriam 1804).

62. Michelman, *supra* note 57 at 1015.

63. *Id. See also* Smith, *supra* note 44.

But see Durkin, *Reproductive Technology and the New Family: Recognizing the Other Mother*, 10 J. CONTEMP. HEALTH L. & POL'Y 327 (1993).

64. *See, e.g.*, Wines, *Views on Single Motherhood Are Multiple at White House*, N.Y. TIMES, May 21, 1992, at A1.

See generally LIVING WITH CONTRADICTIONS: CONTROVERSIES IN FEMINIST SOCIAL ETHICS (A.M. Jaggar ed., 1994).

65. Whitehead, *Dan Quayle Was Right*, THE ATLANTIC MONTHLY 47 *passim* (April 1993).

66. *Id.*

67. *Id.*

See generally R. HUGHES, CULTURE OF COMPLAINT: THE FRAYING OF AMERICA (1993); Goodman, *Where Family Values Begin and End,* WASH. POST, Sept. 24, 1994 at A27.

68. Scalia, *Morality, Pragmatism and the Legal Order*, 9 HARV. J. L. & PUB. POL'Y 123 (1986).

69. Niebuhr, *Public Supports Political Voice for Churches*, N.Y. TIMES, June 25, 1996, at 1.

70. Sunstein, *Social Norms and Social Roles*, 96 COLUM. L. REV. 903, 909-910 (1996).

71. Reagan, *Politics and Morality are Inseparable*, 1 NOTRE DAME J. L. ETHICS & PUB. POL'Y 7 (1984).

72. *Id.* at 10.

73. S. BOK, COMMON VALUES 53, 54 (1994).

74. T. HAUSER & F. MACCHIAROLA, CONFRONTING AMERICA'S MORAL CRISIS 5 (1995).

75. *Id.* at 15.

76. *Id.* at 17.

77. *Id.* at 18.

78. *Id.* at 39.

79. *See* CONTRACT WITH THE AMERICAN FAMILY 145 (1995).

80. R.H. BORK, SLOUCHING TOWARDS GOMORRAH: MODERN LIBERALISM AND AMERICAN DECLINE 273, 274 (1996).

It is asserted nonetheless that moral values have been weakened by the diminishing influence of religion in the private lives of all citizens. HAUSER & MACCHIAROLA, *supra* note 74 at 41-2.

81. BORK, *supra* note 80 at 125.

82. *Id.* at 132.

83. R. SHATTUCK, FORBIDDEN KNOWLEDGE: FROM PROMETHUS TO PORNOGRAPHY (1966).

84. *Id.;* BORK, *supra* note 80 at 127.

85. Shattuck, *supra* note 83.

86. Hauser & Macchiarola, *supra* note 74 at 44.

87. *Id.* at 71.

88. *Id.* at 73.

89. *Id.* at 73, 75.

90. C. MURRAY, LOSING GROUND: AMERICAN SOCIAL POLICY, 1950-1980, at 224, 225 (1984).

91. *Id.* at 227.

92. *See* D.W. KMIEC, CEASE-FIRE ON THE FAMILY: AND THE END OF THE CULTURE WAR Ch. 9 (1995).

See generally Scott & Scott, *Parents as Fiduciaries*, 81 VA. L. REV. 2401 (1995).

93. R.A. POSNER, ECONOMIC ANALYSIS OF LAW 149-57 (4th ed. 1992).

94. *Id.* at 157.

95. P.L. BERGER & R.J. NEUHAUS, TO EMPOWER PEOPLE: FROM STATE TO CIVIL SOCIETY at 148-9 (1996).

96. *Id.*

97. *Id.* at 164.

98. Senator Dan Coats, *The Project for American Renewal* (1996).

99. *Id.*

100. *Id.*

101. *Id.*

102. *Id.*

103. *Id.*

104. *Id.*

105. *Id.*

106. Namuth et al., *Adultery: A New Furor over an Old Sin*, NEWSWEEK, Sept. 30, 1996, at 54.

In 1991, there were approximately five divorces per ten marriages. U.S. BUREAU OF THE CENSUS, STATISTICAL ABSTRACT OF THE UNITED STATES: 1993 (113th ed.) (4.7 divorces per 9.4 marriages).

107. Namuth, *supra* note 106 at 58.

108. *See* L. BENKOV, REINVENTING THE FAMILY: THE EMERGING STORY OF LESBIAN AND GAY PARENTS (1994).

109. B.R. FURROW, S.H. JOHNSON, T.S. JOST & R.L. SCHWARTZ, BIOETHICS: HEALTH CARE LAW AND ETHICS 961 (1991).

110. *Id.* at 113-14.

111. Fineman, *Masking Dependency: The Political Role of Family Rhetoric*, 81 VA. L. REV. 2181, 2186 (1995).

112. Woodhouse, *supra* note 26, at 286.

113. Will, *And Now Pronounce Them Spouse and Spouse*, WASH. POST, May 19, 1996, at C9.

114. *See generally* M.A. GLENDON, THE TRANSFORMATION OF FAMILY LAW: STATE, LAW AND FAMILY IN THE UNITED STATES AND WESTERN EUROPE (1989).

115. Some of the ideas presented in this chapter derive from a monograph that I authored. *See* G.P. SMITH, II, CHALLENGING FAMILY VALUES IN THE NEW SOCIETY (1996).

Challenging or Restructuring
the Concept of Family

Chapter 2

Feminist Perspectives: Enhancing or Threatening Traditional Values?

Feminist literature on the new reproductive technologies emphasizes two recurrent themes: first, that social changes stemming from these new developments will reveal the existing imbalance of power between men and women,[1] and second, that the primary focus of societal domination and exploitation of women, is on their sexual and reproductive capacities.[2]   The core of discrimination is that, systematically, differences between men and women, whether real or perceived, are turned, as a result of social practices, into advantages for men and disadvantages for women.[3]   Many feminists contend that once women gain control over their procreative capacities, they will have made an essential step toward gaining control over their bodies and participate as equals in social, economic, and political life.[4]

Women have established significant reproductive rights in recent years, including the right to avoid pregnancy through the use of contraceptives,[5] the right to become pregnant through artificial insemination, and the right to terminate their pregnancies through abortion.[6] As the judiciary begins to incorporate this new technology into the existing legal framework, emphasis on individual rights—reproductive freedom and bodily integrity in particular—must continue to be protected. "According to feminist arguments, these rights should not be overridden by possible symbolic harms or speculative risks to potential children."[7] The recent use of Norplant by judges as a legal remedy to protect the future children of women convicted of child abuse presents a significant danger of doing just this. By ordering a woman to have a chemical implanted into her body, a court not only violates a woman's fundamental right to decide whether to bear children but also takes away any choice she may have to use other, less drastic methods of birth control.[8] Proponents of Norplant as a condition of probation argue that the probationer is not forced to accept the device; merely it is offered as an alternative to incarceration and the individual is free to make an informed choice.[9] However, there may be doubt as to whether one can really make an informed, voluntary choice when faced with the daunting alternative of prison.

Similar concerns arise in the context of surrogacy agreements. "One of the actual conditions that perpetuates the exploitation of woman is her economic status."[10] Women earn generally far less than men and are often relegated to what society considers "women's employment."[11] Economic exigencies may force some women to seek out surrogacy arrangements when they might otherwise not do so. Feminists agree that women should be able to engage in potentially risky behavior so long as they are able to give voluntary and informed consent.[12] However, a strong element of feminist theory is that women cannot provide fully informed consent until after they have given birth.[13] Other feminists, however, caution that this is a very dangerous argument to make because it represents a step backward for women to argue that they are incapable of making decisions.[14] The inherent evil of surrogacy, according to most feminists is that it is a form of prostitution, in which the woman is exploited, and her reproductive capacity becomes a commodity.[15]

Another area in which women are struggling to break free from conventional gendered roles and male-dominated institutions is the arena of marriage. Entering into marriage with another woman affords women the power to assume the social roles of men and thus make greater strides toward equality in a primarily male-dominated society.[16] However, as women struggle for the freedom to enter into same-sex marriages, they collide with the heterosexual definitional equation of marriage,[17] which forms a self-enclosed system inaccessible to single-gender couples who desire equal protection of the laws for their intimate relationships.[18] The summary denial of homosexual marriage limits the fundamental right to marry, deemed to inhere in the individual, as an exclusive privilege granted to heterosexuals.[19] To prove their suitability to marry, homosexual couples will either have to deny the importance of the sexual aspect of their marriage or diminish the significance of their sexual orientation.[20] From a feminist perspective, it is discriminatory to force homosexuals to declare an essential aspect of their humanity as irrelevant in order to secure the freedom to marry.

This chapter examines feminist perspectives on the new reproductive technologies. Specifically, it analyzes three distinct areas: the Norplant condition, surrogate motherhood, and same-sex marriages. Additionally, because of feminist concerns of inequality, exploitation, and commodification of women in pornography, and because of the negative consequences this has on sustaining traditional family values, it too is considered. This chapter, then, seeks to build comprehensive framework for subsequent analysis of the specific problems raised here. Insofar as possible, it was thought advisable to present a broad codification of feminist perspectives in one place and then proceed to illustrate how these views are effecting change in contemporary family values throughout the remaining chapters in this book.

Feminism

As observed, feminism originated and developed as a basic demand for equality between the sexes. As such, it seeks to cast off the inegalitarian nature of marriage, owing inherently to the differing roles of the male and the female in procreation, and in its place structure a new social ethic.[21] Today, however, most women are not struggling for this type of feminist equality; rather, they seek simple equity and fairness in the distribution of burdens—professional, social, and marital.[22]

Women have been "oppressed"—traditionally—through motherhood, particularly so since procreativity is regarded as the object of male domination.[23] Because of this view, then, the housewife has been termed a "parasite,"[24] with her role in the traditional marriage being likened to "slavery"![25] Indeed, since children account for a very significant portion of women's biological inequality with men, feminists argue for a total transformation of male consciousness, a new division of labor within the family unit (through shared or joint parenting), together with a number of state support programs for working women.[26] The "simple" goal of contemporary feminism may be seen, hence, as an effort to not only advance domesticity as unfashionable, if not shameful, but to recast, if not destroy, the traditional notion of family values by marginalizing the role of housewives and nonworking mothers merely and thereby devaluing their very status in the family itself.[27]

The Epistemology of Feminism

As conceived classically, epistemology is the study of knowledge. Contemporary epistemologists concern themselves with attempting to give accounts of what knowledge is.[28] Attacks by feminists on classical epistemology tie to the fact that the context of Western philosophy—and especially notions of reason and rationality and its uses in critical analysis—are essentially male biased.[29] Because classical epistemology has never taken seriously the "epistemic desires of women," it must be regarded as suspect, and even fraudulent, for it has misrepresented itself as that "which is desired by all persons."[30] The feminist critics of classical epistemology maintain women only desire one thing: "a theory of knowledge which is juxtaposed to men's, one that privileges emotion and is committed to subjectivity."[31] Indeed, the radical feminist dismisses any "rational" challenge to the correctness of her epistemology because, she contends, these challenges are but commitments to "male reasoning" and must therefore be dismissed as illegitimate.[32] Because classical epistemology is male biased, feminists assert their unique epistemology must avoid this inherent weakness by accepting that "emotions are epistemologically indispensable," realizing "that subjectivity and the specificities of cognitive agency can and must be accorded central epistemological significance," and believing that epistemological "contextualization is related to and dependent upon bodily awareness of context through senses."[33]

Sadly, all too often, the "victimization" of females by a male-dominated society has been manufactured as such in some minds because females have been denied biological, social, economic, and professional parity with heterosexual, white middle-class males.[34] The fact of victimizaton is as much biological as social. Andrea Dworkin framed this issue succinctly when she observed that the key to understanding the "lower human status" of women in social and gender relations is found in the act of sex, for the domination of women by men is seen dramatically in "that slit which means entry into her" through intercourse.[35]

Man words are said to be a source of great offense and even victimizaton because they are gender-specific and thus insulting to women. Thus, the word *mankind*, implies females are not humans.[36] The feminist assault on all words which have man as a prefix or suffix is simply overreactionary and not based on logic and truth, for anyone familiar with the history of language knows full well that in Old English, and Anglo-Saxon, the suffix *man* was gender neutral, referring as such to all people equally.[37] So too, in various degrees are antagonism, self-doubt, moral intimidation, and even levels of confused and misdirected empathy engendered in male egos when demands are made and insisted upon in the name of political correctness that the pronoun *he* can never stand alone as gender neutral, but must be linked with the pronoun, *she*.

Indeed, it is quite difficult for men to counter effectively such fulminations of the radical feminists. To do so and to suggest what ideas are perceived as untruths and exaggerations in radical feminism philosophy subjects the male naysayers "to heated accusations of being hostile to women and their rights . . . and wishing to reduce them to subordinate positions."[38] Accordingly, most men, because of their fears of being the subject of such heavy allegations, "choose circumspection."[39] While the man of reason may be male, rationality must be viewed as still sex/gender neutral.[40] Surely, the "possibility" still exists that philosophy is unbiased and seeks perennial truths through a method of universal reason.[41]

Types of Feminism

There are said commonly to be three types of modern feminist thought: liberal, radical, and cultural.[42] They all share the same goal, however, namely to end women's inequality.[43] Achieving that goal is different for the liberal feminist who thinks one way and the cultural feminist who thinks another way. Interestingly, radical feminists think far differently than the other two groups on a considerable number of contradictory points. In some cases, the very concept of thinking—as the verb *think*—is used conventionally—is taken as but an act of patriarchal deceit.[44]

Generally, feminist thought may be taken as encompassing "liberal, Marxist, radical, socialist, multicultural, global, ecofeminist, existentialist, psychoanalytic, cultural or post modern" philosophies.[45] The politics of liberal, radical, and cultural feminism is rooted in part by the way feminists themselves view the ontologies associated with these strains or, in other words, the differing notions of what makes an individual a "self" and how that self relates to others.[46] Consequently, feminists adopt a female ontology and reject male ontologies asserting that, particularly in medicine and science, no objectivity is found because these two fields are androcentric or, in other words, directed toward perceiving and advancing only the interests of males.[47]

The liberal feminists assert that all reproductive-aiding technologies should be made available (regardless of marital status), providing no harm occurs to anyone through the use of these procedures. Further, they maintain that there is a valid legal right for two or more consenting adults, to contract with one another to procreate a child in a collaborative manner. For example, once informed consent has been secured for a surrogacy contract, it must be honored—regardless of the difficulties in enforcement.[48]

The radical feminists do not endorse a contract approach to surrogation and, if anything, favor a total ban on commercial surrogate motherhood.[49] Contrariwise, cultural feminists advocate new policies that not only create but also strengthen when appropriate the bonds between women as a social grouping as well as among women, children, and men. Viewing women within gynocentric collaborative reproductive contexts, cultural feminism would seek to provide a woman with a long-sought child, but in a noncommercial setting either as a gift of love or as a result of a monetary transaction mutually agreed upon and guided more or less by altruistic values.[50]

NORPLANT

The promise of Norplant as a foolproof, long-lasting contraceptive that requires little thought and works for almost everyone was so seductive that the message spread with amazing speed after the Food and Drug Administration (FDA) approved it for public use in December 1990.[51] However, the device was no sooner proclaimed to be "the most effective contraceptive ever made available"[52] than it became the focus of embittered controversy across the country. Only weeks after the FDA's approval, THE PHILADELPHIA INQUIRER printed an editorial suggesting that Norplant could be an effective means of solving the problem of poverty among blacks and called for incentives for welfare mothers to receive it.[53] Thus, in the politically charged arena of fertility and reproductive rights, Norplant has become the issue of the day.[54]

The coercive possibilities of Norplant have spurred much controversy regarding legislative and judicial authority to restrict an individual's reproductive choices. After Norplant's creator, Dr. Sheldon Segal, learned of the INQUIRER controversy, he expressed outrage that "a device intended to enhance reproductive freedom might be used coercively to restrict it."[55] As soon as Norplant was introduced, state legislatures rushed to develop monetary incentive programs to encourage low-income women to use the implant.[56] For example, in 1991 legislatures began to introduce the idea of "bonus" programs that not only would reimburse the full cost of Norplant but also provide a cash bonus to women receiving public assistance who accept the device.[57]

While proposed legislation involving Norplant has raised questions about the propriety of state intervention, the Norplant controversy has also raised the specter of great judicial abuse. Specifically, the use of Norplant by judges as a legal remedy in child abuse cases has ignited heated debate about the constitutionality of compelling Norplant as a condition of probation, or as part of a plea agreement.[58]

What Is Norplant?

Norplant is a contraceptive device consisting of six matchstick-size capsules that are implanted beneath the skin of the woman's upper arm. Implantation and removal of Norplant require minor surgery.[59] According to its manufacturers, after the device is implanted, a woman can leave her physician's office, and enjoy worry-free contraception for five years.[60] After approximately five years, however, the levonorgestrel runs low and the Norplant capsules must be removed. The capsules are extracted under local anesthesia through a small incision at the initial insertion site.   Within one week of its removal, the level of progesterone is almost undetectable in the bloodstream and women revert to their natural state of fertility before using the device.[61]

Though family planning advocates and members of the medical community have hailed Norplant as "a contraceptive victory for women," it is not without disadvantages.[62] An overwhelming majority of women using Norplant experience irregular bleeding, prolonged periods, and other menstrual fluctuations.[63] There might also be headaches, acne, weight gain, or depression associated with using the device. In addition, when Norplant entered the market, it contained a package insert warning that the device is potentially dangerous for women who have heart problems, high cholesterol, high blood pressure, diabetes, acute liver disease, breast cancer, or a history of blood clots. In July 1994 the FDA and Norplant manufacturer, Wyeth-Ayerst, expanded this list of possible negative reactions. The list, ranging from heart attacks to strokes, is based on complaints from actual Norplant users.[64]

Court-ordered Birth Control?

The heated controversies surrounding Norplant have grasped the public's attention and inspired wide debate on the question of whether judicially imposed contraception by any method is appropriate.[65] The rising tide of child abuse and the ineffectiveness of traditional means of combatting this social tragedy have spurred recent controversial recommendations involving Norplant from the judiciary.[66] Specifically, the advent of Norplant has stimulated commendable interest in the implementation of mandatory birth control policies to punish abusive and drug-addicted mothers, and to thwart the increasing number of babies addicted to drugs.[67] However, while such actions are no doubt motivated by legitimate concerns, they also raise significant constitutional issues. Opponents of mandatory contraception as a condition of probation argue that such conditions are beyond the statutory authority of courts,[68] violate a woman's fundamental right to privacy, [69] and constitutes thinly disguised unauthorized eugenic sterilization.[70]

SURROGATION—THE MAJOR ISSUES

In traditional bioethical analysis, liberals view new reproductive technologies as beneficial, because they increase the options available to infertile couples, whereas conservatives object to these methods on moral and religious grounds, finding that they upset the status quo.[71] Feminist analyses of reproductive technologies examine power, control and choice.[72] However, even among feminists there is disagreement about the morality of surrogacy and the alternative modes of reproductive technology. Some feminists regard the choices as new reproductive freedoms that offer significant potential for expanding women's autonomy,[73] whereas other feminists fear that modern reproductive technology provides yet another means for society to continue to control women through their reproductive capacities and to devalue and exploit women by reinforcing the ideological tendencies to view women as "fetal containers" or "mother machines."[74]

Surrogate parenting is a scientific extension of the natural ability to reproduce.[75] A couple may take advantage of this alternative when the woman is infertile, or would be at high risk during pregnancy.[76] While the term, *surrogate motherhood*, can refer to a number of different situations, including the situation where gestation occurs in a womb of a woman other than the egg donor, it is used generally to describe the woman who conceives a child by assisted conception, carries the resulting fetus to term, and relinquishes all parental rights to the sperm donor at birth, in accordance with a contract executed before the child's conception.[77]

Contract Law Versus Family Law

Surrogate motherhood is controversial in a number of areas. There is a general consensus that surrogacy contracts should be viewed in light of either contract law or family law; however, deciding which legal paradigm to apply creates perhaps the central difficulty in deciding how to treat such contracts.[78] Some commentators believe that there will be difficulty no matter what law is applied, because the uniqueness of surrogacy renders appeal to past legal decisions unhelpful in resolving how to treat this novel situation.[79] Indeed, surrogacy does not simply involve regulation of the family, as one of the main elements is that a woman carries the baby of a man to whom she is not married. Therefore, it is false that only "family" issues are involved.[80]   However, because the surrogate does not provide an everyday "service," it is also false that surrogacy arrangements fall *exclusively* within the realm of contract law.[81]

It is too simplistic to conclude that surrogacy must be covered entirely by one area of the law to the exclusion of another. Family law covers more than the simple regulation of the family, and contract law covers more than the provision of standard goods and services.[82] Therefore, reliance on both areas of the law may be necessary. Indeed, family law traditionally relies on contract law in areas other than the controversy surrounding surrogacy contracts.[83]

Some commentators suggest that surrogacy is essentially a contract for gestational services.[84] However, this argument was specifically rejected by the Supreme Court of New Jersey in the controversial decision *In re Baby M*.[85] There, the court found the surrogacy contract at issue to be unenforceable, and turned the case into a custody battle, by determining what arrangement was in the "best interest of the child."[86]

Public Policy Concerns

One of the main concerns of feminists over surrogacy contracts is that women may be harmed when their reproductive capacities are treated as commodities and sold on the market.[87] Historically, women have been discriminated against and exploited by men.[88] Many people fear that surrogacy contracts have the potential to subject future generations of women to the same oppressed fate if they are treated merely as reproductive machines.[89] In turning the womb into a commodity, many feminists fear that society will continue to value women primarily for their reproductive abilities.[90] Opponents of surrogacy maintain that the surrogate is treated as an emotionless, unfeeling machine whose only purpose is to create a life and then vanish.[91] Conducting the reproductive process in this manner runs the risk of "[ridiculing] the basic human value applied to procreation."[92] Proponents of surrogacy, however, maintain that the woman is able to disassociate herself from the emotional attachment because of the honorable act she is performing.[93]

Another argument condemning surrogacy, which is gaining favor particularly among radical feminists, is the claim that the surrogate is somehow coerced or compelled, and that her consent is only superficially voluntary.[94] Adherents to this line of reasoning assert that because the surrogate has been raised in a male-dominated society, and has been conditioned to view her functions primarily as procreative and maternal, her choices are merely "the legacy of [a] socio-psychological framework of social conditioning."[95] These pressures influence a woman's decision, and push her into believing that surrogacy is simply a natural progression of that function. The only freedom left for the woman is to "prostitute herself."[96]

Most feminist writers view surrogacy as a form of slavery or prostitution, in which the surrogate is enticed by the offer of money.[97] One of the most often cited reasons for the exploitative nature of surrogacy is that women may feel compelled by economic pressures to become surrogates.[98] For example, poor women may feel pressure to become surrogate mothers in order to increase the family's income. Similarly, one commentator notes that "society places a greater premium on a woman's childbearing role than it does on her employment prospects. Given that childbearing is the prime function for which women are valued, it is not surprising that some women only feel special when they are pregnant and assert that they love reproducing."[99] Some feminists argue, however, that it is men who perpetuate the notion that women love to be pregnant.[100] "Men are controlling not only what choices are open to women, but what choices women learn to want to make. Women may have a will to be pregnant[,] . . . but [they] have the potential to want other things as well."[101] This potential, feminists allege, is one that is largely unfulfilled.[102]

Legislative Responses

Many have called upon the legislatures to respond to the issue of surrogacy arrangements. As lawmakers have slowly begun to respond to the need for regulation, growing concern about exploitation may have facilitated decisions to hold surrogacy contracts unenforceable or even to criminalize surrogacy.[103] At least three states have outlawed surrogacy,[104] while a number of other states have passed laws prohibiting the enforcement of surrogacy contracts.[105] Many of these statutes are premised on the notion that women who become surrogates are exploited by the intended parents with whom they contract, and by society in general.[106]

REBUTTING FEELINGS AND FEARS

As seen, the current statutes regulating surrogacy contracts are based on a fallacious perception that the practice, itself, presents very serious—indeed, intolerable—risks to women (including physical risks, psychological risks and symbolic ones as well such as objectification and commodification) and should therefore be discouraged.[107] Put simply, there is insufficient evidence that surrogacy is harmful and that, as practiced currently, it promotes objectification and commodification.[108] The evidence also does not show that money is an overpowering coercive force in the decisions made by women to become surrogates.[109] The risks which do occur to surrogates are rare in number and are not different significantly from those assumed under ordinary circumstances by all women in their daily lives.[110]

Those feminists who criticize surrogation as nothing more than acts of exploitation demean a woman's right of intellectual choice to become a surrogate and seek to, essentially, patronize all surrogates as a group.[111] The alleged gender inequality existing within surrogation is no more pervasive than seen within all aspects of contemporary society.[112] Furthermore, surrogation is simply not akin to prostitution,[113] nor is the act properly considered as a form of "baby selling."[114]

This latter argument is argumentation by epithet, for a surrogate mother may not be viewed correctly as "owning" a baby any more than may the genetic father be so viewed. What the surrogate sells is not the baby, but rather her parental rights.[115] In this regard, the surrogate mother is no different from a woman "who agrees in a divorce proceeding to surrender her claim to custody of the children of the marriage in exchange for some other concession from her husband—or from a sperm donor who receives cash, but not parental rights, in exchange for his donation."[116]

No doubt the most substantial risk to cohesive family relations in a surrogacy contract comes not from the actions by either set of parents, but from the uncertain legal status which (in situations where a ban is imposed) may well result in the children born of the contract being stigmatized as the product of a criminal act. And, in those incidents where the contract is unenforced, the child may be subjected to years of litigation in order to determine who will be adjudicated his legal parents.[117]

The insistent, ubiquitous, and unsubstantiated claims of gender inequality, commodification, incommensurability, and coercion should not be accepted as reasons for prohibiting surrogate contracts.[118] Rather, surrogacy should be viewed properly as an affirmation of family values, for it allows for a continuation of genetic ties across the generations and alleviates the heartache of childlessness.[119]

SAME-SEX MARRIAGES

Providing a woman the opportunity to marry another woman affords women, as a class, the power to assume the social roles of men and thus makes greater strides toward equality in a primarily male-dominated society.[120] While most feminists agree that same-sex couples should be entitled to the identical legal and economic benefits of marriage that heterosexual couples are furnished with, some feminists strongly oppose the legalization of gay and lesbian marriage. For example, one feminist writer "believe[s] that the desire to marry in the lesbian and gay community is an attempt to mimic the worst of mainstream society, an effort to fit into an inherently problematic institution that betrays the promise of both lesbian and gay liberation and radical feminism."[121] She contends that the pro-marriage position would accept, rather than challenge, the current institution of marriage, and that the process would be profoundly destructive to the lesbian and gay community. Moreover, any effort to legitimize lesbian and gay marriage would work to persuade the heterosexual mainstream that lesbians and gay men seek to emulate heterosexual marriage as currently constituted.[122]

Most feminists believe, however, that only by marrying will gay and lesbian couples validate the significance of their relationships, and that marriage is the issue most likely to lead ultimately to a world free from discrimination against lesbians and gay men.[123] The inability of homosexuals to marry directly contributes, it is maintained, to the discrimination they experience because of the belief that they are "promiscuous sexual deviants."[124] Because their intimate relationship is the root of their exclusion, marriage sanctioned by the state is "a core means of inclusion for homosexuals that the state may not deny without serious justification."[125] The denial of homosexuals' right to marry "perpetuates their suffocation in 'the closet.'"[126]

The Right to Privacy

Marriage operates essentially as a "relational right," enabling individuals to relate intimately to one another, and to the wider community.[127] This relational right is conceived of and protected by the Court under the guise of the right of privacy. Feminists argue generally that the constitutional right of privacy requires states to sanction and recognize same-sex marriages. Viewed functionally, the legal institution of marriage is a binding commitment between two intimately related adults, "a commitment which sustains the relationship between such adults by structuring their dealings with each other and with third parties."[128] In this sense, marriage is indifferent to the relative genders of its participants.[129] Therefore, because marriage does not inherently exclude homosexual couples, the fundamental right to marry, which derives from the constitutional right of privacy, should also extend to such couples.[130]

The answer to any question usually depends on how it is framed.[131] "Should the issue be framed in terms of a (more general) fundamental right to marry or in terms of a (more specific) fundamental right to marry someone of the same sex?"[132] Framing the issue on a broader level of generality would appear to confer the right to marry on same-sex couples, but this at the same time forces homosexuals to diminish the significance of their sexual orientation. From the feminist perspective, "it is discriminatory to force homosexuals, as a precondition to their access to fundamental rights, to declare the irrelevance of an essential aspect of their humanity."[133]

The feminist quest is to facilitate judicial vision and compel the courts to react meaningfully to inequality.[134] "By connecting imaginatively with the human dimension of social inequalities, the judiciary may . . . resolve moral dilemmas—on human, not just legal terms."[135] In the process of this exploration, it is necessary that courts recognize the notion of equality is in need of expansion in order to defeat a self-enclosed system that is inaccessible to single-gender couples who desire equal protection of the laws of the their intimate relationships.[136]

PORNOGRAPHY

Pornography denotes "a sexually graphic representation, verbal or pictorial, heterosexual or homosexual, designed to titillate or arouse the reader or viewer."[137] This said, some have found a positive value in pornography—arguing as such that in a male-dominated culture the only way for the average woman to learn what appeals to male sexuality is for her to have access to those representations which males, in turn, find sexually appealing and interesting.[138] Indeed, the core value presented within the inevitable debate which follows a discussion of pornography is recognition of liberty and freedom in contemporary society and the extent to which it will be restrained.[139]

The school of radical feminism argues that liberty and freedom mask the real nature of pornography—namely, the nature of equality in the arena of human sexuality.[140] Accordingly, it is argued that in order to alleviate the subordination of women to men, pornography should be eliminated totally. This achievement, in turn, would have a positive effect in the overall struggle to eliminate not only sex discrimination but also the market devaluation of women's work and sexual harassment.[141] For the radical feminist, then, official tolerance of pornography not only elevates the speech of those with social power to define women *over* the efforts of women to define themselves but also makes it impossible for women to speak sexually—this because they are regarded as but *objects* of the moment, subordinated to the ideas and power of the male subject.[142] This inequality results in women being depicted and viewed as not only sexual objects, but as things or commodities.[143] This position has come under serious criticism because of its lack of documentation.[144]   Nevertheless, its supporters are very committed and vociferous in their advocacy of it.[145]

Because pornography "eroticizes" male dominance, it is seen by feminists as a "core constitutive practice" of gender discrimination.[146] Pornographic movies that present portrayals of female criminal assault and rape, in particular, are really not so much about rape (although it is depicted graphically, it is rarely confronted) as it is taken as entertainment. As the depictions of rape have grown more lurid, they would appear to present a singular function: namely, to raise the "violence quotient"—for by taking such a long time to unfold on the screen, rape becomes a sexy "kind of violence."[147]

Feminists seek to reconstruct society's legal and governmental norms from a higher moral position advancing, as such, feminists objectives. As observed, pornography is taken as not only commodifying women but also as fragmenting and fetishizing and alienating the bodies of women.[148] Accordingly, the attack by feminists on pornography is made on the basis that it is an insidious form of power and to be discounted totally as an inherent right of expression.[149] Obscenity laws are viewed within the patriarchal system as speech protection for men and deterrents to free speech for women.[150]   Pornographic harm is seen as an infringement of First Amendment guarantees against victimization by unfair expressions.[151]   Indeed, for feminists, pornography is, simply, a form of sex discrimination.[152]

Toward a New Norm of Behavior

The rhetoric of contemporary feminism is tied, inextricably, to responding to the "woman question" or, in other words, grappling with the extent to which (assisted) reproduction enhances women's productive liberty or restrains it. Of course, the "woman question" comes into direct focus as well when pornography is considered, for it is in this area of interest that it is asserted by leading feminists that women are misrepresented and trivialized—with the law failing consistently to distinguish between rape from intercourse and between categories of prurience and offensiveness.[153] What is needed, it is argued, is for philosophical-aesthetic objectives to prevail over legal-governmental norms which would in turn have the effect of bringing about a "total aesthetic transformation of [the] manipulative being" and an ending of the present culture of pornography.[154]

Deconstructing or Reconstructing

Often the clarity of thought and expression needed to understand a position is lacking in feminist discourse and never more so than in the advocacy of an aesthetic dialectic in pornography. The inherent problem here is that there is no practical way by which a translation between the philosophical-aesthetic conception of pornography as objectification and the actual operations of legal and governmental institutions may be effected. In other words, there cannot be equivalence recognized and implemented between the feminist definition of pornography and an all- encompassing right never to be discriminated against.[155]

The aesthetic dialect advocated by the feminists here is, in actuality, but

> a means of *withdrawing* from the legal-governmental field and of orienting oneself to another set of concerns: those of the self conceived as the problematic interface of the two sides of the dialectic. In fact, the dialectic is an ethical weapon directed against positive law and government. It aims to problematise their normative regulation of conduct and attributes by picturing "complete" human development as the dialectical neutralization of all positive norms and the recovery of "wholeness" from the fragments.[156]

Intellectually, this dialectic might be viewed as noble and aspirational in purpose and vision. Taken from the standpoint of practical implementation, however, it is not achievable, simply because of its failure to structure a mechanism to achieve its goal—deconstruction of the present legal system—and because of majoritatrian society's reluctance to accept the premise of the dialectic in the first place.[157]

CONCLUSIONS

In essence, perhaps the goals of contemporary feminism are three: to develop a new social milieu which guarantees for women that their societal worth is independent of their biological ability to have children; to encourage and promote new medical research policies and practices which commit more economic resources into preventing infertility than in finding "cures" for it; and promote the development of environmentally safe work places which, in turn, will have the effect of preventing conditions which contribute to infertility.[158] Surely the second and third goals are commendable—and perhaps even achievable within the foreseeable future. The first goal is, no doubt, the most problematic.

As has been seen throughout this chapter, all too often the specific taxonomy of feminism is laden in verbosity and philosophical confusion—almost in a way defying understanding for those who do not speak the language of feminism. For many, the effort required to "learn" feminist philosophy is simply not worth the time which must be invested for achievement of the goal. While, no doubt, many of the concerns of the feminist philosophy are valid, the feminist movement is not advanced or understood by its seclusion within obfuscation. Indeed, when ideas, theories, and policies are not put within a level of ready comprehension, they become distrusted, feared, and misunderstood and without the reach of the average, ordinary, reasonable man.

Mary Ann Glendon has concluded that "official feminism" is out of touch with the real concerns of most women today, which are not gender issues at all but rather jobs and families. Thus, the primary concern for men an, women alike is how to structure a decent family life without suffering excessive career disadvantages.[159]

Feminist perspectives challenge the traditional notions of family and demand their reevaluation. This in itself is good and even healthy. When, however, these perspectives offer no real, *constructive*, and reasonable suggestions for reformation but dwell instead on a subjective desire for deconstruction as a noble goal in and of itself, the philosophy of feminism loses its intellectual integrity. A philosophy or school of thought need not have a *practical* goal of any nature, yet here it should allow an understanding of the weaknesses of the present institution—the family—and promote reasonable ways to correct those perceived weaknesses within present social structures. It is one thing to advocate a revolution. It is quite another to have a framework for principled decision making in place to translate the goals of the revolution into success.[160]

NOTES

1.   Wikler, *Society's Response to the New Reproductive Technologies: The Feminist Perspective,* 59 SO. CAL. L. REV. 1043 (1986).

2.   *Id.*

3.   Becker, *Four Feminist Theoretical Approaches and the Double Bind of Surrogacy,* 69 CHI. KENT L. REV. 303, 304 (1993).

4.   *See generally* FEMINIST PERSPECTIVES IN MEDICAL ETHICS (H.B. Holmes & L.M. Purdy eds. 1992).

5.   *Griswold v. Connecticut,* 381 U.S. 479, 485-6 (1965).

6.   *Roe v. Wade,* 410 U.S. 113, 154-6 (1973).

7.   *See* Leiber, *Selling the Womb: Can the Feminist Critique of Surrogacy Be Answered?* 68 IND. L. J. 205, 213 (1992).

8.   Ginzberg, *Compulsory Contraception as a Condition of Probation: The Use and Abuse of Norplant*, 58 BROOK. L. REV. 979, 1016 (1992).

9.   *Id.*

10. G. COREA, THE MOTHER MACHINE 228 (1985).

11. *Id.*

12. Leiber, *supra* note 7 at 216.

13. *Id.*

14. *Id.*

15. *Id.* at 223.

16. Polikoff, *We Will Get What We Ask For: Why Legalizing Gay and Lesbian Marriage Will Not Dismantle the Legal Structure of Marriage*, 79 VA. L. REV. 1535, 1539-0 (1993).

17. *See, e.g., Singer v. Hara*, 552 P. 2d 1187, 1189 (Wash. Ct. App. 1974).

18. Lewis, *From This Day Forward: A Feminine Moral Discourse on Homosexual Marriage,* 97
YALE L. J. 1783 (1988).

19. *Id.*

20. *Id.*

21. Cohen, *Rhetoric, The Unnatural Family and Women's Work*, 81 VA. L. REV. 2275 (1995).

22. Fox-Genovese, *Feminism, Children and the Family*, 18 HARV. J. L. & PUB. POL'Y 503 (1995).

23. Hanigsberg, *Homologizing Pregnancy and Motherhood: A Consideration of Abortion*, 94 MICH. L. REV. 371, 417 (1995).

24. B. FRIEDAN, THE FEMINIST MYSTIQUE 271, 274 (1963).

25. Graglia, *The Housewife as Pariah*, 18 HARV. J. L. & PUB. POL'Y 509, 513 f.n. 31 (1995) (quoting Hillary Rodham Clinton).

See also R.H. BORK, SLOUCHING TOWARD GOMORRAH: MODERN LIBERALISM AND AMERICAN DECLINE 223 (1996).

26. Fox-Genovese, *supra* note 22 at 504.

27. Graglia, *supra* note 25 at 512.

28. E.R. KLEIN, FEMINISM UNDER FIRE 51 (1996).

29. *Id.* at 64.

30. *Id.* at 63.

31. *Id.*

32. *Id.* at 65.

33. *Id.* at 54.

34. R. HUGHES, CULTURE OF COMPLAINT: THE FRAYING OF AMERICA 17 (1993).

35. A. DWORKIN, INTERCOURSE 123 (1987).

36. Hughes, *supra* note 34 at 21.

37. *Id.* at 22.

38. Bork, *supra* note 25 at 224.

39. *Id.*

40. Hughes, *supra* note 34 at 62.

41. Klein, *supra* note 28 at 227.

42. Tong, *Feminist Bioethics: Toward Developing a Feminist Answer to the Surrogate Motherhood Question*, 6 KENNEDY INST. ETHICS J. 37, 38 (1996).

Others have classified the division as being among traditional, liberal, and relational feminism. *See, e.g.,* Ortiz, *Feminism and the Family*, 18 HARV. J.L. & PUB. POL'Y 523, 524 (1995).

See generally Rhode, *Feminist Critical Theories*, 42 STAN. L. REV. 617 (1990).

43. Ortiz, *supra* note 42 at 523.

44. Polsby, *Ozzie and Harriett Had It Right*, 18 HARV. J. L. & PUB. POL'Y 531 (1996).

45. Tong, *supra* note 42 at 36.

46. *Id.* at 39.

47. *Id.* at 41.

48. *Id.* at 43.

49. *Id.*

50. *Id.* at 44.

51. Hilts, *U.S. Approves Contraceptives Planted in Skin*, N.Y. TIMES, Dec. 11, 1990, at A1.

52. *Better Birth Control; A Hormone Implant Promises Safe, Long-Term Contraception; Don't Let Politics Block It*, NEWSDAY, Dec. 15, 1990, at 18.

53. Kimmelman, *Poverty and Norplant: Can Contraception Reduce the Underclass*, PHIL. INQUIRER, Dec. 12, 1990, at A18. The INQUIRER apologized publicly later that month. *See An Apology: The Editorial on Norplant and Poverty Was Misguided and Wrongheaded*, PHIL. INQUIRER, Dec. 23, 1990, at C4.

54. Parker, *Politics: A Bitter Pill for Reproductive Rights*, ORLANDO SENTINEL, Feb. 25, 1994 at E1 (reasoning that Norplant risks unjustified condemnation due to the misguided actions of the overzealous few).

55. Arthur, *The Norplant Prescription: Birth Control, Woman Control, or Crime Control*, 40 UCLA L. REV. 1, 5 (1992).

56. *See, e.g.,* H.R. 1860, 97th GEN. ASSEMBLY, 2d Reg. Session, 1992 Tennessee (offering women receiving welfare benefits $500 stipend for using Norplant); S 2909, 52nd Leg. Reg. Sess., 1992 Washington (mandating Norplant insertion in women whose babies are born with fetal alcohol syndrome or addicted to drugs).

57. *See* Coale, *Norplant Bonuses and the Unconstitutional Condition Doctrine*, 71 TEX. L. REV. 189 (1992).

58. *See, e.g.,* Neuborne, *In the Norplant Case, Good Intentions Make Bad Law*, L.A. TIMES, Mar. 3, 1991, at M1; Queenin, *Judge Orders Birth Control for Abusive Mother*, L.A. TIMES, Jan. 30, 1991, at B6.

59. Shoupe & Mishell, *Norplant: Subdermal Implant System for Long-Term Contraception*, 160 AM. J. OBSTETRICS & GYN. 1286 (1989).

60. Arthur, *supra* note 55 at 90-1.

61. *Id.* at 91, n. 34.

62. Ballard, *The Norplant Condition: One Step Forward or Two Steps Back?*, 16 HARV. WOMEN'S L. J. 139, 142 (1993).

63. *Id.*

64. *See* Reynolds, *Women Suffering from Norplant Arm-Twisting*, USA TODAY, July 15, 1994, at 15A.

65. Arthur, *supra* note 55 at 7.

66. Saunders, *Banning Motherhood: An Rx to Combat Child Abuse?*, 26 ST. MARY'S L. J. 203, 207 (1994).

67. *Id.*

68. Arthur, *supra* note 55 at 7.

69. *Id.*

70. *Id.*

71. Bender, *Teaching Feminist Perspectives on Health Care Ethics and Law: A Review Essay*, 61 CIN. L. REV. 1251, 1265 (1993).

See generally FEMINISM AND BIOETHICS: BEYOND REPRODUCTION (S. Wolf ed. 1996).

72. *Id.*

73. Leiber, *supra* note 7.

74. *Id.*

75. *See* Coleman, *Surrogate Motherhood: An Analysis of the Problems and Suffestions for Solutions*, 50 TENN. L. REV. 71, 75 (1982).

76. Recht, *"M" is for Money: Baby M and The Surrogate Motherhood Controversy*, 37 AM. U. L. REV. 1013, 1025-26 (1988).

77. *See* Mandler, *Developing a Concept of The Modern Family: A Proposed Uniform Surrogate Parenting Act*, 73 GEO. L. J. 1283, 1284 (1985).

78. Strasser, *Parental Rights Terminations: On Surrogate Reasons and Surrogacy Policies*, 60 TENN. L. REV. 135, 138 (1992).

79. *Id.*

80. *Id.* at 138.

81. *Id.*

82. *Id.*

83. *Id.*

84. *Id.*

85. 537 A.2d 1227 (N. J. 1988).

86. *Id.* at 1258.

87. Recht, *supra* note 76 at 1021.

88. *Id.*

89. *Id.* at 1022.

90. Leiber, *supra* note 7 at 213.

91. *Id.*

92. Recht, *supra* note 76 at 1023.

But *see* Comment, *Contracts to Bear a Child*, 66 CAL. L. REV. 611, 614 (1978) (arguing that a reasonable woman is capable of weighing the risks and benefits of becoming a surrogate, which distinguishes her from an unthinking machine).

93. *Id.*

94. Hill, *Exploitation*, 79 CORNELL L. REV. 631, 639 (1994).

95. *Id.* at 639-40.

96. *Id.*

97. Leiber, *supra* note 7 at 211.

See Allen, *Surrogacy, Slavery, and the Ownership of Life*, 13 HARV. J. L. & PUB. POL'Y 139, 147-8 (1990).

98. Hill, *supra* note 94 at 638.

99. Leiber, *supra* note 7 at 215.

100. *Id.*

101. *Id.*

102. *Id.*

103. Hill, *supra* note 94 at 642.

104. *See id.* (citing MICH. COMP. LAWS ANN. §722.857(2) (West 1993) (declaring surrogacy involving minors, mentally ill or mentally disabled women a felony); UTAH CODE ANN. §76-7-204(1)(d) (1991) (misdemeanor); WASH. REV. CODE ANN. §26.26.250 (West 1993) (gross misdemeanor). In a fourth state, surrogacy has been declared to be illegal by the State Attorney General. OP. ATTY. GEN. No. 83-162 (Sept. 26, 1983) (construing surrogacy to violate child trafficking laws). New York imposes a civil penalty for entering into surrogacy contracts and felony sanctions for any subsequent violations. N.Y. DOM. REL. §123(2)(b) (McKinney 1993).

105. *Id.* (noting that many states have opted for nonrecognition of surrogacy contracts). *See e.g.,* ARIZ. REV. STAT. ANN. §25-218 (1991); IND. CODE ANN. §31-8-2-1 (Burns 1993) (voiding surrogate contracts entered into after March 14, 1988); KY. REV. STAT. ANN. §199.590(3) (Michie/Bobbs-Merrill 1988); LA. REV. STAT. ANN. §168 B:23 (IV) (1992) (providing for judicial facilitation of surrogacy but permitting recision); N.D. CENT. CODE §14-18-05 (1992); TENN. CODE ANN. §36-1-114(b)(3)(A) (1992).

106. Hill, *supra* note 94 at 642.

107. Andrews, *Beyond Doctrinal Boundaries: A Legal Framework for Surrogate Motherhood*, 81 VA. L. REV. 2343 (1995).

108. *Id.* at 2361, 2375.

See Epstein, *Surrogacy: The Case for Full Contractual Enforcement*, 81 VA. L. REV. 2305, 2326 (1995).

109. Andrews, *supra* note 107 at 2365.

110. *Id.* at 2354.

111. Posner, *The Ethics and Economics of Enforcing Contract of Surrogate Motherhood*, 5 J.
CONTEMP. HEALTH L. & POL'Y 21 (1989).

112. Epstein, *supra* note 108 at 2329.

113. Posner, *supra* note 111 at 24-8.

114. *Id.*

115. *Id.* at 28. Epstein, *supra* note 106 at 2308.

116. Posner, *supra* note 111 at 28.

117. Andrews, *supra* note 107 at 2358.

118. *Id.* at 2341.

119. *Id.* at 2324.

120. Polikoff, *supra* note 16.

121. *Id.* at 1536.

122. *Id.*

123. *Id.* at 1535.

124. Lewis, *supra* note 18 at 1798.

125. *Id.*

126. *Id.*

127. *Id.*

128. Hohengarten, *Same-Sex Marriage and The Right of Privacy*, 103 YALE L. J. 1495 (1994), (citing *Jones v. Hallahan*, 501 S.W. 2d 588, 589 (Ky. 1973)).

129. *Id.*

130. *Id.*
Hohengarten contends that the privacy concern of the "right" of privacy is not sexual conduct, but the formation of families. *Id. See also* Comment, *To Love and Honor All the Days of Your Life: A Constitutional Right to Same-Sex Marriage*, 43 CATH. U. L. REV. 907 (1994).

131. Hohengarten, *supra* note 128 at 1508.

132. *Id.*

133. Lewis, *supra* note 18 at 1785.

134. *Id.* at 1788.

135. *Id.*

136. *Id.* at 1783, 1788.

137. R.A. POSNER, OVERCOMING LAW 359 (1995). *See also* R. A. POSNER, SEX AND REASON, Ch. 13 (1992).
Chief Judge Posner has gone so far as to suggest "pornography may be both a substitute for and a complement to rape—the former, to the extent that pornography makes masturbation a more satisfying substitute for sexual intercourse; the latter, to the extent that it stimulates desire for sexual intercourse, of which rape of course is one form." R.A. POSNER, ECONOMIC ANALYSIS OF LAW 158 (4th ed. 1992).

138. Littleton, *Old Wine in Nude Skins* (reviewing D. A. Downs, THE NEW POLITICS OF PORNOGRAPHY (1990), 69 TEX. L. REV. 497, 511 (1990);

Clear, *Pornography Saved My Marriage*, SHE Mag., Mar. 1996, at 116. *But see* Dworkin, *Against the Male Flood: Censorship, Pornography and Equality*, 8 HARV. WOMEN'S L. J. 1 (1985).

See also Scheller, *P C Peep Show: Computers, Privacy and Child Porn*, 27 J. MARSHALL L. REV. 989, 996 (1994) (suggesting that pornography is but a healthy expression of repressed feeling and fantasy and allows people to become more comfortable with their sexuality).

139. D. A. DOWNS, THE NEW POLITICS OF PORNOGRAPHY 32 (1990).

140. Littleton, *supra* note 138 at 498. *See generally* C.A. MACKINNON, FEMINISM UNMODIFIED (1987); A. DWORKIN, WOMAN HATING (1974).

141. *Id. See* C. Itzin, A Legal Definition of Pornography, in PORNOGRAPHY, WOMEN, VIOLENCE AND CIVIL LIBERTIES 435 (C. Itzin ed. 1992); A. DWORKIN, PORNOGRAPHY: MEN POSSESSING WOMEN (1981).

142. Littleton, *supra* note 138 at 499, 500, 508. *See generally* C.A. MACKINNON, ONLY WORDS (1993).

143. *Id.*

See generally C. A. MACKINNON, TOWARD A FEMINIST THEORY OF THE STATE (1989).

144. Dworkin, *Women and Pornography*, N.Y. REV. BOOKS, Oct. 21, 1993, at 36.

145. *See* Dworkin, *supra* note 138.

146. MACKINNON, FEMINISM UNMODIFIED, *supra* note 140 at 146, 148-49, 152.

147. Gifford, *Movie Violations: Once Taboo, Rape Is Depicted, Often Graphically in Today's Films*, WASH. POST, Feb. 11, 1996, at G5.

148. I. HUNTER, D. SAUNDERS & D. WILLIAMSON, ON PORNOGRAPHY: LITERATURE, SEXUALITY AND OBSCENITY 231, 234 (1993).

149. *Id.* at 233.

150. *Id.*

151. *Id.* at 235, 241.

152. *Id.* at 233.

See generally Meyer, *Sex, Sin and Women's Liberation: Against Porn-Suppression*, 72 TEX. L. REV. 1097 (1994).

153. MACKINNON, *supra* note 140 at 234-37.

154. *Id.*

155. Hunter, *supra* note 148 at 237.

156. *Id.* at 234.

157. *See generally* LIVING WITH CONTRADICTIONS: CONTROVERSIES IN FEMINIST SOCIAL ETHICS (A.M. Jaggar ed. 1994).

158. Tong, *supra* note 42 at 51.

159. Glendon, *Feminism and the Family: An Indissoluble Marriage*, COMMONWEALTH, Feb. 14, 1997, 11 at 12.

160. Bork, *supra* note 25 at 193.

Reproductive Privacy or Social Responsibility: Toward a New Genetic Family

Chapter 3

Domestic Partnerships and Same-Sex Relationships

While homosexuals and lesbians, to be sure, have children and raise families—with bisexuals often having children with primary sexual partners—on the whole, the children of gay people come through prior relationships, artificial insemination, surrogacy, and adoption, not as a direct consequence of their own primary sexual relationships.[1] These "families of choice," then, substitute for blood families within the gay family structure, and they have become a permanent part of contemporary society, forcing the courts in turn to deal with not only the offspring of lesbian coparents but also to determine support, visitation, inheritance, and all the other conventional rights that stem from heterosexual marriage.[2]

A 1988 study conducted by the American Bar Association estimated that between eight and ten million children were being raised in gay and lesbian households.[3] Some social scientists estimate that ten thousand children are being born each year to lesbian mothers who conceive by means of artificial insemination.[4] These trends, together with a gripping permissiveness in a society as a whole regarding social relationships, are forcing the law itself to redefine the state of marriage. Thus, if these new relationships differ substantially from traditional marriage yet carry the same incidents as marriage, it is argued they may be termed "marriage."[5]

The traditional characteristics of marriage (e.g., sexual exclusivity) are no longer mandated legally. Indeed, contemporary marriage is best defined as "some sort of relationship between two individuals, of indeterminate duration, involving some kind of sexual conduct, entailing vague mutual property and support obligations, a relationship which may be formed by consent of both parties and dissolved at the will of either."[6] As this transformation occurs through individual state statutes and judicial decisions, little consideration is given by the courts and legislatures to the real effect of these actions on marriage as an institution.[7]

Sadly, a growing ambivalence concerning marriage is seen in major U.S. Supreme Court decisions and other jurisdictions which all have the effect of diminishing marriage as a social institution. Thus, while an expansive reading of *Griswold v. Connecticut*[8] and *Eisenstadt v. Baird*[9] forces a conclusion that a zone of privacy—largely immune to state control—protects the acts of both married *and* unmarried persons, a subsequent 1986 case, *Bowers v. Hardwick*,[10] upheld a Georgia state statute prohibiting homosexual conduct between consenting adults in private. Care was taken, however, by the court to emphasize the *Griswold* right of privacy did not resemble an alleged "right" of homosexuals to engage in sodomy.[11]

CONSTITUTIONAL ARGUMENTS FOR VALIDATION

There are several major legal arguments advanced to maintain the position that prohibiting same-sex marriages is a violation of the U.S. Constitution. The first such argument holds the Establishment Clause of the First Amendment to the Constitution, as applied to the states by the Fourteenth Amendment, is violated by a prohibition of this type. Since this position is said to reflect both the traditional Christian view of marriage together with the Judaeo-Christian abhorrence of homosexual conduct, it is said to improperly codify an established religious attitude and thus be in contravention to the Establishment Clause itself.[12]

While this argument appears to be historically efficacious, as a constitutional argument it has been rejected soundly by the courts. Although neglecting to set out the specific legitimate and secular purposes served by forbidding homosexuals and lesbian marriage relationships, the cases seem to hint at three: to enforce a code of traditional morality based as such on very deep emotions shaped by religious views which hold same-sex actions are immoral; to discourage citizens—and especially the young—from becoming homosexuals themselves and thereby being excluded by mainstream society and incurring great societal hardships (a type of *parens patriae* position), and to safeguard the traditional view that only those marriages are valid which are aimed at producing children.[13]

Whether it is time to seek to transform marriage from a religious institution into a purely secular one[14] and begin to accept the position of the American Psychiatric Association set out in 1973 that homosexuality is not properly characterized as a mental illness but rather as a sexual orientation disturbance[15] or, presently, as perhaps having a biological or genetic component,[16] are very complex and heavy questions which cannot be answered with definitiveness. This is the case simply because society has not chosen to come to grips with the consequences of recognizing that a reformulation of the traditional family is already going on presently. By refusing to evaluate new currents in social thought, many states are allowing their courts—rather than the legislatures—to shape policy here.

Another constitutional argument attacking the prohibition against same-sex marriage holds that it is a violation of the Equal Protection Clause of the Fourteenth Amendment for a state to deny by reason of sex the right to marry.[17] Discredited as a part of the doctrine of substantive due process, this argument has not been persuasive at all.[18] Yet, it has been suggested that under Equal Rights Amendments to various state constitutions, a homosexual or lesbian citizen could argue that the right to marriage should be regarded as an absolute right since most of these statutory rights mandate they cannot be abridged because of sex.[19] Since the U.S. Supreme Court has shown itself keen to eliminate sex-based classifications through the authority of the Equal Protection Clause, this argument might well have merit here.[20]

Traditionally, the U.S. Supreme Court has held that a legislative classification which results in the denial of a fundamental right—here, marriage—[21]may only be sustained when it has been shown that compelling state interest directs this course of action. In testing the extent of the state interest in structuring such a legislative scheme, the challenged state law is subjected to "strict scrutiny."[22]

In assessing the validity of such legislative classifications, current decisions by the Supreme Court suggest it will weigh societal interests in validating a particular statutory classification with the injury inflicted allegedly on these individuals subjected to the legislation. Accordingly, if societal interests are deemed more substantial than the harms, the prohibitory scheme within the challenged states should be upheld.[23] It would seem likely, in view of the level of antagonism and nonacceptance by the public in general toward homosexuality, that the interests of homosexuals in recognizing same-sex marriages would not be held superior to those of the public.[24]

STATE JUDICIAL RESPONSES

The Hawaii Supreme Court, in *Baehr v. Lewin*,[25] has recently addressed the issue of same-sex marriages. The appellants had filed a complaint at the trial court level seeking a declaration that the statute governing valid marriage contracts, as interpreted by the Department of Health (DOH),[26] was unconstitutional as it permitted only couples of the opposite sex to obtain marriage licenses.[27] The complaint averred that such interpretation denied plaintiffs their right to privacy under the state constitution[28] as well as to the equal protection of the laws and due process of law under the state constitution.[29] The circuit court, in dismissing the complaint, concluded that plaintiffs, as homosexuals, were not denied their rights to due process nor, as homosexuals, did they constitute a suspect class for equal protection analysis; that there existed no fundamental right to homosexual marriage; and that the relevant marriage statute "is obviously designed to promote the general welfare interests of the community by sanctioning traditional man-woman family units and procreation."[30]

Due Process Challenge

The Hawaii Supreme Court, in its due process analysis, observed that the U.S. Supreme Court declared that "the right to marry is part of the fundamental 'right to privacy' implicit in the Fourteenth Amendment's Due Process Clause"[31] and that the issue in the instant case was whether this right to marry extended to same-sex couples.[32] After analyzing the federal constitutional history relevant to marriage,[33] the Hawaii Supreme Court concluded that "the federal construct of the fundamental right to marry—subsumed within the right to privacy. . .—presently contemplates unions between men and women."[34] Thus, the Hawaii statute did not violate the state constitutional guarantee of a right to privacy–this because same-sex marriages are not a fundamental right.[35] The court refused wisely to structure such a new right by observing that the right to same-sex marriage is not rooted in the traditions of society and thus did not implicate "fundamental principles of liberty and justice . . . ;"[36] nor is the right "implicit in the concept of ordered liberty, such that neither liberty nor justice would exist if it were sacrificed."[37]

An Equal Protection Claim

In its equal protection analysis, the Hawaii Supreme Court first noted that "marriage is a state-conferred legal partnership status" which entitles the couple to exclusive benefits.[38] The complainants argued that the DOH's refusal of the marriage license on the basis that the applicants were of the same-sex, deprived them of such benefits given to other traditional married couples. Using a strict scrutiny standard, the court agreed and held that the marriage statute, on its face, discriminated against same-sex couples' access to the benefits of marital status, pursuant to the Equal Protection Clause of the Hawaii Constitution.[39] Accordingly, the court remanded the case and ruled that, under the strict scrutiny standard, the DOH would have to overcome the burden of demonstrating that the marriage statute furthered compelling state interests and was narrowly drawn to avoid unnecessary abridgments of constitutional rights.[40] Applying strict scrutiny is a major blow to the institution of marriage and a victory for gay rights. In effect, this "converted all homosexual issues into gender issues" thereby opening the floodgates for future homosexual rights issues.[41]

The court supported its reasoning by observing that the definitional argument against same-sex marriages—that marriage by definition means a relationship between a man and a woman—is "circular and unpersuasive."[42] The court made a further attempt to justify its position by citing extensively to *Loving v. Virginia* where the U.S. Supreme Court held that Virginia's miscegenation laws were unconstitutional on both equal protection and due process grounds.[43]

Concurrence and Dissent

The concurring opinion filed by Judge James A. Burns made the astute observation that the Hawaii constitution's reference to "sex" includes all aspects of a person's "sex" that are "biologically fated."[44] Thus, on remand, the complainants must show, as a factual matter, that sexual orientation is biologically fated and thus protected against discrimination by the state constitution.[45]

The dissent relied on the following contentions: (1) the definition of marriage refers to a relationship between a man and woman, (2) *Loving v. Virginia* is distinguished on the premise that the holding referred to racial discrimination, (3) homosexuals are not a "suspect class," and (4) the benefits that the complainants seek can be set forth by the legislature.[46] Judge Heen argued eloquently that such benefits could be afforded to same-sex couples "without rooting out the very essence of a legal marriage."[47] It is predicted that the case will not be settled finally until sometime in 1998. Since it rests on state law, no appeal may be taken to the U.S. Supreme Court. It is also predicted that the constitutionality of anti-gay marriage laws will be litigated in the states anywhere from ten to fifteen years.[48]

The Federal Response

The first federal challenge will no doubt arise over the issue of whether states are required to recognize same-sex marriages from Hawaii under the *Baehr* case (as it is anticipated ultimately the Hawaii Supreme Court will validate such acts) under Article IV of the federal Constitution or, specifically, the Full Faith and Credit Clause.[49] Essentially, this clause requires each state to honor the other's acts, records and judicial proceedings.[50] There is one significant loophole to the seeming rigidity of this requirement for federal uniformity; that is, if a substantial public policy is offended by the foreign state's law, the forum state need not apply the foreign law. Thus, the effect of this exception would allow a forum state to apply its own marriage laws and invalidate a same-sex marriage contracted in another state.[51]

A persuasive argument can be made that even if invalidated, particular *incidents* of marriage could nonetheless be validated. Accordingly, allowing inheritance rights would not be a serious infringement on the forum state's policies against same-sex marriage because refusing an inheritance claim would, after death, have not deterrence on the original prohibited conducted (i.e., the same-sex marriage itself).[52] This argument gains strength when it is realized that many of the incidents of marriage are not even provided by the states. Rather, private enterprises are undertaking more and more of this responsibility. The question then to be posited is, Does the state have any interests challenged or compromised by allowing a claim to be made by a same-sex couple of "spousal coverage under an employment pension plan, or an employee health insurance package, or even a private insurance plan that might have a reduced premium for spouses?"[53] On its face, this argument is fair and reasonable. The only ultimate concern is that if all or many of the incidents of marriage are recognized legally, does this not in effect give a stamp of approval, by the state, to conduct which is nonetheless still prohibited?[54]

BEHAVIORAL OR GENETIC DISPOSITION

In a 1995 case in the District of Columbia two years after *Baehr v. Lewin*, while finding valid the District's marriage statute—and thus not sustainable to a constitutional challenge by two homosexual men that their civil rights were being denied by its enforcement—one of the members of the three-judge panel deciding the case took great pains in his opinion (which was both a concurrence and dissent) to urge the case be remanded on the point of the preventability or immutability of homosexuality.[55] This issue was crucial for the judge in determining whether homosexuals were treated as a suspect classification by the ordinance in question. It also remains, without question, the determining issue in all cases of this type for it helps shape a reasonable response to the parallel concern of the practical consequences of exposing children to the influences of homosexual or lesbian households with their parents. In this case in the District of Columbia, if it were shown that the two homosexuals were treated as a suspect class, a constitutional challenge could then be made that this same-sex couple was being denied Equal Protection of the laws as guaranteed by the federal Constitution.

Even if it were to be shown by testimony from knowledgeable experts, on remand, that homosexuals do indeed have an irreversible (genetic) sexual orientation[56] and thereby constitute either a suspect or quasi-suspect class, the District of Columbia could meet this legal challenge of stricter or intermediate scrutiny here by demonstrating a substantial or compelling reason for withholding recognition of same-sex marriages.[57] While homosexual orientation is not antisocial, such *behavior* is considered antisocial and perhaps this, together with a concern that such relationships if validated legally could influence the sexual orientation and behavior of children, would be taken as sufficient justification for recognizing any statutory scheme prohibiting these associations or relationships.[58] If, however, the government was unable to show some actual prejudice to the public as a consequence of recognizing same-sex marriages—for example, a predictable increase in antisocial conduct—then there would be no sound basis for asserting a valid public interest in withholding legal recognition of same-sex marriages.[59] If sexual orientation were found to be a learned or culturally determined phenomenon,[60] and thus subject to therapeutic change, the government would need only meet a standard of rationality. In other words, in reviewing any challenged legislation prohibiting same-sex marriages, the courts would determine whether a simple rational basis existed for state action in enacting such legislation[61]—and this would surely be found.

What is overlooked in all of this analysis is the fact there could be no more compelling reason to forbid marital legitimization of same-sex relationships than, as Justice William O. Douglas of the U.S. Supreme Court said in 1941: "Marriage *and* procreation are fundamental to the very existence and survival of the race."[62] This is, no doubt, the central point to this whole consideration: traditional heterosexual marriage and the promise of procreation. Inextricably linked to the acceptance of this as the linch pin to American society is the social uneasiness, indeed fear, of the consequences of the social development of offspring in same-sex "marriages." Perhaps it will never be established with certainty that being raised by same-sex parents is a developmental hazard. Common sense, however, should dictate any possible error here should be made in favor of not risking a maladjusted or broken childhood because of some "feeling" that a child should always remain with his family—be it traditional or nontraditional in design. Each case, then, should be decided on its own facts and not guided by one definitive policy. There should, however, be a very strong presumption that a heterosexual upbringing for a child is, for reasons of social maturation, preferred over a homosexual childhood environment.

The Supreme Court of Virginia held in 1995 that a lesbian mother's conduct was immoral and because she practiced "active lesbianism," she could not regain custody of her son from her own mother and the child's grandmother. The court determined further that the child could, indeed, be harmed by virtue of the "social condemnation" attached to such relationships, which in turn would inevitably affect negatively his relationship with his young peers and the community at large.[63] In a word, then, his "best interests" demanded he be raised in a normal environment which could best be provided to him by his grandmother.[64]

In the first study to follow from childhood to adulthood young people raised in lesbian families, it was found that while those children from lesbian families were more likely to explore same-sex relationships—and especially so if their childhood family environment was one characterized by an openness and acceptance of lesbian or homosexual relationships—the large majority of children growing up in lesbian family relationships were identified clearly as heterosexual.[65] Interestingly, while the findings of this investigation present no decisive evidence that one's parents have a critical or determining influence on his sexual orientation as a child, the findings do nonetheless indicate that by creating social climates of acceptance or rejection of homosexuality within the family unit, parents may very well have some impact on childhood sexual experimentation as heterosexual, homosexual, or lesbian.[66]

Custodial Factors

Traditionally, at common law, there was an almost absolute right of a father to custody of his children unless it could be showed he was either corrupt or a danger to them.[67] Gender equality has eroded this position so that now there is a presumption that the welfare of a child of tender years is best served by placing him in his mother's custody.[68] Another competing presumption, which is considered a lesser form of gender discrimination, is that child's welfare is best advanced and maintained by placing him with the custodial parent who, before divorce, was his primary caretaker or, in other words, that parent having primary responsibility for his day-to-day care.[69]

What seems to be the ultimate standard emerging today in contemporary society for both determining custodial rights *and* settling adoption cases is the best interests and welfare of the child standard.[70] Indications of parental unfitness could be shown by presenting evidence, for example, that one parent was living "a disorganized, violent life harmful to the child" and one that involved "periods of neglect or abuse."[71] Claims of sexual immorality as a grounds for termination of parental rights are generally rejected because they either do not comply with stated statutory grounds for termination or because allegations of immorality do not affect a parent's competence to provide child care.[72] In adoption cases, sexual orientation is, however, a relevant factor for judicial consideration of a candidacy for adoption since it is recognized as having a bearing on emotional stability and moral character.[73] In the District of Columbia, however, a nondiscrimination adoption policy exists as to gays and lesbians who wish to make application for child adoption;[74] indeed, a specific policy has been developed to recruit applicants from these two groups.[75]

In an interesting child custody case involving a nine-year-old girl, the Virginia Supreme Court held in 1985 that because of the father's "immoral and illicit homosexual relationship" in the same residence of the child, joint custody would be disallowed inasmuch as the father was determined to be unfit and an improper custodian. It was held to be in the child's best interests to protect her from the "burdens" imposed by her father's conduct. Recognizing that the living conditions which the child must endure when in her father's custody were "not only unlawful but also impose an intolerable burden upon her by reason of the social condemnation attached to them," and that this would "inevitably afflict her relationships with her peers and with the community at large," the court found ample reason for justifying its action here.[76]

A Comparative Approach

In July 1996 three judges at the Court of Sessions in Edinburgh, Scotland, overturned an earlier ruling refusing permission to a thirty-four-year-old homosexual nurse and his boyfriend of ten years to adopt a severely handicapped five-year-old child who had been taken care of by them for some eighteen months since 1994. The unmarried mother of the child relinquished her parental rights at his birth. Holding that since present law did not prohibit adoption of a child by a single person—homosexual—or otherwise—and, furthermore, that the court should be guided by the fundamental principle of promoting the welfare of the child, it was determined, with the support of the social work department, that the adoption would be approved. To do otherwise, the court observed, would be to remove the child from a secure home environment and place him in state services.[77]

This case was decided correctly and shows a balanced and reasonable approach to dealing with the issue of sexual morality in adoption cases. The facts of this case are rather unique, however, and a generalized acceptance of a definitive rule of law here would be obviously not dictated. In every case the need should always be to secure the welfare of the child and thereby allow it to develop in as "normal" an environment as possible given its particular physical, medical, or social needs.

CHANGING VALUES

"Values come into being" through "the exercise of moral choice."[78] If the choice, itself, is perceived as immoral, then—arguably—the core values giving rise or forcing the choice could be viewed as improper and not subject to social approbation. For example, it has been suggested that, as to biblical or heterosexual marriage, which has been sanctified by God, there can be no valid moral assertion of equality by those advocating same-sex marriage, for such an assertion is immoral in the first instance.[79] The counter libertarian argument is that freedom of association for homosexuals and lesbians should never be shaped or limited by religious and moral principle,[80] and, further, that law and society should treat sexuality as but a "morally indifferent subject" and consequently regard sexual preferences as having no greater moral significance than, for example, preferences for food, and thus not a profound statement about life.[81]

While customs do, indeed, "change with an evolving social order,"[82] it is for representative institutions, not the courts, to chart this change.[83] Indeed, the whole democratic process, tied inherently to political debate and resolution, will be broken if the judiciary assumes a role of authoritarianism which has the effect of shoving representative bodies away from their role of policy makers.[84] In a word, judicial preemption of political deliberations cannot be countenanced particularly so in reference to new policies toward marriage.[85] Political debate and consensus are central to an ordered society; judicial fiat is not. Perhaps same gender marriage validation "is in the womb of time," but presently its actual birth is still quite premature.[86]

A temporary solution designed to both "buy time" for contemporary American society to begin a national debate of the issue here and, at the same instance, serve as a fair and equitable compromise for the present would be for recognition in contract law of a domestic partnership—with "contractual vows," as such, being entered into by the parties guaranteeing that neither will be denied pension, insurance, health, inheritance benefits, or other state deductions available to the heterosexual marriage contract.[87] Matrimony, then, would not be available for same-sex relationships, for it would remain a religious institution.[88] Of course, the danger in this proposal is that action of this nature would most certainly be viewed by some advocates as but the "wedge" in the secular door to full matrimonial recognition by state and church alike.[89] The basic dilemma is to find a realistic approach to family relations which maintains strength for the vast majority of Americans who recognize the ideal, nuclear monogamous family, yet faces the reality of the widening gap between the ideal and the real-world situation which sees wide variances in both gender and ethnic preference and which recognizes family disruption, through divorce, as the real problem rather than family structure.[90] This idea of a domestic partnership contract would allow the state to not only extend greater economic benefits to same-sex couples willing to enter into such a contract, but also avoid forcing the state to recognize morally that relationships of this order must be classified as marriage.[91]

Love Has No Bounds?

While affirming the centrality of traditional marriage, it has been urged that all faiths accept that the love of God can be lived and witnessed in a variety of relationships. Specifically, as to the Anglican community, it has been suggested that unmarried but loving heterosexual and homosexual couples should be welcomed into it.[92] Others have concluded that because marriage is for people who love and homosexuals can love as "naturally" as heterosexuals, marriage therefore should be allowed for them as well.[93] Indeed, by permitting gay marriages, society could reaffirm its hope "that people of all kinds settle down into stable unions"[94] and thereby validate a structure for promoting "virtue, stability and commitment" oftentimes found lacking in the gay culture itself.[95] As important a consideration is the opportunity to expand and nurture kinship through validated same-sex relationships. This is thought particularly significant because within this group of people is to be found those who are most unlikely to be supported by children in their old age.[96]

A 1996 national survey of religious identity and political opinion titled *The Diminishing Divide: American Churches, American Politics* polled 1,975 adults and found 65 percent of them opposed to same-sex marriages. A NEWSWEEK poll of the same year of 779 people, found 58 percent of those surveyed were opposed to the idea of legally sanctioning gay marriages, with a third of the respondents holding the contrary opinion: namely, such relationships should be legalized.[97] Given this national—attitude combined as such with the movement in thirty-two state legislatures to introduce proposals prohibiting gay marriages and refusing to honor those in other jurisdictions[98]—it is safe to conclude that social acceptance of homosexuality will not, in the foreseeable future, be seen in American society.[99] Indeed, until homosexuality is viewed as a "normal" variant of human sexuality and is accepted in the personal and private sphere of family members, friends, neighbors and colleagues, society as a whole will never condone its practice as a valid lifestyle.[100]

Social Concerns

William J. Bennett has responded to the arguments advancing a societal need to recognize same-sex marriages by observing that traditional marriage is the "keystone in the arch of civilization."[101] To fail to recognize this historically validated fact would bring long-range social damage to society and promote a societal indifference about heterosexuality and homosexuality which in turn would play havoc particularly with teenagers as they seek to sort out their sexual identities at this crucial state in their psychosocial development and go on subsequently to become either adjusted or maladjusted adults.

He points out that marriage should not be taken as an arbitrary construct and to hold heterosexuality and homosexuality as separate and *not* equivalent does not mark one as an intolerant bigot. Since most homosexuals do not follow a single moralistic model in their relationships and, indeed, are almost unrestrained in them more so than the "normal" ideal of heterosexual married couples, Bennett fears recognizing same-sex marriages would give rise to unbridled promiscuity and thus contribute to the overall decline of society.[102] Sexual relativism would reign supreme with no lines drawn and moral distinctions made between traditional and nontraditional, same gender "marriage" relationships. Thus, in an approved same-sex relational society, a bisexual, for example, wishing to marry two other people would not be censored because to do so would be a denial of that person's sexuality. Similarly, a father and a daughter could marry as could two sisters or men who wish to enter into consensual polygamous arrangements.[103] Social and ethical chaos would be both the mark and the result of a new permissive society which legitimizes same-sex marriages as legal marriages.

Popularizing Same Sex "Marriages"

On March 25, 1996, 175 couples came in tuxedos and wedding dresses, clutching flowers and each others' hands for confirmation *and* acceptance of their same-sex union. Mayor Willie L. Brown, Jr., the mayor of San Francisco, pronounced them "domestic partners" under the city's same-sex marriage law. This law gives gay couples the same rights to a city-sanctioned wedding as heterosexual couples and even provides marriage certificates, though they are entirely symbolic.[104] Under a city ordinance adopted five years ago, those couples who register their domestic partnerships are, in turn, allowed to share their health plans if they are city employees with their partners. They are also allowed equal hospital visitation rights and to take bereavement leave when one of the partners die.[105]

Of the March 25 ceremonies, P. J. Johnson, a spokesman for Mayor Brown, said, "If partnership, commitment and monogamy are what we value, then this (mass) ceremony confirms these values." These couples "share what straight couples share. *They are in love.*"[106] And, in today's obsessive culture of political correctness, who [but the bravehearted] can dare challenge what is done in the name of love!

One such stalwart, Art Crowley, executive director of the Sacramento-based Committee on Moral Concerns, complained that this mass ceremony was "challenging the whole moral foundation of the greatest country there ever was." Of the participants in the same-sex ceremonies, he continued by observing, "They crave public acceptance. They have to bring it out onto the public square and have everybody agree to what they do. Most people will think of this as just another crackpot scheme in California."[107]

In the January 6th, 1996, edition of THE ECONOMIST, the cover shows two plastic male figures dressed in tuxedos, and holding hands atop a wedding cake underneath the words "Let them wed."[108] In its lead article of this issue, the question is put directly: will marital anarchy result as a consequence of allowing homosexuals and lesbians to "marry"? The question is answered in the affirmative, so to speak, if same-sex unions were but arbitrary configurations or mere parodies of "real" marriage. But, *the truth* is revealed (without authoritative documentation) that countless same-sex couples, "especially lesbian ones, have shown that they are as capable of fidelity, responsibility and devotion as are heterosexual couples."[109] Thus, it is maintained, that "permitting gay marriage could reaffirm society's hope that people of all kinds settle down into stable unions."[110]

While admitting the question of children in homosexual households and adoption is a thorny one, it is urged that this issue should be separated from the validitation of such marriages in and of themselves. Sadly, the "children issue" is an inextricable part of the central issue of validating same-sex marriages. There are, as has been seen, both honest fears and doubts regarding the creation of an environment which could well lead to an acceptance or condonation of child abuse.[111]

If contemporary society is not yet ready for legally validating same-sex relationships, it is commonplace to argue the San Francisco approach: namely, merely recognizing the same-sex relationships as domestic partnerships—for in this way, various business and health benefits can be shared.[112] On its face, such an argument should not be problematical—for it advances a goal of shared responsibility. However, for the gay or lesbian, such social structures as domestic partnerships present a unique opportunity for them: public recognition. And, the hope, of course, is that over time, that recognition will be validated by the legislatures or courts. Thus, what might be though of as but a humane and loving accommodation or but approving "an index for belonging," actually is fraught with first-order complexities and might well be seen, in reality, as the beginning of the slippery slope to societal oblivion with the destruction of its very bulwark—the heterosexual family unit.[113] Yet, if only one or two major incidents of marriage (e.g., heath insurance and retirement benefits) were made available to proven long-term relationships, perhaps the slope would in fact become but a level field and just possibly a more humane one as well.

STATE PROHIBITIONS

Most state courts which have ruled against permitting same-sex marriages have relied on the definitional nature of marriage; in other words, marriage can only be entered into by two persons of the opposite sex.[114] By June 1997, 11 additional states had anti-gay marriage bills pending in current legislative sessions and another 12 had blocked, defeated, withdrawn or killed such bills. Since 1995, 25 states in all have enacted anti-gay marriage laws.[115]

Access to Assisted Reproductive Technologies

If same-sex couples were granted the right to marry, would the constitutional rights to procreation and marital privacy extend necessarily to these couples?[116] Although the Supreme Court has established the precedent of procreative autonomy, one commentator makes the trenchant observation that "it cannot be argued from [the right to procreative autonomy] that there must exist a corresponding fundamental right to reproduce or to use artificial reproductive technology."[117] Yet, if the state legislatures were to extend the definition of marriage to same-sex couples, reproductive technologies such as artificial insemination and *in vitro* fertilization, surrogacy, and, in the distant future, cloning, would nonetheless arguably be within these couples' constitutional reproductive autonomy rights.[118] Indeed, it has been maintained that since the U.S. Supreme Court in *Eisenstadt v. Baird*[119] supported the right of an individual's exercise of her autonomy to control decisions regarding her procreative capacities to prevent pregnancy without regard to marital status, it follows that a single woman, lesbian or otherwise, has a fundamental right to control her reproductive system to conceive with the aid and benefit of the new reproductive technologies.[120]

Drawing from the rule of the case in *Bowers v. Hardwick*,[121] however, it has nonetheless been argued cogently that state legislation which limits the procreative technologies of the "new biology" to married couples can "be sustained under the less demanding test of rationality."[122] For, under the rational basis test, it is evident that the state's interest in promoting the traditional family unit is related rationally to limiting the reproductive technologies to traditional married couples.[123]

Lesbian Self-Insemination

Lesbians have the practical option of obtaining donor semen from a private source, either directly or through a third party.[124] While this approach allows the woman the greatest degree of control and freedom from government intervention, it also allows, both as a practical and a legal matter, the donor and the biological mother to assert rights and enforce responsibilities which could lead to custody disputes between the parties.[125] The possibility that the biological mother, the child, or the state might pursue the donor for support and the possibility that the donor might seek custody of the child most likely reduce the frequency of self-inseminations.

CONGRESSIONAL AFFIRMATIONS

U.S. Senator Don Nickels of Oklahoma's introduction of the Defense of Marriage Act (S. 1740) seeks to re-affirm the traditional view of heterosexual marriage by allowing the states to refuse to recognize same-sex marriages across state boundaries. In the act which was passed on September 11, 1996,[126] and which President Clinton chose wisely, from a political point of view, to sign when it reached his office,[127] marriage, under federal law, is defined simply as a "legal union between one man and one woman as husband and wife."[128] Thus, even if a state were to recognize gay marriages, the partners would not be eligible for survivor benefits under federal veterans, Medicare, or Social Security programs. This new legislation, interestingly, merely restates existing law—for the states have never had a federal obligation to recognize marriages solemnized in other states that are contrary to public policy (e.g., bigamous, under age, and common law marriages).[129] Still, a possible constitutional challenge to the legislation's validity as a consequence of its enactment will, no doubt, be made on the grounds it abridges the guarantee that each state give "full faith and credit" to the final decrees of other states.[130]

The Defense of Marriage Act shows clearly, I submit, the national concern over the need to preserve the traditional values of heterosexual family life. Indeed, these values will never be expanded to embrace legal *and* social recognition of same-sex relationships so long as the majority of right-thinking people in America do not accept, or even condone, the gay and lesbian code of moral behavior (or, misbehavior, as the case may be).[131]

Popular Responses

Locally, in the day-to-day arena of life, defending traditional heterosexual marriage is a prime objective of the Christian Coalition. Led by Ralph Reed, the coalition comprises white evangelical Christians, conservative Roman Catholics and mainline Protestants who constitute an army of 1.7 million members from more than one thousand seven hundred local chapters in all fifty states—expanding at the rate of a chapter a day.[132]

In its *CONTRACT WITH THE AMERICAN FAMILY*, the coalition presents a blueprint for addressing what is thought to be the most pressing issues in American politics today: the breakdown of the family, the fraying of the social fabric, the coarsening of the culture, and a decline in civility.[133] The American family is caught in the midst of culture war where its very direction is found to be rooted in radical individualism. Both spouses and children go their separate ways as autonomous units—often discarding all perception of moral truth. Rights are brandished over duties.[134]

To foster greater stability for marriage contracts, the coalition seeks a greater accommodation of the historic role of faith in these relationships, restoring or rebuilding, as such, the time honored tradition of civil religion where religious values are seen as the core of prime mover in all daily actions. To build on this return to religious values, the coalition would seek to advance its goal of strengthening marriage by abolishing the "no fault" divorce laws that allow men to marry and father children and then simply abandon them as they choose.[135]

Reform of the divorce laws should be achieved in such a way to encourage couples to stay together—particularly when children are involved. To this end, waiting periods before a divorce can be granted should be established, also accompanied by a requirement of court appointed counseling, as a way to place the law firmly on the side of marriage.[136] Churches and synagogues can also do more to prepare young couples for the pressure of modern marriage and offer a loving atmosphere where those young marriages in trouble can find counseling and healing.[137]

CONCLUSIONS

In America, religion has always been viewed as the structure upon which moral order is based. Morality's foundation is in turn based on religion itself.[138] Given that the primary goal of politics is to advance and maintain moral order, it can be thus seen that politics and morality enjoy an almost inextricable relationship.[139] And, this relationship preordains a tension which, depending on one's view, either solidifies the spiritual ethic in traditional marriage or serves to rigidify, if not destroy, a humane and more contemporary approach to loving, unstructured relationships.

The depth of this tension is seen clearly by the suggestion that the advocate of same-sex marriage and domestic partnerships demand: namely, more tolerance. Yet, tolerance or recognition of this lifestyle would have the effect for fundamentalists or those traditional Christians of delegitimizing their faith, demonizing them and relegating the Bible to little more than a form of intolerance hate literature.[140] Shaping an accord that balances both positions here is admittedly a precarious undertaking. Yet, as observed previously, perhaps one or two incidents of marriage might be recognized for those same-sex relationships or domestic partnerships which have stabilized more or less, after a reasonable period of practice. Surely, dual coverage for same-sex partners in an employment pension plan or health insurance package would not be unduly threatening to continued legal recognition of traditional heterosexual marriage.[141] As noted previously, matrimony would remain a religious institution and not be available for same gender relationships.[142] This accommodation or balance could then serve as a structure for sustained debate within the state legislatures as they seek to shape their individual policies on this contentious issue.

NOTES

1. Eskridge, *The Many Faces of Sexual Content*, 37 WILLIAM & MARY L. REV. 47, 60 (1995). See generally Sustein, *Homosexuality and the Courts*, 70 IND. L.J. 1 (1994).

2. Durkin, *Reproductive Technology and The New Family: Recognizing the Other Mother*, 10 J. CONTEMP. HEALTH L. & POL'Y 327, 328 (1994).

3. Gilfether, *Homosexual Parents Redefine Images of Family*, THE PLAIN DEALER, Dec. 2, 1995, at 2E.

4. Kolata, *Lesbian Partners Finds the Means to Be Partners*, N.Y. TIMES, Jan. 30, 1989, at A13.

See Note, *Looking for a Family Resemblance: The Limits of the Functional Approach to the Legal Definition of Family*, 104 HARV. L. REV. 1640, 1641 (1991) (observing that the traditional nuclear family is becoming an American anachronism).

5. H.J. CLARK, JR., THE LAW OF DOMESTIC RELATIONSHIPS IN THE UNITED STATES at 30 (2d ed. 1988).

6. *Id.*

7. *Id.* at 31.

8. 381 U.S. 479 (1965).

9. 405 U.S. 438 (1972).

10. 106 S. Ct. 2841.

11. CLARK, *supra* note 5 at 27-9.

12. *Id.* at 77-8.

13. *Id.* at 78.

14. Hunter, *Marriage, Law and Gender: A Feminist Inquiry*, 1 LAW & SEXUALITY 9 (1991).

15. CLARK, *supra* note 5 at 77, n. 13.

16. R.A. POSNER, SEX AND REASON 101-08 (1992); Henry, *Born Gay?*, TIME Mag., July 26, 1993, at 36; Burr, *Homosexuality and Biology*, THE ATLANTIC, Mar. 1993, at 47.

17. CLARK, *supra* note 5 at 78.

18. *Id.*

19. *Id.* at 79.

20. *Id.* at 79, 80.

21. *See Boddie v. Conn.*, 401 U.S. 371 (1971); *Loving v. Virginia*, 388 U.S. 1 (1967); *Griswold v. Conn.* 381 U.S. 479 (1965).

22. CLARK, *supra* note 5 at 79.

23. *Id.*

24. *Id.*

25. 852 P.2d 44 (Haw. 1993).

26. The DOH contended that the state's marriage laws address the union between a man and a woman; that the state is under no obligation to grant homosexual unions official approval; the state's marriage laws help foster the family unit and the proper environment for nurturing the development of children; and homosexuals are neither a suspect nor a quasi-suspect class. *Id.*

27. *Id.* at 48.

The DOH based its conclusion on its reading of several sections of the HAWAII REVISED STATUTES (HRS) §572-1 (1985):

(3) The *man* does not at the time have any lawful *wife* living and that the *woman* does not at the time have any lawful *husband* living;. . .

(7) The marriage ceremony be performed in the State by a person or society with a valid license to solemnize marriages and the *man* and *woman* to be married. . .

Id. at 49 (emphasis added).

28. Article I, Section 6 of Hawaii Constitution provides:

The right of the people to privacy is recognized and shall not be infringed without the showing of a compelling state interest. The legislature shall take affirmative steps to implement this right. *Id.* at 50, citing HAW.

CONST. Art. I, §6 (1978).

29. Article I, Section 5 of the Hawaii Constitution provides:

No person shall be deprived of life, liberty or property without due process of law, nor be denied the equal protection of the laws, nor be denied the enjoyment of the person's civil rights or be discriminated against in the exercise thereof because of race, religion, sex or ancestry. *Id.* citing HAW. CONST. Art. I, §5 (1978).

30. *Id.* at 53-4. As one commentator has observed, same-sex marriages cannot be protected by the federal Constitution because it is "out of harmony with the purpose of male-female psychological and physiological differences." See Marciano, *Homosexual Marriage and Parenthood Should Not Be Allowed*, in CURRENT CONTROVERSIES IN MARRIAGE AND FAMILY 293, 294 (H. Feldman et. al., eds. 1985).

31. *Baehr*, 852 P.2d at 55, citing *Zablocki v. Redhail*, 434 U.S. 374, 384 (1978). Such fundamental rights are drawn from the traditions of our society and as Justice Scalia observed, the Court must "prevent future generations from lightly casting aside important traditional values—not to enable this Court to invent new ones." *Michael H. v. Gerald D.*, 491 U.S. 110, 122 n. 2 (1989), *reh'g denied*, 110 S. Ct. 22 (1989).

32. *Baehr*, 852 P.2d at 55. Arguably, however, the extension—by the judiciary branch—of the category which contains fundamental rights, brings the court into the tenuous position of engrafting legislative pronouncements onto precedent. See Schanck, *The Only Game in Town: An Introduction to Interpretative Theory Statutory Construction, and Legislative Histories*, 38 KANS. L. REV. 815, 820 (1990).

33. In *Maynard v. Hill*, the Court described marriage as "the most important relation in life," and as "the foundation of the family and of society, without which there would be neither civilization nor progress." 125 U.S. 190, 205-11 (1888). In *Meyer v. Nebraska*, the Court explained that the right "to marry, establish a home and bring up children," is a fundamental liberty interest protected by the Due Process Clause. 262 U.S. 390, 399 (1923). In *Skinner v. Oklahoma*, marriage was denoted as "fundamental to the very existence and survival of the race." 316 U.S. 535, 541 (1942). More recently, in *Cleveland Board of Education v. LaFleur*, the Court declared that "the freedom of personal choice in matters of marriage. . . is one of the liberties protected by the Due Process Clause of the Fourteenth Amendment." 414 U.S. 632, 641 (1974). This freedom of choice, however, has not been extended to the *right* of homosexual to marry. *See* Comment, *Let the Legislatures Define the Family: Why Default Statutes Should Be Used to Eliminate Potential Confusion*, 40 EMORY 571, 582 (1991).

34. *Baehr*, 852 P.2d at 56. *But see*, Jaff, *Wedding Bell Blues: The Position of Unmarried People in American Law*, 30 ARIZ. L. REV. 207, 225 (1988) (arguing that if the choice to marry is fundamental, then under *Eisenstadt*, that choice must be protected regardless of how it is resolved).

35. 852 P.2d at 57.

36. *Baehr*, 853 P.2d citing at 57, *Griswold v. Connecticut*, 381 U.S. 479, 493 (1965) (Goldberg, Jr., concurring). Judges, in determining which rights are fundamental, must look "to the 'traditions [collective] conscience of our people' to determine whether a principle is so rooted [there] . . . as to be ranked as fundamental" and "cannot be denied without violating those fundamental principles of liberty and justice which lie at the base of all our civil and political institutions." *Id.*

37. *Baehr*, 852 P.2d at 57, n. 16, citing *Palko v. Connecticut*, 302 U.S. 319 (1937). *See generally, Developments in the Law—The Constitution and the Family*, 93 HARV. L. REV. 1156, 1271-83 (1980) (exploring the boundaries of constitutional protection for families and marital relationships).

38. *Baehr*, 852 P.2d at 58. Such benefits include, for example, the following: (1) a variety of state income tax advantages, (2) public assistance from the DOH, (3) various property rights advantages, (4) the right to spousal support, (5) the right to bring a wrongful death action, and (6) the benefit of exemptions of real property from attachment or execution. *See, e.g., Note, Looking for a Family Resemblance: The Limits of the Functional Approach to the Legal Definition of Family*, 104 HARV. L. REV. 1640, 1642 (1991).

39. *Baehr*, 852 P.2d at 59. The court first explained that the extent of permissible state regulation of marriage is subject to constitutional restraints. *Id.*, citing *Zablocki v. Redhail*, 434 U.S. 374, 388-91 (1978). Further, Hawaii expressly denotes in its Constitution that no person can be discriminated against on the basis of sex. *See supra* note 26. As the relevant statute refers to the applicants for a marriage license as husband and wife and man and woman, the court thus found discrimination on the basis of sex. HAW. REV. STAT. §572-1 (1978).

40. *Baehr*, 852 P.2d at 68. Essentially, the Hawaii Supreme Court is arguing that the statute discriminates on the basis of gender. In other words, the statute allows people of opposite gender to marry but does not allow people of the *same* gender to marry. The U.S. Supreme Court has, interestingly, applied an intermediate level of scrutiny to gender classifications. *Craig v. Boren*, 429 U.S. 190 (1976), *reh'g denied*, 429 U.S. 1124 (1977). To withstand a constitutional challenge, a gender-based classification must thus "serve important governmental objectives and must be substantially related to the achievement of those objectives." *Id.* at 198. The Hawaii Supreme Court, in derogation from precedent, has chosen a different path by applying strict scrutiny.

On retrial, the state of Hawaii endeavored to show that continuing to refuse to grant marriage licenses to same-sex couples protects any children arising from or within such associations from social and psychological burdens of adjustment they would not otherwise have in traditional heterosexual families. Keen, *Hawaii Testimony Assesses Kids' Role in Marriage Issue,* WASH. BLADE, Sept. 20, 1996, at 1.

41. Leo, *Gay Rights, Gay Marriage*, U.S. NEWS & WORLD RPT., May 24, 1993, at 19.

42. *Baehr* at 68.

43. *Id.* at 61-2, citing *Loving v. Virginia*, 388 U.S. 1, 10-2 (1967).

44. *Baehr* at 69.

45. *Id.* at 70.

46. *Id.* at 71-4.

47. *Id.* at 73. Judge Heen cautioned the majority not to manufacture a civil right unsupported by precedent. Rather, it was for the legislature to express the will of the people in deciding whether traditional marital benefits should be extended to same-sex couples. *Id.* at 71-4.

48. Reske, *A Matter of Full Faith*, 82 A.B.A.J. 32 (1996).

On December 3, 1996, a circuit court judge in Honolulu, Hawaii, ruled the state could not prohibit same-sex marriages. This specific ruling was appealed directly to the state supreme court and adds further delay and another level of confusion to efforts to resolve, definitively, the matter. Judge Kevin S.C. Chang found there was no credible evidence that the optimal development of children would be affected adversely by same-sex marriages. It was determined further that the present state statute prohibiting same-sex marriages did not further any compelling state interest. WASH. POST, Dec. 4, 1996, at 1.

See Hansen, *More Battles Ahead over Gay Marriages,* 83 A.B.A.J. 24 (1997).

49. Reske, *supra* note 48.

50. *See* Note, *'Til Death Do Us Part: Granting Full Faith and Credit to Marital Status,* 68 SO. CAL. L. REV. 397 (1995).

51. *Id.*

52. Henson, *Will Same-Sex Marriages Be Recognized in Sister States?,* 32 J. FAM. L. 551, 599 (1993-4).

53. *Id.* at 581-82.

Swedish Law treats same-sex couples the same as heterosexual cohabitants—both in terms of jointly acquired property and inheritance rights. *Id.* at 596, n. 153.

54. *Id.* at 582.

55. *Dean v. District of Columbia,* 653 A.2d 307, 355-56 (D.C. App. 1995) (Ferren, J.).

56. Some studies conclude homosexuality has a genetic or hormonal basis and is virtually unchangeable. Pool, *Evidence for Homosexual Gene,* 261 SCIENCE 291 (1993). See also Hammer, et al., *A Linkage Between DNA Markers on the X Chromosome and Male Sexual Orientation,* 261 SCIENCE 321 (July 16, 1993); Bailey & Pillard, *A Genetic Study of Male Sexual Orientation,* 48 ARCH. GEN. PSYCHIATRY 1089, 1093 (Dec. 1991); A. P. Bell et al., SEXUAL PREFERENCE: ITS DEVELOPMENT IN MEN AND WOMEN 212-5, 216 (1981).

57. *Dean v. District of Columbia, supra* note 55.

58. *Id.*

59. *Id.*

60. Blumstein & Schwartz, *Intimate Relationships and the Creation of Sexuality,* in HOMOSEXUALITY/HETEROSEXUALITY: CONCEPTS OF SEXUAL ORIENTATION 307-20 (D. P. McWhirter et al., eds. 1990). *See also*

C. BURR, A SEPARATE CREATION (1996).

61. Blumstein & Schwartz, *id.* at 346.

62. *Skinner v. Oklahoma*, 316 U.S. 535, 541 (1941) (emphasis added).

63. *Bottom v. Bottom*, 457 S.E. 2d 102, 108 (Va. 1995).

64. *Id.*

65. Golombook & Tasker, *Do Parents Influence the Sexual Orientation of Their Children? Findings from a Longitudinal Study of Lesbian Families*, 32 DEVELOPMENTAL PSYCHOLOGY 3 (1996).

66. *Id.* at 10.

67. CLARK *supra* note 5 at 797.

68. *Id.* at 799.

69. *Id.* at 801.

70. *Id.* at 909 *passim.*

71. *Id.* at 904.

72. *Id.*

73. *Id.* at 909 *passim.*

74. Campbell, *Doors Open for Gays Who Want to Adopt*, THE WASH. BLADE, Aug. 13, 1993, at 1.

75. *Id.*

76. *Roe v. Roe*, 324 S.E. 2d 691, 694 (Va. 1985).

77. Cramb, *Homosexual Wins Court Fight to Adopt Handicapped Boy*, THE DAILY TELEGRAPH, July 27, 1996, at 7.

78. P. BOBBITT, CONSTITUTIONAL INTERPRETATION 179 (1991).

79. Safire, *Same-Sex Marriage Nears*, N.Y. TIMES, April 29, 1996, at A27.

80. Epstein, *Caste and The Civil Rights Laws: From Jim Crow to Same-Sex Marriage*, 92 MICH. L. REV. 2456, 2475 (1994). *See* Friedman, *Same Sex Marriages and the Right to Privacy: Abandoning Scriptural, Canonical, and Natural Law Based Definitions of Marriage*, 35 HOW. L.J. 173 (1992).

81. R.A. POSNER, SEX AND REASON 181 (1992). Even with this posture, Judge Posner posits that in some cases, prohibition against recognition of same-sex marriages should be retained. *Id.* at 309-12, 417-20. *See* Colker, *An Embodied Bisexual Perspective*, 7 YALE J.L. & HUMANITIES 163 n. 4 (1995).

82. *Baehr v. Lewin*, 852 P.2d 44, 63 (Haw. 1993).

83. Will, *And Now Pronounce Them Spouse and Spouse*, WASH. POST, May 19, 1996, at C9.

84. *Id.*

85. *Id.*

86. *Id.*

87. Safire, *supra* note 79; Epstein, *supra* note 80 at 2474, n. 57.

See Baker & Judge, *Where IBM Goes, Others May Follow: It Sees Same-Sex Benefits as a Low-Cost Way to Draw Talent*, BUSINESS WEEK at 39 (Oct. 7, 1996), (detailing how IBM designed a medical benefits program extending these specific benefits to its employees' same-sex partners but *did not* extend to unmarried heterosexual couples).

88. Safire, *id.*

89. *See* Epstein, *supra* note 80 at 2474 (arguing that if enforceable same-sex contracts are recognized, so too should marriage be "accepted").

90. P. L. KILBRIDE, PLURAL MARRIAGES FOR OUR TIMES: A REINVENTED OPTION? 11, 26 (1994).

91. Colker, *supra* note 81 at 186.

92. Barbash, *Anglican Panel Eases View on 'Living in Sin,'* WASH. POST, June 7, 1995, at A24. *See* Bruni, *In the Edge of a Storm over Gay Clergy,* N.Y. TIMES, Mar. 16, 1996, at 23 (acknowledging an Anglican minister's own homosexual relationship as a *positive* influence on his congregation as a magnet for diversity).

93. Rauch, *For Better or Worse?* NEW REPUBLIC, May 6, 1996, at 18.

94. THE ECONOMIST, Jan. 6-2, 1996, at 14.

95. *Id.* at 71.

See also, Macedo, *Morality and the Constitution: Toward Synthesis for Earthbound Interpreters,* 61 U. CIN. L. REV. 29, 46 (1992) (observing same gender relations are characterized just as are heterosexual relationships: by love, companionship and closeness).

96. Rauch, *supra* note 93 at 23.

See A. SULLIVAN, VIRTUALLY NORMAL: AN ARGUMENT ABOUT HOMOSEXUALITY 23 (1995).

97. Kaplin & Klaidman, *A Battle, Not the War,* NEWSWEEK, June 3, 1996, at 25.

98. *Id.* at 29.

99. *See* B. BAWER, A PLACE AT THE TABLE (1993).

100. *Id.*

101. Bennett, . . . *But Not a Very Good Idea, Either,* WASH. POST, May 21, 1996, at A19.

102. *Id.*

Others have noted, on average, the lack of stability in same-sex relationships and the grimmer life prospectus for the average homosexual. POSNER, *supra* note 81 at 305-7.

103. Kaplin & Klaidman, *supra* note 97 at 27.

104. Boudreau, *Brides, Grooms & Partners,* WASH. POST, Mar. 26, 1996, at A3.

See also 2 Dozen Same Sex Marriages in Midtown, N.Y. TIMES, June 17, 1997, at B4 (regarding a symbolic civil ceremony).

105. *Id.*

See generally Genovesi, *Human and Civil Rights for Gays and Lesbians,* AMERICA, April 22, 1995, at 15.

106. *Id.*

107. *Id.*

108. THE ECONOMIST, Jan. 6, 1996, at 13.

109. *Id.* at 14.

110. *Id.*

111. *See* Smith, *Nudity, Obscenity and Pornography: The Streetcars Named Lust and Desire*, 4 J. CONTEMP. HEALTH L. & POL'Y 155 (1988).

112. O'Brien, *Domestic Partnership: Recognition and Responsibility*, 32 SAN DIEGO L. REV. 163, 207 (1995).

113. *See* G.P. SMITH, II, CHALLENGING FAMILY VALUES IN THE NEW SOCIETY (1996).

On July 8, 1997, the state of Hawaii validated a new category of legally recognized relationships—"reciprocal beneficiaries"—for lesbian and gay couples. The statute requires private employers who provide family health coverage for their married heterosexual workers to offer the same coverage to reciprocal beneficiaries (e.g., two adults over the age of 18 prohibited legally from marrying) and their dependents. Act 383, codifed as HAW. REV. STATS. §§ 572C-1-572C-7 (1997).

See generally, Sunstein, *Homosexuality and the Constitution*, 70 IND. L.J. 1 (1994).

114.   Virginia and Massachusetts statutory laws prohibits same-sex "marriages." *See, e.g.,* MASS. GEN. LAWS ANN., ch. 151B §4 (West Supp. 1995); VA. CODE ANN. §20-45.2 (Michie 1995). See also ARIZ. REV. STAT. §25-125 (1991); FLA. STAT. ANN. § 741.04 (West 1986); GA. CODE ANN., §19-3-30 (1991); HAW. REV. STAT. § 572-1 (Supp. 1994); IDAHO CODE § 32-301 (Supp. 1995); IND. CODE ANN. § 31-7-1-2 (Burns 1987); LA. CIVIL CODE ANN. art. 89 (West 1993); N. H. REV. STAT. ANN. §§ 457:1-:2 (1992); TEX. FAM. CODE ANN. § 1.01 (West 1993); UTAH CODE ANN. § 30-1-2 (1995).

115. On the Internet, *see Human Rights Campaign, Status of Legislation to Deny Equal Marriage Rights to Gay People* (June 6, 1997), http://www.hrc.org/issues/marriage/marstate.html.

See also Keen, *Three More States Ban Same-Sex Marriages: Michigan, Delaware and North Carolina Bring the Total, to 14*, WASH. BLADE, June 28, 1996, at 1.

See Note, *A More Perfect Union: A Legal and Social Analysis of Domestic Partnership Ordinances*, 92 COLUM. L. REV. 1164 (1992).

116. *See, e.g., Eisenstadt v. Baird*, 405 U.S. 438, 452-5 (1972); *Griswold v. Connecticut*, 381U.S. 479, 485-6 (1965).

117. G.P. SMITH, II, BIOETHICS AND THE LAW 209 (1993).

118. *See* Post, *The Question of Family: Lesbians and Gay Men Reflecting a Redefined Society*, 19 FORDHAM URB. L. J. 747 (1992).

119. 405 U.S. 438, 453 (1972).

120. Durkin, *Reproductive Technology and the New Family: Recognizing the Other Mother*, 10 J. CONTEMP. HEALTH L. & POL'Y 327, 341 (1994).

121. 478 U.S. 186 (1986).

122. Smith, *supra* note 117 at 211, citing *Maher v. Roe*, 432 U.S. 464, 478 (1977).

123. Smith, *id.* at 229.

124. A. BARAN & R. PANNOR, LETHAL SECRETS: THE SHOCKING CONSEQUENCES AND UNSOLVED PROBLEMS OF ARTIFICIAL INSEMINATION 132 (1990).

See Smith, *A Close Encounter of the First Kind: Artificial Insemination in Flux*, 17 J. FAM. L. 41 (1978).

125. *See* O'Rourke, *Family Law in a Brave New World: Private Ordering of Parental Rights and Responsibilities for Donor Insemination*, 1 BERKELEY WOMEN'S L.J. 140, 143 (1985).

126. Yang, *Senate Passes Bill Against Same-Sex Marriage*, WASH. POST, Sept. 11, 1996, at 1. The Senate vote of approval was 85 to 14 and the House 342 to 67.

127. Purdum, *President Would Sign Legislation Striking at Homosexual Marriage*, N.Y. TIMES, May 23, 1996, at A1. The president signed the legislation September 21, 1996. *See* Barber, *President Quietly Signs Law Aimed at Gay Marriage*, WASH. POST, Sept. 22, 1996, at A1. Public Law 104-199, 28 U.S.C. A. §1783C (1996).

128. S. 1740, Sec. 7(a). On May 7, 1996, the duplicate House Bill 5396 was introduced by Representative Robert L. Barr with 96 cosponsors.

129. *See* Dunlap, *Fearing a Toehold for Gay Marriages, Conservatives Rush to Bar the Door*, N.Y. TIMES, Mar. 6, 1996, at A13. Similar legislation is pending in Alabama, Alaska, California, Colorado, Georgia, Idaho, Illinois, Iowa, Kentucky, Maryland, Missouri, Rhode Island, South Carolina, Tennessee, Virginia, Washington, Wisconsin and Wyoming. South Dakota and Utah already have such laws. *Id.*

130. Vobejda, *Same-Sex Marriage Become Political Issue,* WASH. POST, May 23, 1996, at A14.

131. Kaplin & Klaidman, *A Battle Not the War*, NEWSWEEK, June 31, 1996, at 25.

132. Balz & Brunstein, *God's Fixer*, WASH. POST, Mag., Jan. 28, 1996, at 8.

133. *See* CONTRACT WITH THE AMERICAN FAMILY (1995).

134. D.W. KMIEC, CEASE FIRE ON THE FAMILY 127 (1995).

135. R. REED, POLITICALLY INCORRECT: THE EMERGING FAITH FACTOR IN AMERICAN POLITICS 125-32 (1994).

136. *Id.* at 258-59.

137. *Id.*

See also Raspberry, *Marriage Mentors,* WASH. POST, Jan. 12, 1996, at A15 (suggesting church appointed "mentoring couples" be used more extensively whereby newlyweds are exposed to couples with solid marriages who in turn "teach" the fundamental of successful marriage to them).

138. Reagan, *Policy and Morality are Inseparable*, 1 NOTRE DAME J. L. ETHICS & PUB. POL'Y 7-10 (1984).

139. *Id.*

140. Duncan, *Homosexual Marriage and The Myth of Tolerance*, 10 NOTRE DAME J.L. ETHICS & PUB. POL'Y 587 (1996).

141. Interestingly, recent studies show that Republicans in their twenties favor homosexual couples having the same benefits as married heterosexual couples by roughly four to one—a far higher ratio than among older Republicans. Chandler & Brossard, *The Other Gap in the GOP*, WASH. POST, Aug. 17, 1996, at D1.

See also Editorial, *Gay Rights, Corporate Style*, BUSINESS WEEK at 70 (Oct. 7, 1996) (detailing a growing phenomena among a number of American corporations—including IBM, Harley Davidson, Charles Schwab, Coors Brewing, Dow Chemical, Walt Disney, Microsoft and Time Warner—in extending medical benefits to same-sex couples. Only one to two percent of all potential beneficiaries have signed-up for the benefits program. Interestingly, most same-sex couples have dual incomes and each has his or her own insurance. Put simply, cost is viewed as the major concern for extending these benefits since lifetime medical expenses for HIV patients are approximately $119,000 and there is a real concern that same gender couples are more prone to getting this disease than heterosexual couples).

142. *See* Baker & Judge, *supra* note 88.

Chapter 4

Testing the Limits of Procreational Autonomy

Although the question of whether an ovum that has been fertilized is a baby or has the "moral certainty" of becoming one should not be viewed as a uniquely "Catholic" or religious question,[1] but rather as a question best answered by scientists,[2] the fact remains that ethicists and theologians have been grappling with this very question for quite some time.[3] This question and its "answers," together with their various permutations, structure the framework upon which today's laws are interpreted and future ones enacted.

The official teaching of the Catholic Church is simple and direct: at *all* stages of life, from fertilization through adulthood, human life is to be accorded equal protection.[4] Yet, prominent Church theologians continue to question this official magisterium by positing that, based on their studies of the advances of reproductive biology,[5] "truly human life" cannot be recognized until two or three weeks after fertilization.[6] Accepting this position would thus condone the right to perform tests on excess frozen embryos—undertaken as such to conduct genetic experiments—with the end result being the abortion (or death) of the embryo upon completion of the experiment. For some, this action is abhorrent; for others, it is recognized as a scientifically humane undertaking, grounded in utilitarianism, whose singular purpose is to explore the science of genetics with the hope of improving the genetic profile or genetic pool of mankind of ridding it of inheritable diseases.[7]

The issue of when individuality is established biologically and when the law should, accordingly, protect such individuals, was determined by the U.S. Supreme

Court in *Roe v. Wade,*[8] when it held, in essence, that the *full* protection of the laws could not be extended to a fetus until it was born.[9] Interestingly, in March 1983 Mr. Chief Justice, Sir Harry Gibbs, of the Australian High Court, ruled "that a foetus has no right of its own until it is born and has a separate existence from its mother."[10] The common law tied the commencement of life to the time when an unborn first moved in the womb or, in other words, when it quickened.[11] Thus, it was only after the fetus quickened that its destruction could be classified as murder.[12]

The new reproductive biology, in all its complexity, promises untold opportunities for resolving heartbreaking problems of infertility and will clearly expand the meaning of the very term *procreational autonomy* as a reference to both unmarried and married women. Still, the new biology presents equally untold problems for the physician, lawyer, ethicist, theologian and, for that matter, the average person.[13] This chapter considers, essentially, one major medical, legal, ethical, and religious challenge of the new reproductive biology: *in vitro* fertilization (IVF). It will first survey the force of religion in shaping new attitudes and directions in this area and then summarize the ethical and philosophical concerns about the use and development of IVF procedures. The now famous case of the frozen "orphan" embryos of Melbourne, Australia will serve as a focal paradigm for analysis and point of reference to the work of two study commissions—the Waller Committee in Australia and the Warnock Committee in England—that have charted investigative parameters for work and experimentation in IVF procedures. Finally, the chapter probes the complications of complete utilization of IVF by unmarried women and its devastating effect on the sanctity of the family unit. It concludes that so long as procreation continues to remain the central driving force in a marital relationship and, indeed, in a progressive society, men will undertake new and sometimes controversial endeavors—with or without state or religious approval—in order to expand the period of fecundity and combat infertility. The state must begin to regulate the field now, rather than allow it to develop haphazardly.

LAW AND RELIGION: PARTNERS OR ANTAGONISTS?

That faith and religion have played a dynamic role in the political life of the United States is a given.[14] Indeed, the very "bedrock of moral order is religion."[15] Thus, politics and morality become inseparable.[16] "And as morality's foundation is religion, religion and politics are necessarily related. We need religion as a guide; we need it because we are imperfect."[17] Religious values have, throughout history, played an important part in public policy debates.[18] In fact, today's democratic commitment to pluralism is nurtured and sustained as a consequence of that insistence on recognizing the inviolability of individual conscience.[19] To exclude societal values, which are grounded in a religious base, from the public arena would pose a serious threat to the very principle of pluralism.[20]

An obvious distinction must be made between moral and religious principles and the subsequent application of those principles in the public forum. Principles may be agreed upon, yet without sacrificing Catholic integrity, disagreement may exist as to their political application.[21] Indeed, *Dignitatis Humanae*, the Second Vatican Council's Declaration on Religious Freedom, affirmed specifically the principle of religious freedom for Catholics and non-Catholics alike, and foreswore the use of coercion of any nature in forcing the exercise of a particular act of faith.[22] From the time of Archbishop John Carroll to the present, the fundamental principle of the separation of church and state has always been accepted by the American hierarchy.[23] Yet, while all churches have tried to avoid political involvement with the state, they have refused steadfastly to limit their participation in the formation of national moral policies.[24]

Basil Cardinal Hume, the Archbishop of Westminster in England, has observed that the crisis of modern society is to be found in "the abandonment of objective moral principles and the dogmatism of permissiveness."[25] Perhaps this is but another way of observing that as to Americans at least, emotions and prejudices commonly override reason.[26] There can be little doubt that the self-centered doctrine of "me" is important and all-consuming to many members of modern society. Perhaps in no greater area of concern than procreation do emotions rise to high and often uncontrolled levels, for it appears that an inextricable concomitant of procreation is abortion.

The depth of ferment and controversy within the Roman Catholic Church was displayed in early 1985, in the results of a private survey of Roman Catholic theologians and biblical scholars from three important Catholic organizations—the Catholic Theological Society, the Catholic Biblical Association and the College Theology Society. The survey revealed that 62 percent of those polled (almost 500 persons, including 325 priests and religious) refused to equate abortion with murder; 49 percent acknowledged that, on some occasions, abortion can be recognized as a moral choice; and 49 percent believed that there are times when an act of abortion should be left legally to the pregnant woman.[27]

Given this disparity of attitudes among the clergy and the ranking theologians, it is easy to understand how the laity are bewildered as they consider the mysteries of IVF and how their fundamental attitudes and perceptions concerning abortion will be translated into similar problem areas of the new reproductive biology. Tragically, the percentage of Catholics supporting the legalization of abortion countenanced by *Roe v. Wade*[28] has continued to rise since the decision in 1973; today, 10 to 12 percent of Catholics agree with the official church teaching that abortion is always wrong.[29]

The problem of abortion cannot truly be passed off as another government failure, for no administrative agency or department within government is *forcing* women to have abortions.[30] And, as observed, the statistics demonstrate clearly that Catholics support the "right" to abortion proportionately with the rest of the population and thus ignore the teaching of the Church that such acts are sinful.[31] What is evident in the efforts to criminalize abortion is perhaps little more than a plea to the government "to make criminal what we believe to be sinful because we ourselves cannot stop committing the sin."[32] Accordingly, perhaps the better view here is to recognize that "[t]he failure is not Caesar's. This failure is our failure, the failure of the entire people of God."[33]

The goal set by the members of the pro-life movement has been nothing less than a total prohibition of abortion. Yet, the feasibility of obtaining this goal in a pluralistic society is doubtful, to say the least.[34] In answer to the question whether Catholics would choose to cooperate with other likeminded Americans of similar ethical persuasion in working for a more restrictive abortion law, one would hope that they would cooperate; for surely there would be no compromise of the fundamental belief in the sanctity of all human life.[35] "We should continue to hold ourselves to a higher standard than we can persuade society at large to write into law."[36]

Additional Teachings from Rome

In 1987 the Vatican's Congregation for the Doctrine of the Faith issued its "Instruction on Respect for Human Life in its Origins and on the Dignity of Procreation: Replies to Certain Questions of the Day" wherein, with full papal approval, it called on governments to enact laws against surrogate motherhood, embryo and sperm banks, donation of sperm or ovum between unmarried persons and embryo experimentation. Even with a husband's sperm, a married woman may not utilize IVF or artificial insemination in order to become pregnant. The then U.S. Senator, Albert Gore, Jr., termed the Vatican's position on effecting a total ban on technological conception to be "impractical and unwise."[37]

Veritas Splendor, or "The Splendor of Truth," which was issued as a papal encyclical in 1992, declared certain acts, such as abortion, were simply morally wrong, and, furthermore, decisions to pursue such acts could not be justified morally according to standards of proportionality or balancing because the object of these actions make them intrinsically evil under all circumstances.[38]

The year 1992 also saw the issuance by Rome of a new universal catechism—the first in more than four centuries—designed to maintain the unity of faith and fidelity to Catholic doctrines. In particular, the document condemned artificial insemination by a donor as "gravely dishonest" and while categorizing homologous insemination "as less worthy of condemnation," it nonetheless condemned such acts as "morally acceptable." The catechism also declares, as to genetic engineering, that it "is immoral to produce human embryos destined to be exploited as though they were disposable biological matter."[39]

It remained for the pope's most current encyclical, *Evangelium Vitae*, or "The Gospel of Life," issued in 1995, to underscore with unmistakable clarity, the Vatican's position that the experimental use of human embryos or fetuses is a crime against their dignity. Addressing the three main areas of the life of the embryo in terms of medical research as IVF, abortion, and euthanasia, and linking them for the first time in such a document, the encyclical condemns embryo research and genetic manipulation which lead to fetal death. It does accept life-enhancing operations on a fetus within the womb, so long as the baby's life is not threatened directly. IVF is permissible under certain very limited circumstances when, for example, the Gamete Interfallopian Transfer technique is following, allowing eggs, as such, to be mixed with a husband's sperm and transferred immediately to the womb so that no embryo is grown outside the body.[40]

TO BE OR NOT TO BE?

The issue of abortion, as it rises in the process of IVF, becomes topical during the laparoscopy (or procedure whereby eggs are removed from a woman's reproductive tract). Following this procedure, eggs that may have been produced in response to drug therapy for superovulation are stored for subsequent fertilization and implantation or experimentation.[41] If all the eggs are fertilized by the sperm from a married woman's husband and placed in her uterus, there is no problem. But when some eggs are stored for later efforts to impregnate—should the first attempt fail—or for the purpose of genetic experimentation, the contentious issue of abortion rises to the fore. Ethical complexities attend each of the many variations on the basic IVF theme. When, for example, artificial insemination is used to fertilize a married woman's egg with the sperm of a man other than her husband because her husband's sperm is defective, a serious ethical issue is posed. The same is true when a third party surrogate carries an embryo to term for a genetic mother who is unable to do so for herself or when a single woman seeks to avail herself of IVF procedures.

By way of summarizing broadly, attention is now drawn to what might be termed as the "ethical morality" of IVF or the benefits and the harms of its use.[42] The most obvious benefit of the procedure is that it circumvents infertility and thereby allows those married couples with a strong desire to have children of their own to raise a family and to bring fulfillment and happiness to their marriage. Should it be determined conclusively that frozen embryos can be used without damage to the resultant child, IVF will enable women who so wish to pursue careers and then have children by using embryos created some years earlier—thereby reducing the chance of producing a child with Down's syndrome. Outside the scope of family expansion, IVF could be used to provide embryos that could be used in scientific and medical experiments, not only in cancer research but also as a source of obtaining embryonic tissue used in the treatment of diseases such as diabetes and to harvest organs for transplantation.

There are several major objections to IVF. The first is tied to the concern that separating sex from procreation is inherently wrong. The practice of IVF followed by embryo transfer to the uterus of the married woman severs the very connection between sex and reproduction. The second major objection maintains that IVF is morally wrong because it involves the risk of harm to the individual who is subsequently brought into existence. The harm (although not documented factually) could be either in the nature of physical damage or abnormality resulting from the IVF process or from the subsequent process of transferring the embryo to the genetic mother's or birth mother's womb (in the case of a surrogate) or from psychological harm that might inure to the infant born of the total process.

The third objection holds that the use of IVF as a means to produce embryos to be used for experiments or as sources of tissue and organs—as opposed to being implanted—is wrong because it subjects the embryo to pain. This objection would have considerable merit where experiments were, in fact, to be conducted on substantially developed fetuses. When conducting such scientific interventions with embryos in the first several weeks of their development, such embryos probably do not experience pain, owing to the absence of a critical nervous system.[43]

The fourth objection is that even though IVF may be properly viewed as neither wrong in itself nor wrong because of its effects on those immediately involved, it may be wrong because of the "slippery slope" to which it is likely to lead. Thus, IVF together with embryo transfer may lead to unimpeded use of surrogate mothers as substitutes for genetic mothers, the dissolution of the family unit by the use of the process by women who do not wish to marry or have sexual relations with a man, or even lead to the development of artificial wombs (ectogenesis) whereby women no longer need to have "contact" with their children until after they are, so to speak, born.[44]

Finally, as noted previously, the last objection to the IVF process is that it involves either the destruction or freezing of embryos not implanted. In the former situation, an action morally akin to abortion is committed, but in the case of freezing there may or may note be a comparable action, for such depends on whether it is possible to thaw the embryo successfully and on whether it is likely that the embryo will ultimately be implanted. The only apparent way to resolve these uncertainties would be to continue with limited experimentation in the field, using lower animal life forms.

Values in Conflict

Some would seek to abandon science and reason in favor of mysticism, hermeneutics, and transcendental rapture. Sadly, they fail to comprehend that ignorance, not knowledge assures misery and that the employment of science for inhumane reasons, not science in and of itself, threatens global survival. Reduced to its most fundamental level, then, what is seen is that the pivotal questions confronting the science of human experimentation are two in number: who will *control* its products and what purposes will be employed to achieve this end.[45]

The improvement of human well-being has been, for the most part, the single motivating force in the quest to ensure that all citizens, especially young children, will be safe from all forms of disease, not only genetic and congenital disorders but uterine infections and a formidable host of other birth defects as well.[46] Since the 1930s, for example, human fetal tissue has been an invaluable research tool for molecular biologists as a source of human cell lines. In turn, these cell lines have been widely used in advanced research on viruses and in the preparation of vaccines (notably, the polio vaccine) against them. More recently, successful research has been conducted on fetal tissue transplants in living subjects for therapeutic purposes, and for developing treatments for Parkinson's disease, diabetes and radiation-induced anemia. What makes fetal tissue so particularly useful for transplantation is the fact that it not only grows rapidly and is very adaptable, but it also induces a limited immune response from the host.[47]

The Federal Position

In 1978 the then Department of Health, Education and Welfare (HEW) (now the Department of Health and Human Services [HSS]) and its Ethics Advisory Board decided to study the complex ethical, legal, social, and scientific issues raised by IVF procedures.[48] The final report of the department was ultimately "buried in the bureaucracy."[49] Yet today, given the sometimes strident pro-life mood of a vocal segment of society, there is pessimism that a strong positive movement will occur at the federal regulatory level.[50] Hearings were conducted in August 1984 on the issue of embryo transfers and the legal, ethical, and medical responses to such procedures.[51] Although no firm or conclusive steps were taken as a consequence of these hearings, they served to focus attention on the need for continuing dialogue in this area.

Because of a *de facto* moratorium set in 1975, no federally funded research was undertaken on IVF.[52] Even though the 1979 Report of the Ethics Advisory Board of HEW concluded that federal support of research on humans designed to establish the safety and the effectiveness of IVF procedures would be ethically permissible so long as certain conditions were met,[53] the report was never accepted nor the moratorium ended[54] until 1993 when President Clinton lifted the moratorium in January.[55] He determined subsequently that the National Institutes of Health (NIH) could not allocate any financial resources for the specific creation of human embryos for research purposes—this, in spite of an advisory committee's proposal to the contrary.[56] And, interestingly, the House Appropriations Committee voted in July 1995 to ban the use of federal funds for human embryo research.[57] In the year following this 1993 presidential action, the federal government, through the National Institute of Neurological Disorders and States, approved the first grant for fetal tissue research in over fifteen years.[58]

In making these two decisions, the president was guided by the work of two federal committees studying human embryo research. The first committee submitted its report on September 28, 1994, and concluded that fertilized human eggs could be used for federally financed research if the embryos were no older than fourteen days. The panel determined human embryos, in the every early stage of development, simply did not share the same moral status as infants and children.[59]

This first committee report also concluded that research using human embryos should only be conducted when animal or unfertilized cells could *not* be used and, further, that the number of embryos used in the experiments be kept to a minimum. It was urged that a review panel be constituted to review requests for funding such embryo research. Payment of donors for embryos—as well as experimentation on embryos calling for the use of eggs harvested from aborted fetuses—were found unacceptable. The cloning of embryos for uteral implantation was also forbidden.

The committee maintained further researchers should be allowed to create embryos in test tubes solely for research purposes when no other method was available for obtaining results of "outstanding scientific and therapeutic value."[60] Interestingly, over the years embryo research has gone on apace at private in vitro fertilization clinics, without government regulation, with the surplus embryos being deprived from infertility treatments that would have otherwise been discarded.[61]

The second NIH advisory panel presented its report in December 1994 and concurred with the previous committee's finding that human embryo research should go forward with federal funding. Under suggested committee guidelines, most of the research which should qualify for federal funding would involve surplus embryos created in test-tube pregnancy programs which have not been implanted in wombs.[62] Strong congressional opposition has been mounted by Congressman Robert K. Dornan to curtail federal support of such research terming it nothing more than "bizarre experiments on living human embryos."[63]

Among the guidelines proposed for embryo research by this committee—drawn, as such, from the work of the previous committee—were: an understanding that donors of eggs or sperm must give their informed consent to the research purpose; that most embryos should be obtained from IVF clinics which routinely create "spare" embryos; an allowance that eggs and embryos may be obtained for research from women undergoing pelvic surgery as well as dead women–again, if informed consent has been obtained; that parthenotes, or eggs "activated" without sperm through parthenogenesis, be used in research; and that any research plan hold the promise of conferring a significant scientific or clinical benefit.[64]

It should be noted that the involvement of the federal government and HHS is presently structured by general regulations protecting human subjects which apply to any IVF research, development, or other related activities that might in the future be conducted by the department, or by the federal government outside the department.[65] To ensure additional protection in research projects that involve fetuses and/or pregnant women, the department's Ethics Advisory Board has been required to review every such proposal for IVF "as to its acceptability from an ethical standpoint."[66]

Subsequent specific protections have been provided to fetuses who are the subject of proposed experimentation and IVF research.[67] Although limited to research efforts funded in whole or in part by the federal government,[68] these guidelines make a significant distinction with regard to potential legal rights of implanted embryos.[69] The distinction is apparent in the definition of a fetus as "the product of conception from the time of implantation (as evidenced by any of the presumptive signs of pregnancy, such as missed menses, or a medically acceptable pregnancy text. . .)."[70]

As a consequence of this structured definition, research undertaken on fetuses *in utero* and *ex utero* has been prohibited unless the purpose of the activity is to either meet the particular health needs of the at-risk fetus, or there is minimal real or potential harm to the fetus by the research, and the purpose is to obtain biomedical knowledge not otherwise obtainable.[71] Research undertaken on nonviable fetuses *ex utero* has been prohibited unless either vital functions will not be maintained artificially, experimental activities that would terminate vital functions are not used, or the research purpose is to obtain otherwise unobtainable significant biomedical knowledge.[72] The obvious implication of these restrictions on embryonic and fetal research is that the scientific pursuit of mankind has been significantly handicapped. Private research into the mysteries and the opportunities of the new reproductive biology has continued over the years. But, without a balanced, regulated scheme and sources for federal research funding, the initiative and the momentum for scientific advancement is curtailed. With the reentry of the federal government into the field as a consequence of the lifting of the moratorium on fetal experimentation and the anticipated promulgation of new regulations for research, however, the critical balance may well be achieved.

A BASIC RIGHT TO PROCREATE—FOR WHOM?

As modern society continues to evolve and change, so too do many of its values, including privacy.[73] Autonomy, self-representation, personhood, identity, intimacy and dignity are all essentials of privacy.[74] The extent to which these essentials play a role in shaping a degree of sexual, procreational autonomy must surely remain largely fluid and flexible, for to attempt to define them with precision would challenge and erode any efficacy that they may enjoy.[75] The right of the state to control and shape the behavior of both individuals and groups regarding the birth of children is always an area of high emotion and legitimate concern.

The most widely held view is that private conduct between consenting adults or, for that matter, personal conduct of any nature, should be regulated only to the extent necessary to prevent harm to others.[76] Conformity is thus not a value of momentous concern and certainly not a value worth pursuing.[77] The counter or conservative view is that the business of law is to suppress vice and immorality simply because if violations of the very moral structure are indulged and promoted, such actions would surely undermine the whole basis of society itself.[78] Under the former view, the state would be justified—arguably—in acting to control personal decision making, if not for the need to prevent illegitimates from proliferating then to prevent the ultimate economic harm to society of having to help bear the expenses associated with the maintenance and education of a fatherless child born of artificial insemination. Similarly, the prevention of harm theory could be invoked in surrogation where the state, by preventing such acts, seeks to maintain the dignity and continuity of the family unit.

The Foundation

The first case to address tangentially what has now come to be regarded as a fundamental right to procreate was *Buck v. Bell*.[79] In *Bell*, the Supreme Court upheld a Virginia statute that permitted the sterilization of inmates in state institutions who suffered from a hereditary form of insanity or imbecility.[80] This opinion, authored by Justice Holmes, was written *before* the development of the fundamental right/compelling state interest standard.[81] Thus, it must be determined whether the Court's opinion implicitly recognized the existence of a compelling state interest, or whether the Court merely failed to perceive procreation as a fundamental right.[82] The latter appears to be the case; indeed, it has been suggested that the Court's pervasive emphasis on the state's right to promote the general welfare approximates a rational basis standard of judicial review.[83]

In *Skinner v. Oklahoma*,[84] the Supreme Court again considered the validity of compulsory sterilization laws. Unlike the Court in *Bell*, which found no equal protection violation,[85] the *Skinner* Court struck down Oklahoma's Habitual Criminal Sterilization Act on equal protection grounds. The statute provided for the sterilization of habitual criminals—anyone convicted of three felonies—but did not consider felonies which arose from the violation of the prohibitory laws, revenue acts, embezzlement, or political offenses.[86] The Court recognized initially that marriage and procreation are fundamental to both the existence and survival of mankind.[87] It then proceeded to observe, however, that a classification distinguishing larcenists from embezzlers, for purposes of criminal sterilization, represented a form of invidious discrimination. Consequently, the Court subjected the classification to strict scrutiny and found it violated the equal protection clause.[88]

Although a number of Supreme Court decisions[89] have since cited the *Skinner* case as at least validating, if not in fact creating, a constitutional right to procreate,[90] it is important to recognize precisely the contours of that right. In both *Bell* and *Skinner*, the Court was confronted with sterilization statutes. Sterilization, unlike other methods of control over human reproduction, is irreversible.[91] Thus, in discussing the procreative "right" affected by Oklahoma's Habitual Criminal Sterilization Act, the *Skinner* Court aptly observed that this "right [was] basic to the perpetuation of a race."[92] Given this background, the procreative right recognized in *Skinner* was simply a right to remain fertile, *not* an uninhibited right to engage in potentially procreative conduct. Subsequent decisions which have focused on a fundamental right to privacy have further delineated the contours of this right.

Searching for a Fundamental Right to Sexual Privacy

Nowhere in the Constitution is there mention of a right to privacy. Nor is any right of sexual freedom found within the gambit of procreative rights recognized by the Supreme Court; nor for that matter has the Court fashioned a general right of personal privacy which is sufficiently broad based to permit sex outside marriage.[93]

In *Griswold v. Connecticut*,[94] however, the Supreme Court, for the first time, recognized a constitutionally protected zone of privacy and invalidated part of a Connecticut statute forbidding the use of contraceptives by married persons.[95] The protection of this aspect of procreative autonomy "was largely subsumed within a broad right of marital privacy"[96] which "stressed the unity and independence of the married couple and forbade undue inquiry into conjugal acts."[97] From this, however, it cannot be argued that there must exist a corresponding fundamental right to reproduce or to use artificial reproductive technology.[98] For, as Justice Goldberg made clear in his concurring opinion, *Griswold* "in no way interfere[d] with a State's proper regulation of sexual promiscuity or misconduct," and thus the constitutionality of Connecticut's statutes prohibiting adultery and fornication remained beyond dispute.[99]

In *Eisenstadt v. Baird*,[100] the Supreme Court was confronted with construing a Massachusetts statute that prohibited the distribution of contraceptives to unmarried persons. In holding that the statute violated the Equal Protection Clause of the Fourteenth Amendment, the Court observed, "If the right of privacy means anything, it is the right of the *individual*, married or single, to be free from unwarranted governmental intrusion into matters so fundamentally affecting a person as the decision whether to bear or beget a child."[101] Accordingly, the *Eisenstadt* Court fleshed out the procreative skeleton of *Griswold*, which initially appeared confined to the so-called "scared" precincts of relations between married persons.[102] This decision, however, did no more than refine a qualified right to procreative autonomy blurred by the *Griswold* Court's emphasis on the marital relation.[103]

In *Roe v. Wade*,[104] the Court addressed squarely an integral part of the individual's right to procreative autonomy when an unmarried woman in a class action suit challenged the constitutionality of the Texas criminal abortion laws. The Court articulated a new source of privacy derived from the fourteenth amendment's standard of personal liberty and inherent restrictions on state action and held that this right was sufficiently broad to embrace a decision made by a woman whether or not to terminate her pregnancy.[105] The Court, however, went further to state that it was *not* recognizing "an unlimited right to do with one's body as one pleases."[106]

The final pertinent case of interest in this area is *Carey v. Population Services International*.[107] In *Carey*, the Supreme Court invalidated a New York statute which regulated the sale and distribution of contraceptives to minors and stated that "at the very heart of [the] cluster of constitutionally protected choices," recognized in the previous privacy cases,[108] was "the decision whether or not to beget or bear a child."[109] This decision is particularly instructive on the question of the unmarried woman's right to artificial insemination or IVF procedures, for it examines the previous privacy cases and delineates the extent of the individual's right to procreative autonomy.

It has been suggested that since a woman has a right to terminate her pregnancy and to use contraceptives, *a posteriori*, the conduct required to bring about those procreative choices must also be protected.[110] The Court's opinion in *Carey* indicates, however, that this is simply not the case.

First, with regard to contraception and abortion, the Court made clear that it is "[the] individual's right to decide to *prevent conception* or *terminate pregnancy*" that is protected.[111] Such unequivocal language, however, lends little or no support to the argument that a concomitant right to conceive is also protected. Second, the Court emphasized that its decision did not encompass any constitutional questions raised by state statutes regulating either sexual freedom or adult sexual relations.[112] This reading of *Carey* is supported by a later decision of the Court which stated that if "the right to procreate means anything at all, it must imply some right to enter the only relationship in which the [s]tate . . . allows sexual relations to legally take place."[113]   Thus, the lesson from the Court's decisions in *Skinner, Griswold, Eisenstadt, Roe,* and *Carey* is plain: "procreative autonomy . . . includes both the right to remain fertile and the right to avoid conception,"[114] but absolutely *nothing more*.

State Justification for Intervention

Since the unmarried woman's decision to be artificially inseminated or to participate in an IVF procedure does not fall within the gambit of any recognized fundamental right, state statutes limiting this procreative technology to married women "[may] be sustained under the less demanding test of rationality."[115] Under this test, the distinction drawn must be "rationally related" to a "constitutionally permissible" objective.[116] In employing this rather relaxed standard, courts must be sensitive to the fact "that the drawing of lines that create distinctions is peculiarly a legislative task and an unavoidable one."[117]

Absent a suspect classification or the infringement of a fundamental right, the Supreme Court has recognized that legislation "protecting legitimate family relationships" as well as both the regulation and protection of the family unit are "venerable concerns of the state."[118] Statutes limiting the availability of artificial insemination to married women and those which might (indeed, should) be drafted to limit the use of IVF procedures to married women, fall squarely within this classification.

As early as 1888, the Court recognized marriage as "the foundation of the family and society, without which there would be neither civilization nor progress."[119] Recently, the Court observed that "a decision to marry and raise a child in the traditional family setting must receive . . . protection."[120] Thus, although certain aspects of an individual's right to procreative autonomy have correctly been divorced from the familial and marriage relationship, the Court has also implicitly recognized that, whenever possible, childbearing should take place within the traditional family unit.[121] An unmarried woman's decision to seek artificial insemination or to participate in an IVF procedure goes directly against the tide of these pronouncements.

An instructive analogy may be made to the law of adoption. Adoption statutes, like the statutes regulating artificial insemination, have their genesis in state law.[122] Although all states currently allow adoption by unmarried adults,[123] it occurs only in rare cases. In *In re Adoption of Infant H.*,[124] an unmarried middle-age woman sought to adopt a thirteen-month-old child, for whom parental care by a young couple was available. In rejecting her application, the court observed:

> Adoption by a single person has generally and in this Court's experience been sought and approved only in exceptional circumstances, and in particular for the hard-to-place child for whom no desirable parental couple is available. In the universal view of both experts and laymen, while one parent may be better than none for the hard-to-place child, joint responsibility by a father and a mother contributes to the child's physical, financial and psychic security as well as his emotional growth. This view is more than a matter of present convention, anthropologists pointing out that the institution of marriage, which is a method of signifying commitment to such joint responsibility, evolved in response to the need for two-parent care of children.[125]

This observation applies with equal force to artificial insemination for an unmarried woman as well as her participation in an IVF program.[126] Indeed, if a state may reasonably regulate unmarried adults in their quest to adopt children, it would be anomalous to suggest that it could not regulate the use of a procreative technology designed to bring children into the world.

More important, however, the unmarried woman's access to artificial insemination, IVF and, thus, surrogation, directly undermines not only the concept of marriage, but the family as well and hence the very foundation of society.[127] The courts have repeatedly recognized the desirability of having a child reared within a traditional family unit. Moreover, it is clear that the marital relationship serves as the very genesis of the family unit.[128] Accordingly, the inherent procreative potential of this union,[129] together with the stability that this provides to the social fabric,[130] would be dealt a mortal wound by permitting unmarried women to assert total procreational autonomy through the use of the new reproductive technologies.[131]

Another argument made against state intervention is that action taken by the state in this area of procreational autonomy seeks to paint with too broad a brush when it limits artificial insemination to married couples or withholds approval or licensure of IVF procedures unless one is married. Although the Supreme Court has failed to formulate a concrete definition of the family, *Moore v. City of East Cleveland*[132] represents a clear extension of procreation that is routinely afforded to the "nuclear" family to one recognized as a "quasifamilial group."[133] In *Moore*, a zoning ordinance which limited an area to single-family dwellings was challenged by a woman who shared her home with her two grandsons. The Court merely recognized that the extended family occupies a place in American tradition similar to that of the nuclear family and thus is to be guaranteed protection by the Constitution.[134]

As the procreation and privacy cases clearly illustrate by analogy, however, the fact that a mother and her offspring may find protection within the nuclear family structure does not imply a right to freely bring about that condition, nor does it demonstrate that the limitations placed on artificial insemination, or on IVF for that matter, with respect to unmarried women are in any way irrational or unreasonable. Thus it assuredly demands an expanded definition of family in order to contend that statutes limiting artificial insemination or the new reproductive technologies to married women are not rationally related to a constitutionally permissible objective. The line of demarcation may be drawn imprecisely, but the Constitution is not offended "simply because the classification 'is not made with mathematical nicety or because in practice it results in some inequality.' "[135]

CONCLUSIONS

The legal system, by protecting such relationships as kinship and formal marriage, promotes not only those interests of private parties, but the interests of society in those social and political structures which ensure a long-term individual view of liberty.[136] In judicial decisions affording familial and marital relationships a higher degree of constitutional protection, traditions have played a pivotal role. In the procreative field, the Supreme Court has carved out a limited degree of autonomy for the individual.

As this chapter has demonstrated, a woman's fundamental right to privacy or procreation does not encompass a right to artificial insemination or use of new reproductive technologies, such as IVF, or surrogation. Accordingly, statutes limiting the use of these new reproductive technologies need only be rationally related to the promotion of a constitutionally permissible state interest. A state's desire to promote the raising of children in the *traditional* family setting while at the same time promoting the institution of marriage and the family is an unquestionably permissible, if not laudable, objective.

Thirty years ago, Justice Felix Frankfurter cautioned: "Children have a very special place in life which the law should reflect. Legal theories and their phrasing in cases readily lead to fallacious reasoning if uncritically transferred."[137] The legislature, in limiting the practices and use of the new biological technologies to married women, have taken—and should continue to take—this admonition seriously. The extended use and application of these procedures primarily through artificial insemination and surrogation must be controlled strictly by legislative design. Surrogation should only be tolerated by a married woman, with her husband's actual consent, and then only under proper medically supervised standards. As a medical aid to infertility, IVF and surrogation should then be allowed by as last relief adjuncts to medical treatment of this impediment and not as a popular or novel experience to be championed on street corners and at political gatherings.

A legislative program designed to validate, and thereby license, the IVF process and its inextricable use and reliance on surrogation for married women, as well as the married surrogates participating therein, would not only seek to protect the health and well-being of the issue born but also would assure the safety of the surrogate. Such a legislative program would ideally include provisions shaping the rights and determining the extent of the liabilities of the contracting parents in the IVF-surrogate compact *vis-à-vis* the infant and also give due consideration to shaping the sphere of responsibility for various types of errors that intermediaries—such as doctors and lawyers—might commit in facilitating the whole process. Ideally, the specific policy matters coincident with the administration of an IVF-surrogation program, once structured, would be implemented by an administrative body or licensing board, where the policies and standards for evaluating and processing her requests for surrogate mothering would be both comprehensive and equitable in their design and utilization.[138]

The new reproductive biological techniques for parenthood portend an enormous opportunity of untold significance for humanity and demand the need for a searching inquiry into the parameters for future development.[139] The legislative branch of government is far better equipped to deal with this inquiry than is the executive or judicial, and is potentially a more responsive forum for posturing and advocacy by the various religions which must assume their roles as stalwart guides in the search for insightful, yet humane, lawmaking responses.[140] Thoughtful study and a cautious plan of action are needed now, before advancing complexities become genuine crises that overwhelm, confuse, and confound the role of the rule of law in meeting the challenges of the brave and pluralistic new world of tomorrow which, in actuality, are already here.

NOTES

1. Blum, *Moral Foundations of American Democracy*, 1 NOTRE DAME J.L. ETHICS & PUB. POL'Y 65, 67 (1984).

2. M. TOOLEY, ABORTION AND INFANTICIDE chs. 5-7 (1983).

3. Tauer, *The Tradition of Probabilism and the Moral Status of the Early Embryo*, 45 THEOLOGICAL STUD. 3 (1984).

4. SACRED CONGREGATION FOR THE DOCTRINE OF FAITH, DECLARATION ON ABORTION (1975). *See* Noonan, *Abortion and the Catholic Church: A Summary History*, 12 NAT. L.F. 85 (1968).

5. Diamond, *Abortion, Animation and Biological Hominization*, 36 THEOLOGICAL STUD. 305 (1975). *See* TOOLEY, *supra* note 2, chs. 5-7.

6. *See* the writings of McCormick, Curran, Di Ianni and Rahner, as cited in Tauer, *supra* note 3, at 3 nn. 1-4.

7. *See generally* OFFICE OF TECHNOLOGY ASSESSMENT, IMPACTS OF APPLIED GENETICS: MICROORGANISMS, PLANTS AND ANIMALS (1981).

8. 410 U.S. 113 (1973).

9. It is only when the fetus reaches a "compelling" point of viability or that time when it "presumably has the capability of meaningful life outside the mother's womb" that the state's interest in protecting fetal existence will be asserted. *Id.* at 163-4. It is at the third trimester of development that the state's interest becomes controlling.

For a chart presenting the stages at which the life of a person could begin *see,* B.R. FURROW ET AL., BIOETHICS: HEALTH CARE AND ETHICS 44 (1991).

10. *Attorney General for Queensland ex rel. Kerr v. T.,* 57 A.L.J.R. 285 (Austl. 1983).

And in Canada, Mr. Justice Matheson of the Saskatchewan Court of Queen's Bench held that a fetus was not to be regarded as a person within the meaning of the law and thus not within the scope of the term *everyone* as used in the Canadian Charter of Rights and Freedoms. The charter provides, in pertinent part, that "[e]veryone has the right to life . . . and the right not to be deprived thereof except in accordance with the principles of fundamental justice." *Borowski v. Attorney-General of Canada,* 4 D.L.R. 4th 112, 121 (1983) (quoting CAN. CHARTER OF RIGHTS AND FREEDOMS § 7).

11. Gavigan, *The Criminal Sanction as It Relates to Human Reproduction: The Genesis of the Statutory Prohibition of Abortion,* 5 J. LEGAL HIST. 20 (1984).

Over the past fifteen years, some states have expanded the common law rights of the fetus by recognizing it can be an independent victim for purposes of criminal law. FURROW, ET AL., *supra* note 9 at 45.

12. Gavigan, *id.* at 21. The present position is summarized:

A child is not considered in law to be in being, so as to be the subject of a charge of murder or manslaughter, until the whole body of the child is extruded from the womb and has an existence independent of the mother. Whether the child has an independent existence turns upon whether it has an independent circulation, and has breathed or has a capacity for independent breathing. But a child may have an independent existence even though it has not drawn breath and even though the umbilical cord is not severed. In relation to the law of homicide a person continues in being until his being is extinguished by death. 11 HALSBURY'S LAWS OF ENGLAND para. 1153 (4th ed. 1976).

But see D. HEYD, GENETHICS: MORAL ISSUES IN THE CREATION OF PEOPLE (1992).

13. *See* Smith, *Intrusions of a Parvenu: Science, Religion and the New Biology,* 3 PACE U. L. REV. 63 (1982).

14. Reagan, *Policy and Morality Are Inseparable,* 1 NOTRE DAME J.L. ETHICS & PUB. POL'Y 7 (1984).

15. *Id.*

16. *Id.* at 10. Indeed, it has been stated that, "The state must be subject to the higher law of God." C. RICE, BEYOND ABORTION: THE THEORY AND PRACTICE OF THE SECULAR STATE 135 (1979).

17. *Id.* *See* J. ELLIS, AMERICAN CATHOLICISM 156 (2d ed. 1969); R. NEUHAS, THE NAKED PUBLIC SQUARE: RELIGION AND DEMOCRACY IN AMERICA (1984).

18. Hyde, *Keeping God in the Closet: Some Thoughts on the Exorcism of Religious Values from Public Life,* 1 NOTRE DAME J.L. ETHICS & PUB. POL'Y 33, 36 (1984).

19. *Id.* at 43.

20. *Id.*

21. McBrien, *The Church and Politics,* 1 NOTRE DAME J.L. ETHICS & PUB. POL'Y 57, 64 (1984).

22. *Id.* at 59.

23. ELLIS, *supra* note 17, at 157.

24. R. Drinan, *Religion and Politics in the United States in the Next Fifteen Years 20* (paper delivered at the Conference on Religion and Politics at Kenyon College, April 18-21, 1985).

25. LONDON TIMES, June 6, 1985, at 12. As Joseph Cardinal Ratzinger has observed, "Economic liberalism creates its exact counterpart, *permissivism*, on the moral plane." J. RATZINGER, THE RATZINGER REPORT OF THE CHURCH 83 (1985). He continued by stating, "Separated from motherhood, sex has remained without a locus and has lost its point of reference." *Id.* at 84.

26. ELLIS, *supra* note 17, at 159.

27. Anderson, *Catholic Scholars Express Varied Abortion Views,* WASH. POST, Feb. 9, 1985, at B6.

See the Freedom of Access to Clinics Entrance Act, where criminal sanctions are imposed for actions by individuals which threaten, intimidate or interfere with those individuals obtaining or providing reproductive health services (e.g., abortion) relating to the termination of a pregnancy whether these services be provided in a hospital, clinic or physician's office. 18 U.S.C.A. §248(a)(e) (1994).

28. 410 U.S. 113 (1973).

29. Hyer, *U.S. Bishops Rebuke Dissenters on Abortion,* WASH. POST, Nov. 17, 1984, at D10.

30. Cuomo, *Religious Belief and Public Morality: A Catholic Governor's Perspective,* 1 NOTRE DAME J.L. ETHICS & PUB. POL'Y 13, 26 (1984).

31. Hyer, *supra* note 29.

32. Cuomo, *supra* note 30, at 26.

33. *Id.*

34. ˈHesburgh, *Reflections on Cuomo: The Secret Consensus,* 1 NOTRE DAME J.L. ETHICS & PUB. POL'Y 53, 56 (1984).

35. *Id.*

36. *Id.*

37. Hyer, *Vatican Basis Many Birth Technologies: Test Tube, Surrogate Fertilization Banned* WASH. POST, Mar. 11, 1987, at A1.

38. McCormick, *Veritas Splendor and Moral Theology,* 169 AMERICA 8 (Oct. 30, 1992).

39. Riding, _New Catholicism for Catholics Define Sins of Modern World_, N.Y. TIMES, Nov. 17, 1992, at A1.

40. Gledhill & Laurance, _Pope Sets Limits on Treatment for Fertility_, N.Y. TIMES, Mar. 18, 1995, at A1. _See_ 24 ORIGINS, Documentary Service 690-727 (April 6, 1995).

41. _See generally The New Origins of Life_, TIME Mag., Sept. 10, 1984, at 46 _passim_.

42. _See generally_ R. McCORMICK, HOW BRAVE A NEW WORLD? chs. 1, 16 (1981); TEST-TUBE BABIES: A GUIDE TO MORAL QUESTIONS, PRESENT TECHNIQUES AND FUTURE POSSIBILITIES (W. Walters and P. Singer, eds. 1982) [hereinafter cited as TEST-TUBE BABIES].

43. TOOLEY, _supra_ note 2, chs. 5-7.

44. TEST-TUBE BABIES, _supra_ note 42, chs. 8, 11. _See generally_ D. KELLY, THE EMERGENCE OF ROMAN CATHOLIC MEDICAL ETHICS IN NORTH AMERICA (1979).

45. J. F. FLETCHER, HUMANHOOD: ESSAYS IN BIOMEDICAL ETHICS 93 (1979).

46. _Id. See also_ Eisenberg, _The Social Imperatives of Medical Research_, 198 SCIENCE 105 (1977).

47. Greely et al., _The Ethical Use of Human Fetal Tissue in Medicine_, 320 NEW ENG. J. MED. 1093 (1989). It is between the sixth and eleventh weeks of gestation that nearly 80 percent of all individual abortions are performed. Thus, neural and other tissue are at a sufficiently developed state that it may, with success, be retrieved and transplanted. For those abortions performed between fourteen and sixteen weeks, pancreatic tissue is of particular value in diabetes research. Robertson, _Rights, Symbolism and Public Policy in Fetal Tissue Transplants_, 18 HASTINGS CENTER RPT. 5 (Dec. 1988).

48. Ethics Advisory Board of the Department of Health, Education and Welfare, Report and Conclusions: HEW Support of Research Involving Human in Vitro Fertilization and Embryo Transfer, 44 Fed. Reg. 35,033 (1979). _See_ McCormick, _Who or What Is the Preembryo?_ 1 KENNEDY INST., ETHICS J. 1 (Mar. 1991).

49. Krause, _Artificial Conception: Legal Approaches_, 19 FAM. L.Q. 185, 190 (1985).

50. This pessimistic, although realistic, view is tied to a perception that it would be far better to hold in abeyance any strong movement at this time for fear of its possible linkage with the right-to-life controversies and would thus give rise to the real possibility that it would never be allowed to be evaluated in a calmer atmosphere. Abramowitz, _A Stalemate on Test-Tube Baby Research_, 14 HASTINGS CENTER RPT. 5 (Feb. 1984).

51. _See Hearings on Human Embryo Transfer, Subcommittee on Investigations and Oversight, U.S. House of Representatives' Committee on Science and Technology_, 98th Cong., 2nd Sess. 142 (1984).

52. Abramowitz, *supra* note 50.

53. Ethics Advisory Board, *supra* note 48 at 35,057. Among these conditions were that the embryo be sustained in vitro beyond the implantation stage and that IVF, followed by embryo transfer, be used only by married couples who donated their sperm and ova. Abramowitz, *supra* note 50.

54. Abramowitz, *supra* note 50 at 6. *See* Fletcher & Ryan, *Federal Regulations for Fetal Research: A Case for Reform*, 15 L. MED. & HEALTH CARE 126 (1987).

55. Weekly Comp. Pres. Doc., Jan. 2, 1993, at 87.

56. Weekly Comp. Pres. Doc. Dec. 2, 1994, at 2459.

See Schwartz & Devroy, *Clinton to Ban U.S. Funds for Some Embryo Studies*, WASH. POST, Dec. 3, 1994, at A1; Marshall, *Human Embryo Research: Clinton Rules out Some Studies*, 266 SCIENCE 1634 (Dec. 9, 1994).

57. N.Y. TIMES, July 22, 1995, at Sec. 1, p. 8.

58. *Fetal Tissue Research Grant Awarded*, WASH. POST, Jan. 5, 1994, at A3.

Interestingly, under the National Institutes of Health Revitalization Act of 1993, it is a criminal offense for any person to solicit or otherwise acquire human fetal tissue for purposes of transplantation affecting interstate commerce if it is obtained from an induced abortion, as a consequence of a promise

to donate tissue to a specified individuals (or relative of the donating individual), or obtained for a valuable consideration as part of the costs associated with performing an abortion. 42 U.S.C. §289g-2 (1993). *See* Maroney, *Bioethical Catch-22: The Moratorium on Federal Funding of Fetal Tissue Transplantation Research and the NIH Revitalization Amendments*, 9 J. CONTEMP. HEALTH L. & POL'Y 483 (1993).

59. *Federal Panel Urges U.S. to Drop Its Ban on Financing of Human Embryo Research*, N.Y. TIMES, Sept. 28, 1994, at B7.

See also Angier, *Rules Due on Disputed Embryo Research*, N.Y. TIMES, Sept. 6, 1994, at C1.

60. *Medicine and Health: Committee Backs Embryo Testing*, FACTS ON FILE WORLD NEWS DIGEST, Nov. 3, 1994, at A3.

61. *Id.*

See Milch, *In Vitro Fertilization and Embryo Transfer: Medical Technology plus Social Values equals Legislative Solutions*, 30 J. FAM. L. 875 (1991-92).

62. Wetzstein & Price, *Panel OKs Research on Human Embryos: Clinton Rejects Creating Them for Labs*, WASH. TIMES, Dec. 3, 1994, at A2.

63. *Id. See also supra* note 60.

64. *Id. See generally Symposium: What Research? Which Embryos?*, 25 HASTINGS CENTER RPT. 36 (Jan.-Feb. 1995).

65. 45 C.F.R. §§ 45.101-124, 46.301-306(g), 46.401-409 (1991).

66. 45 C.F.R. § 46.204(d) (1991). *See also* 45 C.F.R. § 46.205 (1991).

67. 45 C.F.R. §§ 46.102-206 (1985). In vitro fertilization is defined as "any fertilization of human ova which occurs outside of the body of a female, either through admixture of donor human sperm and ova or by any other means." §

46.203(g) (1991).

68. 45 C.F.R. § 46.101(a) (1991).

69. Blumberg, *Legal Issue on Nonsurgical Human Ovum Transfer* 251 J.A.M.A. 1178 (1984).

70. 45 C.F.R. § 46.203(c) (1991).

71. 45 C.F.R. §§ 46.208(a) (1)-(2) (1991).

72. 45 C.F.R. §§ 46.209(b) (1)-(3) (1991).

73. L. TRIBE, AMERICAN CONSTITUTIONAL LAW § 15-2 (1978).

74. *Id.* § 15-2 at 889.

75. *Id.* § 15-2 at 892.

76. H.L.A. HART, LAW, LIBERTY AND MORALITY 57 (1963).

77. *Id.*

78. P. DEVLIN, THE ENFORCEMENT OF MORALS 25 (1965). *See* Dworkin, *Lord Devlin and the Enforcement of Morals*, 75 YALE L.J. 986 (1966).

79. 274 U.S. 200 (1927).

80. *Id.* at 207.

81. Comment, *Artificial Human Reproduction: Legal Problems Presented by the Test-Tube Baby*, 20 EMORY L.J. 1045, 1054 (1979).

82. *Id.*

83. Note, *Legislative Naiveté in Involuntary Sterilization Laws*, 12 WAKE FOREST L. REV. 1064, 1071 (1976).

Writing for the Court in *Bell*, Justice Holmes stated:

We have seen more than once that the public welfare may call upon the best citizens for their lives. It would be strange if it could not call on those who already sap the strength of the State for these lesser sacrifices, often not felt to be such by those concerned, in order to prevent our being swamped with incompetence. It is better for all the world, if instead of waiting to execute degenerate offspring for crime, or to let them starve for their imbecility, society can prevent those who are manifestly unfit from continuing their kind. *Buck v. Bell*, 274 U.S. at 207.

84. 316 U.S. 535 (1942).

85. The *Bell* Court has used a revolving door rationale in rejecting the claim of equal protection:

[T]he law does all that is needed when it does all that it can, indicates a policy, applies it to all within the lines, and seeks to bring within the lines all similarly situated so far and so fast as its means allow. Of course so far as the operations enable those who otherwise must be kept confined to be returned to the world, and thus open the asylum to others, the equality aimed at will be more nearly reached. 274 U.S. at 208.

86. *Skinner v. Oklahoma*, 316 U.S. at 537.

87. *Id.* at 541.

88. *Id.*

89. *See, e.g., Cleveland Bd. of Educ. v. LaFleur*, 414 U.S. 632, 640 (1974).

90. Comment, *supra* note 81 at 1056. Indeed, it has been suggested that this case has been incorrectly interpreted since "the *Skinner* Court neither denied the state's right to sterilize nor established a constitutional right to procreate. Rather, the Court expressly declared that the scope of the states' police power was unaffected by its holding." *Id.*

91. *See Relf v. Weinberger*, 372 F. Supp. 1196, 1199 (D.D.C. 1974).

92. *Skinner v. Oklahoma*, 316 U.S. at 536.

93. Hafen, *The Constitutional Status of Marriage, Kinship, and Sexual Privacy—Balancing the Individual and Social Interests*, 81 MICH. L. REV. 463, 538 (1983).

94. 381 U.S. 479 (1965).

95. The Court observed that "specific guarantees in the Bill of Rights have penumbras, formed by emanations from the guarantees that help give them life and substance." *Id.* at 484. Thus, it is those "[v]arious guarantees [which] create zones of privacy." *Id.*

96. Note, *Eugenic Artificial Insemination: A Cure for Mediocrity?*, 94 HARV. L. REV. 1850, 1867 (1981).

97. Comment, *Developments in the Law—The Constitution and the Family*, 93 HARV. L. REV. 1156, 1183 (1980).

98. Comment, *supra* note 81 at 1058.

99. *Griswold v. Connecticut*, 381 U.S. at 498-9. But, Professor Laurence Tribe has observed that since *Griswold* recognized as valid individual decisions not to bear a child, read as such and considered with *Skinner*, it forces the conclusion that whether in fact one's body is to be the source of new life must be regarded as a personal decision for the concerned individual *alone*. L. TRIBE, *supra* note 73 at 923.

100. 405 U.S. 438 (1972).

101. *Id.* at 453 (emphasis in original).

102. *Id.*

103. "It has been suggested that the Court's opinion was lacking in candor, for it stated in broad dictum a major extension of the 'privacy right' which could have justified its decision, while purporting to rest on a strained conclusion that the statute involved failed even the minimal rationality test." Comment, *supra* note 97 at 1184.

Under an expansive liberal interpretation, *Eisenstadt* has been held to extend the right of privacy to *all* sexual activities. *E.g., Miller v. Rumsfeld*, 647 F.2d 80, 85 (9th Cir.) (Norris, J., dissenting), *cert. denied*, 454 U.S. 855 (1981).

104. 410 U.S. 113 (1973).

105. *Id.* at 153. This right, however, was not absolute and the degree of involvement allowed would be continued on the length of the pregnancy. "[P]rior to approximately the end of the first trimester, the abortion decision and its effectuation must be left to the medical judgement of the pregnant woman's attending physician." *Id.* at 164. After this stage, the "State may . . . regulate the abortion procedure to the extent that the regulation reasonably relates to the

preservation and protection of maternal health." *Id.* Finally, after viability, the state may protect fetal life and "may go so far as to proscribe abortion during that period, except when it is necessary to preserve the life or health of the mother." *Id.* at 163-4.

Unless scientists develop an artificial womb, no dramatic changes of survival rates for infants before the twenty-fourth week of pregnancy will be recorded. Russell, *Lawyers Question Letting Fetus Viability Shape Abortion Law*, WASH. POST, May 29, 1985, at A4.

106. *Id.* at 154. In support of this proposition, the Court cited *Buck v. Bell*, which led one commentator to observe: "As it is difficult to imagine a more substantial interference with procreation than compulsory sterilization, the limited nature of the recognized procreative
'right' is apparent." Note, *supra* note 96 at 1868.

107. 431 U.S. 678 (1977) (plurality opinion).

108. In addition to the privacy cases already analyzed in this chapter, the Court cited *Cleveland Bd. of Educ. v. LaFleur*, 414 U.S. 632 (1974); *Loving v. Virginia*, 388 U.S. 1 (1967); *Prince v. Massachusetts*, 321 U.S. 158 (1944); *Pierce v. Society of Sisters*, 268 U.S. 510 (1925).

109. *Carey*, 431 U.S at 685.

110. Kritchevsky, *The Unmarried Woman's Right to Artificial Insemination: A Call for an Expanded Definition of Family*, 4 HARV. WOMEN'S L.J. 26, 27-8 (1981).

111. *Carey*, 431 U.S. at 688 (emphasis added).

112. *Id.* at 688 n.5. *See Paris Adult Theatre I v. Slaton*, 413 U.S. 49, 68 n.15 (1973) (implication that state fornication statutes do not violate the federal constitution). *But see* State v. Saunders, 75 N.J. 200, 381 A.2d 333 (1977) (holding that fornication statute involves by its very nature a personal choice and that it infringes upon the right of privacy).

113. *Zablock v. Redhail*, 434 U.S. 374, 386 (1977). *See Doe v. Commonwealth Attorney*, 403 F. Supp. 1199 (E.D. Va. 1975), *aff'd*, 425 U.S. 901 (1976) (summary affirmance of three-judge district court decision holding that the state of Virginia could constitutionally apply its sodomy statute to private sexual conduct between consenting male adults).

114. Comment, *supra* note 97 at 1185.

115. *Maher v. Roe*, 432 U.S. 464, 478 (1976).

116. *Lindsey v. Normet*, 405 U.S. 56, 74 (1972).

117. *Massachusetts Bd. of Retirement v. Murgia*, 427 U.S. 307, 314 (1975).

118. *Weber v. Aetna Casualty & Sur. Co.*, 406 U.S. 164, 173 (1972).

119. *Maynard v. Hill*, 125 U.S. 190, 211 (1888).

120. *Zablocki v. Redhail*, 434 U.S. 374, 386 (1977).

121. *See generally Parham v. J.R.*, 442 U.S. 584 (1979); *Wisconsin v. Yoder*, 405 U.S. 205 (1972).

122. *See, e.g., Ferguson v. Finch*, 310 F.Supp. 1251 (D.S.C. 1970); *In re* Jarboe's Estate, 235 F. Supp. 505 (D.D.C. 1964).

123. Kritchevsky, *supra* note 110 at 31.

124. 69 Misc. 2d 304, 330 N.Y.S.2d 235 (1972).

125. *Id.* at 314, 330 N.Y.S.2d at 245. *Cf. Smith v. Organization of Foster Families for Equality & Reform*, 431 U.S. 816 (1977). In upholding the statutory and regulatory procedures for the removal of foster children from foster homes, the Court stated in *Smith* that: "Whatever liberty interest might otherwise exist in the foster family as an institution, that interest must be substantially attenuated where the proposed removal from the foster family is to return the child to the natural parents." *Id.* at 947.

126. Kritchevsky, *supra* note 110 at 29.

127. *Smith v. Organization of Foster Families for Equality & Reform*, 431 U.S. at 843.

128. Comment, *supra* note 97 at 1270.

129. If approved and encouraged by the state, artificial insemination tends to upset the traditional, totally private, monogamous method of human reproduction. By sanctioning the intervention of a third party (the donor) into the process, the state is approving a trend toward treating reproduction as a social, as opposed to a private, act. Artificial insemination also creates a potential for direct state intervention into the reproductive process. Kindregan, *State Power over Human Fertility and Individual Liberty*, 23 HASTINGS L.J. 1401, 1409 (1972).

130. *Griswold v. Connecticut*, 381 U.S. 479, 486 (1965).

131. *See* Karst, *The Freedom of Intimate Association,* 89 YALE L.J. 624 (1980), where it is maintained that procreation is considered fundamental because it "strongly implicates the values of intimate association, particularly the values of caring and commitment, intimacy, and self-identification." *Id.* at 640. These values may not be found in the unmarried woman's desire to engage in artificial insemination—thus lending further credence and support to a state's interest in limiting the use to married women. *Id.*

132. 431 U.S. 494 (1977).

133. Comment, *supra* note 97 at 1272.

134. *Id.* at 1271.

135. *Dandridge v. Williams*, 397 U.S. 471, 485 (1969) (quoting *Lindsey v. Natural Carbonic Gas Co.*, 220 U.S. 61, 78 (1910)). *But see* M. GLENDON, THE NEW FAMILY AND THE NEW PROPERTY (1981).

136. Hafen, *supra* note 93 at 559.

137. May v. Anderson, 345 U.S. 528, 536 (1952) (Frankfurter, J., concurring).

138. *Razor's Edge, supra* note 39. *See also* Brophy, *A Surrogate Mother Contract to Bear Child*, 20 J. FAM. L. 263 (1981).

139. R. SCOTT, THE BODY AS PROPERTY 221 (1981).

See generally Annas & Elias, *In Vitro Fertilization and Embryo Transfer: Medio-Legal Aspects of a New Technique to Create a Family*, 17 FAM. L. Q. 199 (1983).

140. *See supra* notes 15-0. *See also* Culliton, *Science's Restive Public*, 107 DAEDALUS 147 (1978). *See generally* Marcin, *Justice and Love*, 33 CATH. U.L. REV. 363 (1984).

Intra-Familial and External Discontinuities

Chapter 5

Assisted Reproductive Technologies: Artificial Insemination, Surrogation, and *In Vitro* Fertilization

It has been determined in a 1990 study that in the United States some eighty thousand babies are born through artificial insemination by a donor (AID) each year.[1] The Congressional Office of Technology Assessment issued a 1988 report which found over eleven thousand physicians have performed artificial insemination on approximately 172,000 women each year.[2]

With the startling new advances in reproductive technology, or what has been termed "collaborative conception,"[3] it is now possible for a child to have up to five "parents": an egg donor, a sperm donor, a surrogate mother who gestates the fetus, and the couple who actually raise the child.[4] From reading the biblical account of Sarah directing her husband, Abraham, to conceive a child with the assistance of her handmaiden, Hagar, it is evident that the practice of surrogate motherhood has existed for years.[5]

For many, infertility, sterility, genetic incompatibilities, and/or physical handicaps do not in any way appear to diminish the need for having children in order to have what is regarded as a complete marriage. Adoption is often a long, complicated procedure lasting anywhere from four to six years.[6] For many couples, continuation of the blood line is of central importance. With the assistance of surrogates, such continuation can be achieved anywhere from a year and a half to two years. Married women who share this view have been known to state: "I want my husband's baby even if someone else carries it."[7] It is astonishing and incongruous to realize that, with children in such great demand for some, there presently exists some 400,000 or more unwanted children in foster care arrangements.[8] Tragically, time, circumstances and socioeconomic conditions often change parental attitudes after an infant is added to the family unit—with the result being that the sought after and prized child all too often becomes an unwanted liability.

An early 1969 Harris opinion survey of some sixteen hundred adults from throughout the country concerning advances and applications of the new developing biology revealed a fascinating attitudinal profile. Of all interviewed, 19 percent approved of AID, or heterologous, donor insemination, while 56 percent disapproved of the process.[9] Where the sole method to achieve conception is by use of the AID procedure, that is, obtaining semen from a donor and injecting by syringe into the woman's reproductive tract, 35 percent of those interviewed approved of the technique. Forty-nine percent of the men interviewed in the survey agreed in principle with homologous insemination, that is, taking semen from the husband. Sixty-two percent of the women interviewed approved of pregnancies achieved by the artificial injection of their husbands' semen where physical or psychological difficulties precluded fertilization through sexual intercourse.[10]

Another sampling of public opinion occurred in 1978, shortly after the first recorded *in vitro* success of "Baby Louise Brown's" birth in England, when Gallup conducted a poll to determine American attitudes concerning the process of IVF.[11] The poll revealed public approval of the procedure by a two-to-one margin. A majority stated they would be willing to follow this procedure if they were childless and wished to have offspring. Nationwide, 53 percent would undergo this medical intervention and 36 percent would not.[12] While no sophisticated studies have been conducted regarding the public's acceptance or rejection of surrogate motherhood, there is every indication that it will not be universally accepted or rejected. Rather, a case-by-case response will be forthcoming with the reasons for the initial action being carefully scrutinized.

In a 1994 opinion survey by the Roper Center for Public Opinion Research, 71 percent of those 701 individuals polled said it was wrong for a man to sell his sperm for purposes of artificial insemination.[13] Yet, if the sperm were given as a gift, 59 percent said it would be proper and 35 percent said it would be wrong to assist a couple who could not otherwise conceive in this way.[14] When women in the survey were asked if they would consider paying another woman to be artificially inseminated with their husband's sperm and carrying the baby to term because of their own incapacity to achieve this, 76 percent of the respondents would not consider such actions while twenty percent said they would.[15]

THE ARTIFICIAL FATHER

Generally, in dealing with heterologous AID cases, the donor is unknown. The major issues involve whether the putative father (i.e., the husband of the artificially inseminated mother) becomes the legal father of the artificially conceived child and whether the wife has committed adultery by participating in the act with or without her husband's consent.

In 1948 the New York Supreme Court recognized that a woman artificially inseminated by a third-party donor, with her husband's consent, gave birth to a legitimate child.[16] The woman's husband was "entitled to the same rights as that acquired by a foster parent who has formally adopted a child, if not the same rights as those to which a natural parent under the circumstances would be entitled."[17]

With the case of *Gursky v. Gursky*[18] in 1963, however, a New York trial court held that even though a husband consents to his wife's use of AID, the child is nonetheless illegitimate. In 1968 a considerably more enlightened and contemporary California Supreme Court in *People v. Sorensen*[19] rejected the *Gursky* thesis and held that a husband who gives his consent to his wife's use of AID intervention cannot disclaim his lawful fatherhood of the child for the purpose of child support.[20] The court construed a state penal nonsupport statute to incorporate liability of a consenting father of the AID child—finding a genetic relationship, as such, unnecessary in order to establish the required father-child relationship.[21]

A considerable degree of sophistication was shown by the New York Supreme Court in 1973 with its holding in *Adoption of Anonymous*.[22] Instead of adhering blindly to *Gursky,* the court found a strong state policy favoring legitimacy. Furthermore, the court acknowledged that a child born of consensual artificial insemination by a donor, accomplished during a valid marriage, was legitimate and thereby entitled to enjoy all rights and privileges of a child who was conceived in a natural way by the same marriage.

Since *Sorensen* and *Anonymous*, a growing number of states have passed legislation making legitimate the offspring of AID when the husband consents to the procedure.[23] Twenty-four states have chosen to enact legislation that refuses to treat the donor as the father of a child conceived from artificial insemination.[24] For the majority of states addressing donor insemination, the provisions of the Uniform Parentage Act[25] are followed thereby providing that the donor sperm used by a married couple does not confer recognition on the donor of legal fatherhood of a child conceived by assisted conception so long as the procedure itself is supervised by a licensed physician.[26]

Where states chose not to define the legal rights of the sperm donor, paternity may still be established if it is pursued by the legitimacy statutes as an issue of fact. Thus, courts confronted with such a matter, would consider not only the intent of the parties as substantiated or modified by the parties subsequent behavior, but the placement of the name of the donor on the certificate of birth, for example, or the declaration by the donor of his paternity.[27] What these judicial and legislative actions indicate clearly, then, is that both these branches of government no longer equate AID with adultery as they once did,[28] and may even signal the public's willingness to sanction more startling genetic developments and to legitimate heretofore illegitimate conduct.[29]

In 1977 a New Jersey court held that an unmarried woman, who conceived a child through sperm artificially donated by a friend, was required to allow custodial and visitation rights for the donor despite her wishes but consistent with what was perceived as the best interests of the child. Even though refusing to take a specific position on the propriety of the use of artificial insemination between unmarried persons, the court recognized the donor as the *natural* father, and imposed on him the responsibility to support and maintain the child.[30]

Today, with the social and legal recognition of equality of rights for women, and of their reproductive autonomy granted by the U.S. Supreme Court in *Roe v. Wade,*[31] the issue of the necessity of a husband's consent for an act to be performed on his wife's body has become less significant. Nonetheless, it is to be hoped that married women who contemplate offering to become surrogate mothers, or submit to AID for their personal benefit or desire to have a child, will do so only after consultation with their husbands. Failure to disclose such acts may be tantamount to deceit.[32]

DONOR CONFIDENTIALITY VERSUS THE RIGHT TO KNOW

A rather interesting and far-reaching precedent in the field of adoption law could, if construed broadly, seriously jeopardize donor secrecy in AID cases. A District of Columbia Superior Court Judge ruled that a twenty-two-year-old mother of two living in Takoma Park, Maryland, who was adopted as a child, should be granted permission to see her sealed birth records and thus learn the identities of her natural parents.[33] The plaintiff in this case asserted her "basic right" to know her total historical identity, and also to discover whether hereditary diseases or other health problems were a part of her genetic inheritance.[34]

A comparable argument can obviously be made by the progeny of AID. The argument for disclosure would gain even more persuasiveness in light of dramatic findings presented in the NEW ENGLAND JOURNAL OF MEDICINE.[35] Statistics from a 1979 study showed that sperm from one donor had in fact been used to produce fifty children and thus raised the very real danger of accidental incest among offspring who have the same father.[36] The article also recorded the sloppiness of some doctors in failing to screen genetically the donors who participate in AID procedures. A mere 29 percent of the doctors tested the donors of semen—and then primarily for communicable diseases. Most recipients were inseminated twice per cycle. Seventeen percent of the physicians used the same donor for a given recipient, and 32 percent used multiple donors within a single cycle. Only 37 percent kept records on children, and only 30 percent kept records on donors. The identity of donors usually was carefully guarded to ensure privacy in order to avoid legal complications.[37] Interestingly, most donors have been over time medical students or resident physicians, thus prompting concern by some that eugenic decisions are made by using "superior" genes for donor insemination.[38]

Of 711 physicians likely to perform artificial insemination by donors surveyed to determine their current practices, 471 responded, and 379 reported that they performed this procedure. They accounted for approximately 3,576 births by this means in 1977. In addition to treating infertility, 26 percent of these physicians used the procedure to prevent transmission of a genetic disease, and 10 percent used it for single women. Donors of semen were only superficially screened for genetic diseases and were then matched phenotypically to the recipient's husband.[39]

Subsequent studies have shown the very high degree of carelessness—if, indeed, not negligence—many doctors exhibit in performing AID.[40] Serious legal cases of "wandering sperm" have arisen when women have alleged that due to the negligent actions of sperm banks or physicians or both in administering inseminations, they have been impregnated with wrong sperm.[41] Additional actions growing from such failed undertakings would be for breach of contract if the sperm banks storing the semen failed to maintain its promised viability together with negligence or strict liability for those participating physicians who failed to properly screen the sperm donors and recipients for infectious diseases.[42]

In 1987 a report of the Congressional Office of Technology Assessment found only 10 percent of 1,558 physicians surveyed tested regularly the sperm donations for the HIV virus.[43] The report found an absence of federal regulatory programming[44] in this area and few states[45] with laws screening sperm donations designed, as such, to protect either the female recipients or possible offspring.

Suppose a donor of semen, at age thirty-four, discovers that he is a carrier of the congenital abnormality—Huntington's chorea. His bodily movements become involuntary and his mental abilities become progressively disoriented. Death is certain. Realizing that he was a donor of semen at age twenty-one when he was a law school student, he approaches the physician who administered the artificial intervention and advises him of his condition. The physician advises, regrettably, that his records of the insemination are incomplete. Sensing a grave responsibility, he seeks to learn the identity of those children whom he fathered artificially. He wishes to provide some type of financial assistance for his offspring and/or make provision in his estate for them before he dies. *Quaere:* Should a court of law consider a best interest of the child test, an average ordinary donor's wishes under similar circumstances standard, or a best interest of society test, in ruling on a resolution of this dilemma? If a court-ordered investigation discloses the donor's issue, should they be told of the situation without a revelation of their donor-father's identity? Does the donor in such a hypothetical case as this have a right to know the identity of his progeny even though they were conceived artificially? Why should not the same right to know be provided the donor—in cases of this nature—as the adopted child is being given some jurisdictions to learn the identity of its birth parents? Even without legal validation of the right to know genetic lineage, all too often independent investigatory means are employed and the missing identity established.

Provisions within the Uniform Parentage Act provide that all records involving AID interventions are to be kept "confidential and in a sealed file." Inspection of records is only sanctioned when a court order acknowledges the existence of "good cause."[46] By drawing upon analogous right-to-know parental-identity cases arising in regular adoption areas, "good cause," in order to discern the identity of a donor in artificial insemination cases, could be determined to exist not only for reasons of obtaining complete medical information regarding the child's donor-father but also for such additional reasons such as allowing the AID child to resolve questions of identity and promote social adjustment, establishing a bond of love,[47] promoting a wish to be of genuine assistance and support to a biological family unit,[48] and determining if the rules of intestate succession were applicable.[49]

The Future of Artificial Insemination

As the courts begin to recognize "a best interest of the child test"[50] in deciding vexatious cases involving artificial insemination, it would surely appear that where genetic heritage is brought into question concerning the health and well-being of an AID child, the confidential files (*if* such are maintained) of a participating physician to an AID intervention, should be examined by a judge *in camera* and, where necessary, with the assistance of a geneticist. Although a strong argument against disclosure of the donor's identity can be made,[51] the exigencies and circumstances of each case should be considered. And, where the utility of the good in maintaining the confidentiality of the donor's identity is outweighed by the gravity of the "harm"[52] that will arise as a consequence of disclosure, then the veil of confidentiality should be pierced.

Greater safeguards must be undertaken in order to preserve the integrity and value of artificial insemination as a medico-legal process. If physicians are not sufficiently careful in their supervision and administration of the AID process, then the state must act in order to guarantee higher standards of professional care and competence. When a physician is negligent in properly screening prospective donors for artificial insemination, and a genetic abnormality thus passes undetected to the issue, the physician must always be held liable for the consequences of his error.

In addition to continued judicial activism, legislative implementation should be sought by creating presumptions at law of the legitimacy of issue born of consensual AID and thus clarifying both the legal rights and duties of the husband. To the extent that greater confidentiality of donor records would be strengthened, additional adoptions of the Uniform Parentage Act should be advocated.[53]

THE SURROGATE MOTHER—A PROFILE

The surrogate mother has been regarded correctly as the female counterpart to AID.[54] This concept embraces several processes of surrogate parenthood. One is the embryo implant in which a married woman's eggs are fertilized by her husband's semen *in vitro* and then implanted in specific human female carriers or "incubators." Another process might be the simple use of semen from a married woman's husband and the insertion of that semen into a female donor or surrogate who will, under a bilateral contract for services rendered, carry the issue to term and, after birth, release all her rights to the child by allowing adoption by the biological father and putative mother. Additional situations might arise in which maternally carried dominant genetic disorders exist, where a married woman's eggs would not accept fertilization, or where ovarian failures would arise and prevent the woman from conceiving but which would not preclude her from carrying another woman's embryo.[55] Thus, a reverse surrogate mother situation would exist where a married man's semen was used *in vitro* to fertilize another woman's eggs—with the embryo then being implanted into the married man's spouse.

The attitudes that prompt a woman to become a surrogate mother have been isolated to three or four. Some women possess either a sentimental or a maternal instinct, or a fascination with having a child. Others feel a sense of altruism which advances a wish to help others experience that which has been a part of the surrogate's life. Still others have cited a need for money as a reason for seeking the status of surrogate motherhood.[56]

Policy Issues—Legality of the Bargain

A number of vexatious policy issues are inherent in any consideration of surrogate motherhood. Some issues may be resolved now, others must await the test of time to be both sharpened and clarified before a resolution will emerge.

If an illegal performance promised bilaterally or unilaterally is regarded as being heinous, criminal, or immoral to a high degree, courts normally will not enforce the promise that accompanies such performance.[57] Before such drastic judicial action is taken, however, the court will give due consideration to the degree of the offense, the extent of public harm involved if the bargain is recognized as valid, and the nature of the moral quality of the conduct of the parties to the bargain in light of current community standards.[58] Obviously, as times change, so too does the public policy relevant to the particular issue under consideration or in controversy.[59] Public policy in this context may be defined simply as a legal principle which declares an act either to be unlawful (i.e., that which promotes corruption or immorality) or which has a "tendency" to be injurious to either the welfare, health, or morality of the public.[60]

State Positions

A number of states make it a crime to pay anything of value to a parent in consideration for obtaining consent to adopt or obtain custody of a child and impose a heavy penalty or imprisonment for violation thereof.[61] In this way, some deterrent exists to prevent extensive "black market" operations in adoptions.[62] Since the legality of a contract is tested by, and depends on the place where it is made,[63] a jurisdiction having such a law would hold a contract between a husband and wife with a surrogate mother, in which the latter relinquished her parental rights to an infant born of such a contract for subsequent adoption by the natural father and putative mother, to be illegal and thus invalid. The bargain is an *adoption* contract. Now, if this same contractual relation is viewed as a contract *to bear* a child, less objection and greater acceptance of the contract, itself, should be recognized simply because the purchaser is the natural father of the child. With such a consideration, fears of commercialization become less worrisome as a competing or undermining factor over the interests of the child or the biological mother.[64]

Interestingly, an unmarried man would encounter even less legal entanglement in dealing with a surrogate. Since no wife would be involved, it would be unnecessary for a man to adopt his own child. He would simply pay the surrogate without risk and, as natural father of the child, take custody upon birth without any formal adoption procedure being required.[65]

Perhaps the easiest way in which to avoid the issue of illegality surrounding contracts to adopt a child or to bear one would be to have the contracting parents either make a simple gift,[66] conditional or absolute,[67] or a voluntary declaration of trust to the surrogate mother.[68]

Presumptions of Paternity

The Uniform Parentage Act, although adopted in only eighteen states,[69] presents an initial obstacle to the establishment of paternity in surrogate contract situations. Section 5 of the act controls the use of artificial insemination and provides: "The donor of semen provided to a licensed physician for use in artificial insemination of a married woman other than the donor's wife is treated in law as if he were not the natural father of a child thereby conceived."[70] While it appears rather obvious that this provision was crafted in order to protect anonymous AID donors from all legal responsibility for those children fathered as a consequence of their donations of semen, if the provision is adopted *in toto* this language could well establish a difficulty for the real father under a surrogate contract to establish either paternity or to assert parental rights, such as visitation.

Children born of a validated marital union are presumed to be the legitimate issue of that union.[71] Regardless of their adoption of the Uniform Parentage Act, all of the states have recognized this presumption. Thus, if a surrogate is married, the issue she bears will be presumed, unless rebutted by proof beyond a reasonable doubt, to be the legitimate child or herself and her husband not of the artificial donor of the sperm. If the donor or biological father brought a custody suit and upon proof (again, beyond a reasonable doubt) that he was in fact the biological father, it would then fall to the court to determine which parent or set of parents could better serve the long term interests of the child.[72]

Section four of the Uniform Parentage Act also establishes presumptions of paternity. When, for example, a man, after a child's birth, receives a child under the age of majority into his home and openly holds the child out as his natural child, a presumption arises, which may be rebutted only by clear and convincing evidence, that the man is the natural father of the child.[73] Another provision allows for the establishment of a presumption of paternity when the man purporting to be the natural father acknowledges his paternity of the questioned child by filing a written statement with the appropriate court or administrative agency, informing the biological mother of this public acknowledgment, and no dispute of this acknowledgment occurs. Again, this presumption is to be rebutted only by clear and convincing evidence.[74]

A liberal construction of these provisions of the Uniform Parentage Act could modify the rigidity of the provisions regarding issue born of artificial insemination and thereby enable a surrogate contract father to establish his paternity. To avoid confusion in both interpretation and implementation of the Uniform Act, however, it would be wise to modify the act in such a manner so as to provide a specific provision or state a specific presumption establishing a mechanism for the biological father to establish his unquestioned paternity in surrogate contracts.

Additional Policy Issues

As observed, the parallel relationship between AID and contracts to bear children is inescapable. Yet, while donor identity is generally assured of confidentiality in heterologous insemination, the identity of a surrogate mother is generally known by the contract couple. Appearance, in fact, is often a major consideration, together with the prospective surrogate's medical history, education level, environment and cultural background, in making a judgment as to the suitability of a surrogate.[75] Because of the increased potential for genetic anomalies in births by women over thirty-five years of age,[76] this age is usually the cutoff for surrogate candidacy. The availability of the pool of candidates is, furthermore, normally limited to women who are presently married or have been divorced.[77] Single, unwed women are regarded generally as not suitable simply because their involvement would not only be regarded in some circles as promoting immorality (and perhaps technically adultery)[78] but as a practical matter, an unproven record of birth successes might also promote a further element of uncertainty for the contracting parties which is undesirable. The right of a single, unmarried woman to control her own physical autonomy is an ever-evolving concept measured in proportion to the degree of state interest in preserving the public welfare and morals.[79] The right of a married woman to act or conduct her marital affairs without the informed consent of her husband, specifically to submit herself to surrogate mother status, remains an open-ended question as well.

Perhaps an even more unsettled issue is the extent of the surrogate's autonomy during the period of the pregnancy versus the extent and nature of the right of control of her and the fetus by the biological husband and his wife. If, for example, after agreeing to abstain from uses of alcoholic beverages during the pregnancy, the surrogate does in fact imbibe on a regular basis, could a court order be obtained to stop such consumption?[80] If so, how could it be enforced? By total restraint (i.e., hospital confinement)? Suppose the surrogate did not reveal her propensity to consume alcohol (or unprescribed drugs) and upon birth, the child is born with a genetic impairment or defect which is determined to be as a direct consequence of the actions of the surrogate. Could the surrogate be sued for negligence? Suppose, further, neither the husband nor his wife wish to raise the defective child as their own, and the surrogate does not wish to either. Should a penalty be assessed against all concerned parties because of this "misdeed"? In such a situation, the infant would likely become a ward of the state, and therefore a responsibility of the taxpayers if and until an adoption could be arranged.

Other issues arise in the area of physician negligence. If a physician is negligent in failing to screen adequately a prospective surrogate mother candidate and upon birth the infant is born with a genetic deficiency, might a suit for malpractice be obtained against the attending physician or the surrogate? Suppose a surrogate decides to keep the contract baby. Could she in turn sue the biological father for child support?[81] As a practical matter, it would appear that in a case where a court decreed the biological surrogate mother had a right to keep her child and assuming the mother had insufficient funds to support herself and the child that financial support by the biological father would be in the best interests of the child and of the state. But, *quaere,* given this hypothetical, would it not be arguably best for all concerned to have the child in a stable economic environment with its biological father and his wife instead of being placed and raised in the possibly impoverished environment of its biological mother alone and no adoptive father? Yet another interesting question is raised in the case where the surrogate suffers mental trauma or a complete breakdown after relinquishing the baby to the biological father and his wife. Would the surrogate be able to sue the contracting parents for damages?

Further unanswered issues may arise with changes in the status of the contracting couple. What if the contracting couple divorced or one or both died before the surrogate gave birth? What would be the status of the infant upon birth? Would the contract be voided for impossibility of performance and the child recognized as illegitimate and a subsequent ward of the state? Obviously, if the biological father died, severe difficulty would be encountered in establishing the paternity of the infant. Assume further that upon the death of the biological father, the surrogate decided that she wished to keep the infant that she bore, but the widow wanted her husband's child. Would Solomonic wisdom be called into play dictating the birth mother win out over a widow who might never be able to have a child?[82]

To anticipate or forestall these complexities and others that might arise, it is imperative that a tightly drawn contract be executed which defines the rights and responsibilities of all parties and establishes a mechanism or procedure for assessing damages for violations thereof. Clarity of terms and specification of duties will go far toward assisting a court to construe the provisions of a contract of this nature and, at the same time, to determine the intent of the contracting parties. Absent such a controlling instrument and definitive legislation in the area, it will fall upon the courts to employ a rather traditional equitable balancing test in determining the merits or demerits of each issue in a surrogate contract case; thus, the gravity of the "harm" (economic, social, personal, religious, etc.) of holding one particular way according to the plaintiff's case, will be weighed against the utility of the "good" (economic, social, personal, religious, etc.) in sustaining defendant's case-in-chief. Fluidity and flexibility, then, become the coordinates of action instead of predictability and stability.

Inextricably related to this area of concern are various religious considerations. Indeed, these considerations remain a serious point of contention to a complete understanding, acceptance, and advancement of the aspects of the new human genetic technology. An exegesis or even a mere tentative analysis of them remain beyond the scope of this chapter.[83] Suffice it to state that from the standpoint of maintaining its strengths and efficiency of power, religion must meet change with the same attitude and spirit as does science. Accordingly, while religious principles may be immutable and eternal, the continued expression of those principles require an open, continual development that staves off stagnation.[84]

TOWARD A NEW RIGHT OF FAMILIAL PROCREATION

The courts have slighted or even refused to recognize the mental elements of procreation by acknowledging that the biology of reproduction is controlling over the psychological and, indeed, have chosen traditionally to give little consideration to the motivations of initiating parents.[85] Thus, as might be expected, final decisions in surrogation have included neither an accurate assessment of the child's best interest nor an assessment of adequate care for the child.[86] Adequate care should be but a complement to best interests and not a separate standard of application. With this approach, the "mentally conceiving" (or "initiating") parents would be recognized, of necessity, as holding the priority of right to raise the child[87] without extracustodial visitation rights from the birthing mother. Admittedly, before this approach could be validated, a new right of "familial procurement" would have to be structured whereby the judicial protection of the choice to procreate[88] would be recognized as but a logical analogue to "recognition of a fundamental interest in procuring assistance to overcome a personal inability to procreate."[89] Absent the wide acceptance of this new or coordinate right, the best interests test must, however, remain controlling.

Determining Best Interests

How should the best interests of the child test be developed and, for that matter, applied? Obviously, the test is fact sensitive and defies a uniform standard of application. Yet, a core set of factors may be employed to test, as between competing family and state interests in a surrogation case, the extent to which the best interests of the disputed child would be advanced and recognized as reasonable.[90]

Ideally, the following factors could be weighed in performing the balancing test[91] of determining which of the opposing parties would provide for or guarantee that the infant's best interests would be assured: the character and extent of harm (economic, physical, mental, social, psychological, ethical) that would either befall or so threaten the infant as to jeopardize its well-being; the specific social value that would be continued or, alternatively, abridged if the child were placed with one set of parents as opposed to the other set; the suitability of the character of the opposing parties; the burden (economic or social) that would be placed on the parties *and* the infant if one course of action were pursued over another (e.g., custodial or visitation rights); and the practicability of the ultimate action (i.e., ease of enforcement if parties are in different jurisdictions).[92]

Maintaining Middle-Class Standards

Middle-class standards should never be considered a handicap or negative value for a court to consider in determining from whom a child can receive the most adequate care that, in turn, will ensure its best interests are advanced. A good education, attractive job, and financial security should mean—in the normal course of affairs—that a child being raised within a family environment of this nature will be afforded a more enhanced opportunity for care and growth than would be the case otherwise. It really is just that simple. If the goal of law is to maximize the welfare or utility of all human beings, a *prima facie* case could be posited for according children some measure of legal protection against their parents or those who would assert custodial rights.[93] Efficiency, emotional stability and security are minimal investments for a child's development.[94]

EVOLVING CASE LAW
The Case of Baby M

In 1987 a New Jersey trial court determined that since the state legislature had neither specifically approved nor rejected surrogate parentage contracts, the judiciary itself had certain broad, inherent powers to shape a response to specific problems within this area. Specifically, as presented by the facts of the *Baby M* case, the court enforced a preconception agreement whereby a biological mother, Mary Beth Whitehead-Gould, agreed to relinquish her child conceived through artificial insemination and carried to full term. Mrs. Whitehead was married to another person as was the contracting party, Mr. William Stern. For her services, it was agreed further that Mrs. Whitehead would receive $10,000. After Baby M was born, the biological mother changed her mind and decided she would keep and raise "her" daughter.[95]

Even though determined not to be unfit, the trial judge ordered, as a consequence of the contract, that the biological mother's rights were terminated. It was held further that only the consent of the baby's biological father, William Stern, was necessary for him and his own wife to proceed to adopt Baby M.[96]

The Supreme Court of New Jersey determined that the original contract between Mrs. Whitehead-Gould and Mr. Stern was not legally enforceable.

Consequently, under existing principles of family law, the court held both biological or "natural" parents were the legal parents. Even though granting that the primary custody of the child was to remain with Mr. Stern, the biological and legal father, the court granted Mrs. Whitehead-Gould visitation rights. The court proceeded to rule that in future cases where a surrogate mother might refuse to relinquish her child, contrary to contractual agreement, the child would nonetheless remain with the biological mother, in nearly all cases, until the custody issue was determined.[97]

Variations on a Theme

Robert Moschetta, a thirty-four-year-old man and his wife of nine years, Cynthia, aged forty, decided to hire a surrogate mother to bear them a child. Elvira Johnson, a divorced mother of three, became artificially inseminated and conceived in November 1989. The surrogacy contract stipulated that she was to be paid $10,000 for her services. Shortly before the child was born in May 1990, Ms. Johnson learned of the plans of the Moschettas to divorce. Robert and Cynthia had decided previously not to divulge their marital difficulties to Ms. Jordan until after the birth, but complications arose toward the end of the pregnancy and necessitated the disclosure. Upon the birth of the female child, Ms. Jordan agreed reluctantly to nonetheless let the Moschettas take the baby home—provided they agreed to seek marriage counseling for a least a year and allow her visitation rights, together with full payment of her contract. Six months later, Mr. Moschetta separated from his wife and let her and the surrogate battle for custody of the child, Marissa. Mr. Moschetta asserts Marissa is his legally because he fathered her with his sperm. His wife, Cynthia, maintains the surrogacy contract establishes her rights as the legal mother while the surrogate advances her claim as the biological birth mother.[98]

Ms. Jordan, whom the court initially denied contact with the child, is a native Spanish-speaking woman who admits that she never read the document relinquishing her parental rights before executing it and furthermore states that she would have never signed it if she had understood the focus of the relinquishment and that the child might not be provided with a two-parent environment in which to be raised. A clause in the contract barring a couple from divorcing would have been unenforceable, however.

During the protracted litigation involding this case, Cynthia Moschetta helped raise Marissa by visting with her two days a week and even going so far as to take maternity leave from her regular employment in order to care for and bond with the child when it was born. Additionally, she helped pay for the expenses the surrogate, Ms. Jordan, incurred during the pregnancy itself. Had it been decided that parenting rights are established by raising the child rather than by participating in its birth, a new precedent setting course would have been charted in family law.

As will be remembered, in the *Baby M* case, the New Jersey Supreme Court gave the biological father, William Stern, and the surrogate mother, Mary Beth

Whitehead, parental rights, but Mrs. Stern, who helped raise the baby, was awarded no legal rights. In 1991 there was no definitive and tested appellate court decisional law in California indicating whether surrogacy contracts were legal, let alone delineating the respective rights of a divorcing couple and a surrogate mother.[99] Heretofore, unless it could be proved otherwise, a strong presumption is made that the biological bonding of gestational mother makes her a better mother.[100] Indeed, she "is the legal mother for all purposes" since, quite simply, she has assumed the majority of the risks during the pregnancy.[101]

In 1994, showing rather predictable judicial confusion and indecisiveness on the issue of surrogation, the California Court of Appeal in dealing with the *Moschetta* case, called for "legislative guidance" in assisting it to develop standards for determining legal rights under both "traditional" surrogacy arrangements and "gestational" surrogacy. The court proceeded to define traditional surrogation as an arrangement whereby a woman is impregnated with the sperm of a married man, with a full understanding prior to the completion of the act that the resulting child is to be recognized legally as the child of the married man and his infertile wife. Contrariwise, in cases of gestational surrogacy, sperm given by a married man is united artifically with the egg of his wife, with the resulting embryo being implanted into another woman's womb. The court stated

> Infertile couples who can afford the high tech solution of *in vitro* fertilization and embryo implantation in another woman's womb can be reasonably assured of being judged the legal parents of the child, even if the surrogate reneges on her agreement. Couples who cannot afford *in vitro* fertilization and embryo implantation, or who resort to traditional surrogacy becaue the female does not have eggs suitable for *in vitro* fertilization, have no assurance their intentions will be honored in a court of law. For them and the child, biology is destiny.[102]

Considerable progress in clarifying the "rights" of a gestational surrogate was, however, made by the State Supreme Court in the 1993 California case of *Johnson v. Calvert*.[103]

The Gestational Surrogate

Unlike Elvira Johnson or Mary Beth Whitehead, Anna Johnson had no genetic claim to the baby she was carrying as a surrogate. Rather, she contracted for a $10,000 fee to carry the embryo (fetus) derived from the egg and sperm of Cris and Mark Calvert that had been fertilized in a petri dish. Since Cris had had a hysterectomy and was unable to carry a baby, Anna was hired to perform that biological function. Accordingly, the fertilized embryo was implanted in her womb and she thus became a gestational surrogate. This type of surrogation is on the rise with nearly eighty births being attributed to the process over some three years.[104]

The ethics of gestational surrogacy have focused on whether it is but exploitation of poor women by affluent couples with a coordinate fear that the time is approaching when busy professional women who cannot take the time to conceive and carry a fetus will merely rent another woman's uterus in order to achieve motherhood.[105] If a contract for personal services is entered into freely without fear or coercion, it should, in a free, democratic society functioning as such within a freemarket economy, be allowed. The test is, of course, to assure that there be an absence of coercion in the negotiating or bargaining phase of the contract itself.

On October 22, 1990, Judge Richard N. Parslow, Jr., of the Orange County, California, Superior Court refused the claim of parental rights and custody made by Anna Johnson and ruled that she was a "genetic stranger" to the infant and thus had no legal rights to assert parenthood.[106] Again, this was a valid contract and, absent fraud, should be enforced. Emotional changes of mind simply cannot be countenanced as the rule of the day. Subsequently, the California Supreme Court affirmed, finding that not only was there nothing in the record to support an argument that surrogacy contracts tend to exploit and dehumanize poor women and that they violate state public policy or the constitutional rights of gestational mothers. Accordingly, the court found for Cris Calvert, the genetic mother.[107]

STRUCTURING A NEW FRAMEWORK

Since surrogate parenting is the biological counterpart of AID with the surrogate herself being thus equivalent to the semen donor—it might be hoped that present laws controlling AID would in turn provide a basis for regulating parenthood arrangements in surrogation. Such is not the case, however.[108]

Statutory distinctions exist that allow payment for semen to donors who participate in AID but deny it for surrogate mothers and thus may well be challenged as an unconstitutional denial of equal protection.[109] Further distinction might be found in separating cases involving surrogating practices when there will be no genotypical relationship between the child and the individuals seeking its procreation and those cases in which a womb is "borrowed" to carry a child conceived by persons who will be the biological parents and who propose to integrate fully the child into their family.[110]

In some twenty-three jurisdictions presently, financial compensation (except for certain specific expenses) is prohibited under state adoption laws.[111] While in Michigan payment to a surrogate based on a contract to perform services was held invalid as a contract to sell a baby,[112] the Kentucky Supreme Court reached the opposite conclusion based on constitutional grounds reasoning as such that surrogacy was not baby selling simply because the biological father already had established a legal relationship with the child.[113]

Some commentators have suggested that an unmarried woman's right to AID may derive from a liberal reading of Supreme Court decisions establishing fundamental rights to procreation and privacy.[114] The following discussion summarizes the points of view presented in those cases.

As society evolves and changes, so do many of its values.[115] Autonomy, self-representation, personhood, identity, intimacy, and dignity are all essential to privacy.[116] The extent to which these essentials play a role in shaping sexual, procreational autonomy must surely remain flexible; attempting to define them with precision would challenge and erode any efficacy they might enjoy.[117] The right of the state to control and to shape the behavior of both individuals and groups regarding the birth of children is always an area of high emotion and concern.

The majority view on privacy holds that private conduct between consenting adults or, for that matter, personal conduct of any nature, should be regulated only to the extent necessary to prevent harm to others.[118] Thus, conformity is not a priority and is certainly not a value worth pursuing.[119] The opposing view argues that the business of the law is to suppress vice and immorality.[120] Advocates of this view reason that if violations of society's moral structure are indulged and promoted, the whole basis of society would be undermined.[121]

Arguably, under the majority view, the state would be justified in acting to control personal decision making in the areas of artificial insemination and surrogation for unmarried women. The requirement of harm to others is met because society could suffer economic harm by incurring expenses associated with the maintenance and education of a fatherless child born of artificial insemination. Similarly, the prevention of harm theory could be invoked in surrogation where the state, by attempting to prevent such acts, seeks to maintain the dignity and continuity of the traditional family.

Alternative Legal Approaches

In retrospect, it can be seen that three alternative legal approaches or strategies may be developed by states in order to meet the critical challenges of surrogate motherhood. First, specific legislation that outlaws the practice[122] coupled with stringent enforcement codes could be enacted.[123] This would have the obvious effect of forcing a real "black market" to develop, particularly since the process of becoming a surrogate mother is not an exceptionally difficult one to learn. Furthermore, the enforcement of a law forbidding surrogate motherhood in all forms would be difficult as a matter of policy to enforce. For example, it would be rather distasteful to many to exact a penalty for becoming a mother or to impose a prison sentence for promoting its advancement and implementation. Such would be offensive and morally distasteful to the very policy that both favors and recognizes the family as the bulwark of society.

Second, a legislative program designed to license the procedure and the surrogates participating in it as well as to protect the health and well being of the child, together with the safety of the surrogate, could be enacted. Legislation of this order and dimension would include provisions shaping the rights and determining the extent of the liabilities of the contracting parents in the surrogate compete *vis-à-vis* the infant. Consideration would, additionally, be given to shaping the sphere of responsibility for various types of error which intermediaries (doctors, lawyers, or mere friends of the family) might commit in facilitating the whole process. Courses of action to be taken in many of the other specific policy areas discussed previously would be ideally either tackled legislatively or delegated to administrative decision making by a licensing board constituted in order to set, enforce and implement standards considered relevant.

A third and final strategy would be to purposely allow the very concept or principle of surrogate mothers to develop through case-by-case judicial determination. Obviously, this would yield a crazy patchwork quilt similar to those early and disparate cases dealing with artificial insemination.[124] In some jurisdictions, regrettably, this very process concerning artificial insemination in fact still continues.[125] Judicial activity will of necessity be the order of the day if the state legislatures assume their normal passive role in matters of great moment and controversy, but the preferred approach would be a legislative one.

Practical Consequences

If regulated adequately, the "legitimization" of the status of surrogate mothers, involving a legislative or judicial interpretation, and the corresponding validation of contracts to bear a child, present no insuperable problems to society. It is by realizing the vast dimensions of the 21st century and by preparing for them now that the law assumes its rightful posture as a predictive, rather than a resultative vector of force in a scheme of modern living. Any new change or departure in custom and practice in the philosophies and coordinate actions of biological and technological advances as they impact on social life initially elicit a response of horrified negation. Subsequently with time, this shades into a negation of the acts without horror; then comes a slow, yet nonetheless, perceptible type of curiosity, study and devaluation. This evolutionary thinking process concludes with a slow but steady acceptance and establishment of a new norm or construct.[126]

It is evident that artificial insemination is becoming more widely accepted and approved as a means of family development. The parallels and, indeed, linkage between artificial fathering and surrogate mothering are so obvious that it can be but hoped that wise judges and informed legislatures will give official recognition to this method which is also designed to further and promote the basic unit of society—the family.

IN VITRO FERTILIZATION
Combatting Infertility

An estimated two hundred conception clinics around the United States currently serve two million couples seeking assistance in combatting infertility.[127] These couples expend nearly $1 billion to arrest their condition. Tragically, the national "take home baby rate" from these clinics is between 11 and 14 percent.[128]

From this, the question that becomes uppermost in the hearts and minds of many is whether there is a fundamental or international human right to health assistance in biological reproduction. In recognizing or structuring such a right, would the state be obligated to spend any and all reasonable amounts of money in order to validate the procreative rights of all women—regardless of marital status? Consistent with the fundamental constitutional right to life, liberty and the pursuit of happiness, should the state enforce its protective powers *vis-à-vis* infants at the moment of conception or at some point later in their embryonic development?

In 1983 Sir Harry Gibbs, Chief Justice of Australian High Court, ruled "that a foetus has no right of its own until it is born and has a separate existence from its mother."[129] The common law tied the commencement of life to the time when an unborn first moved in the womb or, in other words, when it quickened.[130] Thus, only after the fetus quickened could its destruction be classified as murder.[131] In the United States, the issue of when individuality is established biologically and when the law should, accordingly, protect such individuals, was determined by the Supreme Court in *Roe v. Wade*.[132] In *Roe*, the Court essentially held that a fetus does not receive the full protection of the law until it is born.[133]

In September 1989 a judge of the Circuit Court for the Fifth Judicial District of Tennessee ruled that life begins at the moment of conception.[134] The court held that seven cryogenically preserved *in vitro* embryos were children, not personal property. Accordingly, the court placed the embryos in the custodial care of the woman who, during marriage, produced eggs subsequently fertilized by her then husband.[135] The only support the court provided for its momentus decision was a reference to the definition of "conception" in WEBSTER'S NEW COLLEGIATE DICTIONARY.[136] Apparently, the court was unpersuaded by the authoritative texts and treatises relevant to the field. Instead, it relied primarily on the testimony of eight witnesses, particularly that of Dr. Jerome Lajeune, a member of the Faculty of Medicine of the University of Paris and the Pontifical Academy of Science at the Vatican.[137]

On September 13, 1990, however, the Tennessee Court of Appeals ruled that awarding the seven fertilized ova to the woman would constitute "impermissible state action" by violating the former husband's "constitutionally protected right not to beget a child where no pregnancy has taken place."[138] The court based its opinion on the U.S. Supreme Court recognition that the decision to "bear or beget a child" is one of protected choice by the Constitution.[139]

Consistent also with state law which recognizes legal protections extending only to viable fetuses, the court remanded the case to the trial court directing a new judgment to reflect the appeals court decision, granting both parties joint control and an equal voice in the disposition of the ova. The court thus held that just as it would be repugnant constitutionally to order the woman to implant the fertilized ova against her will, it would be equally repugnant to order her former husband to bear the psychological, if not legal, burdens of forced paternity.[140] In 1992 the Tennessee Supreme Court affirmed the ruling of the Court of Appeals holding that Mr. Davis could not be forced to become a parent against his will and, thus, the frozen embryos were to remain in storage or be destroyed.[141]

The dilemma of frozen embryos presents no clear course of action for easy resolution.[142] Yet, in the state of Victoria, Australia, alone, there are said to be some two thousand embryos cryogenically preserved.[143] Throughout Australia as many as ten thousand such frozen embryos may exist.[144] Fritze Honduis, the Deputy Director of Legal Affairs of the Council of Europe, has suggested that upwards of twenty thousand embryos are frozen throughout Europe.[145]

A Lack of Consensus

The fact that no clear consensus is evolving on even how to begin a dialogue about frozen embryos, let alone develop a legal response-mechanism to deal with the situation, does not bode well for clarity and direction in this area. Indeed, "the ethical debate is even less focused than the unending rhetorical battle over abortion."[146] Before the legislature and the courts are called upon to develop a definitive framework for principled decision making, objective "hard thinking" is required of the major cross-disciplinary participants in this unfolding drama.[147]

The new reproductive biology promises untold opportunities for resolving heartbreaking problems of infertility and will expand the meaning of "procreational autonomy" for women. It also presents difficult problems for the physician, lawyer, ethicist, theologian, and, for that matter, the average person.[148]

The next section of this chapter explores the major issues confronting the use of assisted noncoital technologies in the United States. It seeks to provide a multifaceted construct that will promote informed and enlightened decision making devoid of as much emotion and sentimentality as possible. The evolving—indeed, fluid—parameters of the new reproductive biology defy a single definitive response. This analysis is premised on the belief that medical and scientific interventions that minimize human suffering (genetically or otherwise induced) and maximize quality of life should be pursued. Most always, the untold benefits of noncoital reproduction outweigh the costs attendant with its experimentation and use.

THE ETHICS OF *IN VITRO* FERTILIZATION

Typically, the IVF and embryo transfer processes begins with drug therapy to produce super ovulation in a woman. Through a procedure called laparoscopy, the resulting eggs are removed from the woman's reproductive tract and then fertilized. An embryo is then implanted in the woman's uterus and, if the implantation is successful, carried to term. The remaining embryos are stored, either for future implantation should the first attempt fail or for use in scientific or medical experiments. Alternatively, IVF may be used without embryo transfer to produce embryos solely for experimental purposes.

Ethical Complexities

Attention is now drawn to what might be termed as the "ethical morality" of IVF, a discussion which explores the benefits and the harms of IVF use.[149] Ethical complexities attend each of the many variations on the basic IVF theme. For example, when artificial insemination is used to fertilize a married woman's egg with the sperm of a man other than her husband because her husband's sperm is defective, a serious ethical issue is posed. Similarly, moral and ethical issues arise when a third-party surrogate carries an embryo to term for a genetic mother or when a single woman seeks to avail herself of IVF procedures. This section of the chapter probes not all of the ethical issues raised by IVF but instead proceeds selectively.

The most obvious benefit of IVF is that it circumvents infertility and allows persons with a strong desire to have children to rear a family. If it is determined conclusively that frozen embryos can be used without damage to resultant children, IVF could enable women who wish to pursue careers to bear children using embryos created some years earlier, thereby reducing their chance of producing a Down's syndrome child. Beyond family expansion, IVF could be used to provide embryos for scientific and medical experiments. Embryos could be used in infertility, genetic, and cancer research; as a source of obtaining embryonic tissue used in the treatment of diseases such as diabetes; and to harvest organs for transplant.

There are several major objections to IVF. The first is that separating sex from procreation is inherently wrong. IVF, followed by embryo transfer to the uterus of the married woman, severs the connection between sex and reproduction. The second objection is that IVF is morally wrong because it involves an abnormal risk of harm to the individual subsequently brought into existence. Physical damage or abnormality (although not documented factually) could result from IVF or from the subsequent transfer of the embryo to the woman's womb. Furthermore, psychological harm might inure to an infant born of the total process.

The third objection is that using IVF as a means to produce embryos for experiments or as sources of tissues and organs subjects the embryo to pain. This objection would have considerable merit where experiments were conducted on substantially developed fetuses. When conducting such scientific interventions with embryos in the first several weeks of their development, such embryos probably do not experience pain, owing to the absence of a critical nervous system.[150]

The fourth objection is that although IVF may not be inherently wrong or wrong because of its effects upon those immediately involved, it may be wrong because of the "slippery slope" to which it is likely to lead. IVF together with embryo transfer may lead to unimpeded use of surrogate mothers as substitutes for genetic mothers, cause the dissolution of the family unit when women who do not wish to marry or have sexual relations with a man use this technique, or even lead to the development of artificial wombs, severing the mother-child connection.[151]

The strongest objection to the IVF process is that the unimplanted embryos will eventually be destroyed—an action morally akin to abortion. When embryos are not implanted in the woman's uterus they must be used for scientific experimentation, frozen, or destroyed. Generally, antiabortionists view all scientific experimentation using embryos as morally wrong since it necessarily leads to the embryos' destruction. However, at a recent meeting of the American Society of Human Genetics, a new procedure was revealed which might ease the high tension associated with prenatal genetic testing.[152] This procedure is designed to discover genetic defects in the human egg *before* fertilization. Although considered promising, this procedure must itself undergo further testing. Once validated, this could well take the "sting" out of some moral objections to experimentation and use of IVF and embryo implants as assaults on the right to life. Indeed, the General Counsel for the National Right to Life expressed his opinion that the test was proper since it did not involve "the taking of innocent human life."[153]

Moral Dilemmas

The freezing of embryos also poses difficult moral dilemmas. If frozen embryos cannot be thawed successfully, a decision to thaw would lead to the destruction of the embryos. Moreover, even if successful thawing can be accomplished, the decision to experiment, implant, or destroy arises again. Quite clearly, the ethical dilemma involves very real problems. For example, would a woman whose first implantation was successful be required to keep the remaining embryos frozen in perpetuity to avoid their destruction? The only apparent way to resolve the uncertainty about freezing techniques would be to continue with limited experimentation in the field, using lower animal life forms.

Religious Overtones

Religious values have historically played an important part in public policy debates.[154] Indeed, the very "bedrock of moral order is religion."[155] "And as morality's foundation is religion, religion and politics are necessarily related. We need religion as a guide; we need it because we are imperfect."[156]

Faith and religion have played a dynamic role in the political life of the United States.[157] Today's commitment to democratic pluralism is nurtured and sustained as a consequence of recognizing the inviolability of individual conscience.[158] For some, politics and morality become inseparable.[159] To exclude societal values grounded in a religious base from the public arena would pose a serious threat to the very principle of pluralism.[160] What this commitment to pluralism means, however, is that no definitive posture can ever emerge relative to assisted noncoital reproduction.

REGULATION IN THE UNITED STATES

The extent to which U.S. states may validly regulate IVF procedures and embryo transfers depends on whether these acts are viewed as fundamental rights. Thus, the threshold question is whether they are "rights" guaranteed by the Constitution as part of the "right to marital privacy."[161]

Various Supreme Court decisions seem to grant "the right . . . 'to marry, establish a home and bring up children'" as among those liberties granted by the fourteenth amendment.[162] Based on these cases, it could be argued that any state regulation on IVF and embryo transfers would be an intrusion on the fundamental right to marital privacy.[163] "[I]f the decision to beget a child is a protected area of privacy, presumably the actual method of begetting also would be protected. Thus, any statute affecting this delicate area would have to serve a compelling state interest and must do so by the least restrictive means."[164]

A more conservative analysis of the Supreme Court decisions in this area recognizes, at the threshold, that the right to privacy is not explicitly mentioned in the U.S. Constitution. No right of sexual freedom is found within the gambit of procreative rights recognized by the Supreme Court nor has the Court fashioned a general right of personal privacy which is sufficiently broad based to encompass sex outside marriage.[165]

Legislative Positions among the States

It is doubtful that Congress could ever enact effective legislation on the legal status of an embryo because society is not of a singular mind. Nor is there a consensus as to when "life" should be legally protected. Judicial interpretation of this issue has aroused national debate with the decision in *Roe v. Wade*.[166] Despite the lack of agreement regarding when life begins, those children born of an IVF procedure using either a donor ova or donor sperm should be recognized as children of the family in which they were born. No issue of illegitimacy should be raised nor should the donors be held to any level of financial support of the child. Similarly, the child should have no right of inheritance against the donors. The best interests of the IVF child are served and, more important, the strength of the family unit is enhanced and its stability assured by following this course.[167]

After *Roe*, some twenty-five states enacted fetal research laws[168] designed primarily to control research on aborted fetuses.[169] Several statutes extend their protective coverage to research on embryos.[170] If cumbersome safeguards effecting excess embryo preservation are required, the initiation of medical scientific programs utilizing IVF procedures could be discouraged.[171] Moreover, in a number of these states, the very legality of IVF as a medical procedure to overcome infertility is in question.[172]

Only Pennsylvania[173] and Louisiana[174] have statutes regarding IVF. Pennsylvania's law simply monitors IVF by requiring anyone conducting the procedure to file quarterly reports with the state Department of Health fully describing the processes involved.[175] In 1986, the Louisiana legislature decreed that, "[a] viable *in vitro* fertilized ovum is a juridicial person" that cannot be destroyed[176] and furthermore—that such an ovum "cannot be owned by the *in vitro* fertilization patients who owe it a high duty of care and prudent administration."[177] If a renunciation of parental rights by the IVF patients occurs, the "ovum shall be available for adoptive implantation."[178] Sadly, no other state statutes clarify the legal status of IVF children.[179]

Illinois had a statute which prohibited selling or experimenting upon a "fetus produced by the fertilization of a human ovum by a human sperm unless such experimentation is therapeutic to the fetus thereby produced."[180] However, the statute was struck down subsequently as being unconstitutionally vague and restrictive of women's fundamental right to privacy.[181]

U.S. Government's Position

The HHS has the responsibility for regulating human subjects involved in research conducted or funded by HHS or other federal agencies, including research and development relating to IVF.[182] The HHS Ethics Advisory Board reviews every proposal concerning research projects involving fetuses or pregnant women. The board examines the research projects' "acceptability from an ethical standpoint."[183] HHS regulations specifically protect fetuses that are the subject of proposed experimentation and IVF research.[184]

Although limited to research efforts funded in whole or in part by the federal government,[185] these guidelines made a significant distinction with regard to potential legal rights of unimplanted embryos.[186] The distinction is apparent in the definition of "fetus": "the product of conception from the time of implantation (as evidenced by any of the presumptive signs of pregnancy, such as missed menses, or a medically acceptable pregnancy test)."[187]

As a consequence of this structured definition, research undertaken on fetuses *in utero* and *ex utero* is prohibited unless the purpose of the activity is either to meet the particular health needs of an at-risk fetus or to obtain biomedical knowledge not otherwise obtainable, but then only if the harm posed to the fetus is minimal.[188] Research undertaken on nonviable fetuses *ex utero* is prohibited unless vital function are not maintained artificially, experimental activities that would terminate vital functions are not used, or the research purpose is to obtain otherwise unobtainable significant biomedical knowledge.[189] The effect of these restrictions on embryonic and fetal research is that the scientific pursuit of knowledge is significantly handicapped. Because of this *de facto* moratorium, no federally funded research on IVF has been undertaken since 1975.[190] Private research into the mysteries and the opportunities of the new reproductive biology continues.[191] But without a balanced regulatory scheme and sources for federal research funding, the initiative and the momentum for scientific advancement is curtailed.

Both as a response to Louise Brown's extracorporeal birth in 1978 and to a grant application for IVF research, HSS and its Ethics Advisory Board decided to study the complex ethical, legal, social and scientific issues raised by IVF and embryo transfer.[192] Their report concluded that federal support of research on human IVF, in order to establish both the safety and the effectiveness of IVF procedures, would be permissible ethically so long as certain conditions were met.[193] The report was ultimately "buried in the bureaucracy."[194] Yet, due largely to the leadership of then-Congressman Albert Gore of Tennessee, hearings were conducted in August 1984 on the very issue of embryo transfers and the legal, ethical, and medical responses to such procedures.[195] Although no firm or conclusive steps were taken as a result of these hearings, the hearings served to focus attention on the need for continuing dialogue in this area.

Given the oftentimes strident antiabortion mood of a vocal segment of society, strong positive movement will probably not occur at the federal regulatory level.[196] Indeed, on November 2, 1989, the Bush Administration extended the prohibition on support for research involving fetal tissue transplants from induced abortions.[197] The principal reason for such action was that the positive health benefits generated by this research were outweighed by the accompanying complex moral and ethical problems.[198] Dr. Louis W. Sullivan, Secretary of HHS, stated that permitting human fetal research "will increase the incidence of abortion across the country."[199] What is once again evident is the inextricable relationship between abortion and fetal research and experimentation and, even more importantly, the almost inextricable relationship between politics and morality.

On January 22, 1993, President William Clinton lifted the moratorium on federal funding of research involving transplantation of fetal tissue from induced abortions.[200] With the execution of a presidential memorandum, then, untold opportunities have been created for developing effective treatments not only for Parkinson's disease and Alzheimer's but also for disorders such as diabetes and leukemia.

The Human Embryo Research Panel

On September 27, 1994, the Human Embryo Research Panel of the NIH recommended a series of guidelines allowing for a wide range of research on human embryos (developed from test-tube fertilization) with less than fourteen days of developmental age.[201] President Clinton, however, on December 3, 1994, concluded that no federal monies would be expended for research on human embryos. His order did not bar support for studies using fertilized eggs from fertility clinics.[202] Interestingly, when in January 1996 the president signed a continuing resolution to keep the government operating,[203] it incorporated within its provisions a prohibition on the use of federal funds for human embryo research.[204]

The 1994 findings of the Embryo Research Panel were that several areas of scientific research were well within the limits for federal funding and consisted of research involving fertilization, egg activation, maturation and freezing, methods for improving chances of pregnancy, genetic diagnosis before implantation, and the development of embryonic stem cells.[205] Sadly, these vital areas of embryonic research have become linked with the issue of abortion and, indeed, become a captive of it. The reality here is that abortion is truly a political issue and its resolution is unlikely to be resolved by ethical argumentation.[206]

A disengagement of embryonic research from the continuing abortion debate must be undertaken if scientific progress is to be made in combatting the problem of fertilization and improvement made in structuring the effectiveness of the process of *in vitro* fertilization itself.[207] Two major points overlooked totally are the fact that research on embryos *ex utero* need not involve abortion since no pregnancy is necessary for this type of research and, similarly, that a goal of embryonic research is to serve as an aid to increasing the number of pregnancies and thereby reducing the rate of abortion.[208] Put simply, then, ethical research must be shaped by ethical reasoning rather than political vagaries.

The Impact and the Promise of *Webster v. Reproductive Health Services*

In tackling "the most political divisive domestic legal issue of our time,"[209] the Supreme Court, on July 3, 1989, upheld the validity of a Missouri statute which significantly restricts a woman's right to obtain an abortion.[210] The preamble to the challenged statute declares human life to begin at conception[211] and defines conception as "the fertilization of the ovum of a female by a sperm of a male"—in disregard of standard medical tests which equate conception with uteral implantation occurring about six days after fertilization.[212] Thus the statute not only sought implicitly to regulate previable abortions but common forms of contraception such as the IUD and the morning-after-pill as well.[213] Yet a majority of the Court held the preamble did not actually regulate abortion and therefore the scope of its application would have to await testing until a concrete example restricting the appellees' activities was shown.[214] The majority of the court refused "[t]o decide . . . abstract propositions."[215]

It is beyond the scope of this chapter to probe the permutations and interstices of *Webster*. Suffice it to note that *Webster* strongly indicates that a clear majority of the justices are willing to depart from *Roe v. Wade* and thereby curb, if not abolish, the constitutional right of a woman to have an abortion.

What is relevant to the present analysis is Justice Stevens' opinion in *Webster* concurring in part and dissenting in part.[216] Stevens would find the Missouri statute violated the Establishment Clause because of the legislative ("theological") finding in the statute's preamble that endorses the state interest in preserving the life of an embryo during the first forty or eighty days of pregnancy to be at the same level of protection and scrutiny as after viability.[217] Justice Stevens would also invalidate the statute because it violates the right of contraceptive privacy set forth in *Griswold v. Connecticut*.[218] Before reaching this conclusion, however, he develops a thoughtful inquiry into the issue of male versus female ensoulment articulated in the early writings of St. Thomas Aquinas which have been accepted by the Roman

Catholic Church.[219]

What Justice Stevens concludes after analyzing the Aquinas position is most important to a sophisticated understanding of the complex medico-legal-ethical issue of the scope of protection the state should or may extend to research and experimentation of extracorporeal embryos. He states eloquently:

> As a secular matter, there is an obvious difference between the state interest in protecting the freshly fertilized egg and the state interest in protecting a 9-month-gestated, fully sentient fetus on the eve of birth. *There can be no interest in protecting the newly fertilized egg from physical pain or mental anguish, because the capacity for such suffering does not yet exist; respecting a developed fetus, however, that interest is valid.* In fact, if one prescinds the theological concept of ensoulment—or one accepts St. Thomas Aquinas' view that ensoulment does not occur for at least 40 days, *a State has no greater secular interest in protecting the potential life of a sperm or an unfertilized ovum.*[220]

The logic of this position is quite compelling and provides much weight to the position that while the embryo does not theologically have an independent moral status, it is regarded by some as worthy of respect as a "symbol of life."[221] While the embryo might well be treated as "an object of respect," it arguably does not—consistent with this position—gain any type of moral status or recognition until transferred to a uterus.[222] Accordingly, when no transfer occurs, vexatious decisions concerning unused or stored embryos "become occasions to use embryos as a symbol of life or persons generally" are presented.[223] What then must be evaluated is whether the need for preserving such symbols outweighs "the costs to autonomy or future knowledge that symbol-making necessarily involves."[224]

Justice O'Connor, in concurring in part and concurring in the judgment, addressed the concern that the preamble to the challenged statute might prohibit the development and use of IVF by dismissing them as "intimations of unconstitutionality" that were "simply too hypothetical" to address.[225] Regarding the challenge that the statute is violative of *Griswold*, she found nothing in the preamble that would affect a woman's right to practice acts of contraception.[226]

Justice O'Connor stressed that as to the state's interest in protecting potential life, the point of viability was the crucial determination when such interest could be focused by the enactment of regulations designed to achieve that end.[227] "No decision of this Court has held that the State may not directly promote its interest in potential life when viability may differ with each pregnancy."[228] Its "possibility" can thus be determined within a period of testing—as for example here with Missouri's twenty-week period (that was essentially a presumption of viability of twenty weeks—subject to medical rebuttal).[229] As more advanced medical technologies develop, the testing period may commence earlier. Yet, even with an earlier time frame for testing viability, it is well known that fetal lungs do not mature until some thirty-three to thirty-four weeks of gestation.[230] The physician is also aided in the determination of viability by ultra sound examinations that determine gestational age and fetal weight, as well as fetal lung maturity.[231]

The full Court chose not to address the validity of the statute's preamble that recognized life as beginning with human conception. However, the arguments made by Justices Stevens and O'Connor regarding viability and the tone of the other opinions in the case persuasively show that legal protection of personhood under present accepted biological and medical knowledge ought not be extended to unimplanted, extracorporeal embryos. When implanted, as with normal conception, the embryo must develop into a *viable* fetus before full state protections will be accorded to it.[232]

Congressional Action

With the enactment in 1994 of the Freedom of Access to Clinics Entrance Act, Congress, unlike the Supreme Court, has stated boldly and unequivocally that efforts to threaten, intimidate or interfere with persons obtaining or providing reproductive health services (e.g., abortion) are prohibited with criminal sanctions.[233] Health services are defined as including "medical, surgical, counseling or referral services . . . including services relating to . . . the termination of a pregnancy whether the services are provided in a hospital, clinic, doctor's office or other facility."[234]

THE AMERICAN FERTILITY SOCIETY GUIDELINES

In an effort to update and supplement its 1990 Report on Ethical Considerations of the New Reproductive Technology, the Ethics Committee of the American Fertility Society issued, in 1994, its sixty-page report titled "Ethical Considerations of Assisted Reproductive Technology."[235] Although their conclusions and recommendations are not binding policy, they do reflect the serious thinking of one of the nation's preeminent groups in family planning. Thus, from this standpoint, they are of considerable importance.

The committee, while acknowledging artificial insemination by a husband is acceptable, nonetheless called for the development and regulation of reliable sperm bank facilities and concluded the cryo-preservation of human sperm is both ethically and medically acceptable. Donor insemination, although controversial, was also found to enjoy the same status as husband, or homologous, insemination. Again, calling for uniform standards for the collection and preservation of sperm in banks, the committee urged donors to be subject to genetic and health screening and suggested cyro- preserved donor sperm be used over fresh sperm because of the opportunity for more extensive screening and testing. Further, it was recommended that no payment be made to semen donors other than for their time and expenses involved and that the same donor not be used for more than *ten* offspring.[236] This latter point, taken together with the conclusion that single, unmarried women should be entitled to donor insemination, shows a very sad and tragic societal direction for traditional families. Indeed, both recommendations regarding multiple donor use and the availability of donor insemination for single women—if accepted popularly and acted on—would destroy the very notion of the nuclear family and glorify the motto of popular feminism: "My Body, My Choice!"[237]

IVF was found to be not only safe for both mother and child but was also an extension—and, thus, not a radical separation—of procreation and sexual intimacy. If whatever risks involved with the procedure are found acceptable by the participating couple, then its use should be permitted. While recognizing the ethical difficulty with the process which allows the selection of some pre-embryos for transfer and the discarding of others not used, the committee concluded that there was no ethical objection to the discarding of those pre-embryos which were clearly degenerate or abnormal. In order to lessen the rate of discard, adjunctive cryo-preservation programs for maintenance of pre-embryos in excess of those transferred were recommended. With programs of this nature in place, the necessity of selective reduction would be reduced considerably since cryo-preservation would also enable the transfer of a limited number of pre-embryos.[238]

The American Fertility Society's Ethics Committee came out strongly against the use of a surrogate gestational mother for nonmedical reasons (e.g., the genetic mother's convenience). Even though it recognized the inherent controversy involved in the use of surrogation, the committee nonetheless concluded there is a definite role for surrogate gestation in reproductive medicine. Finding that the frequency of use for surrogation is low, and that the morality of the process is less an issue than the possible exploitation of the surrogates, it was urged that surrogate gestational motherhood programs should nonetheless have their protocol approved by a properly constituted ethics committee or institution review board. Furthermore, a full and voluntary informed consent must be obtained from the surrogate as well as the participating couple and those participating professionals should not receive any type of finder's fee for participating in the program; instead, they should only receive whatever customary fees allowed. It is preferable that surrogates, in turn, make no payment beyond compensation for their expenses and inconveniences—with only rare cases being allowed for compensation beyond this standard.[239]

Complex and unresolved ethical, social, and psychological issues prevented the committee from endorsing fully the use of this new reproductive technology. Although finding its use appropriate where it offers the only *medical* solution to infertility for a couple of whom the woman has no uterus, is incapable of producing eggs, or is unwilling to pass on a genetic defect that she carries, it nevertheless cautioned against the potentially negative effects of the procedure on not only the surrogate gestational mother and the couple but the resulting child as well, the possibility of *in utero* bonding between the surrogate and the fetus, the need for thorough screening of the surrogate and the degree of appropriate care which must be exercised by her during the period of her pregnancy.[240]

CONCLUSIONS

In exploring the noncoital reproductive sciences, a balance should be struck between the unfettered use of science for individual satisfaction and the promotion and maintenance of the social good. Thus, embryo research and experimentation which contributes to the goal of minimizing human suffering and maximizing the social good deriving therefrom must be pursued in a reasonable manner. As long as the central driving force in marital relationships continues to be procreation, and the family unit remains at the core of a progressive society, efforts will be pursued which seek to expand the period of fecundity, combat infertility, and ensure that inherited genetic deficiencies are not passed on to future generations. Genetic experimentation and planning, in conjunction with eugenic programming, are more rational and humane than alternatives to population regulation through death, famine, and war or an abdication of genetic autonomy to the countervailing doctrines of gene sovereignty and biological determinism.[241]

Socially responsible scientific inquiry should be restrained only when the scientist "is clearly able to foresee that the particular line of work is leading to a kind and scale of dangers" that would constitute a "limitation" or, in other words, presents "dangers of cataclysmic physical or psychological proportions for mankind as a whole."[242]

While some would view research and experimentation in human embryology and reproductive biology as promoting a genetic disaster or cataclysm, the better view is that such work advances the goal of minimizing human suffering and maximizing the quality of purposeful and meaningful existence free of inherited genetic disabilities.[243] Certain aspects of the new human reproductive biology (e.g., cloning) might well require greater degrees of reasonable self-restraint. By and large, however, the nature and degree to which restraint is mandated must be determined by the individual scientist.

Preemption of scientific work in human reproductive biology by the state is shortsighted and repressive of the principle of free scientific inquiry.[244] Instead of developing a scientific regulatory scheme relying on legislative prohibition, rule-making committees within the pertinent medical and scientific profession should be established to monitor and control scientific inquiry. Perhaps the best model would be a simple organization approached easily on a consultative and advisory basis and designed to assist biologists, scientists and medical researchers in making their own decisions.[245]

Included in the Health Research Extension Act of 1985[246] were provisions to create a Biomedical Ethics Board and a Biomedical Ethics Advisory Committee to report on human genetic engineering and on the federal rules on human fetal research.[247] If totally funded, the Committee would have also studied the ethical, social, and legal implications of human genome mapping, genetic testing, eugenics and gene therapy.[248] These bodies would have perhaps provided some continuity with the now defunct President's Commission for the Study of Ethical Problems in Medicine and Biomedical and Behavioral Research by advancing efforts to study, evaluate, and organize responses to the new reproductive biology.

President Clinton renewed hope in the scientific community during the summer of 1996 by issuing an executive order creating a new National Bioethics Advisory Committee charged with studying ethical issues arising from experiments on human biology and behavior. More specifically, the commission will consider how best to use and manage genetic information—derived from the Human Genome Project—as well as explore the scientific, legal, and ethical implications of patenting human genes.[249] Whether the Commission's work will meet with greater success than its most recent precedessor depends in large part on the degree to which politics can be disengaged from the ultimate recommendations it will make.

It remains for lawyers to become more aware and, indeed, educated to the challenges and complexities of these new scientific and technological advances in reproductive biology. If they fail to achieve this level of awareness and education, "they will increasingly lack understanding of the questions to be asked, let alone answers to be given."[250] And, one such open-ended question remains: To what extent, if at all, is there a fundamental constitutional or international human right for procreative liberty, health assistance in biological reproduction, and the point in the biological developmental chart that mandates the state to extend its protection to "life?"

While ever mindful of the perhaps unavoidable mixture of religion into science and the new laws of reproductive biology, every step must be taken to ensure as pragmatic a view as possible is adhered to in the ultimate structuring of legislative responses and judicial interpretation. Scientific objectivity, if not verifiability, should be not an ideal but a given in this area of decision making.

In the final analysis, it is well to remember that the world is forever changing. Consequently, practices which seem weird and unnatural to those of the current adult generation will no doubt be seen as less so to the next generation.[251] With this caveat is in mind, law, science, and medicine should continue in their present cooperative alliance which allows them to be proactionary rather than reactionary and thus to develop frameworks for principled decision making in dealing with the myriad problems associated with the assisted reproductive technologies now rather than later.[252]

NOTES

1. Fracassini, *The Regulation of Sperm Banks and Fertility Doctors: A Cry for Prophylactic Measures*, 8 J. CONTEMP. HEALTH L. & POL'Y 275, 293 (1992).

Previous estimates set the figure at 20,000. L.B. ANDREWS, NEW CONCEPTIONS (1984).

2. Fracassini, *suprs*, at 294, n. 107. *See* Lichtbau, *Artificial Insemination Raises Fears,* L.A. TIMES, Aug. 10, 1988, at 1.

Still other sources have found about 200,000 women are inseminated medically each year. B.R. FURROW ET AL., BIOETHICS, HEALTH CARE LAW AND ETHICS 114 (1991).

3. Robertson, *Procreative Liberty and the Control of Conception, Pregnancy and Childbirth,* 69 VA. L. REV. 405, 424-26 (1983).

4. Andrews, *The Stock Market: The Law of the New Reproductive Technologies,* 70 A.B.A.J. 50, 56 (1984).

5. Genesis 16:1-16. *See* Smith, *Through a Test Tube Darkly: Artificial Insemination and the Law,* 67 MICH. L. REV. 127 (1968).

6. Krucoff, *Private Lives: The New Surrogates,* WASH. POST, Sept. 24, 1980, at B5.

See H. RAGONE, SURROGATE MOTHERHOOD: CONCEPTION IN THE HEART (1994).

7. *Id.*

8. J.C. WESTMAN, CHILD ADVOCACY 276 (1979).

9. There are two principal ways undertaken for human artificial insemination: homologous and heterologous. When semen is secured from a wife's husband and artificially injected by instrument into her reproductive tract, the process is termed homologous or AIH. When semen is obtained from a third-party donor, the process is referred to as heterologous or AID. Artificial insemination, as a technique for improved animal husbandry, occurred as early as 1322, while the first reported case of human artificial insemination was in 1799. Not until the early part of the 20th century were recorded instances of donor insemination observed. Smith, *supra* note 5 at 128-29.

10. Smith, *For unto Us Is Born a Child—Legally,* 56 A.B.A.J. 143 (1970).

11. Weintraub, *First Test-Tube Baby Born in British Hospital,* WASH. POST, July 15, 1978, at 1. *See* T.M. GARRETT, H.W. BAILLIE & R.M. GARRET, HEALTH CARE ETHICS: PRINCIPLES AND PROBLEMS, Ch. 8 (2d ed. 1993).

In vitro fertilization is the procedure employing a laparoscope that seeks to remove eggs from the ovaries of a female and fertilize them outside the body. Once fertilization is achieved, the embryo is then implanted in the uterus of the female. *See* J.N. LASKER & S. BORG, IN SEARCH OF PARENTHOOD: COPING WITH INFERTILITY AND HIGH-TECH CONCEPTION (1994).

12. G. GALLUP, 5 THE GALLUP OPINION INDEX, No. 161 (Dec. 1978). *See* R.H. BLANK, THE POLITICAL IMPLICATIONS OF HUMAN GENETIC TECHNOLOGY 152 (1981).

13. High Technology Fertility Survey, done by Princeton Survey Research Associates and distributed by the Roper Center for Public Opinion Research, *Family Circle* Mag., Sept. 20, 1994 at 67.

14. *Id.*

15. *Id.*

16. Strnad v. Strnad, 190 Misc. 786, 787, 78 N.Y.S.2d 390, 391-92 (Sup. Ct. 1948).

17. *Id.*

18. 39 Misc. 2d 1083, 242 N.Y.S.2d 406 (Sup. Ct. 1963).

19. 68 Cal. 2d 280, 437 P.2d 495, 66 Cal. Rptr. 7 (1968). *See also* Smith, *supra* note 10.

20. 68 Cal.2d at 283-84, 437 P.2d at 498, 66 Cal. Rptr. at 10.

21. *Id.*

22. 74 Misc. 2d 99, 345 N.Y.S.2d 430 (Sup. Ct. 1973).

23. *See, e.g.,* CONN. GEN. STAT. §§ 45a-771 (1991); FLA. STAT. ANN. § 742.11 (West 1996 Supp.); TEX. FAM. CODE ANN. § 151.103 (Vernon 1996); VA. CODE § 64.1-8.1 (1995).

24. *See, e.g.,* CAL. FAM. CODE § 7613 (Deering 1994); MASS. GEN. LAWS ANN. ch. 46 §4B (West 1994); N.Y. DOM. REL. § 73 (McKinney 1994). *See* Hollandsworth, *Gay Men Creating Families Through Surro-Gay Arrangements: A Paradigm for Reproductive Freedom,* 3 AM. U. J. GENDER & L. 183, 208, n. 108 (1995).

Another author counts thirty-five states as having amended their statutes in order to allow the preconception intent of the parties to govern in artificial insemination cases. Accordingly, in such states, the sperm donor is not taken to be the legal father of the issue. Rather, the consenting husband of the sperm recipient is recognized as the father for all legal purposes. Andrews, *Beyond Doctrinal Boundaries: A Legal Framework for Surrogate Motherhood,* 81 VA. L. REV. 2343 at 2371, n. 131 (1995).

In egg donor situations, the egg recipient, or intended mother, is recognized as the legal mother in some five states. *Id.* at n. 132. *See, e.g.,* FLA. STAT. ANN. § 742.11 (West Supp. 1995); TEX. FAM. CODE ANN. §§ 12.03A to .03B (West Supp. 1995).

25. UNIF. PARENTAGE ACT §§ 5(a) to 6(b), 9B UNIF. LAWS ANN. 287, 301-02 (1987).

26. Thirteen states have adopted these specific provisions of the act. *See* Hollandsworth, *supra* note 24 at 210, n. 110. Eighteen states are listed, however, as having adopted the Act *in toto.* 9B UNIF. LAWS ANN. 16 (1996 Supp.).

27. Hollandsworth, *supra* note 24 at 211, nn.'s 121-22.

28. *See Orford v. Orford,* 58 D.L.R. 251 (Ont. Sup. Ct. 1921); *Doornbos v. Doornbos,* 23 U.S.L.W. 2308 (unreported decision of Super. Ct. Cook County, Ill., Dec. 13, 1954) (held that use of AID without a husband's consent was adultery). In *MacLennan v. MacLennan,* 1958 Sess. Cas. 105, decided in Scotland, AID was recognized as being an adulterous act. And in England, in 1949 case, a marriage was annulled, and the issue born from the use of an homologous insemination (by the husband, himself, not a donor) were held to be illegitimate. *L. v. L.,* [1949] 1 All. E.R. 141.

29. Smith, *The Medicolegal Challenge of Preparing for a Brave Yet Somewhat Frightening New World,* 5 J. LEGAL MED. 9 (Apr. 1977). *See also* Shaman, *Legal Aspects of Artificial Insemination,* 18 J. FAM. L. 331 (1980); Keane, *Legal Problems of Surrogate Motherhood,* 1980 SO. ILL. U.L.J. 147, 151-52.

30. *C.M. v. C.C.,* 152 N.J. Super. 160, 377 A.2d 821 (1977). *See* Smith, *A Close Encounter of the First Kind: Artificial Insemination and an Enlightened Judiciary,* 17 J. FAM. L. 41 (1978).

31. 410 U.S. 113 (1973).

32. In New York, it is provided by statute that a written consent must be executed by a married woman seeking to be artificially inseminated and by her husband if the issue therefrom is to be considered legitimate. N.Y. DOM. REL. LAW § 73 (McKinney 1988). *See also* CAL. FAM. CODE, § 7613 (West 1994).

33. Whitaker, *Birth Data Ruled Open to Adoptee,* WASH. POST, Feb. 5, 1979, at C1.

34. R. SCOTT, THE BODY AS PROPERTY 208 (1981).

35. Currie-Cohen et al., *Current Practice of Artificial Insemination by Donor in the U.S.,* 300 NEW ENG. J. MED. 585 (1979).

36. *Id.* at 587.

37. *Id.* at 588. The principal complication would be a possible claim being asserted (with consequent adverse publicity) that the donor should share in the expenses of raising the child or confer testamentary rights of inheritance upon the child. *See* Wadlington, *Artificial Insemination: The Dangers of a Poorly Kept Secret,* 64 NW. L. REV. 777 (1970).

38. *See* Fracassini, *supra* note 1 at 296.

39. Currie-Cohen et al., *supra* note 35, at 585-87.

40. *See* A. BARAN & R. PANNOR, LETHAL SECRETS, THE SHOCKING CONSEQUENCES OF UNSOLVED PROBLEMS OF ARTIFICIAL INSEMINATION (1989); L.B. ANDREWS, NEW CONCEPTIONS 169 (1987); Ziporyn, *Artificial Human Reproduction Poses Medical Social Concerns,* 255 J.A.M.A. 13 (1986).

41. Fracassini, *supra* note 1 at 286, nn.'s 63-64.

See DeStefano, *Sperm Suit Raises Array of Legal Issues,* NEWSDAY, City Ed., Mar. 10, 1990, at 11; *Fertility Doctor Accused of Using his Own Sperm,* WASH. POST, Nov. 20, 1991, at A1.

42. Fracassini, *supra* note 1 at 287 *passim.*

43. Office of Technology Assessment, Artificial Insemination (Background Paper, Summary of 1987 Survey) at 6, 9. *See also Self-Insemination May Carry Risk of HIV Infection,* WASH. POST, Mar. 15, 1995, at A3.

44. *Id.* at 20.

45. *See, e.g.,* OHIO REV. CODE ANN. § 3111.33(B)(1) (Anderson 1988); DEL. CODE ANN., tit. 16, § 2801 (Supp. 1991); IDAHO CODE, § 39-5408 (Supp. 1991). The other states regulating sperm donation were Florida, Georgia, Illinois, North Carolina, New Hampshire, Oregon, Rhode Island, Fracassini, *supra* note 1 at 276, n. 9.

This 1987 study found only four states—Illinois, Indiana, Michigan, and New York—employing their state health departments for licensing and inspecting all sperm banks doing business in their states. Fracassini, *supra* note 1 at 275, n. 4.

Georgia is the only state addressing clearly the potential liability for misperforming artificial insemination procedure. GA. CODE ANN. § 43.34-42 (Michie 1991).

46. Ten or more states have adopted, in essence, the provisions of Section 5 of the Uniform Act.

See e.g., CAL. CIV. CODE § 7005(a) (West 1975); N.Y. CITY HEALTH CODE § 21.07 (1959); WYO. STAT. § 14-3-103(a) (1978). *See* Note, *The Uniform Parentage Act: What Is Will Mean for the Putative Father in California,* 28 HASTINGS L.J. 191 (1976).

47. *In re Adoption of Female Interest,* 5 FAM. L. REP. (BNA) 2311 (1979).

48. *In re Ann Carol* S., 172 N.Y.L.J. 31, Aug. 13, 1974, at 12.

49. 9B UNIF. LAWS ANN. 16 (1996 Supp). *See Spillman v. Parker,* 332 So.2d 573 (La. Ct. App. 1976). *See generally* Wadlington, *Artificial Conception: The Challenge of Family Law,* 69 VA. L. REV. 465 (1983).

50. This was clearly the standard enunciated in *C.M. v. C.C.*, 152 N.J. Super. 160, 167, 377 A. 2d 821, 825 (1977). *See* Smith, *supra* note 30.

51. P. REILLY, GENETICS, LAW AND SOCIAL POLICY 202 (1977).

52. The Currie-Luttrel article cites to carelessness in record keeping by doctors, *see supra* notes 35-37 and accompanying text, thus, the statement "*if* records are maintained." The harms of disclosure would be headed by perhaps a dwindling of the number of donors because they would fear financial demands of support would be made against them. REILLY, *supra* note 51 at 202. *See* Capron, *Tort Liability in Genetic Counseling,* 79 COLUM. L. REV. 618 (1979); *Curlender v. Bio-Science Labs*, 106 Cal. App. 2d 811, 164 Cal. Rptr. 721 (1980).

53. The Uniform Parentage Act has been adopted in eighteen jurisdictions. *See, e.g.*, CAL. FAM. CODE §§ 7600-7730 (West 1994); MINN. STAT. ANN. §§ 257.51-54 (West 1992); and WASH. REV. CODE ANN. § 26.26.010 to .905 (1986). *See supra* note 49.

54. R. BLANK, *supra* note 12 at 68. *See also* G.P. SMITH, II, GENETICS, ETHICS AND THE LAW 110, 124-25 (1981).

55. *Id.*

56. Mann, *Surrogate Motherhood: The Inevitable Conflict*, WASH. POST, Mar. 25, 1981, at C1; Burmiller, *Mothers for Others*, WASH. POST, Mar. 9 1983, at B11; Krucoff, *Focus: The Surrogate Baby Boom*, WASH. POST, Jan. 25, 1983, at C5.

57. A. CORBIN, ON CONTRACTS § 1522 (1962).

N. P. KEANE & D. C. BREO, THE SURROGATE MOTHER (1981) at 117 lists six considerations to be taken into account in both designing and reaching a surrogation contract and at 270-305 presents various model forms to be used in such a surrogate arrangement.

58. CORBIN, *supra* note 57, § 1534.

59. *Id.* § 1315.

60. 15 S. WILLISTON, A TREATISE ON THE LAWS OF CONTRACTS § 1745, n. 1 (1972).

61. *See* CAL. PENAL CODE § 181 (West 1988); MICH. COMP. LAWS ANN. § 710.54 (1996 Supp).

62. *See, e.g., Adoption Hotline Inc. v. State,* 385 So. 2d 682 (C.D. C.A. Fla. 1980); Comment, *Independent Adoption: Is the Black and White Beginning to Appear in the Controversy over Gray Market Allocations?* 18 DUESQUNE L. REV. 629 (1980).

63. WILLISTON, *supra* note 60 at § 1792.

64. Erickson, *Contracts to Bear a Child,* in 1 ETHICAL, LEGAL AND SOCIAL CHALLENGES TO A BRAVE NEW WORLD 100 (G.P. Smith ed. 1982).

65. Krucoff, *Private Lives: The New Surrogate,* WASH. POST, Sept. 24, 1980, at B5.

66. W. RAUSHENBUSH, THE LAW OF PERSONAL PROPERTY § 7.1 (3d ed. 1975).

67. *Id.* at § 7.13.

68. *Id.* at § 7.21.

69. UNIF. LAWS ANN., *supra* note 49.

70. Unif. Parentage Act § 5(b), 9A UNIF. LAWS ANN. 593 (1979). *See* the Uniform Status of Children of Assisted Conception Act (USCACA), 9B UNIF. LAWS ANN. 50 (Supp. 1989); Wadlington, *Baby M: Catalyst for Family Law Reform?,* 5 J. CONTEMP. HEALTH L. & POL'Y 1, 18-19 (1989).

71. Annas, *Contract to Bear a Child: Compassion and Commercialism?,* 11 HASTINGS CENTER RPT. 23, 24 (April 1981).

72. *Id.*; Andrews, *supra* note 24 at 2369, n. 127.

73. Unif. Parentage Act § 4(a).

74. *Id.* § 4(b).

75. Erickson, *supra* note 64 at 611-13.

76. Robinson, *Genetics and Society,* 1971 UTAH L. REV. 487, 489 (1971). *See also* Friedman, *Legal Implications of Amniocentesis,* 123 U. PA. L. REV. 92, 100 (1974).

77. *Id. See generally* Smith, *supra* note 30. Interestingly, however, a sperm bank run by feminists in Oakland, California, has recently opened. It serves all women, regardless of race, marital status, or sexual orientation. *The Birth of a Feminist Sperm Bank: New Social Agendas for* AID, 13 HASTINGS CENTER RPT. 3 (Feb. 1983).

78. *See, e.g., Orford v. Orford,* 58 D.L.R. 251, 257-59 (Ont. Sup. Ct. 1921) and *Doornbos v. Doornbos,* 23 U.S.L.W. 2308 (unreported decision of Super. Ct., Cook County, Ill., Dec. 13, 1954) (held that a woman's use of AID without her husband's consent was adulterous).

79. *See generally* Kritchevsky, *The Unmarried Woman's Right to Artificial Insemination: A Call for an Expanded Definition of Family,* 4 HARV. WOMAN'S L.J. 1 (1981).

80. *See generally* Comment, *Constitutional Limitations on State Intervention in Prenatal Care,* 67 VA. L. REV. 1051 (1981).

81. One of the early "mind change" cases covered a surrogate's desire to keep her biological child, with no issue of support being raised. TIME Mag., June 22, 1981, at 71.

82. *See generally* Curtis, *The Psychological Parent Doctrine in Custody Disputes Between Foster Parents and Biological Parents,* 16 COLUM. L.J. & SOC. PROBS. 149, 157-61 (1980). *See also* Schiff, *Solomonic Decisions in Egg Donation: Unscrambling the Conundurm of Legal Maternity,* 80 IOWA L. REV. 265 (1995).

83. Smith, *Theological Reflections and the New Biology,* 48 IND. L.J. 605 (1973).

84. SMITH, *supra* note 54 at 153.

85. Note, *Redefining Mother: A Legal Matrix for New Reproductive Technologies,* 96 YALE L. J. 187, 194, 195 (1986).

86. *Id.* at 206.

87. *Id.* at 208, n.1.

88. *Griswold v. Connecticut,* 381 U.S. 479 (1965).

89. *Supra* note 85 at 198, 199. *See* Wadlington, *Artificial Conception: The Challenge for Family Law,* 69 VA. L. REV. 465, 508-509 (1983).

90. RESTATEMENT (SECOND) OF TORTS §§ 827(a), 828(a) (1977).

91. *Id.* at § 826(a).

92. *Supra* note 90.

93. R.A. POSNER, ECONOMIC ANALYSIS OF LAW 2d, 111 (1977).

94. *Id.* at 117.

95. 217 N.J. Super. 313, 525 A.2d 1127 (1987).

96. *Id.*

97. 109 N.J. 396, 537 A.2d 1227 (1987).

98. Efron, *A 3-Way Fight for Custody,* L.A. TIMES, Mar. 3, 1991, at 3. On appeal, Mrs. Moschetta lost on her claim as legal mother. *See infra* note 101.

99. Efron, *supra* note 98.

100. Ranii, *Future Shock for Family Law: Can One Child Have 2 Mothers,* NAT'L L.J., Mar. 26, 1984, at 1.

101. Sachs, *And Baby Makes Four,* TIME Mag., Aug. 27, 1990, at 53. On April 18, 1991, an Orange County Superior Court Judge ruled that Ms. Jordan was the legal parent of the baby girl she bore as a surrogate and that since the contract for her services as a surrogate was an exchange of money for a baby in contravention of California law and thus unenforceable, the central issue became a simple custody fight between the biological father and the biological mother (Super Ct. Orange County D324349). Efron & Newman, *Surrogate Mother Gets Rights of Legal Parent,* L.A. TIMES, April 19, 1991, at 1.

On June 10, 1994, the California Court of Appeal allowed Ms. Jordan to retain her parental rights. Thus, she and Mr. Moschetta were recognized as the mother and father of Marissa and Cynthia Moschetta's claim was disallowed. *Moschetta v. Moschetta & Jordan,* 30 Cal. Rptr. 2d 893 (1994).

102. *Moschetta v. Moschetta & Jordan, id.* at 902-03.

103. *Johnson v. Calvert*, infra note 107.

104. Sachs, *supra* note 101. *See* L.B. ANDREWS, BETWEEN STRANGERS: SURROGATE MOTHERS, EXPECTANT FATHERS AND BRAVE NEW BABIES (1989). *See also* Kolata, *When Grandmother Is the Mother*, N.Y. TIMES, Aug. 5, 1991, at A1.

105. *Id. See* Andrews, *Surrogate Motherhood: The Challenge for the Feminists*, 16 L. MED. & HEALTH CARE 72 (1988).

It has been urged that there should be a legal, irrebuttable presumption that the gestational mother should be the rearing mother. G.J. ANNAS, STANDARD OF CARE: THE LAW OF AMERICAN BIOETHICS 70 (1993).

106. Tifft, *Its All in the (Parental) Genes*, TIME Mag., Nov. 5, 1990, at 77.

The Calverts urged that Ms. Johnson be recognized only as a foster parent who cared for their embryo-fetus. Efron, *Surrogate Mother Is Like a Foster, Parent, Calvert Attorney Says*, L.A. TIMES, April 30, 1991, at B7. The California Court of Appeal ruled October 8, 1991, that the gestational surrogate mother had no statutory or constitutional right, in this case, to be declared the child's parent. 286 Cal. Rptr. 369 (1991).

107. *Johnson v. Calvert*, 851 P.2d 776 (Cal. Sup. Ct. 1993).

See generally Polikoff, *The Child Does Have Two Mothers: Redefining Parenthood to Meet The Needs of Children in Lesbian-Mother and Other Nontraditional Families*, 78 GEO. L.J. 459 (1990).

Whether a non-biologic father—here, John A. Buzzanca—can disclaim financial responsibility and legal paternity in a divorce action before a child is delivered by a surrogate under contract with him and his then-wife, has yet to be determined by the California courts. Under present law, a man is deemed to be a father if he is the genetic father, adoptive father, or married to the child's mother at the time the child is born. *See* Majaraj, *California and the West: Surrogacy Case Could Become Legal Benchmark*, L.A. TIMES, Sept. 15, 1997, at A3.

108. Robertson, *Surrogate Mothers: Not So Novel After All*, 13 HASTINGS CENTER RPT., 28 (Oct. 1983).

109. Coleman, *Surrogate Motherhood: Analysis of the Problems and Suggestions for Solutions*, 50 TENN. L. REV. 71, 81-82 (1982). For a more complete historical analysis of the AID cases, *see* Smith, *supra* note 5.

110. Wadlington, *supra* note 89 at 502.

111. The states are: Alabama, Arizona, California, Colorado, Delaware, Florida (exempting stepparents), Georgia, Idaho, Illinois, Indiana, Iowa, Kentucky, Maryland, Massachusetts, Michigan, Nevada, New Jersey (exempting stepparents), New York, North Carolina, Ohio, South Dakota, Tennessee, Utah, and Wisconsin.

See also Katz, *Surrogate Motherhood and the Baby Selling Laws*, 20 COLUM. J.L. & SOC. PROBS. 1 (1986).

112. *Doe v. Kelly*, 106 Mich. App. 169, 307 N. W. 2d 438 (1981), *cert. denied*, 459 U.S. 1183 (1983).

See generally Johnson, *The Baby M Decision: Specific Performance of a Contract for Specially Manufactured Goods*, 11 SO. ILL. U. L. J. 1339, 1342 (1987).

113. *Surrogate Parenting Assoc., Inc. v. Kentucky,* 704 S.W. 2d 209 (Ky. 1986).

The Kentucky legislature subsequently made surrogacy agreements void and unenforceable. KY. REV. STAT. ANN. § 199.590(4) (Baldwin 1993).

114. Annas, *Father Anonymous: Beyond the Best Interest of the Sperm Donor,* 14 FAM. L. Q. (1980).

115. L. TRIBE, AMERICAN CONSTITUTIONAL LAW 892 (1978).

116. *Id.* at 889.

117. *Id.* at 892.

118. H.L.A. HART, LAW, LIBERTY AND MORALITY 57 (1963).

119. *Id.*

120. P. DEVLIN, THE ENFORCEMENT OF MORALS 7 (1965).

121. *Id.* at 24, 25. *See also* Dworkin, *Lord Devlin and the Enforcement of Morals,* 75 YALE L. J. 986 (1966).

122. Eight state legislatures make surrogacy agreements void and unenforceable: D.C. CODE ANN. § 16-401 (1993); IND. CODE ANN. §§ 31-8-1-1 to 8-2-3 (Burns 1994); KY. REV. STAT. ANN. § 199.590 (Baldwin 1993); LA. REV. STAT. ANN., § 9:2713 (West 1991); MICH. STAT. ANN. §§ 25.248(153), 25.248(155) & 25.248(1959) (Callaghan 1994); NEB. REV. STAT. § 25-21, 200 (1993); N.Y. DOM. REL. LAW § 122 (McKinney 1994); N.D. CENT. CODE § 14-18-05 (1991).

Thirteen jurisdictions prohibit the enforcement of paid surrogacy contracts: Arizona, District of Columbia, Indiana, Florida, Kentucky, Louisiana, Michigan, Nebraska, New York, North Dakota, Utah, Virginia, and Washington. Michigan and Washington make determinations here, however, based on the best interests of the child. Florida, Nevada, New Hampshire, New York, and Virginia also make exceptions under certain circumstances and allow expenses of surrogates to be paid. Virginia and New Hampshire, in fact, provide extensive regulatory structures for unpaid surrogacy contracts—including medical and psychological screening and judicial analysis of the surrogate contract before the pregnancy occurs together with a home study of the intended parents as well as the surrogate and her husband. VA. CODE ANN. §§ 20-156 to -165 (Michie Supp. 1994); N.H. REV. STAT. ANN. § 168-13 (1994 & Supp. 1994). *See* Andrews, *supra* note 24 at 2346-48.

123. Some states impose criminal or civil sanctions for agreements involving compensation for surrogate services: D.C. CODE ANN. § 16-402 (1993); MICH. STAT. ANN. §§ 25.248(153), 25.248(155) & 25.248(159) (Callaghan 1994); N.Y. DOM. REL. LAW § 122 (McKinney 1994).

Nineteen states in all have legislation allowing, banning or otherwise regulating surrogate mothers. Andrews, *supra* note 24 at 2346, n. 16.

124. *See supra* note 78 and cases therein together with *supra* notes 18-23 and discussion.

125. The very fact that not all jurisdictions have uniformly adopted legislation conferring legitimacy upon issue born of AID is pertinent to this point. Interestingly, Connecticut has gone so far as to prohibit physicians from performing

AID upon married women unless the husband gives his written consent. CONN. GEN. STAT. § 45a-772 (1993). Arkansas, while not maintaining such a prohibition, is concerned with the legal status of the issue born of an assisted conception arrangement, and, thus, declares as to an unmarried woman using artificial insemination, that for all legal purposes the child of such a woman shall be hers except in the case of a surrogate mother "in which event the child shall be that of: (A) The biological father and the woman intended to be the mother if the biological father is married; or (B) The biological father only if unmarried; or (C) The woman intended to be the mother in cases of a surrogate mother when an anonymous donor's sperm was utilized for artificial insemination." ARK. CODE ANN. §§ 9-10-201 to 202 (Michie 1993).

See Manus, *The Proposed Model Surrogate Parenthood Act: A Legislative Response to the Challenges of Reproductive Technology,* 29 MICH. J. L. REF. 671 (1996) (where the author urges surrogation be placed under strict judicial supervision instead of being eradicated or criminalized).

126. S. KLEEGMAN & S. KAUFMAN, INFERTILITY IN WOMEN 178 (1966).

127. Sanders, *Whose Lives Are These? A Judge Sets a Pro-Life Precedent for Embryos,* TIME Mag., Oct. 2, 1989, at 19.

128. USA TODAY, Aug. 7, 1989, at 1A.

129. *Attorney General for Queensland ex rel. Kerr v. T.,* 57 A.L.J.R. 285 (Austl. 1983).

130. Gavigan, *The Criminal Sanction as it Relates to Human Reproduction: The Genesis of the Statutory Prohibition of Abortion,* 5 J. LEGAL HIST. 20 (1984).

131. *Id.* at 21.

132. 410 U.S. 113 (1973).

133. It is only when the fetus reaches a "compelling" point of viability or when it "presumably has the capability of meaningful life outside the mother's womb," the state's interest in protecting fetal existence will be asserted. *Id.* at 163-64. It is at the third trimester of development that the state's interest becomes controlling.

134. *Davis v. Davis,* No. E-14496, slip op. at 17 (Tenn. Cir. Sept. 21, 1989) (1989 WL 140495). (This case was reversed and remanded by the Tennessee Court of Appeals in September 1990; *see infra* note 138 and accompanying text.)

Louisiana has unique legislation which recognizes the judicial status of a viable IVF human ovum and prohibits its destruction if it develops over a thirty-six hour period. LA. REV. STAT. ANN. § 129 (West Supp. 1990).

135. *See Davis,* No. E-14496 at 20. *See also* WASH. POST, Sept. 22, 1989, at A13 (discussing Judge Young's decision in *Davis* to grant Mrs. Davis custody of the seven "embryo children").

136. *Davis,* No. E-14496 at 17 n. 45.

137. *Id.* at 15.

138. *Davis v. Davis,* C/A No. 180, slip op. at 4 (Tenn. Ct. App. Sept. 13, 1990).

139. *Carey v. Population Services Int'l.,* 431 U.S. 678, 685 (1977).

140. *Davis*, C/A No. 180 at 6.

141. 842 S.W.2d 588 (Tenn. 1992), *cert. denied*, 113 S. Ct. 1259 (1993). *See* Owen, *Davis v. Davis: Establishing Guidelines for Resolving Disputes over Embryos*, 10 J. CONTEMP. HEALTH L. & POL'Y 493 (1994).

Interestingly, the Supreme Court of Israel ruled a childless woman estranged from her husband could have their frozen embryos implanted in a surrogate against the husband's wishes. Greenberg, *Israel's Court Gives Wife the Right to Embryos*, N.Y. TIMES, Sept. 13, 1996, at A10.

142. *See* Curriden, *Frozen Embryos—The New Frontier*, 75 A.B.A. J. 68 (1989) (discussing the history of *Davis* and the "embryonic" state of the law in this area). *See also* WASH. POST, Aug. 15, 1989, at A19 (discussing the trend towards using *in vitro* embryos as weapons in divorce cases).

143. Pirrie, *Re-inventing the Law of Human Life*, WALL ST. J., Sept. 26, 1989, at A26, (discussing the status and ethics of IVF research in Australia and Europe).

144. *Id.*

145. *Id.*

As many as twenty-five hundred unused embryos created for fertility treatments were destroyed in London during the summer of 1996—all consistent with the Human Fertilization and Embryology Act of 1990 directing clinics to destroy unused embryos after five years. Petrie & MacDonald, *Hume Urges Final Rite for Embryos*, THE SUNDAY TELEGRAPH, July 21, 1996, at 1.

146. Elson, *The Rights of Frozen Embryos*, TIME Mag., July 24, 1989, at 63.

147. *Id.*

148. *See* G.P. SMITH, II, THE NEW BIOLOGY, ch. 11 (1989); Noonan, *Abortion and the Catholic Church: A Summary History,* 12 NAT. L. F. 85 (1968).

149. *See generally* MAKING BABIES: THE TEST TUBE AND CHRISTIAN ETHICS (A. Nichols & T. Holgan, eds. 1984).

150. M. TOOLEY, ABORTION AND INFANTICIDE Chs. 5-7 (1983). *See* Robertson, *Rights, Symbolism and Public Policy in Fetal Tissue Transplants*, 18 HASTINGS CENTER RPT. 5 (Dec. 1988).

151. *See* Harvey, *A Brief History of Medical Ethics from the Roman Catholic Perspective*, in CATHOLIC PERSPECTIVES ON MEDICAL MORALS at 129 (E. Pellegrino, J. Langan & J. Harvey, eds. 1989).

152. Purvis, *An Early Warning System*, TIME Mag., Nov. 27, 1989, at 56.

153. *Id.*

154. Hyde, *Keeping God in the Closet: Some Thoughts on the Exorcism of Religious Values from Public Life*, 1 NOTRE DAME J.L. ETHICS & PUB. POL'Y 33, 36 (1984).

155. Reagan, *Politics and Morality are Inseparable*, 1 NOTRE DAME J.L. ETHICS & PUB. POL'Y 7 (1984).

156. *Id.* at 10. *See* J. ELLIS, AMERICAN CATHOLICISM 156 (2d ed. 1969); R. NEUHAS, THE NAKED PUBLIC SQUARE: RELIGION AND DEMOCRACY IN AMERICA (1984).

157. *See* Reagan, *supra* note 155 at 10. *But see* infra notes 201-08.

158. *See* Hyde, *supra* note 154 at 43.

159. Reagan, *supra* note 155 at 10.

160. Hyde, *supra* note 154. *See also* McCormick, *Pluralism within the Church* at 147, Dougherty, *One Church, Plural Theologies* at 169 and Leavitt, *Notes on a Catholic Vision of Pluralism* in CATHOLIC PERSPECTIVE ON MEDICAL MORALS (E. Pellegrino, et al., eds. 1989).

161. *See* J. NOWAK, R. ROTUNDA, J. YOUNG, CONSTITUTIONAL LAW 740 (2d ed. 1983). *See also* Lorio, *In Vitro Fertilization and Embryo Transfer: Fertile Areas for Litigation*, 35 SW. L.J. 973, 983 (1982).

162. *Zablocki v. Redhail*, 434 U.S. 374, 384 (1978). *See also Carey v. Population Services Int'l.*, 431 U.S. 678, 685 (1977); *Roe v. Wade*, 410 U.S. 113, 153 (1973); *Eisenstadt v. Baird*, 405 U.S. 438 (1972).

163. Lorio, *supra* note 161 at 1007-8.

164. *Id.*

165. Hafen, *The Constitutional Status of Marriage, Kinship, and Sexual Privacy–Balancing the Individual and Social Interests*, 81 MICH. L. REV. 463, 538 (1983).

166. *Roe*, 410 U.S. 113.

167. *See generally* Smith, *Through a Test Tube Darkly: Artificial Insemination and The Law*, 57 MICH. L. REV. 127 (1968).

168. *See* Smith, *Assisted Noncoital Reproduction: A Comparative Analysis*, 8 BOSTON UNIV. INT'L. L.J. 21 at n. 143 (1990).

169. *Id.* at n. 144.

See Vetri, *Reproductive Technologies and United States Law*, 37 INT'L. COMP. L.Q. 505, 520 (1988).

170. *See, e.g.*, CAL. HEALTH & SAFETY CODE § 25956(a) (West 1984); MINN. STAT. ANN. § 145.422 (West 1989).

171. Michigan statutes, for example, prohibit research on a live embryo if its life or health may be jeopardized. MICH. COMP. LAWS ANN. § 333.2685 (West 1992). *See also* MINN. STAT. ANN. § 145.422 (West 1989).

172. Andrews, *The Stork Market: The Law of the New Reproduction Technologies*, 70 A.B.A. J. 50, 54-55 (1984). Blumberg, *Legal Issues on Nonsurgical Human Ovum Transfer*, 251 J.A.M.A. 1178 (1984); Flannery, et al., *Test Tube Babies: Legal Issues Raised by In Vitro Fertilization*, 67 GEO. L.J. 1295 (1979).

See also Comment, *In Vitro Fertilization: Insurance and Consumer Protection*, 109 HARV. L. REV. 2092 (1996).

173. 18 PA. STAT. ANN. § 3213(e) (Purdon 1983).

174. LA. CIV. CODE ANN. arts. 129, 130 (West 1990). The U.S. Court of Appeals for the Fifth Circuit in *Margaret S. v. Edwards*, 794 F.2d 994 (5th Cir. 1986), examined the constitutionality of a Louisiana statute that provided, "no person shall experiment on an unborn child or a child born as the result of an abortion, whether the unborn child or child is alive or dead, unless the

experimentation is therapeutic to the unborn child or child." LA. REV. STAT. ANN. § 40.1299.35.13. The court held the statute unconstitutionally vague, because the distinction between experimentation and testing, or between research and practice, is virtually meaningless. *Id.* at 999.

175. *See* 18 PA. STAT. ANN. § 3212 (Purdon 1983).

176. *See* LA. REV. STAT. Civil Code, § 129 (1986).

177. *See id.* § 130.

178. *Id.*

179. *See* Andrews, *supra* note 172.

180. *See* ILL. ANN. STAT. ch. 38, para. 81-26(7) (Smith-Hurd 1989). *See* presently Ch. 720 ILL. COMP. STATS. ANN., Act 510/§12.1 (Smith-Hurd 1993).

181. *See Lifchez v. Hartigan*, 735 F.Supp. 1361 (N.D. Ill. 1990).

The only other decision involving an *in vitro* fertilization procedure was an unpublished case, *Del Zio v. Manhattan's Columbia Presbyterian Medical Center*, No. 74-3588 (S.D.N.Y., *filed* April 12, 1978), which resulted in an award of $50,000 damages to the prospective parents for emotional distress caused by the willful destruction of an embryo produced by IVF. *See* Lorio, *supra* note 161 at 996-97.

But see Kolata, *Clinics Selling Embryos Made for Adoption: Couples Can Even Pick Ancestry for $2,750*, N.Y. TIMES, Nov. 29, 1997, at 1 (reporting on this practice in New York city and particularly at the Columbia Presbyterian Medical College.

182. 45 C.F.R. §§ 46.101-124, 46.301 (1989).

183. *Id.* § 46.204(d) (1989). *See also id.* § 46.205 (1989).

184. *Id.* §§ 46.101-.211 (1985). *In vitro* fertilization is defined as "any fertilization of human ova which occurs outside the body of a female, either through admixture of donor human sperm and ova or by another means." *Id.* § 46.203(g) (1989).

185. *Id.* § 46.101(a) (1989).

186. Blumberg, *supra* note 172.

187. 45 C.F.R. § 46.203(c) (1989).

188. *Id.* §§ 46.208(a)(1)-(2) (1989).

189. *Id.* §§46.209(b)(1)-(3) (1989).

190. *See also* Abramowitz, *A Stalemate on Test-Tube Baby Research*, 14 HASTINGS CENTER RPT. 5 (1984).

191. The Bush Administration extended the prohibition on federal scientists conducting research using fetal transplants, thus effectively continuing the federal government's prohibition of scientific inquiry into and study of the new reproductive biology. *See infra* note 197.

192. Ethics Advisory Board of the Department of Health, Education, and Welfare, Report and Conclusions: H.E.W. Support of Research Involving Human In Vitro Fertilization and Embryo Transfer, 44 Fed. Reg. 35,033 (1979).

193. *See id.* at 35,057. Among these conditions were that the *in vitro* embryo (blastocyst) be sustained no longer than the implantation stage and that IVF be used only by married couples who had donated their sperm and ova. *See also* Abramowitz, *supra* note 190 at 5.

194. Krause, *Artificial Conception: Legislative Approaches,* 19 FAM. L.Q. 185, 190 (1985).

195. *See Hearings on Human Embryo Transfer, Subcommittee on Investigations and Oversight of the House Comm. on Science and Technology,* 98th Cong. 2nd Sess. 142 (1984).

196. Abramowitz, *supra* note 190.

197. Department of Health and Human Services, HHS News (Nov. 2, 1989) (discussing the continuation of a limited moratorium on federal funding of research on human fetal tissue transplants; statement by Louis W. Sullivan, M.D., Secretary of Health and Human Services).

198. *See* WASH. POST, Nov. 3, 1989, at A5 (discussing the ban on federal research on fetal-tissue due to ethical and moral issues).

199. *Id.*

200. Weekly Compilation of Presidential Documents, Jan. 25, 1993, at 87. *See* 42 U.S.C. § 289g-1 (1993).

201. J. Schwarz, *Panel Backs Funding of Embryo Research,* WASH. POST, Sept. 28, 1994, at A1.

202. W. Leary, *Clinton Rules Out Federal Money for Research on Human Embryos Created for That Purpose,* N.Y. TIMES, Dec. 3, 1994, at 8.

203. H.R. 2880, Sec. 128.

204. 142 CONG. REC. *5443 (1996).

205. *See* G. Annas et al., *The Politics of Human Embryo Research—Avoiding Ethical Gridlock,* 334 N. ENG. J. MED. 1329 (1996).

206. *Id.*

207. *Id.*

208. *Id.* at 1331.

209. *Webster v. Reproductive Health Services,* 109 S. Ct. 3040, 3079 (1989).

210. Polls show 70% of Americans believe that abortion should be a decision for women to make alone. Yet more than 50% also think the act to be inherently wrong. Cassidy, *U.S. Abortion Ruling Divides a Nation,* SUNDAY TIMES (London), July 9, 1989, at C4.

211. *Webster,* 109 S. Ct. at 3047.

212. *Id.*

213. *Id.*

214. *Id.* at 3050. Reproductive Health Service, which brought the action against the Missouri Attorney General, was not affected by the *Webster* decision because it is a private facility. Since such privately operated clinics perform 87 percent of all abortions, *Webster* will have little impact. If a clinic is, however, on public land, *Webster* would apply. Cassidy, *supra* note 210. *See also American Survey: The Fearful Politics of Abortion,* THE ECONOMIST, July 8, 1989, at 31.

215. *Webster*, 109 S. Ct. at 3050.

The viability testing provision of the statute requires physicians to determine fetal viability if the pregnant woman is more than twenty weeks pregnant. If deemed viable, the fetus may not be aborted unless its mother's life is in danger. The majority held that this provision was consistent with the exercise of a physician's professional judgment and complimentary to the state's interest in protecting human life. *Id.* at 3055.

A simple ultra sound examination can determine gestational age, fetal weight and fetal lung maturity which in turn allows a physician to determine whether a fetus is viable. Smith et al., *Assessing Gestational Age*, 33 AM. FAM. PHYSICIAN 215, 219-20 (1986).

216. *Webster,* 109 S. Ct. at 3079-85.

217. *Id.* at 3081.

218. 381 U.S. 479 (1965).

219. *Webster*, 109 S. Ct. 3083.

220. *Id.* (emphasis added).

See Schiff, *Solomonic Decisions in Egg Donation: Unscrambling the Conundrum of Legal Maternity*, 80 IOWA L. REV. 265 (1995).

221. Robertson, *Extracorporeal Embryos and the Abortion Debate*, 2 J. CONTEMP. HEALTH L. & POL'Y 53, 59-60 (1986).

222. *Id.*

223. *Id.* at 60.

224. *Id. See also* Robertson, *Procreative Liberty and the Control of Conception, Pregnancy and Childbirth*, 69 VA. L. REV. 405 (1983).

225. *Webster,* 109 S. Ct. at 3059.

226. *Id.*

227. *Id.* at 3062 (citing *Thornburgh v. American College of Obstetricians & Gynecologists*, 476 U.S. 747 (1986)).

228. *Id.*

229. *Id.* at 3061.

230. *Webster,* 109 S. Ct. at 3063.

231. *Id.* Chief Justice Rehnquist noted that the *Webster* District Court found uncontradicted medical evidence that a 20-week-old-fetus was not viable, and furthermore, that the earliest point in pregnancy where a reasonable possibility of viability exists was between 23½ to 24 weeks of gestation. *Webster*, 109 S. Ct. at 3055. However, the district court also recognized that there was a four week margin of error in determining gestational age, thus giving support for the commencement of testing at 20 weeks. 662 F. Supp. 407, 420 (W.D. Mo. 1987).

In *Roe*, which is still controlling, the Court acknowledged that viability was "usually placed" at or around seven months (or twenty-eight weeks) but on occasion may occur as early as twenty-four weeks.

232. *See generally* Smith, *Intimations of Life: Extracorporeality and the Law*, 21 GONZ. L. REV. 395 (1986).

233. 18 U.S.C. §248(a) (1994).

234. 18 U.S.C. §248(e)(5).

235. 62 FERTILITY AND STERILITY 1 S (Nov. 1994).

236. *Id.* at 418-38.

The society also suggested semen be quarantined for 180 days and be retested for the AIDS virus and that it be reexamined again two or three days prior to actual insemination; that the use of fresh semen be eliminated; that only donors under the age of fifty be accepted; that participating couples be informed of the possible adverse emotional and psychological consequences; that a proper consent form be executed by the couple or single woman; and that the confidential records of donors be certain to exclude their names from all requests from any resulting offspring. *See also* American Fertility Soc'y, *New Guidelines for the Use of Semen Donor Insemination*; 1990, 53 FERTILITY & STERILITY No. 3 at 4 S (Supp 1. 1990).

237. *See* G.P. SMITH, II, CHALLENGING FAMILY VALUES IN THE NEW SOCIETY (1996).

See also J.A. ROBERTSON, CHILDREN OF CHOICE: FREEDOM AND THE NEW REPRODUCTIVE TECHNOLOGY (1994); Fracassini, *The Regulation of Sperm Banks and Fertility Doctors: A Cry for Prophylactic Measures*, 8 J. CONTEMP. HEALTH L. & POL'Y 1, 13 *passim* (1989).

238. *Supra* note 235 at 358-68.

239. *Id.* at 678-708, 738.

240. *Id.*

241. Smith, *The Province and Function of Law, Science and Medicine: Leeways of Choice and Patterns of Discourse*, 10 U. NEW SO. WALES L.J. 103, 123 (1987).

242. Stone, *Knowledge, Survival and the Duties of Science*, 3 AM. U.L. REV. 231, 240 (1973).

243. *See generally* Delgado & Miller, *God, Galileo and Government: Toward Constitutional Protection for Scientific Inquiry* in 1 ETHICAL, LEGAL AND SOCIAL CHALLENGES TO A BRAVE NEW WORLD at 231 (G. Smith, ed. 1982).

244. *See* Nelkin, *Threats and Promises: Negotiating the Control of Research*, 107 DAEDALUS 191 (1978).

245. *See* Edwards & Sharpe, *Social Values and Research in Human Embryology*, 231 NATURE 87, 90 (1971).

246. Health Research Extension Act of 1985, Pub. L. No. 99-158, 99 Stat. 820 (1985).

247. Capron, *Bioethics on the Congressional Agenda* 19 HASTINGS CTR. RPT. 22 (1989).

248. *Id.* at 23.

249. Weiss, *Clinton Names 15 to Advisory Panel on Ethics in Human Experimentation,* WASH. POST, July 20, 1996, at A9.

250. Kirby, *Human Rights—The Challenge of The New Technology*, 60 AUST. L.J. 170, 181 (1986).

251. Posner, *The Ethics and Economics of Enforcing Contracts of Surrogate Motherhood,* 5 J. CONTEMP. HEALTH L. & POL'Y 21, 24 (1989).

252. G.P. SMITH, II, THE NEW BIOLOGY: LAW, ETHICS AND BIOTECHNOLOGY (1989).

Chapter 6

Incest and Intrafamilial Child Abuse

Incest may be defined as an "illicit sexual relationship between persons in degrees of consanguinity excluded from such relationship by socially determined regulation."[1] It occurs within three basic dyads: mother-son, father-daughter, and full siblings.[2] Incest, not cannibalism, was universally recognized as the world's first taboo.[3] Because of this, it has been suggested that incest may well "have been built into the human mechanism from the very beginning."[4] Thus, in it most basic form, incest is regarded as inbreeding.[5]

Professor Edward O. Wilson of Harvard University, regarded as the modern father of sociobiology, has cautioned that inbreeding at either the brother-sister level or parent-child level increases drastically the incidence of homozygosity and genetic defects.[6] Therefore, if any psychological barriers to incest exist or any inborn propensity that directs mating beyond the circle of closest relatives is recognized, a net reproductive biological advantage will occur. Accordingly, if all other things remain equal, those individuals either having or expressing a genetic propensity to avoid incest by whatever means will contribute more healthy offspring to the next generation than those either lacking the propensity or failing to express it.[7] Natural selection will then remain the rule rather than the exception, and the opportunity for genetic stability will be enhanced.

Studies of African baboons reveal a breeding system that virtually rules out the possibility of incest. Other apes and monkeys have also demonstrated a built-in incest taboo, though on a lesser scale. Macaque monkey mothers, for example, avoid mating with their sons, and it is believed that chimpanzees do likewise. But, interestingly, gibbons are not equally self-constrained; a gibbon father deprived of his wife will mate with his daughter and a widowed mother with her son.[8] It is far beyond the scope of this article to probe the Freud-Westermarck debate regarding whether people's desire to commit incest requires it to be prohibited, or whether it is an improper act that is naturally inhibited.[9] Instead, what is important to a contemporary study of the issue is an appreciation of the two central methodological problems inherent in any examination of incest: the heretofore limited opportunities for empirical research and the coordinate universality of the basic variables at work.[10] Because of these inherent weaknesses in any study of the subject, it will be impossible for some to accept the time-honored premise that incest is indeed disruptive, if not ruinous, to the whole of society. Such individuals will be content to show that there are already significant amounts of consensual incest activity that may well be beneficial and supportive of family cohesion,[11] and that one can, over time, adapt to the initial trauma normally associated with it.[12] These individuals advocating relaxation of incest prohibitions argue that society unwisely and unnecessarily imposes social guilt and stigma on the innocent victims of the act. "The shame they suffer is not natural guilt, but rather the effects of social banishment."[13]

Regardless of this perspective, the underlying dynamics of incest clearly illustrate that the female participant is always the victim and never the partner. Incest is child abuse and rape.[14] Parent-child incest inherently involves a "fundamental betrayal of trust,"[15] which no amount of social-psychological theorizing can explain away or render acceptable through tolerance. Simply stated, to condone or accept an abolition or relaxation of the social and legal prohibitions against incest is to invite the slow but sure dissolution of the family as the foundation of the social fiber of America, the nation's *elan vital*. While consanguineous, or same-blood, relations found in the three basic incest dyads should not be tolerated, marriages between collateral relatives of affinity (those having a relational status only by marriage) could be allowed because, as such, they are outside the bounds of the nuclear family and accordingly pose no threat to its continuation nor threaten to significantly pollute the gene pool.

To varying extents, child sexual abuse has been a part of every culture and, indeed, every generation.[16] Only within the last decade has public attention been focused on it, however.[17] Aided in no small part by investigative print and broadcast media, the degenerate and pathetic realities of some family life patterns have been publicized and found shocking.

Researchers must undertake a more sophisticated study to determine the etiology of child abuse and thereby attack the inherent reasons for its alarming development. Definitional precision must be utilized in refining existing legislation in this area and, when necessary, in drafting new remedial plans. Legal practitioners must seek to develop closer professional ties with mental health care professionals and learn to better utilize their skills and expertise when coping with the aftermath of child abuse litigation.

As observed, there is an inextricable relationship between incest and child abuse. The combined continuance of incest and intrafamilial child abuse presages the imperilment, if not collapse, of the bulwark of the social order—the family. Individuals simply must be made to understand that incest and child abuse are intolerable. Society must impose severe punishment for offenses of this nature. Of course, where possible, rehabilitation must be sought as well; if there is no effort to educate and retrain, the venomous cycle of repetition will recur. The abused, over time, become abusers themselves.

Incest as a social phenomenon can be best studied and analyzed at different cross-cultural levels. These include biological, psychological, and sociological perspectives,[18] as well as literary, canonical, and legal ones. Especially important is the literary perspective, for it is the popular literature of the day (in all its permutations) that perhaps best chronicles contemporary culture.

CROSS-CULTURAL PERSPECTIVES
Historical

While study of the origins and ends of the incest taboo is the central focus of anthropology, psychology prefers to deal with clinical studies of actual incest offenders. History takes yet a broader focus and studies the incidence of incest set within the context of world events, especially humanity's efforts to evade, ignore, challenge, and manipulate the taboo.[19] Although history shows that the incest taboo has been abrogated and sanctioned from time to time (usually very narrowly and under ascribed circumstances), such an occurrence is the exception rather than the rule.[20]

Incestuous marriages in ancient times were permitted within the royal families of several Eastern countries—notably Egypt in the fourth dynasty, 2700-2650 B.C., and Persia and Caria in the third and fourth centuries B.C., as well as Japan and Korea. After the initial introduction of consanguineous marriages in the fourth dynasty in Egypt, they emerged again in the eighteenth or sixteenth century B.C. In fact, for a period of three hundred years under the reign of the Ptolemies, royal incest was practiced with considerable fervor. It was not until Cleopatra's death (herself a wife to two full brothers) that the tradition was broken. Under subsequent Roman rule, however, the custom of sibling marriage was passed to the common people where it continued until abolished by the Emperor Diocletian in 295 A.D.[21]

In the Western world, only the Incas and the Hawaiians sanctioned incest.[22] When disclosed, incidents of incest occurring from time to time in Greece and Rome could easily "wreck a career or destroy a dynasty."[23] Prohibitions against incest became more strongly entrenched in the West with the end of the Greek and Roman empires. This was due to both the Christianization of the Western world and the Judaeo-Christian faith's abhorrence of incest.[24]

Interestingly, in certain biblical accounts, incest was not only tolerated but actually condoned. Notable here was the union of Adam and Eve, the marriages of their children, Lot's incest with his daughters, Tamar's incest with her father-in-law, Judah, and Abraham's marriage to his half-sister, Sarah.[25] These early biblical accounts of incest were justified on the grounds that they were necessary for the survival of the race.[26] With the introduction of the Mosaic laws, incest for Jews and Christians alike was condemned unequivocally.[27] Not only were past incidents of incest in the Old and New Testaments censured, but Leviticus and Deuteronomy defined its parameters narrowly and forbade its practice.[28]

Titillating Secrets and Advertising Ploys

Whether subtly or directly, the advertising industry has exploited the popular curiosity about incest. Wide use within the industry and subsequent public acceptance point clearly to the fact that "we are drawn to contemplate, for reasons ranging from titillation to revulsion, sexual acts in fiction which we would abhor, or at least avoid, or profess to avoid, in reality."[29] All too often, however, the heretofore separate worlds of the figurative and the real become ultimately indistinguishable if not merged:[30]

> What we imagine in fiction has a tendency to become what we must confront in reality. But knowledge works both ways. The impact of simply hearing a terrible secret often enough makes it first less terrible, and then less of a secret. As long as incest is hidden by the mantle of secrecy, as long as it is an unspeakable subject, it will continue to have potency far in excess of what may be necessary for the general welfare.[31]

The Literary Focus—Past and Current

Literature presents a frozen cultural time zone. Current social problems are presented and explicated. In a sense, literature incorporates the three previous approaches—anthropological, psychological and historical—used in the study of incest.[32] The critical difference in approach is to be found "in the writer's interest in incest not only as a reality, but also as a symbol, his concern with the multitude of directions in which incest points."[33]

Historically, incest abounds in Western literature. It first appeared in Homer's works, then in those of Aeschylus, and subsequently it constituted a dominant them in *OEDIPUS THE KING* by Sophocles.[34] The same consequence always attended its practice: disaster.[35]

While the literature of the Middle Ages paid scant attention to incest as a theme, the Renaissance revitalized it as a literary focus. The Neoclassical period found incest an occasional source of exposition, but the theme was always muted.[36] The Gothic works of drama and literature of the late eighteenth and early nineteenth centuries revived the theme of incestuous relationships and focused on the unconscious way in which they were consummated and the swift punishment that ensued.[37]

The literature of the Romantic period saw a continuation of incest as a literary theme. Incest often was idealized even when it was committed consciously and when it signified not only alienation and isolation but also narcissism.[38] Now, near the close of the twentieth century, it is quite obvious in retrospect that the theme of incest has thrived throughout literary history and will probably continue to thrive in the future. In some current works, the act of incest is "committed knowingly and deliberately by a couple fully aware of their blood relationship."[39]

American Themes—Faulkner's Paradigm

Incest as a literary theme pervades American literature.[40] William Faulkner realized and developed the theme in a number of his works: *ABSALOM, ABSALOM; FLAGS IN THE DESERT; THE SOUND AND THE FURY; THE WILD PALMS; KNIGHTS GAMBIT; PYLON; THE UNVANQUISHED; GO DOWN, MOSES; SANCTUARY; AS I LAY DYING;* and *MOSQUITOES*. Faulkner's pervasive use of incest in these works is as a metaphor for "the original evil . . . the Fall of man."[41] Faulkner associated incest with countless disasters—alcoholism, promiscuous behavior, catastrophic marriages, dismal and sterile lives, fratricide, exile, and suicide.[42] Although he drew from studies of incest in anthropology, psychology, and history, Faulkner appears to have gained his most important insights from literature, especially Somerset Maugham and Lord Byron in *FLAGS IN THE DUST*, Sherwood Anderson in *THE SOUND AND THE FURY* and Oscar Wilde in *SANCTUARY*.[43] Thomas Mann and Milton were also strong sources of inspiration; "Faulkner owes much to *Paradise Lost* and its concept of incest as a metaphor for the original sin."[44]

Contemporary Subplots

When literature is viewed as an expression of the "external communal psyche," contemporary society remains much as it was in the nineteenth century *vis-à-vis* the incest problem.[45] While art and its sister media have been "energized by incest," the social sciences are not of one posture in placing and evaluating it within modern society. In this regard, interdisciplinary study holds great promise for continued investigation and analysis.[46]

Current literatures also shows decisively that the family, as a structured unit, is becoming less and less structured. As for the issue of incest, deep-seated anxieties and conflicts exist and are being examined in greater depth. This study can only be of positive value, for it raises to a conscious level of discourse what has heretofore been both voluntarily and, depending on the social strictures of the day, involuntarily muted.

Language, Popular Culture, and Fairy Tales

In phrases of popular language and jokes, aversions to forbidden behavior patterns show clearly the popular distaste that the incest taboo holds. For example, unconscious linguistic triggers of revulsion are to be found in the phrase "He's old enough to be her father." While at first blush innocuous, this observation is pejorative in that it evokes the father-daughter paradigm.[47]

A multitude of folk, popular, and country-western songs address "baby" or "daddy" and lament the emotional heartache of displaced fathers and daughters.[48] Jokes also embody popular cultural attitudes toward incest. In *Mountain Mother*, the line goes, "My, Billy, your prick is bigger than Dad's!" Billy: "Yes, that's what sister always says."[49] In addition, the mountain definition of a virgin is "[a] girl who can run faster than her brother; or, a girl who has no brother."[50]

Mother-son incest incurs the "linguistic wrath" of "the most obscene and ferocious curse" in the English language (and a good number of other languages as well) with the assertion that one is a "mother-fucker." In this characterization, social and familial outrage are combined at fever pitch.[51] This is one "of the first curses learned, so potent that its occurrence can change any movie to an 'X' rating, so ferocious that no artist has ever softened it in art, and yet, it is also profoundly paradoxical."[52]

The Saga of Little Red Riding Hood

Even within the range of popular children's stories there are overtones of dominant forbidden relationships. In the tale of Little Red Riding Hood, for example, father-daughter incest is suggested.[53]

> One morning Little Red Riding Hood sets off from her mother's house to take her grandmother some cakes and wine. When she gets to the woods, she meets a wolf who asks where she's going and she tells him. She is not frightened by the wolf, in fact, at most she is maybe a little uncomfortable. The wolf tells her to linger a while and pick some flowers for grandmother and, even though she had been told earlier by her mother not to dally, she does. Meanwhile the wolf goes to the grandmother's, swallows her whole, and waits between the sheets for the next morsel—the granddaughter. She comes; they perform the famous litany about large ears, eyes, hands, and mouth, and Little Red Riding Hood is soon gobbled up. Just happening by is the good woodman; he finds the wolf in a post-prandial snooze, breaches the wolf's intumescent stomach, and safely delivers both Little Red Riding Hood and her grandmother. The connections with giving birth are clear and reinforce the sexual allegory. They fill the wolf's stomach with stones, and when he awakens he falls over and dies.[54]

Bettelheim argues that the reason this fairy tale has remained so popular over the years is, quite simply, because "it addresses the problems of a young girl's sexual initiation."[55]

The fact that the girl-child must travel from mother's house (there is no mention of father) past a wolf to whom she is attracted (surely his questions belabor the obvious, for he knows the way to grandmother's house, and if he had only wanted to eat Little Red Riding Hood he could have consumed her then) until she comes to her destination ("grand" mother's bed, complete with that wolf).[56]

Bettelheim notes that while the wolf is not the seducer (even though he does eat Little Red Riding Hood) she, herself, is "profoundly implicated," for "she gives the wolf directions, then dallies sufficiently for him to be abed before she arrives, and certainly she can't be that ingenuous about grandmother's lupine appearance."[57]

The implied moral from this story "is that Little Red Riding Hood had best be careful not to lose her 'little red cap,' her 'girdle,' her 'cestus,' to the first man she meets, because we all know who that *first* man will be. She should work together with her (grand) mother to make sure this particular wolf is kept from the door, or, more appropriately, from the bed."[58]

The mother and daughter do not work together in this fairy tale, for the wolf dispatches "the surrogate mother before the (grand) daughter can be his."[59] Since the major parties have unconsciously colluded with the wolf, the woodsman or "good father" so to speak, heretofore missing from the family, intercedes. "Rife with associations of pregnancy and birth, the wolf's stomach is cut open," and a rebirth of mother and child occurs.[60]

According to the popular version of the story, to ensure the wolf will not revive, the woodsman fills his belly with rocks. In other, unsanitized versions, however, the bad little girl must be punished.[61] "But the good woodsman belongs in the tale, for he reminds us what Little Red Riding Hood has done may be wrong, yes, but not immoral or even unexpected. Little Red Riding Hood has followed bad advice; her trust has been violated; she has not been vigilant. She will not let such careless seduction happen again."[62]

Art

It has been suggested that much of what appears in the twentieth century as horrific, poetic, literary, and artistic familial imagery was formulated initially by Francisco de Goya, 1746-1828, a Spanish artist regarded as "the master of the modern macabre."[63] His paintings, especially *Los Caprichos* and *Saturn Devouring Man*, were regarded as archetypes of horror and bizarre family romance.[64] Edvard Munch, 1863-1944, a Norwegian painter, drew upon de Goya's themes that in turn were of significance to existential philosophy. "His series of lamias, female vampires, whose bodies literally enwrap and twine around their male victims while their mouths hungrily suck the life-force from the victim, are on the surface a conscious reiteration of the *'la belle dame sans merci'* theme of romanticism. Lurking under this theme is a displacement of forbidden sexual passion."[65]

The predominant question then, as always, is, Does art merely imitate life and mirror its anxieties, frustrations and titillations, or does life imitate art?

Movies

From the 1920s to the 1950s, films dealing directly with incest were few indeed.[66] This revealed a sensitivity to the message of the cultural history of that period that could best be described as: "Incest is un-American."[67] However, from the 1960s to 1981, more than one hundred movies explored every aspect of incest in the historical setting, from *Caligula* to *Blame It on Rio*.[68] First as a book in 1955, and later as a movie, Vladimir Nabokov's *Lolita* opened pathways that had been closed for over a century.[69] Sibling incest was discarded for an in-depth analysis of father-daughter incest. In *Lolita*, innocence is demythologized and sexual indulgence becomes the watchword.[70] "Lolita has become an eponym for the sexually manipulative child, not because this was her role in the novel or film . . . but because that is the role we seem to *want* her to perform."[71]

The themes of popular culture, particularly fascination with family instability, have appeared repeatedly in subplots of television programs such as *Dynasty, Falcon Crest*, and *Dallas*. These programs complement incest taboos explored previously in afternoon "soap operas" appearing on the major television networks.[72] In 1983 NBC adapted the best selling novel *Princess Daisy* into a television movie that explored the repercussions of the molestation by a "sour-faced Englishman" of his American half-sister.[73] In 1984 ABC demystified father-daughter incest when it aired *Something about Amelia*.[74]

Given the continued public fascination with vicariously exploring social and legal taboos such as incest, future television programming is expected to pander to such interests by delivering more and more shock-oriented themes exploring these and other dark and fascinating subjects (e.g., homosexuality, lesbianism, pedophilia).

Canon Law

Nineteenth-century English religion codified, in the 1761 Book of Common Prayer, thirty types of people with whom one could not engage in sex. Although purporting to track what the scriptures forbade, the book was in reality theologically questionable, for biblical injunctions and prohibitions were indeed nothing if not irregular and inconsistent. Of those individuals listed, almost 50 percent have no genetic linkage to the individual. Consequently, the list makes little biologic sense. Equally interesting is the fact that there is no mention made of first and second cousins.[75]

Civil Law: The English Heritage

Only after 1908 did incest become recognizable as a crime in England and punishable by the civil authorities.[76] Up to this time, while accusations of incest were, if credible, sufficient to yield social ostracism for its participants, the charge of homosexuality was far more serious. Though sinful in the eyes of the Church, incest was not unspeakable and even had a fascinating vogue in the literature of the day.[77] Lady Annabella Byron's divorce action against her husband, Lord Byron, was based on allegations of Byron's homosexuality and incest with his half-sister, Augusta.[78] And Henry VIII's famous divorce from Anne Boleyn was tied to charges of treason, adultery, and her alleged incest with her brother, George, Viscount Rochford.[79]

While the penalty for conviction of homosexuality was the gallows, incest was an issue of family strife. When it was presented to the courts, they deferred to "the feeble coercion of the spiritual (i.e., ecclesiastical) court," consistent with canon law.[80] In 1813 the sentencing power of the ecclesiastical courts was limited by Parliament to six months of imprisonment.[81]

THE AMERICAN LEGAL POSITION
Civil

With the exception of Alabama, every American jurisdiction has enacted civil prohibitions against consanguineous marriages.[82] These statutes fall broadly into one of two categories: those restricting marriage between persons related within the fourth degree of consanguinity (thereby prohibiting marriages by first cousins), and those prohibiting marriage in any degree of lineal consanguinity. Since, however, union "between lineal relatives that is not covered under a general prohibition against marriage between persons with the third degree of consanguinity is not likely to occur, the unlimited nature of such statutory prohibitions is of little practical significance."[83] Although subject to wide criticism as to the justification of restrictions on marriages by first cousins, such statutory prohibitions still exist in more than half of the states.[84]

There has been a rather significant modern trend to abolish affinity restrictions. Some sixteen states restrict union between certain individuals who are related only by affinity.[85] Generally, these statutes prevent marriage of the spouse of certain lineal kin of one's spouse.[86] Nowhere in the nation, however, do there remain any prohibitions against marrying the spouse of one's nonlineal kin (e.g., the spouse of one's brother or sister).[87] Uncle-niece and aunt-nephew marriages are prohibited in eighteen states, with no explicit distinction between uncles or aunts by marriage and those by blood.[88]

In many states, incorporation by reference is the means through which respective criminal codes absorb civil consanguinity and affinity marriage prohibitions. In this way, sexual relations between parties to a void marriage are a criminal as well as a civil offense. Forty-eight states have enacted legislation criminalizing either sexual intercourse or cohabitations between a man and woman who are related, within certain degrees, to each other.[89] And in forty-six of the states, incest is a felony.[90]

Those marriages entered into in violation of affinity or consanguinity restrictions are generally regarded as void.[91] In six states, the marriages are regarded as voidable, and in another six states, they will be taken as void or voidable.[92] Most states have tempered the consequences of nullifying a marriage by legitimizing the offspring and empowering the courts of jurisdiction to grant alimony.[93] Significant deterrents still do exist but are beyond the scope of this chapter.[94]

While it has been recommended that the law distinguish "between siblings and lineal relatives, on the one hand, and collateral relatives, on the other, in deciding whether the defect renders the marriage void or voidable," a more simplified approach would be to "prohibit entirely all marriages between lineal relations and siblings and to permit all marriages between collateral relations."[95] Since such an arrangement would threaten neither the cohesiveness of the nuclear family nor the integrity of the gene pool, collateral relation marriages should be allowed.

THE GENERAL PSYCHOPATHOLOGIES OF INCEST AND CHILD ABUSE
Child Abuse—The Statistical Toll

Researchers estimate that in 1963, 150,000 children were victims of child abuse and neglect in the United States. In 1989 more than 2.4 million were suspected victims of abuse and neglect and were reported to state authorities.[96] Nonetheless, many apparently maltreated children seen by teachers, social workers, and police are not in fact reported. An estimated fifty thousand children with severe, observable injuries requiring a form of hospitalization go unreported. In fact, a 1981 study conducted by the U.S. HHS found "most abused and neglected children are not now being identified and helped."[97] Lack of substantiated evidentiary proof of the abuse and concerns of unwarranted intrusions into familial privacy generally are acknowledged as the reasons for failure to report incidents of alleged abuse or neglect.[98]

In West Yorkshire, England, the police reported that in the span of just two months in 1989, more than six hundred cases of alleged child abuse—half of which were sexual—had been referred to them and their newly formed domestic violence and child abuse unit.[99] The statistics, which were acknowledged to be perhaps "the tip of the iceberg," did not reveal the actual number of the cases of alleged abuse that resulted in children being removed from their parents' care.[100]

Scope of Abuse

Seriously harmful parental behaviors include not only sexual abuse (e.g., vaginal, anal, and oral intercourse) and sexual exploitation (e.g., child prostitution and pornography) but physical battering, endangerment and neglect, medical neglect, emotional abuse, developmental neglect, improper ethical supervision, educational neglect, and abandonment.[101] A less common, but equally serious, form of child abuse is asphyxia.[102] Of the approximately two thousand cases of sudden infant death syndrome reported in Britain each year, between 2 percent and 10 percent of these babies are thought to have died as a direct result of asphyxia or, in other words, being smothered by a parent.[103]

For the health care professional, child sexual abuse is defined as "the exposure of a child to sexual stimulation inappropriate for the child's age, level of psychosexual development, or role in the family."[104] Child abuse statutes broadly define abuse as including not only physical and sexual assault but also physical neglect and psychological abuse.[105] As will be seen, structural or definitional problems plague efforts to efficiently enforce state statutes regulating the reporting of suspected incidents of child abuse.[106]

No doubt one of the truly frightening aspects of the new found or newly surfaced interest in intrafamilial sex abuse is the revelation, as more statistical information becomes available about its practice, that the incidence of incest is increasing exponentially. Oddly, this phenomenon is occurring just at the time when both considerable interest exists to maintain the laws against incest and contrary forces are building to subvert the social and legal taboo. Thus, the central questions to be posited are, "Is this because our methods of discovery are revealing what has always been present? Or is it because once we start to learn about such behavior, we start to accept it while denying it? Could increased incidence be both the cause and the effect of curiosity?"[107]

It remains to be discovered whether or not there is a correlation between what is done and what is purportedly done, and what in fact is prohibited and what is claimed to be prohibited.[108] It is distressing to be reminded that but a few generations ago adultery was punishable by death because it was regarded to be so disruptive to the social fabric of the day that to ignore or condone it would bring about the collapse of society itself.[109] History, of course, has shown that adultery has grown in popularity. It is no longer punishable by death, and society still flourishes in spite of it.

Whether modern incest follows along the social pathway of toleration or acceptance set by adultery remains to be determined. That determination will depend on the basic acceptance of the traditional values associated with the family, nature, sex roles, society, and self.[110] It can only be hoped that the wise, humane and sophisticated majority of Americans will safeguard the fundamental integrity of the family unit and, indeed, preserve it through the continued enforcement of the laws against incest.

Incest—The Alarming Statistics

The growing frequency of incest is alarming. With father-daughter incest constituting two-thirds of all reported cases, traditional estimates of the crime place the range from one to two cases per million population. More recent studies place the figures as high as five thousand cases per million per year. One current study found the incidence of incest jumped from one case per million in the early part of the 20th century to one case per twenty today.[111] It has been estimated that familial *and* nonfamilial sexual abuse affects anywhere from between 10 percent to 30 percent of the total population.[112]

What these reports appear to be charting is not only a more accurate form of reporting but also an increase in the frequency of incest as well as more generalized forms of intrafamilial sexual abuse. In turn, what these two conclusions indicate is an apparent lessening of the vigor of the incest taboo.[113]

The General Effects of Incest

Given that the nuclear family is the bulwark of the social order, incest taboos seek to preserve that unit from social disruption and, indeed, destruction. Unrestricted sexual impulses are of such a nature that if unabated they would be "socially disruptive" to the very fundamental bonds of kinship (within the nuclear family) on which all social development is built.[114] Accordingly, if incest were allowed, not only would the family unit collapse but so too would the kinship system and thereafter the entire social order.[115]

It is a part of human nature to find sexual attractiveness within the family.[116] Indeed, Freud's basic assumption was that this sexual attraction between males and females is "omnipresent" and, if not held in check, totally destructive. Thus, "if incest is not prohibited, it will be the rule."[117] One popular television commentator, Phil Donahue, acknowledged that the natural, sexual "feelings" (or primal force of love) that exist among parents and children "must be lived with *and* repressed; otherwise, it might occur."[118]

Even though a good number of adults may well have occasional erotic thoughts involving their children under the age of eighteen years, current research reveals that only from 1 percent to 5 percent fulfill those urges.[119] Currently, although ninety percent of those offenders are men, it is thought that the number of female perpetrators, when discovered, will be quite high as well—principally because females traditionally have far greater and closer access to children than males.[120]

Initially most incidents of sex abuse are confined to "fondling and undressing."[121] Over time, however, these incidents may escalate. While at first "a father may turn to his daughter one night for affection, and find himself with his hand on her panties, over time he may have intercourse with her, her sisters, and other children."[122] Recently, an Atlanta-based psychiatrist released a controversial study of approximately six hundred offenders and found that "the average number of hands-on offenses committed against boys was 281 times outside the home, plus another 78 times inside the home. The median number of offenses, however, was 10.1 outside plus 5.2 inside; some of his sample had committed phenomenal numbers of offenses."[123]

Maternal-Neonatal Incest

Although overt sexual abuse of newborn infants is rarely reported and the etiology incidence is thus unavailable for evaluation,[124] the Perinatal Center for Chemical Dependence of the Northwestern Memorial Hospital of Northwestern University's Medical School in Chicago, Illinois, in an effort to provide a comprehensive care program for chemically addicted women and their infants, has discovered both interesting and alarming data about this current area of concern.[125]

From group therapy sessions with twenty-five women in its first program conducted in 1983, the Center found that incestuous maternal-neonatal activity was motivated primarily by either loneliness, recent alienation from sexual partners, or long-term isolation from peers and family, along with a chemically dependent "borderline" personality.[126] The cases studied in depth reveal that the definitive factors predisposing a woman to abuse her child sexually remain unknown or inconclusive at best and "seem to indicate that social alienation and isolation of the mothers, common characteristics of substance abusers in general, were significant facts in the molestation of their newborn infants."[127] Sadly, the long range and more devastating effect of these maternal patterns of conduct may appear later in childhood with the consequence being that today's molested child could be predisposed easily to become tomorrow's molester[128] and remain damaged psychologically for life.[129]

Behavioral Modifications

The psychopathology of the victims of child abuse includes pain of all dimensions: depression, suicidal tendencies and actual attempts, eating disorders, drug and alcohol dependencies, prostitution, multiple personalities, and a host of other problems and disorders.[130] For the child who has been assaulted only once, his or her behavioral changes parallel to a large degree those arising from other psychic trauma. There is increased parental clinging, withdrawal from social activities, refusal to leave the home, crying, disturbances in sleep, and school phobias.[131]

Long-term chronic molestation produces a different symptomology and is the most prevalent type of incest. In such cases, the child must develop coping strategies since his or her daily survival will oftentimes depend upon this very mechanism. What is thus seen is "a greater tendency to identify with the aggressor, and to internalize the type of behavior of which the child has been a victim."[132] The child's symptoms will include depression, precocious sexual knowledge, pseudomaturity, sexual advances toward adults and other children, rolereversal with adults, and acting-out behaviors. As indicated, this symptomology is most commonly found in cases of incest where tender and innocent appearing gestures of affection precede greater degrees of intimacy and subsequent digital or coital intrusion.[133]

Research regarding the long-term harmfulness of incest remains inconsistent. Some studies show the individual consequences to victimized daughters or sons to be serious, producing long-term psychosexual consequences to their lifetime development.[134] Others reach the conclusion that not all incestuous relationships are traumatic to the participating children,[135] and furthermore that they may be more stabilizing to some familial relationships than disruptive of them.[136]

Genetic Repercussions

When consummated with issue, consanguineous relationships also raise a problem as to the genetic integrity of the offspring.[137] It is recognized generally that parents who are related closely, genetically, and have inherited a pair of mutual recessive genes associated either with congenital abnormalities or malformations or even lesser mental and physical fitness, are more likely than unrelated parents to pass those negative genes on to their children. Indeed, as a group, the offspring of incestuous relationships more often than not find themselves placed within a group that is physically or mentally handicapped.[138]

No doubt the most striking observable consequence of inbreeding is the reduction of both reproductive capacity and physiological efficiency, a phenomenon termed "inbreeding depression." This phenomenon has been investigated in several animals using different variables of reproductive capacity as well as physiological efficiency. Results from these studies have shown that in cattle, there is a 3.2 percent decrease in milk yield per 10 percent increase in the coefficient of inbreeding; in pigs, a 4.6 percent decrease in the litter size together with a 2.7 percent decrease in weight; in sheep, a 5.5 percent decrease in fleece weight and a body weight decrease of 3.7 percent; in poultry, a 6.2 percent decrease in egg production and 6.4% decrease in hatchability; and in mice, an 8 percent decrease in the litter size per 10 percent increase in the inbreeding coefficient. From this information, the conclusion emerges that, since inbreeding has a tendency to reduce fitness, "natural selection is likely to oppose the inbreeding process by favoring the least homozygous individuals."[139] It has also been shown that "if a trait (e.g., size, intelligence, or motor skill) possesses a degree of heritability, then inbreeding will cause a decline of the trait in the population."[140] Accordingly, the conclusion to be drawn here is that incest inescapably harms higher organisms.

Studies of inbreeding in humans point decisively to the deleterious effect incest has upon the gene pool by the introduction and propagation of detrimental mutations into it.[141] Mental retardation and other severe disabilities (e.g., seizure disorders, cerebral palsy) together with high child mortality percentages, have been common for the progeny of incestuous relationships.[142]

For all of these disadvantages accruing from incest, certain advantages are recognized by biologists and anthropologists. Perhaps the primary one is that with inbreeding, more of the parental genes (assuming for the strength of the gene pool they are positive) will be transmitted to the offspring. Second, kinship altruism will be promoted within the social "family" unit. From relatedness comes a familiarity that, in the animal kingdom, allows for "assortative mating," whereby the animal preference for familiar partners for mating is given validity. Thus, the genetic gamble of mating with a stranger is lessened.[143] Finally, because inbreeding reduces competition among siblings and relatives for mates, this is regarded as another positive effect of incestuous relations.[144]

Yet, even with these advantages, recent research has confirmed convincingly that in most, if not all, of the animal species, incest is either avoided or prevented.[145] The reason for this avoidance by most plants and animals alike is that such inbreeding increases homozygosity that, in itself, runs counter to Mendelian laws of heredity and plays havoc with the maintenance of genetic diversity.[146] For humans, perhaps the simplest reason for maintaining the social and legal prohibitions against incest is that they in turn preserve the family unit, the coordinate kinship system and, indeed, the whole of society.[147]

The Free Sex Movement and Unorthodox Permissiveness

Children are thought by some to be innately sexual. A commonly held belief arising from that position is that repression of such an interest, or of sexuality itself, later breeds psychological damage, producing neurotic and malfunctioning adults.[148] The distressing condonation of these and other excessively liberal ideas by a formalized group that propounds them first appeared in the United States with the founding of the Rene Guyon Society in 1962.[149] This group advocates child-child and child-adult bisexuality starting at age four, five, or six, provided protected sex is available and used through contraceptives. Their appalling slogan is "Sex before eight before it's too late."[150]

A similar organization in America is the Childhood Sensuality Circle whose central focus is to work for acceptance of a child's sexual bill of rights. This bill of rights would stress the child's right to privacy and personal exploration, a coordinate right not only to accurate sexual information but also to "sensual pleasure and choice of sex partner; the right to learn the act of love and grow mentally, spiritually and emotionally and physically as a free uncrippled happy person."[151]

The type of unorthodox permissiveness advocated by these two groups, even in a democratic society, must be held in check and monitored carefully. The undercurrents of their messages promote a licentiousness that, if accepted, could not only lead to the total destruction of any type of cohesive family unit but also to irreparable social and psychological harm to its participants. Incest, pedophilia, and intrafamilial sexual abuse would become the hallmarks of all "familial" relationships and social order would be destroyed. Simply stated, fatal attractions and dangerous, forced liaisons of this nature spell total disaster.

What types of empirical proof must be given to substantiate the consequences of these perverted relationships and the proven fears and concerns to which they give rise?[152] A distracting smoke screen is constructed when it is suggested that the *real* question is a moral one and posits whether "meaningful consent can be obtained from a child."[153] This question's foundation derives from thin research suggesting that (1) children are not always appalled by sex,[154] (2) they are sometimes in fact seductive and not deserving of "the cloak of innocence,"[155] (3) a number are "highly sexed" and need "a continuous sexual outlet," and (4) they are not always the manipulated party in adult sex.[156]

The uncertainties in any research of this nature, however, even when based on limited actual observations, far outweigh the validity of the sweeping conclusions sought to be drawn from them about the morality of actual or implied consent. The law simply does not recognize a child of tender years as having the reasoned capacity to give consent to an act legally considered to be (self) abusive. Thus, until the laws are changed on this point—and a safe and informed opinion is that they will *not* in the foreseeable future be altered—society must initiate methods to identify, counsel, rehabilitate to the degree possible, and, when necessary, punish child abusers. Programs designed to "educate" the public to the positive values of intrafamilial sex simply smack of a "space cadet" mentality and are surely light years away from ever being taken seriously and supported.[157]

Since the acute and long-term psycho-noxious effects of child sexual abuse and specifically incest remain the focus of much debate,[158] what is needed to assess their effects are controlled studies of the behavior and history of children involved in such relationships and an assessment of these sexually abused individuals as they have matured into adulthood.[159] Child abuse studies and evaluations need to be specifically tied more to actual *clinical* assessments and less to empirical ones meshed in hypotheticals. Careful, retrospective reviews of records from the hospital, the mental health care center or the court are of value but must not be prioritized over the actual clinical observations.[160]

Given the state of flux in the research regarding incest and child abuse, it is apparent that no sweeping conclusions can or should be made about either the need to lessen the acceptance of incest or the preferred treatment modalities for child abusers. What is certain, however, is that both of these issues present very serious challenges to the social fabric of contemporary society.

Profiling the Child Abuser

Although there are a number of different causes for the maltreatment of children, four factors are most frequently associated with abusing parents. First and foremost is the aberrant nature of the parents' own childhoods.[161] Research studies conclude that those parents who, during their own childhoods, were nurtured aberrantly "are more likely to abuse or neglect their children than individuals who receive normal, appropriate care."[162]   Second, prior to maltreatment, early attachment problems between mother and child are likely to have existed. Well-functioning families develop a pattern of interaction that promotes a child's growth and development, thereby building a parental relationship. The abusing parent, however, did not as a child participate in such a familial environment.[163]

The third character trait exhibited among abusing parents is a tendency toward aggression in social relationships. Although little conclusive understanding exists to explain why some people are prone to violence, it may well be related to aberrant child rearing. Several studies conclude that those individuals who have developed a history of adult violence "are more likely to abuse young children than are people without such a history."[164]

Finally, the typical abusing parent is under significant levels of stress stemming from a plethora of such every day life problems as finances, health, marriage, employment, difficult or ill children, poor family interaction, and social isolation. When any number of these factors combine rather spontaneously, a connection between the level and intensity of stress and maltreatment occurs. Generally, "stress seems to increase the risk of maltreatment among individuals whom we might already consider to be at risk based on personal history, or personality traits."[165]

PROGRAMMATIC FAILURES OF CHILD ABUSE PREVENTION PROGRAMS
The Four Major Causes

Little concrete action has been undertaken by federal and state governments to develop and implement child abuse prevention programs. Those treatment programs that have been structured for known abusing or neglecting families have also been less than successful.[166] The four major problems confronting the development of such successful prevention programs are tied to society's inability to agree upon definitions of abuse or neglect. This is an especially difficult first obstacle to overcome with regard to neglect, since the term and the concept are generally left undefined by state legislative programs.[167] Physical abuse is also problematic in that it may be defined either in terms of the extent of injury, the manner of its occurrence, the intent of the person causing the injury, the likely prospect of future injury or even some combination of all these elements.[168]

> We allow parents, and others, to hit children. Abuse is "inappropriate" hitting. However, there is great variation in the types of situations considered inappropriate by people involved in the child protection system. Without a clear-cut definition of abuse, we do not know what it is that we are trying to prevent and we do not have a means of adequately assessing the effectiveness of prevention programs.[169]

Even with an acceptable definition of abuse in place, a second obstacle to an effective child abuse prevention program remains. This is a failure to develop a consensus theory of the causes of physical abuse.[170] No simple cause can be cited verifiably as *the* reason for maltreatment.[171] Regrettably, there remains little understanding of the real reasons why a particular set of parents abuse their children.[172] Absent a validated causal theory, no strong basis appears for choosing a particular set of strategies for intervention.[173]

The third difficulty encountered in the development of a strategy is targeting the at-risk population that may have the "disease."[174] While a considerable amount of research has been undertaken to identify the actual factors that can predict those parents most likely to abuse their children, these research instruments also identify a large number of at-risk parents who never do become abusers.[175] It therefore becomes necessary "to either abandon targeting effects or accept the costs of mislabeling a large number of parents."[176]

Finally, the strategist who seeks to shape and coordinate a prevention program is handicapped by a "paucity of evaluative research regarding past and current prevention programs."[177] The strategist is also faced with inescapable reality that "there is very little adequate research with that shows a reduction in child abuse or neglect as the result of *any* prevention program."[178]

The Changing Standard of Veracity for the Accuser

Over the years, the veracity of a child's allegation of sexual abuse was routinely disputed.[179] Today, however, a complete shift to the opposite extreme position has occurred. The acceptance of all child allegations of abuse as *prima facie* evidence of an act of abuse itself appears to be the reality of practice. All too often, explosive, non verifiable allegations of this nature are placed within an atmosphere reminiscent of the Salem witch-hunts and the McCarthy anti-Communist hearings.[180]

Sexual misconduct or abuse allegations made by a child, especially one between the ages of two and seven, normally lack clarity, celerity, certainty, and consistency. Simply stated, children of this age group, classified in the preoperational period of development, do not have mental structures adequate for logical or abstract thought.[181] Even with these weaknesses, a child's allegations should nonetheless be taken seriously to the extent that they form a starting point from which further and more elaborate details of the alleged misconduct may be elicited.[182]

CONSTITUTIONAL PROTECTIONS

The federal government and each of the fifty states have laws that shield social agency case files on child abuse from disclosure.[183] The crucial constitutional issue here is when an investigation into an allegation of child sexual abuse should become a criminal prosecution. When does a criminal defendant's right to disclosure of witnesses and evidence by the prosecution arise under either the Due Process Clause of the Fourteenth Amendment or under the Compulsory Process Clause? Writing for a divided majority of the Supreme Court, Justice Lewis Powell in *Pennsylvania v. Ritchie* endeavored to strike a balance between the public's valid interest in confidentiality and the rights of criminal suspects to know the evidentiary facts of the case against them. The Court held that the trial judge will review *in camera* any confidential records that the defendant requests and release any material evidence he or she finds necessary to meet the defendant's right to be fully informed.[184]

In 1988, writing for a six to two majority of the High Court, Justice Antonin Scalia ruled in *Coy v. Iowa* that a state statute's generalized presumption that a child victim of sexual abuse will suffer trauma as a result of testifying in the presence of the accused does not outweigh the right of the criminal defendant to a direct confrontation under the Sixth Amendment.[185] This right of confrontation was declared to be a "literal" or "core" right.[186] Yet, the right of a defendant to cross-examine witnesses in order to exclude statements made out of court was described as but an implied right.[187] Although she joined the majority in holding that exceptions to this core right of confrontation exist only on case-specific findings of necessity in order to advance an important public policy,[188] Justice Sandra O'Connor insisted that a broad exception should be recognized in order to "shield a child witness from the trauma of courtroom testimony."[189]

While eight justices agreed on the existence of sixth amendment guarantees of witness confrontation at trial by a defendant in *Coy*, they differed on the scope of this encounter right. Thus it remains unclear whether the *Coy* rule, as a rule of procedure duly designed to maintain the very adversary nature of the criminal proceeding, guarantees in the first instance a right to have witnesses testify at trial and, additionally, whether it applies uniformly to all testifying witnesses or instead only to some. Since the Court was unwilling to grant an absolute right of face-to-face confrontation, the states may continue to fashion legislative exceptions that can accommodate the perceived needs of children in cases of sexual abuse. To this end, exceptions to *Coy* should be guided by *Globe Newspaper Co. v. Superior Court*[190] where the Court held "the minor victim's age, psychological maturity and understanding, the nature of the crime, the desires for the victim and the interests of the parents and relatives" were factors of central importance in deciding the constitutional validity of protective legislation in this area.[191] In light of *Coy*, preexisting legislation permitting a child's testimony to be taken in a separate room and either transmitted to the courtroom via closed circuit television or be videotaped for subsequent viewing by the jury,[192] should be reconsidered with a view to its constitutional correctness.

In a five to four opinion delivered June 27, 1990, in the case of *Maryland v. Craig*, a majority of the Supreme Court held through Justice O'Connor that the face-to-face confrontation requirement of the Sixth Amendment may be dispensed with, consistent with the GLOBE newspaper standard,[193] when such action would protect the victims of alleged child abuse from trauma and the witness's testimony is otherwise assured.[194] The confrontational denial must be conditioned on the finding of necessity that such a confrontation would threaten the child accuser's welfare, that the child would be traumatized by testifying in the defendant's presence and, furthermore, that the trauma suffered by the child witness if he or she testified be more than *de minimis*.[195] Thus, a Maryland statutory scheme allowing a child witness to testify outside the courtroom via closed circuit television was sustained. In a strong dissent, Justice Scalia criticized the "interest balancing" test of the majority and instead adhered to the conviction that face-to-face confrontation with witnesses appearing at trial is an indispensable element of the Sixth Amendment's guarantee of the right to confront one's accusers.[196]

Interestingly, in 1991 the state of Virginia joined with a group of eight other states[197] (since then expanded greatly) in enacting legislation which extended the statutes of limitations for initiating civil actions against incest and childhood sexual abuse offenders.[198] Under prior Virginia law, such actions had to be initiated before the victim reached twenty years of age.[199] One proposal would have extended the deadline to age twenty-eight.[200] There is no statute of limitations on felony criminal charges, however.[201] California enacted similar legislation which took effect January 1, 1991, extending the statute of limitations in abuse cases from age nineteen to age twenty-six and in certain cases allows victims to file a civil suit at whatever age the discovery of injury is made. Accordingly, this type of suit may be filed up to three years after an adult is able to establish a connection between his or her current psychological, physical, or emotional problems and the earlier molestation.[202]

The central question confronting legislative extensions of this statute is whether allowing the statute of limitations to be recalculated in order to allow incest and child abuse survivors to sue anywhere from ten to thirty years after the fact promotes justice for the survivors or injustice for the accused.[203] The director of the National Center for Child Abuse in Virginia argues that the chances of maintaining criminal charges against offenders a number of years after the primary offense occurred are negligible. "[P]ersuading a jury to consider an old claim . . . is easier when money, rather than jail time is at stake."[204] In modern society, perhaps it is correct that "money is the way people are held accountable."[205]

Since survivors of incestuous relationships may experience severe and complicated mental (and even physical) problems later in life, it seems only equitable to allow them to seek redress for their injuries when those injuries manifest themselves.[206] Consequently, in this regard, these state efforts at procedural extensions of the statute of limitations are to be commended as yet another strong weapon in the arsenal against incest and child abuse.

GOALS AND TREATMENT STRATEGIES

Restoration of a functional family unit as a treatment goal is *not* a realistic one to pursue in cases where a more disturbed family is evidenced. Rather, more successful management goals are directed toward not only preserving the present capacity for mental growth of the incestuous daughter but also toward developing future opportunities for sustained growth. To promote these goals, successful treatment pursues steps that seek a resolution by the daughter of her conflicts over her initial disclosure of the incestuous relation and the subsequent separation of her father from the family unit. These steps include adapting to a new environment structured outside the incestuous daughter's heretofore nuclear family setting, reestablishing peer relationships for her, and improving academic performance records in school.[207]

Treatment Procedure

What is the course of treatment for the individual sexually attracted to children? Dr. Martin Malin, a sexologist in Bethesda, Maryland, who is also associated with the Johns Hopkins University Sex Disorder's Clinic, tells his patients that their treatment is like learning to speak a foreign language. "Years of therapy and drugs will never rid you of your native language. However, you can learn to speak another language—but you'll speak it with an accent." Sadly, Dr. Malin observes that the first choice of sex for the pedophile will always be children.[208] Largely because of this phenomenon, it has been suggested that as to abusive mothers, sterilization be considered as a remedy for child abuse.[209]

Most psychotherapists require special training in treating sex offenders, for it is a skill most simply do not have.[210] Individual therapy, the goal of which is to assist the patient in understanding what precipitated his aberrant behavior, may be combined with a group setting where, with other sexual offenders, a child abuser may more fully explore the full degree and consequences of individual actions.[211] During initial attempts to structure a program of therapy, the chronic compulsive molester may be confined for three to four weeks and, if having a high testosterone level, medicated with the drug Depo-Provera, which lowers the sexual drive to a level equivalent to prepubescence.[212]

Therapy may continue for one to four years or until the therapist thinks the offender is ready to be released. Because incest is a family disorder, therapy is given not only to the offender but is offered as well to the victim, the nonoffending spouse, and other siblings. Generally, the offender is removed from the home and reunited within his family *if and when* the other members of the family are comfortable with his return.[213] Family support groups, such as Parents United based in California, serve as helpful adjuncts to a sound program of therapy.[214]

While sexual abuse treatment centers set their success rate at 80 to 85 percent (and 96 percent for incest), some have questioned the accuracy of the figures.[215] A member of the Federal Bureau of Investigation has observed that the patient success or failure rate is based either on self-reporting by patients or their simply getting caught. Accordingly, some reoffended without ever getting caught.[216] For the sake of argument, even assuming a 50 percent success rate, is there any real consolation for society in knowing that half of the individuals receiving treatment will theoretically molest children again?

First-order solutions would appear to be deceptively simple, yet present a vexatious conundrum: society can choose either to continue an obviously weak program of therapy (yet hope to strengthen it) and teach the abusers how to control themselves, or incarcerate the offenders in a prison system ill-prepared to offer hope of rehabilitation. Both of these solutions appear to be negatively focused, accepting and passive. Surely there must be another approach.

A New Working Partnership—Law and Mental Health

It has been suggested that a well-qualified and experienced mental health professional can assist greatly in the legal process while also aiding the child-victim. For the health professionals to be effective, however, significant control must be ceded to them over both the investigatory and the therapeutic phases of the case. The health worker must have a broader mandate than being used as a detective. Indeed, the therapist must determine whether the alleged abuse is verifiable. Even if there is no verification, the mere existence of an allegation of sexual molestation is sufficient evidence in and of itself to signal an at-risk child and verify the need for counseling either for the family as a group or the individual members within it.[217] Therapy is thought to be more effective when two therapists work as a team—one for the child and one for the parents.[218] They, in turn, will consult with each other and, when appropriate, with other professionals such as teachers and counselors of the child.[219] After the attorneys reach a formal agreement with the therapists that memorializes the conditions of their employment and use by the lawyers, the initial task for the health professionals is to undertake a preliminary assessment of the allegations of abuse and make a recommendation regarding interim visitation.[220]

The second phase of the therapeutic assessment brings the team of therapists and family court service professionals together in a collaborative instead of adversarial relationship. To conduct a thorough assessment of the child's interests, an "ordinary" custody evaluation can take at least several months to complete. If protective measures are in place for the child, there is no real need to rush the investigation.[221]

The third phase brings the expertise of the therapists together with that of the legal profession in formulating recommendations for the disposition of the case at bar consistent with all pertinent statutory guidelines. It is at this stage that, if a determination is made that the child should have his or her own legal advocate, one is appointed. The court may, in turn, conduct hearings as to the scope of the child's interests and the best way to ensure their continuance, with the therapists testifying only as court-appointed experts or on behalf of the child.[222]

After the development and presentation of a comprehensive plan, together with an advocacy of the child's best interests, the final disposition must provide for a subsequent review hearing within six months or less and, if needed, a continuing jurisdiction by the court, with the assistance of the child's therapist, "for a sufficiently safe period of time."[223] In safeguarding the needs of a sexually abused child, the therapists must nevertheless be ever mindful that, especially as to incest, a mother may be overreacting to marginal evidence of its occurrence and displaying reactions of overprotectiveness of her child *or* excessive suspicion and vengeance toward the separated or divorced father.[224]

CONCLUSIONS

The media and expressive arts, as barometers of the communal psyche, show clearly that by many measures family stability is under increasing stress and challenge. The fascination with and study of incest reveal deep-seated anxieties regarding the unity and integrity of the family structure and the sexual links within it. Fascination should prompt serious further study of the dynamics or vectors of force at work in this area. Critical self-examination of the strengths and the weaknesses of the nuclear family is much preferred to its total destruction and the resulting lawlessness and disorder that would arise in its perilous aftermath. With the family comes a kinship system and the whole of social order.

The social stigmas and legal prohibitions against incest must continue so long as the self-examination continues. New, enforced laws against intrafamilial child abuse should go hand in hand with the continuing study of incest. Consistent with the constitutional principles of freedom of association and of contract, civil and criminal sanctions probably should be modified to allow marriages between collateral relatives. Such marital relationships present no undue threat to the cohesiveness of the nuclear family or to the genetic balance and integrity of the societal gene pool. But consanguineous marriages between lineals, especially in the three dyads of father-daughter, mother-son, and full siblings, must be condemned, disallowed, and punished. These clearly incestuous acts of inbreeding would destroy the basic foundation of the family unit and contribute significantly to weakening society's genetic profile.

Endeavoring to correct the societal problems that give rise to and promote child abuse will take more time, greater professional commitment and renewal by the legal and health care professions. To ensure success, local and state governments must create a greater financial base from which to draw. Until these three components are placed in equilibrium, corrective or implemental actions through the present system must continue. Old laws must be reanalyzed and new ones proposed to correct existing weaknesses. Definitional precision must be sought in delineating child and physical abuse and the circumstances and evidentiary proofs that will sustain convictions thereunder. Child protective systems can be only as efficient as the laws that structure them.[225]

Uppermost in any ongoing examination of child abuse should be the sad reality that abused children will be left with profound psychosocial maladjustments throughout their lives and may very well develop in later life into child abusers themselves.[226] To prevent this end, researchers must conduct more sophisticated clinical research and less empirical study to probe the etiology of child abuse and develop effective programs to combat it.

Severe punishments must be continued for wrongdoing involving child abuse. At the same time, the criminal justice system should seek to fine tune the balance of protections afforded the public's interest in safeguarding the privacy of children who have been abused already, and prevent further trauma to them while protecting the accused's right to fair standard of procedural due process when he or she is prosecuted for child abuse or incest. Indeed, one study has proven clearly that the greater the likelihood that incest offenders will be brought to trial, the greater the deterrent effect on potential violation.[227]

When punishment is in fact meted out, to the extent possible, it must be fair and embody plans for rehabilitation (if such can be hoped for realistically). Allowing greater ease in recovery of civil damages for incest and child abuse would also be a positive step. This would act as a reinforcing social benefit to both present and potential victimized plaintiffs by inviting a public reconsideration, and thus a heightened awareness, of the real plight and horror of the victims and also of where the real blame is to be fixed in tragic cases of this nature.[228]

Society cannot be held totally liable for the potential or subsequent acts of child abuse because of its failure to teach lower socioeconomic and undereducated mothers to bond with their newborns.[229] Individual values and responsibilities have to be taught and assumed in the total maturational process. The first to teach such values and responsibilities is the family, second are the schools, and third are formalized religious or ethics instructors. It is rather simpleminded, indeed, to blame society for the total breakdown in those values conducive to and promotive of child abuse. In the final analysis, it should be remembered always that individuals constitute society, and *they* must be held accountable for their *own* actions.

NOTES

1. Fortune, *Incest*, in 7 ENCYCLOPEDIA OF THE SOCIAL SCIENCES 620 (1937). *Compare* Mead, *Incest*, in 7 INT'L ENCYCLOPEDIA OF SOCIAL SCIENCES 115 (1968).

2. J. SHEPHER, INCEST: A BIOSOCIAL VIEW 28, 108 *passim* (1983). *See also* J. HERMAN, FATHER-DAUGHTER INCEST (1981).

3. R. TANNAHILL, SEX IN HISTORY 29 (1980). *See* R. RUBIN & G. BYERLY, INCEST: THE LAST TABOO (1983).

4. TANNAHILL, *supra* note 3 at 28.

5. *Id. See also* A. ELLIS THE ORIGIN AND DEVELOPMENT OF THE INCEST TABOO (1964).

6. SHEPHER, *supra* note 2 at xi. *See also* J. BECKSTROM, SOCIOBIOLOGY AND THE LAW (1985); E. WILSON, ON HUMAN NATURE (1978). Smith, Book Review, 25 J. FAM. L. 773 (1987) (reviewing J. BECKSTROM, SOCIOBIOLOGY AND THE LAW (1985)).

7. SHEPHER, *supra* note 2 at xi. *See generally* Herrnstein, *IQ and Falling Birth Rates*, ATLANTIC MONTHLY 73 (May 1989).

8. TANNAHILL, *supra* note 3 at 29.

9. SHEPHER, *supra* note 2 at 3. *See, e.g.,* S. FREUD, TOTEM AND TABOO (1931); E. WESTERMARCK, THE HISTORY OF HUMAN MARRIAGE (5th ed. 1921). *See also* K. MEISELMAN, INCEST: A PSYCHOLOGICAL STUDY OF CAUSES AND EFFECTS WITH TREATMENT

RECOMMENDATIONS (1978).

10. SHEPHER, *supra* note 2 at 4.

11. J. TWITCHELL, FORBIDDEN PARTNERS: THE INCEST TABOO IN MODERN CULTURE 15 (1987).

12. *Id.* at 16.

13. *Id.*

14. *Id.* at 17.

15. *Id.* at 18.

16. M. DE YOUNG, THE SEXUAL VICTIMIZATION OF CHILDREN (1982); J. BOSWELL, CHRISTIANITY, SOCIAL TOLERANCE, AND HOMOSEXUALITY: GAY PEOPLE IN WESTERN EUROPE FROM THE BEGINNING OF THE CHRISTIAN ERA TO THE FOURTEENTH CENTURY (1980); F. RUSH, THE BEST KEPT SECRET (1980).

17. DE YOUNG, *supra* note 16; RUSH, *supra* note 16.

18. *See* TWITCHELL, *supra* note 11 at 243; R. GREEN, SEXUAL SCIENCE AND THE LAW 155-75 (1992).

19. C. HALL, INCEST IN FAULKNER: A METAPHOR FOR THE FALL (1986).

20. *Id.* at 2.

21. *Id.* at 5.

22. *Id.* at 6.

23. *Id. See generally* BOSWELL, *supra* note 16.

24. *See* HALL, *supra* note 19, at 6.

25. *See* Gen. 2:22-25; Gen. 17:26; Gen. 37; Gen. 19:30-38. *See also* Davis, *Incest in the Bible,* 7 NEW CATHOLIC ENCYCLOPEDIA 419 (1967).

26. *See* HALL, *supra* note 19 at 6.

27. *Id.*

28. The following incestuous unions were for example prohibited: those of son and mother; of a man with the wife of his father (Lev. 18:8, Deut. 27:20), with the mother of his wife (Deut. 27:23), with his granddaughter or his wife's daughter or granddaughter (Lev. 28:10, 17), with his sister or half-sister (Lev. 28:9; Deut. 17:22; *but see* Gen. 20:12); of a nephew with his aunt (Lev. 18:12-14; Exod. 6:20); and of a man with his daughter-in-law or his sister-in-law (Lev. 18:15-16; 20-21). Penalties for incest included death (Lev. 20:11-17).

29. TWITCHELL, *supra* note 11 at 31.

30. *Id.* at 31.

31. *Id.* at 32.

32. *Id.* at 8.

33. *Id.*

34. *Id.*

35. *Id.* at 9.

36. *Id. See* M. TAYLOR, SHAKESPEARE'S DARKER PURPOSE: A QUESTION OF INCEST (1982).

37. *Id.* at 10, 195. The most popular or basic incest scenarios were to be found in Milton's PARADISE LOST. *Id.* at 80.

38. *Id.* at 10. The "poeticization" of sibling incest reached a high point of discovery and elucidation in the works of Percy Bysshe Shelley, 1792-1822. *See also* TAYLOR, *supra* note 36, at 162.

39. HALL, *supra* note 19 at 11 (referring to, among others, Somerset Maugham's THE BOOK BAG; Iris Murdoch's THE SEVERED HEAD; Robert Jeffers' TAMAR; and Thomas Mann's THE BOOK OF THE WALSUNGS).

40. TWITCHELL, *supra* note 11 at 195.

41. HALL, *supra* note 19 at 89.

42. *Id.* at 90.

43. *Id.* at 91.

44. *Id.*

45. *Id.* at 239. *See also* TWITCHELL, *supra* note 11, Ch. 4.

46. HALL, *supra* note 19, Ch. 14.

47. TWITCHELL, *supra* note 11 at 53.

48. *Id.*

49. *Id.*

50. *Id.*

51. *Id.* at 54.

52. *Id.*

53. *Id.*

54. *Id.* at 54, 55.

55. *Id.* at 55 (citing B. BETTELHEIM, THE USES OF ENCHANTMENT (1975)).

56. *Id.*

57. *Id.*

58. *Id.*

59. *Id.* at 55-56.

60. *Id.*

61. *Id.*

62. *Id.* at 56-67. Another corollary to Little Red Riding Hood is the fable of Beauty and the Beast. *Id.* at 57-59. Bettelheim interprets the moral of this story to be that sex must be experienced by the child as disgusting as long as sexual longings are attached to the parent, because only through such a negative attitude towards sex can the incest taboo, and with it the stability of the human family, remain secure. But once detached from the parent and directed to a partner of a more suitable age, in normal development, sexual longings no longer seem beastly—to the contrary, they are experienced as beautiful. *Id.* at 58 (quoting from B. BETTELHEIM, THE USES OF ENCHANTMENT (1975)).

63. TWITCHELL, *supra* note 11 at 50.

64. *Id.* at 51.

65. *Id.*

66. *Id.* at 24.

67. *Id.* at 236.

68. *Id.* at 24-26. *See* Kael, Movie Review, THE NEW YORKER, Feb. 20, 1984, at 115 (reviewing *Blame It on Rio*).

69. TWITCHELL, *supra* note 11 at 225.

70. *Id.* at 238.

71. *Id.*

72. *Id.* at 21.

73. *Id.*

74. *Id.*

75. *Id.* at 129. *See also* A TABLE OF KINDRED AND AFFINITY, wherein "whosoever are related, are forbidden in Scripture and our Laws, to marry together." *Id.* at 129. *See also* J. GOODY, THE DEVELOPMENT OF THE FAMILY AND MARRIAGE IN EUROPE at Ch. 4 and App. 3 (1983).

76. Punishment of Incest Act, 165 ENGL. REP. 451, 8 EDW. 7, c. 45 (1908). For carnal knowledge of a female, whom he knows to be his granddaughter, daughter, sister or mother, a man's punishment is imprisonment for not more than seven years. If an allegation in the indictment proves the female was under 13 years of age, the imprisonment may be for life or any shorter term. 11 (1) HALSBURY'S LAWS OF ENGLAND § 510 (1990). *See* the Criminal Justice Act of 1988 regarding other sentencing options, 12 HALSBURY's STAT. 1159 (1989). *See also* A. DIAMOND, THE EVOLUTION OF LAW AND ORDER 21 (1951).

77. L. CROMPTON, BYRON AND GREEK LOVE: HOMOPHOBIA IN 19TH CENTURY ENGLAND 223 (1985).

78. *Id.*

79. TWITCHELL, *supra* note 11 at 130-31. *See* J. RIDLEY, ELIZABETH I: THE SHREWDNESS OF VIRTUE, 19-27 (1987).

80. W. BLACKSTONE, 4 COMMENTARIES OF THE LAWS OF ENGLAND 64 (1769).

81. 23 STAT. 297, 53 GEORGE III, c. 127 (1814). Under Scottish law, theoretically, incest was punishable by hanging until 1887. L. CROMPTON, *supra* note 77 at 223 n.55.

82. L. WARDLE, C. BLAKESLEY & J. PARKER, 4 CONTEMPORARY FAMILY LAW: PRINCIPLES, POLICY AND PRACTICE §2:06 (1988).

83. *Id.*

84. *Id.* at §2:07.

85. *Id.* at §2:09.

86. *Id.*

87. *Id.*

88. *Id.* at §2:10.

89. *Id.* at §2:12.

90. *Id. See* Sklar, *The Criminal Law and the Incest Offender: A Case for Decriminalization*, 7 BULL. AM. ACAD. PSYCHIATRY & L. 69 (1979).

91. L. WARDLE, C. BLAKESLEY & J. PARKER, *supra* note 82 at §2:13.

92. *Id.*

93. *Id.*

94. *Id. See also* Ch. 16 & §2:16. *See generally* Bratt, *Incest Statutes and The Fundamental Right of Marriage: Is Oedipus Free to Marry?* 18 FAM. L.Q. 257 (1984).

95. *Id.*

96. Rich, *Child-Abuse Cases Total 2.4 Million*, Wash. Post, July 21, 1990, at A6; Besharov, *Introduction*, PROTECTING CHILDREN FROM ABUSE AND NEGLECT: POLICY AND PRACTICE 3 (D. Besharov, ed. 1988) [hereinafter PROTECTING CHILDREN]. In 1985, the figures were set at 1.9 million. Besharov, *supra.*

97. Meriwether, *Child Abuse Reporting Laws: Time for a Change*, PROTECTING CHILDREN, *supra* note 96, at 9 n.2 (referring to NATIONAL STUDY OF THE INCIDENCE AND SEVERITY OF CHILD ABUSE AND NEGLECT: STUDY FINDINGS, U.S. DEPT. OF HEALTH & HUMAN SERVICES Pub. No. (OHDSO 81-3025) at 34 (1981)).

98. *Id.* at 10. *See generally* R. GEISER, HIDDEN VICTIMS: THE SEXUAL ABUSE OF CHILDREN (1979).

See also Jones, *Reliable and Fictitious Accounts of Sexual Abuse to Children*, 2 J. INTERPERSONAL VIOLENCE 27-45 (1987).

99. Sapstead, *County's Police Receive 600 Reports Alleging Child Abuse*, THE TIMES, May 13, 1989, at 3.

100. *Id. See generally* R.A. POSNER, SEX AND REASON 395-404 (1992).

101. Besharov, *The Need to Narrow the Grounds for State Intervention*, PROTECTING CHILDREN, *supra* note 96 at 90.

102. Meadow, *ABC of Child Abuse: Suffocation*, 298 BR. MED. J. 1572 (1989).

103. *Id.*

104. Brant & Tisza, *The Sexually Misused Child*, 47 AM. J. ORTHOPSYCHIATRY 80, 81 (1977).

105. Besharov, *The Legal Aspects of Reporting Known and Suspected Cases of Child Abuse and Neglect*, 23 VILL. L. REV. 458, 473 (1978).

106. Thoenes & Pearson, *A Difficult Dilemma: Responding to Sexual Abuse Allegations in Custody and Visitation Disputes*, PROTECTING CHILDREN, *supra* note 96 at 93.

107. TWITCHELL, *supra* note 11 at 39.

108. *Id.* at 40.

109. *Id.*

110. *Id.*

111. Henderson, *Is Incest Harmful?*, 28 CAN. J. PSYCHIATRY 34 (1983). *See* Duggan, *Daughter Accuses Father of 16 Years of Incest*, WASH. POST, June 27, 1990, at 1.

112. Churchman, *Is Child Abuse a Disease?*, WASH. POST, Oct. 4, 1988, at D5.

113. Henderson, *supra* note 111.

114. SHEPHER, *supra* note 2 at 140 (explaining Malinowski's classical functional explanation of the incest theory.

115. *Id.*

116. B. MALINOWSKI, SEX AND REPRESSION IN SAVAGE SOCIETY 81-82 (1927).

117. SHEPHER, *supra* note 2 at 136.

118. *Phil Donahue Show*, CBS Network, Jan. 2, 1989. Mr. Donahue aired another program that was devoted to the problems encountered by the progeny of incest. *Sally Jessy Raphael,* ABC Network, considered problems of incest on her program of Jan. 6, 1989. On August 23, 1989, Geraldo Rivera devoted his ABC network program to the topic of surviving incest.

119. Churchman, *supra* note 112.

120. *Id.*

121. *Id.*

122. *Id.*

123. *Id.*

124. Chasnoff et al., *Maternal-Neonatal Incest*, 56 AM. J. ORTHOPSYCHIATRY 577, 578-79 (1986).

125. *Id.*

126. *Id.* at 579.

127. *Id. See also* Egeland & Vaughn, *Failure of "Bond Formation" as a Cause of Abuse, Neglect and Maltreatment*, 51 AM. J. ORTHOPSYCHIATRY 78 (1981).

128. Chasnoff et al., *supra* note 124 at 579.

129. Henderson, *supra* note 111 at 36-37; Sloane & Karpinski, *Effects of Incest on the Participants*, 12 AM. J. ORTHOPSYCHIATRY 666 (1942).

130. C. COUTOIS, HEALING THE INCEST WOUND (1988); S. BUTLER, CONSPIRACY OF SILENCE: THE TRAUMA OF INCEST (1978).

131. Bresee, et al., *Allegations of Child Sexual Abuse in Child Custody Disputes: A Therapeutic Assessment Model*, 56 AM. J. ORTHOPSYCHIATRY 560, 565 (1986).

132. *Id.* at 566.

133. *Id.*

134. COUTOIS, *supra* note 130; Henderson, *supra* note 111; Browning & Boatman, *Incest: Children at Risk,* 134 AM. J. PSYCHIATRY 69 (1977); Ferenzi, *Confusion of Tongues between Adults and the Child*, 30 INT'L J. PSYCHOANALYSIS 225, 228 (1949); Sloan & Karpinski, *supra* note 129.

135. A Massachusetts psychologist, Nicholas Groth, having tested more than three thousand sex offenders over a 22 year period, has concluded that *not* all incidents of sexual abuse are traumatic for the child participant. Churchman, *supra* note 112.

136. Henderson, *supra* note 111; Yorokoglu & Kemph, *Children Not Severely Damaged by Incest with a Parent*, 5 J. AM. ACAD. CHILD PSYCHIATRY 111 (1966). *See also* Weimer, *A Clinical Perspective on Incest*, 132 AM. J. DIS. CHILD 123 (1978).

137. G.P. SMITH, II, GENETICS, ETHICS AND THE LAW Chs. 1, 2 (1981).

138. Henderson, *supra* note 111 at 35; Nakashima & Zakus, *Incestuous Families*, 8 PEDIATRICS ANN. 300 (1979); Adams, *Incest: Genetic Considerations*, 132 AM. J. DIS. CHILD 124 (1978).

139. SHEPHER, *supra* note 2 at 90.

140. *Id.*

141. *Id. See* C. LUMSDEN & E. WILSON, PROMETHEUS FIRE (1983).

142. SHEPHER, *supra* note 2 at 92. *See also* Bashi, *Effects of Inbreeding on Cognitive Performance*, 266 NATURE 440 (1977); R. ALEXANDER, DARWINISM AND HUMAN AFFAIRS (1979).

143. SHEPHER, *supra* note 2 at 93-98.

144. *Id.* at 98.

145. *Id.* at 104.

146. *Id.* at xii, 132.

147. *Id.* at 140; B. MALINOWSKI, THE SEXUAL LIFE OF SAVAGES IN NORTH-WESTERN MELANESIA (1929).

148. Plummer, *The Paedophile's Progress: A View from Below*, PERSPECTIVES ON PAEDOPHILIA 121 (B. Taylor ed. 1981). *See generally* J. MONEY & P. TUCKER, SEXUAL SIGNATURES: ON BEING A MAN OR A WOMAN (1977).

149. Plummer, *supra* note 148.

150. *Id.*

151. *Id.* at 122. In the United Kingdom, the Paedophile Action for Liberation (P.A.L.) operated as an "outreach" support group until 1977 when its operations ceased. A successful counterpart, the Paedophile Information Exchange (P.I.E.) is still active and promotes law reform and public "education" programs. *Id.* at xi, 123.

152. SHEPHER, *supra* note 2 at 4.
See HORNER & GUYER, *Prediction, Prevention and Clinical Expertise in Child Custody Cases in Which Allegations of Child Sexual Abuse Have Been Made*, 25 FAM. L. Q. 381 (1991).

153. G. WILSON & D. COX. THE CHILD LOVERS: A STUDY OF PAEDOPHILES IN SOCIETY 129 (1983).

154. T. O'CARROLL, PAEDOPHILIA: THE RADICAL CASE 22 (1980).

155. *Id.* at 45.

156. *Id.* at 156.

157. *See supra* note 151 discussing the "education" programs in the United Kingdom.

158. Orr, *Incest* 132 AM. J. DIS. CHILD 1045 (1978).

159. Henderson, *supra* note 111 at 38.

160. De Young, *A Conceptual Model for Judging the Truthfulness of a Young Child's Allegations of Sex and Abuse*, 56 AM. J. ORTHOPSYCHIATRY 550, 555 (1986).

161. Wald & Cohen, *Preventing Child Abuse—What Will It Take?*, PROTECTING CHILDREN, *supra* note 96 at 298.

162. *Id.* at 299.

163. *Id.*

164. Wald & Cohen, *supra* note 161 at 300 n.13 (citing Altemeier et al., *Antecedents of Child Abuse*, 100 J. PEDIATRICS 823 (1982)).

165. Wald & Cohen, *supra* note 161 at 301.

166. Wald & Cohen, *supra* note 161 at 295.

167. *Id.* at 296.

168. *Id.*

169. *Id.*

170. *Id.* at 297.

171. *Id.*

172. *Id.*

173. *Id.* at 296.

174. *Id.* at 297.

175. *Id.*

176. *Id.*

177. *Id.* (emphasis added).

178. *Id. See* Younes & Besharov, Appendix, *State Child Abuse and Neglect Laws: A Comparative Analysis*, in PROTECTING CHILDREN, *supra* note 96.

179. *See* M. KENDRICK, ANATOMY OF A NIGHTMARE (1988); J. MASSON, THE ASSAULT ON TRUTH: FREUD'S SUPPRESSION OF THE SEDUCTION THEORY (1984); Yeaza, *Child-Abuse Prosecutions Prove to Be Troublesome,* Wash. Post, April 11, 1990, at A-6. *See generally* Moss, *Are the Children Lying?*, 73 A.B.A.J. 59 (1987).

180. R. UNDERWAGER & H. WAKEFIELD, SEXUAL ABUSE 59 (1985). *See also* A. Rosenfeld, *Fantasy and Reality in Patient Reports of Incest*, 40 J. CLIN. PSYCHIATRY 159 (1979).

181. De Young, *supra* note 160 at 551. *See generally* Tuerkheimer, *Convictions Through Hearsay in Child Sexual Abuse Cases: A Logical Progression Back to Square One*, 72 MARQ. L. REV. 47 (1988).

182. De Young, *supra* note 160 at 553. *But see* Avery, *The Child Abuse Witness: Potential for Secondary Victimization*, 7 CRIM. JUST. J. (1983).

For a tragic account of another incident of sexual abuse, see Cochrane, *Abused by the Experts*, NEW STATESMAN & SOCIETY 28 (June 2, 1989). *See supra* notes 130-133.

183. *Pennsylvania v. Ritchie*, 480 U.S. 39, 60 f.n. 17 (1987). *See* Besharov, *supra* note 105 at 508-12.

184. *Ritchie*, 480 U.S. at 61.

185. *Coy v. Iowa*, 487 U.S. 1012 (1988).

186. *Id.* at 1017.

187. *Id.* at 1020 (citing *Ohio v. Roberts*, 448 U.S. 56, 63-65 (1980)).

188. *See, e.g., Ohio v. Roberts*, 448 U.S. 56 (1980).

189. *Coy,* 487 U.S. 1022. *See* Bjerregaard, *Televised Testimony as an Alternative in Child Sexual*
Abuse Cases, 25 CRIM. L. BULL. 164 (1989). *See generally* CHILDREN AS WITNESSES (H. Dent & R. Flin eds. 1992).

190. 457 U.S. 596 (1982).

191. *Id.* at 607. *See* Comment, *Videotaping the Testimony of Children: Necessary Protection for the Child or Unwarranted Compromise of the Defendant's Constitutional Rights?,* 1986 UTAH L. REV. 461 (1986).

192. R. EATMAN & J. BULKEY, PROTECTING CHILD VICTIM/WITNESSES 31-36 (1986).

193. 457 U.S. 596 (1982).

194. 110 S.Ct. 3157 (1990).

195. *Id.*

196. *Id.* at 3171, 3173. On remand, the Supreme Court of Maryland reversed Craig's conviction finding that the trial court failed to make particularized determinations that were necessary to warrant issuance of an order allowing the allegedly abused six-year-old child in question to give her testimony through closed circuit television. *Craig v. State,* 588 A.2d 328 (Md. 1991). It has been suggested that *Craig* might well have overruled *Coy, sub silentio.* *See generally* Small & Schwartz, *Commentary: Policy Implications for Children's Law in the Aftermath of Maryland v. Craig,* 1 SETON HALL CONST. L.J. 109 (1990).

Finding that a child's testimony outside of a defendant's presence violates their state constitution, several states have refused to follow the finding of *Craig.* R. MNOOKIN & D.K. WEISBERG, CHILD, FAMILY AND STATE 423 (3d ed. 1995).

See generally King, *The Molested Child Witness and the Constitution: Should the Bill of Rights be Transferred into a Bill of Preferences?* 53 OHIO STATE L. J. 49 (1992).

197. Mithers, *Incest and the Law,* N.Y. Times, Oct. 21, 1990, §6, at 44, col. 2. In 1991 the states were: Alaska (ALASKA STAT. §09.10.140 (1990), *amended by* ALASKA STAT. §09.55.650 (1990)); California (CAL. CIV. PROC. CODE §340.1 (West 1982), *amended by* 1990 CAL. STAT. 1578); Colorado (COLO. REV. STAT. §18-6-401.1 (1990)); Iowa (House File 2408 §2, adding IOWA CODE ANN. §614.8A (West Supp. 1991)); Maine (14 ME. REV. STAT. ANN. §752-C (1989)); Montana (MONT. CODE ANN. §27-2-216 (1989)); New Hampshire (N.H. REV. STAT. ANN. tit. 62, Crim. Code, ch. 639 (1989)); and Washington (WASH. REV. CODE §4.16.340 (1990)). Other states with similar legislation include Connecticut, Massachusetts, Nebraska, and New Jersey.

198. Baker, *Va. Senate Considers the Trauma of Incest: Bill Giving Victims of Childhood Sexual Abuse More Time to Sue Draws Dramatic Testimony,* Wash. Post, Jan. 27, 1991, at B10. *See* Note, *Civil Incest Suits: Getting Beyond the Statute of Limitations,* 68 WASH. U.L.Q. 995 (1990).

The 1991 Virginia legislation mandated a period of ten years after the disability is lost in which to maintain an action for sexual abuse during infancy. Act of July 1, 1991, ch. 674, 1991 VA Acts. In a bold move in 1995, Virginia amended this legislation so that the action for sexual abuse during infancy or incompetency arises "when the fact of the injury and its causal connection to the sexual abuse is first communicated to the person by a licensed physician, psychologist or clinical psychologist." 2 VA. CODE ANN. §8.01-249 (1995 Cum. Supp.).

199. Under previous Virginia law, a personal injury action was to be brought within two years after the cause accrued, with minors permitted to disregard the time during which they were within the age of minority as any part of the statute of limitations. Va. Code Ann. §8.01-243 (Supp. 1990).

200. Baker, *supra* note 198 at B10.

201. *Id.*

202. CAL. CIV. PROC. CODE §340.1 (West 1995).
See Chira, Sex Abuse: The Coil and Truth of Memory, N.Y. Times, Dec. 5, 1993, at E3. *See also* Note, *Tolling the Statute of Limitations for Adult Survivors of Childhood Sexual Abuse*, 76 IOWA L. REV. 355 (1991).

203. Mithers, *supra* note 197 at 44.

204. *Id.*

205. *Id.*

206. *See* Baker, *supra* note 198 at B10.

207. Molnar & Cameron, *Incest Syndromes: Observations in a General Hospital Psychiatric Unit,* 20 CAN. PSYCHIATRIC J. 373 (1975). *But see* Comment, *Killing Daddy: Developing a Self Defense Strategy for the Abused Child*, 137 U. PA. L. REV. 1281 (1989); Solin, *Displacement of Affection in Families Following Incest Disclosure*, 56 AM. J. ORTHOPSYCHIATRY 570 (1986).

208. Churchman, *Is Child Abuse a Disease?*, WASH. POST, Oct. 4, 1988, at D5.

209. Comment, *Sterilization: A Remedy for the Malady of Child Abuse*, 5 J. CONTEMP. HEALTH L. & POL'Y 245 (1989).

210. Churchman, *supra* note 208.

211. *Id.*

212. *Id.*

213. *Id.*

214. *Id. See generally* Comment, *Killing Daddy, supra* note 207.

215. Churchman, *supra* note 208.

216. *Id.*

217. Bresee et al., *supra* note 131 at 561, 567. *See also* Myers et al., *Expert Testimony in Child Sexual Abuse Litigation*, 68 NEB. L. REV. 1 (1989).

218. Bresee et al., *supra* note 131 at 561.

219. *Id.*

220. Bresee et al., *supra* note 131 at 568.

221. *Id.* A battery of psychological tests, together with an analysis of behavioral signs observed both at home and at school, can be utilized as an effective complement to reaching a therapeutic assessment. *But see* Tuerkheimer, *supra* note 181. *See also* De Young, *supra* note 160, at 564-65.

222. Bresee et al., *supra* note 134, at 568. *See* Comment, *The Admissability of Expert Testimony in Intrafamily Child Sexual Abuse Cases*, 34 U.C.L.A. L. REV. 175 (1986).

223. Bresee et al., *supra* note 131 at 568.

224. *Id.* at 563.

225. *See supra* notes 166-84.

226. *See supra* notes 128, 129, 162, 164, 208.

See generally CHILDREN, RIGHTS AND THE LAW (P. Alston et al., eds. 1993).

227. Herman, *An Economic Analysis of Incest: Prohibitions, Behavior and Punishment*, 25 ST. LOUIS U.L.J. 735 (1982). *See also* Vachss, *How We Can Fight Child Abuse*, PARADE, Aug. 20, 1989, at 14.

228. *See* Note, *Statutes of Limitations in Civil Incest Suits: Preserving the Victim's Remedy*, 7 HARV. WOMEN'S L.J. 189 (1984).

229. *See* Comment, *Sterilization, supra* note 209. *See also* Egeland & Vaughn, *supra* note 127.

Chapter 7

Pornography and Obscenity

Today sex is packaged in every and all ways possible—from the gleeful banterings of Dr. Ruth Westheimer's about "Good Sex,"[1] through flagrant displays of revealing undergarments now worn as outer garments by such perennial teen role models as Cyndi Lauper and Madonna,[2] tightly contoured and suggestive Calvin Klein jeans,[3] on television,[4] cable,[5] the movie screen,[6] videos,[7] and in suburban boutiques.[8] No-holds-barred sensualism and extempore eroticism become the focal points for advertising and nudity—and its various degrees—an all-too-often erotic cue for lust. First, one part of the female (or male) body is uncovered and found erotic; and then another part is discovered, creating what has been referred to as "shifting erogenous zones."[9]

Living for the moment's prevailing passion[10] and for hedonistic pleasure—considered the sole object of desire—[11]threatens to be overwhelming for many.[12] Packaging sex, in all its various products, is big business. In New York City, for example, the marketing of sex as an industry is a significant part of the city's economy and a lucrative tourist attraction as well.[13] Not only does it generate business dollars and tax revenues, it employs a large number of people as well.[14] Sadly, one person's vulgarity is another's lyric.[15]

Western society has, over the years, sought to develop various standards to suppress the viewing and commercial dissemination of explicit materials.[16] The dilemma, however, remains. As much as dilemmas cry for resolution, being what they are, they resist it.[17] This is especially the case here as the quest for a "decent society" is forever balanced against the right of free expression, with the First Amendment[18] always being viewed as prescribing common sense[19] by those who seek its protection.

In 1986 Maine became the first state in the nation to conduct a referendum on whether pornography should be restricted. More specifically, the question on the ballot asked: "Do you want to make it a crime to make, sell, give for value or otherwise promote obscene material in Maine?"[20] The results revealed, by a two to one majority, that the residents of Maine did not want any restrictions placed on their right to enjoy obscene material.[21] This outcome should come as no surprise; for although a 1986 Harris poll found 41 percent of Americans support "reasonable censorship" of obscene or pornographic materials, 35 percent opposed censorship and 24 percent expressed ambivalence, or a "we don't think it matters" attitude.[22]

If, as the Surgeon General of the United States concluded in 1986, pornography is "blatantly antihuman" and poses a clear and present danger to the health of America,[23] what should be done to prevent human sexuality from descending to the level of starkness or that "of animals other than man?"[24] Modern society's ongoing debate about pornography and obscenity focuses upon several major themes or questions: the nature of the relationship between that which is considered obscene and that taken as pornographic and the standards used to delineate and judge these two. Additional concern is given to a study of the relationship between the words and images of pornography, in the broad context, with violence against women (or, stated otherwise, is pornography the theory and rape the practice), male attitudes toward women generally, child abuse, and specifically consumer desensitization where the common culture accepts violence against women as merely routine.[25]

These dynamic themes present a background for analysis of the modern dilemma of society in dealing with obscenity and pornography, and specifically the need to preserve a decent, moralistic society while guaranteeing a free right of expression, dissent and moral independence. Although laboratory studies reveal violent pornography may very well promote aggression toward women, the integrity of these conclusions in unstructured social situations is yet to be established.[26] While some caution must obviously be taken in imposing blanket restrictions on pornography, on the issue of child pornography there can be no hesitancy in eradicating its dissemination and use. The benchmark for ultimate decision making in this area of concern must forever be the standard of reasonableness which, in turn, dictates a case-by-case balancing of individual freedom of expression against the societal right to decency and moral integrity.

NUDITY: YESTERDAY, TODAY, AND TOMORROW

Insofar as recorded history is concerned, the concept of nudity belongs to the ancient Greeks and their participation in athletic competitions.[27] Those who competed in stadia did so entirely in the nude and thereby freed themselves of cumbersome garments during their competitions. Body freedom, then, was a tolerable activity for the sportsman. But this freedom almost totally vanished with the Dark Ages.[28]

For more than fifteen centuries, with one single and rather markable exception, nudity was taboo. That exception was made in 1043 by a Saxon countess, Lady Godiva, who rode naked through her husband's village to protest a levy of taxes which he had made on the local peasants.[29] Both in Europe and America, the eighteenth and nineteenth centuries were characterized by a strikingly morbid fear of nudity. Throughout the major part of the world, some form of "covering up" was mandatory. Nudity became an integral part, or at least a significant element, of public morality.[30]

In America Anthony Comstock came into power and asserted himself as a symbol of extremism in the censorship of anything pertaining to nudity. Every instance of indecency was attacked—books, plays, pictures, and some.[31] Anything approaching nudity was challenged. "He violently objected to circus posters that depicted acrobats in tights."[32] Congressional legislation embodying Comstock's personal standards of decency was passed in 1873 and was enforced substantially for eight years.[33] Under this legislation, the U.S. Post Office undertook actions that suppressed every form of nudity—even the American nudist magazine, SUNSHINE AND HEALTH, first published in 1933.[34]

During this same time frame, Church authorities in Spain, Portugal, and Italy banned nudity in every form—even in the case of young infants.[35] In England Queen Victoria established a pattern of public conservative conduct that bore her own name.[36] The concept and practice of nudity was, prior to World War I, premature at best.[37]

Nudity took hold and was nurtured after 1918—promoted in large part by the heavy poverty confronting the German nation following its defeat in the war. For the city dwellers, the countryside and the woods provided a free opportunity for swimming and frolicking *au naturel*. Sexual emotions were in no way aroused from these group activities.[38] With the gradual recovery of the nation, the ranks of the German nudist swelled to such an extent that by 1926, it was estimated some 50,000 active *Lichtfreuden* (or light friends) could be found. The idea and philosophy of nudism soon began to spread to other European countries—especially Switzerland, England, and France.[39] *Freikorperkultur* (or free body culture) is commonly thought of as being introduced into the United States in 1929 by Kurt Barthel.[40]

Tolerance and Volatility

The public response to nudity under certain prescribed conditions is today somewhat amazing in its degree of tolerance and also is volatility.[41] More and more "free" beaches where swimsuits are "optional" appear to be spreading in California and elsewhere.[42] In Austin, Texas, an apartment house was provided with a "liberated environment" where nudity was allowed in all public areas.[43] Nudist resort areas or camps are also developing and providing new dimensions for social nudism in tennis courts, teen centers, pools, jacuzzis, and so on.[44]

Yet, prudity raised its conservative head nationally with NEWSWEEK's cover of June 7, 1982, that showed a colored picture of William Bailey's, *Portrait of S.*, a frontal oil painting of a woman nude to the waist.[45] So offensive was this striking reproduction considered to be by a surprising number of people that it was banned outright in some distribution outlets, and, in Washington, D.C., the magazine was pulled from the display racks of all 131 Giant supermarkets. The cover was used to introduce the reader, assuming he so wished, to a lead story on the revival of realism in art. NEWSWEEK editor Lester Bernstein, could find nothing whatsoever of any pornographic nature in the cover.[46] Above the reproduction on the cover was the line, "Art Imitates Life–The Revival of Realism." Mr. Bernstein observed, "I thought this was 1982." He continued, "[T]his just tells you that there are a lot more people around who haven't been inside a museum than you might expect. I expected that there might be some objections, but I felt that it was a beautiful painting illustrating a distinguished article of art criticism. Any different view of it is in the eye of the beholder."[47]

In trying to discern why there was such an uproar over the cover, Meg Greenfield opined that it very probably was due in large part to the "women's movement" that has insisted as of late "that the female body—its appearance, reality and workings—not be regarded as either (1) fit subject only for cheesecake reveries or (2) a collection of vaguely disgusting glands and functions not to be contemplated by polluted society."[48] Decrying this false perception of the liberationist contemporary society, Ms. Greenfield observed that today there are practically no limitations on what society will purvey to the public.[49] The new candor of the day tolerates "[a]dvertisements . . . [that] prey fairly explicitly on unspeakable instincts having to do with adult lust for children and . . . for fooling around in groups of more or less than two."[50] Continuing in her analysis of the openness of today's society, she comments, "[T]he women on some of those daytime call-in shows and the articles in some of those ancient mass-circulation homemakers' magazines deal overtly and clinically in sexual desires and practices in a way that would make the cover female on NEWSWEEK blush."[51] Finally, she concludes, with sage wisdom, that "[w]e will put up with the distant, the alien, the exotic and, yes, the present-day kinky. It's the rest that unnerves us. *Reality has become the last dirty picture.*"[52]

Female and Male Erotica

There is, rather obviously, a significant number of women who are attracted to male erotica and who frequent male "strip" clubs of the Chippendale vintage.[53] Originally chartered in West Los Angeles, Chippendales now has an outlet in New York and allows women to visit in a cocktail lounge atmosphere and be served and entertained by young bare-chested men, wearing white collars and cuffs and black tights and boots. This attire is exchanged for more revealing costumes during the entertainment or floor show.[54] Many of the emancipated women of today have shown their freedom and attitudes regarding sexuality by developing popular male magazines. PLAYGIRL is perhaps the most popular women's magazine that shows men in nude and often suggestive poses—designed obviously to either titillate or to entertain.

To live in contemporary society, then, is to submit oneself to a "cult of physical perfection and desirability."[55] Indeed, to live in the 90's is to be subjected to "a blizzard of images of human nudity, of semi-nudity, of pretty girls in uplifting bras, of all-boy bands in tight pants of languid androgynes advertising unisex perfumes."[56] Nudity, in the same instance, titillates, amuses, destructs, or confuses, for nudes are always "about" something. Their meanings go beyond straightforward depictions of the human body.[57] Personal "hang-ups"—more than philosophical convictions—all too often create what the British author, John Cleese, terms "a great fear of being carried away, of losing control, not being able to put the brakes on."[58] Put simply, people cannot handle pleasure. Thus, heavy sexual context is far too often read into images that are totally incorrect.[59] The *implications* of nudity, in the final analysis, become the determinants of social outcrys for government regulation. The image of a man or woman showering alone is thought acceptable. When soap is added and the single images wash their private parts, with voice-overs suggesting how pleasurable the soap feels, sexual arousal is suggested.[60]

In France displays of attractive female nudes are not taken as either pornographic or as a form of exploitation of women. Rather, the beauty of the human body is not regarded as a means by which men oppress women; rather, it is the way that women assert their power over men.[61]

Fears of Sexual Emotions

This "fear of being carried away" by one's sexual emotions when being exposed to erotic displays of nudity has been validated legally by what is termed the principle of secondary effects.[62] Not only has criminal activity been found to be associated with areas where pornographic adult is conducted,[63] but, more particularly, it has given rise to secondary effects such as "prostitution, sexual assault and associated crimes."[64] Nude dancing, for example, carries an "erotic message" and "is likely to produce the same pernicious secondary effects as the adult films displaying 'specified anatomical areas.'"[65] Indeed, the U.S. Supreme Court has found a correlation with nude dancing and "other evils" thereby justifying recognition of the very principle of secondary effects.[66]

Most Americans have, during their formative years, cognitively allied nudity and sex and, indeed, a learned association between the two has built up.[67] Undeniably, sex is but a normal part of life.[68] Nudism is, however, neither a cult nor a religion nor exhibitionism. Rather, it should be viewed properly as but healthy-mindedness with respect for the human body and human relationships.[69]

Sadly, popular and ingrained ideas hold that there is something not only wicked and daring but also thrilling in viewing the exposed body of a member of the opposite sex.[70] Sensations arise that have nothing to do with the body itself.

If this were not so, classical statues could be taken as producing the same effect. In the normal and intelligent person, these sensual feelings are dispersed immediately and nudity is thus properly regarded in a plain and common light.[71] Accordingly, obscenity should be viewed correctly as but

> an attitude or predisposition of the viewing and accusing mind which is only delusionally read into, or ascribed to that which is accused of being obscene. The emotional intensity which accompanies our accusations is an exact measure of our personal guilt—often unconscious over similar past offense committed by us, or over some suppressed or perhaps craving to indulge in the condemned act. . . . *Every passionate accusation is at the same time a confession.*[72]

THE EARLY AND ENDURING PRINCIPLES

Certain ancient perennial principles lay at the core of constitutional governance in the United States.[73] Perhaps the most controlling of these principles is the recognition of mankind's "fallen human nature"[74] and the coordinate need to be guided by "republican virtue" if survival of this form of governance is to be assured.[75] The society structured during the period of the nation's founding, thus recognized limitations on "lewdness" or "public indecency" simply because such acts would, it was believed, threaten the very core of a virtuous society.[76] In adopting the common law that criminalized public indecency, the willful exposure of obscene print, and what was termed "grossly scandalous affairs," the Founders went on record as being opposed to all forms of "open and notorious lewdness."[77] And, interestingly, this same generation witnessed the passage by the federal government and the states of not only the Fourteenth Amendment to the Constitution, but also, at the federal level, the Comstock Act. As noted previously, the Comstock Act assessed criminal liability for the use of the mails to distribute or promote "obscene, lewd, lascivious, indecent, filthy or vile articles."[78] Thus, it is seen historically that

> *some* control of speech by government, certainly on the state level, was entirely consistent with the common law and the political theory of the Founders' generation, as well as with the actual language of the First Amendment. This is true whether the focus be the role of criminal law in maintaining public decency, the Founders' concern about responsible or virtuous use of freedom, or the unique brand of federalism they created.[79]

Because of the dynamic role that faith and religion have played in the political life of the United States, politics and morality have, indeed, become inseparable.[80] The very commitment of the United States to pluralism is both nurtured and sustained as a result of a firm insistence on a continuing recognition of the inviolability of individual conscience.[81] Thus, if efforts were successful in excluding societal values that are regarded as inherently religious in their core, from the public arena, a serious threat would be made to the very principle of pluralism itself.[82]

Popular Culture

Although popular comment admits that one can never legislate morality,[83] and that private immorality harms no one[84] other than perhaps those participating in it, in reality it is postured that the very nature of the existence of society is threatened by such acts.[85] The reason given for this position is that society comprises not only a community of political ideas but moral ideas as well. Consequently, while "not every deviation from society's stated morals threatens its existence, every such deviation is at least capable of such a threat, and so cannot be put beyond the law."[86] Accordingly, the spread of pornography threatens the Constitution in that it allows disorder to spread among individual lives to such an extent that society becomes morally corrupted, wounded, and possibly even endangered.[87] "Every human organization has an inner life of shared purpose and values, and if too many of its members reject those purposes and discard those values, the inner life is shattered. In other words, when a critical mass of citizens who reject society's beliefs and norms develops, that society falls apart."[88]

The central inquiry for the committed conservative is: what happens to the political character of young men and women who, over many years, indulge themselves "without inhibition, in today's hard-core, animalistic, predatory pornography?"[89] If good character is acknowledged as the well-spring of rightful conduct, then moral sensibility must be structured by objective standards of truth.[90]

> Moral sensibility is composed of many elements, including a person's conscious values, his sense of respect for other persons, his ease in setting aside present comfort for future reward, his sense of right and wrong, and the degree of his commitment to honor and decency. It includes conscious principles, half-conscious attitudes and beliefs, and subconscious feelings. Moral sensibility is the psychic and intellectual bases for character.[91]

A Right of Moral Independence

One strategy of analysis acknowledges that even if a community were to be made worse off as a consequence of a failure to censor pornography, it is still inherently wrong to either censor or, for that matter, restrict its use or dessimation simply because such a restriction "violates the individual moral or political rights of citizens who resent the censorship."[92] The only justification, then, for suppressing pornography is when it harms someone.[93] Harm can either be taken as a form of direct physical damages to particular individuals, or injury to their property or financial interests, or broadened to include mental distress or annoyance, or even damage to the general cultural environment.[94] If the general value of free expression is recognized, it has been argued that "a presumption [should be made] against censorship or prohibition of any activity when that activity even arguably expresses a conviction about how people should live or feel, or opposes established or popular convictions."[95] This presumption would not have to be recognized as absolute and might well be overcome by a direct showing that "the harm the activity threatens is grave probable, and uncontroversial."[96] Such a presumption should, however, be strong if it is to protect adequately the long term goal of guaranteeing the best conditions for human development.[97]

Professor Ronald Dworkin opines that the inherent or pivotal issue in any analysis of pornography is a structuring of a right of moral independence and its recognition as such.[98]   "The right of moral independence is part of the same collection of rights as the right of political independence, and it is to be justified as a trump over an unrestricted utilitarian defense of prohibitory laws against pornography, in a community of those who find offense just in the idea that their neighbors are reading dirty books."[99] The right is not derived as a consequence of the recognition of a general right to liberty but rather as the consequences of equality,[100] and its application is tied to a fundamental balancing process that weights constraints on individual liberty against gains to others of such a restriction.[101]

The Neoconservative Attitude

The "New Right," led by Robert H. Bork, endeavors to reduce all claims and assertions for morality to a more central claim for "gratification."[102] Thus, when clashes occur between a majoritarian assertion of power to regulate—here, pornography—and a counterassertion of minority interests for freedom of ideas and dissemination of them, it is to be regarded as but a clash between two competing groups, each of which seeks the gratification of certain needs, values or interests.[103] Essentially, any want that people have, to that degree of wanting, has some social value.[104]

Judge Bork recognizes First Amendment protections for political speech that are within the bounds of established order. He does not extend those protections to either academic or literary expression or any other forms.[105] Chief Justice William H. Rehnquist is a close philosophical companion with the judge when he acknowledges that personal moral judgments are just that—*personal*—until they are given, in some form or other, a legal sanction.[106] Finally, Chief Judge Richard A. Posner of the U.S. Seventh Circuit Court of Appeals, in responding to his contemporary judicial understanding of "value judgments," acknowledges that many judicial decisions are based on value judgments instead of being grounded in technical evidentiary proofs, and thus not readily verifiable. Consequently, such determinations "are not always profitably discuss[ed]."[107] It is maintained that because these theorists of the New Right seek to reduce rights claims to demands for gratification, distinctions between moral reasons and arbitrary preferences are destroyed.[108] Accordingly, the assertion is that "[i]n telling the majority, those with the strength of numbers, that morality may be ignored (because moral reasons are mere preferences), the New Right calls upon what is worst, not what is best, in the public."[109]

Justice Antonin Scalia finds the noble middle ground in this dilemma and articulates it eloquently when he acknowledges that

> to say that there is a moral obligation to achieve a particular distributive result is not to say that government must undertake the function. And, conversely, to say that distributive justice is a purely moral matter is not to say that government cannot undertake the function. We are left with the usual problem of political choice. Moral perceptions are . . . relevant to that choice. We are more likely to pursue those moral perceptions we feel strongly about.[110]

A classic exercise of the police power is to be found in the state's interest in promoting "morality"—including sexual morality. The dissent by Mr. Justice John Marshall Harlan in *Poe v. Ullman* speaks to this power:

> The very inclusion of the category of morality among state concerns indicates that society is not limited in its objects only to the physical well-being of the community, but has traditionally concerned itself with the moral soundness of its people as well. Indeed to attempt a line between public behavior and that which is purely consensual or solitary would be to withdraw from community concern a range of subjects with which every society in civilized times has found it necessary to deal.[111]

Nor may privacy be considered a mask for actions termed by the state to be immoral.[112]

OBSCENITY VERSUS PORNOGRAPHY

Throughout most of the history of American law, no clear standards for governing obscenity and pornography have been evident.[113]   Indeed, the development of obscenity law "has proceeded with a mixture of moralism and paternalism,"[114] and some have maintained "that the only rational for most obscenity laws is the belief that the government should protect public morals."[115]

Although the terms "*obscenity*" and "*pornography*" have all too often been used interchangeably,[116] there is a proper distinction between these two words. The OXFORD ENGLISH DICTIONARY defines "obscene" as that which is "abominable, disgusting, filthy, indecent, loathsome or repulsive."[117] An obscene act is one that is "offensive to the senses," and expresses or suggests "lewd, unchaste or lustful ideas."[118] "Pornography" is defined as a description of the life activities of prostitutes and their patrons and "the expression or suggestion of obscene or unchaste subjects in literature or art."[119]   And, "sexual appetite" or "desire" is defined accordingly as "a libidinous desire, degrading animal passion."[120]   "Nudity" is simply "the condition or fact of being naked or nude" with the "privy parts" being exposed.[121]

Placing obscenity within contemporary context, Irving Kristol has observed that "[o]bscenity is not merely about sex, any more than science fiction is about science. . . . Obscenity is a peculiar vision of humanity: what it is really about is ethics and metaphysics."[122]

Pornography is regarded as "inherently and purposefully subversive of civilization,"[123] this being the case because it has been shown in some controlled studies that when violent images saturate the minds of the young and impressionable, a number of them are predisposed to violent actions.[124]

In 1896, in *Swearingen v. United States,*[125] obscenity was defined in terms of "sexual impurity" by the U.S. Supreme Court—with the emphasis on sexual and pornographic aspects of the questioned material still permeating definitional inquiries today.[126]   Until 1957, however, the basic legal definition in American courts continued to be that derived from *Queen v. Hicklin.*[127]   *Hicklin* established the test as "whether the tendency of the matter charged a obscenity is to deprave and corrupt those whose minds are open to such immoral influences, and into whose hands a publication of this sort may fall."[128]

Coming of Age

Before *Roth v. United States*[129] in 1957, the obscenity laws were challenged rarely on constitutional grounds.[130]   In *Roth* the High Court reaffirmed its conclusion that "obscenity is of within the area of constitutionally protected speech or press."[131]   More specifically, the Court determined that "sex and obscenity were not synonymous. Obscene material is material that deals with sex in a manner appealing to prurient interest," that is to say, "the material ha[s] a tendency to excite lustful thoughts."[132]   During the 1950s and 1960s that heralded the so-called sexual revolution, criminal prosecutions and constitutional challenges thereto of cases designed to stop the production and distribution of sexually explicit and potentially offensive materials were seen in considerable numbers.[133]   In the ten years that followed *Roth*, a three-part test was developed by the Supreme Court in *Memoirs v. Massachusetts*[134] and was recognized as ushering in an era of minimal regulation of obscenity.[135]

The Supreme Court handed down eight obscenity decisions in 1973 that structured a new and stronger framework for regulating obscenity.[136]   In *Miller v. California,*[137] the Court retained the first element of the basic three-prong test in *Memoirs v. Massachusetts,*[138] and thereby sought to test "whether the average person, applying contemporary community standards' would find that the work, taken as a whole, appeals to the prurient interest [in sex]."[139]   It was with the second and third prongs of the obscenity test that changes were made.

Under *Roth* and *Memoirs*, the concern was to test whether "the material is patently offensive because it affronts contemporary community standards relating to the description or representation of sexual matters."[140] However, under *Miller*, the new inquiry was "whether the work depicts or describes, in a patently offensive way, sexual conduct specifically defined by the applicable state law."[141] Under *Roth* and *Memoirs*, the third test was undertaken to determine whether the work in question was devoid of "redeeming social value."[142] *Miller's* third test or prong was reshaped in order to assess "whether the work, taken as a whole, lacks serious literary, artistic, political, or scientific value."[143] This newly formulated test would allow "fair notice" to those dealing in "materials depict[ing] or describ[ing] patently offensive hard core sexual conduct specifically defined by the regulating state law."[144]

The Court then proceeded to define with specificity the type of sexual conduct that could be regulated by the states: "patently offensive representations or descriptions of ultimate sexual acts, normal or perverted, actual or simulated" and "patently offensive representations or descriptions of masturbation, excretory functions, and lewd exhibition of the genitals."[145] The Court emphasized that these specific examples neither limited nor served as a substitute for state legislative efforts in this area, but rather only as examples of conduct that could be regulated by the state.[146]

Chief Justice Burger took the occasion in *Paris Adult Theatre I v. Slaton*[147] to underscore the authority of the states to regulate obscene material by acknowledging their power "to make a morally neutral judgment that public exhibition of obscene material, or commerce in such material, has a tendency to injure the community as whole, to endanger the public safety, or to jeopardize, in Mr. Chief Justice Warren's words, 'the States' right . . . to maintain a decent society."[148] The courts have, generally, sought to classify pornography by use of the legal terms *obscenity* and *indecency*.[149]

Means of Dissemination

The Supreme Court has never made a distinction between different means of disseminating obscenity, and, therefore, has clearly established that obscenity disseminated by *any* means is not protected.[150] Unresolved constitutional questions remain concerning the regulation of indecent, but not obscene, material over media that are pervasive and easily accessible to children, such as telephone, cable television, computers, and videocassettes.[151]

It was not until *F.C.C. v. Pacifica*[152] that the U.S. Supreme Court dealt with the issue of regulating obscenity over the airwaves. Here, the Federal Communications Commission (FCC) was firmly empowered to regulate indecent, yet nonobscene, broadcasts over both radio and television; it being determined that a radio monologue titled "Filthy Words," presented by George Carlin, had been presented in a patently offensive manner.[153] One major thrust of the decision was to assure a level of protection for children from being exposed to either profane or indecent material through a medium that was readily accessible to them.[154]

In 1983, with its decision in *New York v. Ferber*,[155] the Supreme Court again showed its intent in protecting children from the pervasive and degenerative effects of pornography by upholding a New York State legislative prohibition on child pornography *without* proof of obscenity.[156] In *Ferber,* unlike *Pacifica*, children were afforded protection by a prosecution on the dissemination of child pornography because the material constituted not only acts of sexual abuse of children in progress, but because the pictures, once created, presented a very real and continuing potential for mental and emotional injury, and even blackmail.[157]

THE SCIENTIFIC RESEARCH ON SEXUAL AROUSAL

A significant body of research exists that both studies and documents the immediate effects of pornography and the effect of nudity as an erotic cue.[158] The purpose of this section of the chapter is not to probe with inexhaustive depth this literature but rather merely to evaluate several sources used to make this assertion.

Erotic stimuli include an exceedingly wide range of subjects, including partial nudity, explicit portrayals of sexual relations in unrestrained manner, line drawings, movies, videotapes, and live entertainment.[159] Because of the varying degrees of naturalism presented by the stimuli, it has been posited that immediate arousal value varies with the stimuli and the circumstances under which it is presented.[160] The late Dr. Alfred Kinsey of Indiana University, a pioneer in understanding human sexuality, presented one of the earliest and classic studies of this subject area by conducting large-scale interviews in the 1940s.[161] In his interviews, he not only sought information about the sexual behavior of the respondents, but he sought to elicit information regarding their reactions to erotica.[162] A significant number of those interviewed for this study, men and women alike, reported that they became sexually aroused when presented with material portraying either nudity or sexual acts.[163] Also rated were various materials according to the likelihood of arousal—with their impact varying between the male and female respondents.[164]

Erotica Stimuli

For males, the level of response to the erotic stimuli was tied to the degree of realism portrayed by the stimuli. Thus, the most powerful stimulus for males was the actual observance of sex acts, with floor shows or burlesque next in arousal values and commercial films of least value.[165] The more direct and unambiguous the sexual cue, for the males in the Kinsey sample, the more likely it was found that arousal occurred.[166] Since this study was undertaken prior to revision of the film rating code, it is very conceivable that commercial films rated X or XX, now made available by video reproduction with VCRs, would today not be rated as low in arousal value as they were in the 1940s.[167]

A study presented in 1943 of 280 adolescent boys ranging from eleven to fourteen and fifteen to eighteen years of age asked them to rank some fifteen potentially erotic stimuli on an arousal scale potential. It was determined that the young adolescents found three experiences as having the highest arousal value: sexual conversations among themselves, female nudity, and obscene pictures.[168] For the older adolescent groups (fifteen to eighteen), the stimuli presenting the most arousal were female nudity, daydreaming, and obscene pictures.[169] This study, taken together with the Kinsey work, suggests that the level or number of one's sexual experience affects his or her reactions to erotica.[170] Thus, for those having had a greater level of sexual experience, "more direct representations of sexual activity are found to be arousing."[171]

A 1967 study exploring nudity as an erotic cue has relevance as well. There, two sets of photographs, each portraying similar sexual activities, were presented to the subjects.[172] In one set of pictures, all participants were totally nude, while the other set presented nudity with only an exposure of the genitals. Those interviewed (38 percent) reported a more significant degree of sexual arousal from the photographs showing nudity than from the partially nude set. Thus, despite suggestions nudity contributes significantly to sexual arousal in an erotic stimulus, this study supports the 1948 work of Dr. Kinsey and associates in one important conclusion that "the more explicit the representation of heterosexual intercourse, the higher the rated sexual arousal."[173]

Rank Ordering of Sexual Arousal Properties
by a Group of Male Graduate Students[174]

---

1. Heterosexual coitus in the ventral-ventral position.
2. Heterosexual coitus in the ventral-dorsal position.
3. Heterosexual petting, participants nude.
4. Heterosexual petting, participants partly clad.
5. Heterosexual fellatio.
6. Nude female.
7. Heterosexual cunnilingus.
8. Masturbation by a female.
9. A triad of two females and one male in conjunctive behavior involving coitus and oral-genital activity.
10. Partly clad female.
11. Homosexual cunnilingus.
12. Homosexual petting by females.
13. Sadomasochistic behavior, male on female.
14. Homosexual fellatio.
15. Sadomasochistic behavior, female on male.
16. Masturbation by a male.
17. Homosexual anal coitus.
18. Nude male.
19. Partly clad male.

The Kinsey material on arousal value of varying stimuli for females shows marked differences between male and female responses, even though, as to observing genitals, a substantial number of females and males were aroused.[175] The female respondents to Dr. Kinsey's study reported greater arousal from viewing commercial films or from reading materials in which sexuality is infused and placed within a romantic context. While more direct and sexually explicit expressions that were found to arouse males have less influence on females, this statistic could be thought of as reflecting in part the state of the American culture during the time of the investigation.[176] Indications were found that within a given statistically defined female population, "those who report more masculine interests and values respond more emphatically to erotic stimuli."[177] To some extent, every stimulus exists in the "eye of the beholder," who proceeds to give it meaning and/or actual significance.[178]

Popular Magazines

Various studies of the effect of sex-oriented magazines—CHIC, CLUB, GALLERY, GENESIS, HUSTLER, OUI, PENTHOUSE and PLAYBOY—and rape in 1979 showed a correlation of .63 between the circulation of these magazines and rapes. A similar study of magazine circulation in 1980 showed a .55 correlation, while one conducted between 1980 and 1982 among all the states showed a correlation of .64.[179] Although a plausible interpretation of this data could be that pornography is the *cause* of rape, other sophisticated research merely acknowledges that "the evidence presented allows only that there is a strong association between sex magazine readership and rape, not that one causes the other."[180] The exact degree of influence, direct or indirect, pornography has on known sex offenders is still lacking.[181]

The crucial issue of understanding here in this area of concern is that great care and caution should be given to generalizing from experimental laboratory results to real world situations. Only when laboratory studies of sexual violence have been undertaken that allow the exposure to this type of violence to have been manipulated as an independent variable and field studies completed (testing the level to which consumption of sexually violent material is correlated with subsequent rates of sexual assault or a comparable variable), can a rational conclusion of causality be reached. "So far, there have been no field studies measuring naturally occurring levels of exposure to sexual violence and later sexually violent behavior that would allow us to assess the validity of the laboratory work in this area."[182]

CONTEMPORARY RESPONSES

In 1985, led actively by two powerful political women—Susan Baker, wife of James Baker, then Secretary of the Treasury, and Tipper Gore, wife of then Senator Albert Gore—the campaign against "porn rock" received wide national publicity.[183]

Groups such as the National Music Review Council based in Dallas, Texas, the National Parents and Teachers Association, and the Parents Music Resource Center were mobilized as well to campaign against the "unwholesome" recording companies, radio stations, and producers of rock videos who market musical porn in the marketplaces of the 1980s.[184]

This approach to modern censorship is tied to calls for truth in advertising and labeling that will allow rock and video albums and tapes to be identified as to their degree of "raunchiness" so that parental guidance may be preferred before purchase by underage children (assuming children shop with their parents when such purchases were made). This approach also promotes an enormous pressure on distributing outlets to take the offending products off the shelves as well. This, in turn, creates an equal level of intense pressure for the artist and studios producing X-rated music videos to stop their production of these items. This whole program has been termed "an elegant form of censorship" because it is made to have the appearance of a program in consumer education and information.[185] If this form of self-censorship has success, then it must surely be applauded, for it obviates the need for strong enforcement or censorship policies by the state and federal governments.

> Rock music has become a plague of messages about sexual promiscuity, bisexuality, incest, sado-masochism, satanism, drug use, alcohol abuse and, constantly, misogyny. The lyrics regarding these things are celebratory, encouraging or at least desensitizing . . . . The concern is less that children will emulate the frenzied behavior described in porn rock than that they will succumb to the lassitude of the demoralized literally.[186]

The hottest numbers on the radio dial appear more and more to be those stations where "obnoxious, sometimes lewd, occasionally pornographic morning radio shows" operate.[187] Indeed, over recent years, audience support has grown for the services of disc jockeys who seek to titillate their listeners.[188] One station, KLOL-FM in Houston, Texas, went so far in programming its morning show to encourage their listeners to call it while they were having sex.[189]

In May 1987 the FCC tightened its policy on indecent language and banned references that were explicit as to "sexual and/or excretory activities."[190] Designed to regulate the "extremes" in radio programming, most station managers, however, perceive the new policy directives as ineffective simply because "shock" radio makes far too much money with ready advertisers to be "toned down" or taken off the airwaves.[191]

Ten years after the Baker-Gore "porn rock" campaign, U.S. Senator Robert Dole of Kansas energized and broadened the campaign against smut in 1995 to include not only rock, heavy metal, and "gangsta" rap "music" produced by Time-Warner but Hollywood's movies as well. Both product lines were termed "nightmares of depravity."[192]

As to music, the central question is whether rock, heavy metal, and rap lyrics are representative of a unique American subculture or whether nihilistic lyrics promote behavioral problems.[193]   Stated otherwise, should merely a dimissive attitude be taken regarding the efforts of the lower classes and marginalized groups to drive changes in language, tastefulness, and appropriateness, or should direct action be undertaken to restrain what is regarded by some as a destructive societal force and the "mainstreaming of deviancy" by the entertainment industry?[194]

Increasingly, releases from the music industry glorify guns, violence, and drugs and use sexually explicit language which all too frequently celebrate rape, torture, and even murder—all promoting what some view as a form of social genocide.[195]   History has shown that marginalized groups have always sought to use language as their badge of solidarity or courage in order to resist the efforts of mainstream society to make them conform.[196]   But, query: has the limit to this "freedom" of expression been reached?

Advocating a return to "the politics of virtue," Senator Dole has called for a national debate over the relationship of liberty to virtue.[197]   Fortified by a TIME poll conducted in 1995 by Yankelovich Partners, Inc., which found 70 percent of the public concerned with media representations of sex, the moment is no doubt right for such a debate—one that uncovers the real ugliness of underclass American life and seeks to stop emulative behavior by others of this pathetic group of social misfits.[198]   Indeed, another poll—this time by the Gallup Organization—taken after the Dole speech, found 65 percent of Americans think the entertainment industry is "seriously out of touch with the values of the American people."[199]   Yet, surprisingly, an almost identical percentage agreed that the federal government should *not* be involved in restricting sex and violence presented by the entertainment industry.[200]

Hollywood has, through its productions, begun to produce more and more violent movies which depict graphic rape as a kind of sexual "turn-on." These depictions have grown more and more lurid trapping the viewers amid horror, guilt and titillation. Their sole function is but to raise the "violence quotient."[201]

Jack Valenti, the president of the Motion Picture Association of America, has suggested the solution to resolving the current dilemma of the entertainment industry is to be found with a simple restoration of parental responsibility.[202]   Others have termed this responsibility "private censorship" and called on responsible citizens to rouse themselves from a cultural malaise dominated by sources of questionable entertainment.[203]

Decrying the need for congressional action and regulatory overview by the FCC, Mr. Valenti has cautioned parents, churches, and schools that they must fight the great societal contradiction which, while extolling family values, tolerates aberrations, is fascinated with the bizarre, and fails to reject anything being beyond the pale. "We indulge ourselves in condemning that which is tawdry, and then turn into TV talk shows barren of anything that might remotely resemble worthiness," he said.[204]

Executive and Administrative

The 1970 Presidential Commission on Obscenity and Pornography concluded that when some individuals are exposed to erotic materials, masturbatory, or coital behavior increase, but for the majority, no change in these two behavioral patterns occurs. In any event, the increases of these behaviors disappear generally within forty-eight hours. When masturbation followed exposures to erotica, it occurred most often among those either with established masturbatory patterns or among individuals with established, but unavailable, sexual partners. And, for those individuals increasing coital frequencies following exposure to sexual stimuli, the activation occurred generally among sexually experienced persons with established and available sex partners. Thus, generally, it was determined that established patterns of sexual behavior were stable and not altered substantially by exposure to erotica.[205]

The commission found that pornography was not only harmless but had, in some presentations, a potential therapeutic or "cathartic" value and, second, had no negative effect on adults or on children.[206] Because of the past futility of efforts to legislate in the area of obscenity prevention, the commission concluded that public opinion in America did "not support the imposition of legal prohibitions upon the right of adults to read or see explicit sexual materials."[207] Owing to this lack of consensus concerning the availability of sexually explicit materials, serious problems existed regarding the enforcement of legal prohibitions in the area. Accordingly, the commission found,

> Consistent enforcement of even the clearest prohibitions upon consensual adult exposure to explicitly sexual materials would require the expenditure of considerable law enforcement resources. In the absence of a persuasive demonstration of damage flowing from consensual exposure to such materials, there seems no justification for thus adding to the overwhelming tasks already placed upon the law enforcement system. Inconsistent enforcement of prohibitions, on the other hand, invites discriminatory action based upon considerations not directly relevant to the policy of the law. The latter alternative also breeds public disrespect for the legal process.[208]

This report was rejected by the U.S. Senate by a sixty to five vote and was characterized by President Nixon as "morally bankrupt."[209]

On May 21, 1985, Attorney General Edwin Meese named an eleven-member commission to study pornography and, "if appropriate," propose measures designed to control not only its production, but its distribution as well.[210] The attorney general stated that the very formation of the commission reflected the basic concern that a healthy society has "regarding the ways in which its people publicly entertain themselves."[211] He continued further by observing that "[t]he Commission is an affirmation of the proposition that the purpose of a democracy involves . . . the achievement of the good life and the good society."[212] It is assumed that "good" was a synonym for "virtuous."

Prior to the official release of the 1,960-page final report of the commission in July 1986, advance copies of the conclusion and recommendations showed, among other points, that, based on admittedly "tentative" scientific evidence, a substantial exposure to pornography likely increases the extent to which those so exposed will view either rape or other forms of sexual violence as less serious than they would have otherwise if not exposed to the material.[213] Critics came forward immediately to caution that the conclusions of the commission are not based upon conclusive scientific proof and, further, that social scientists are divided on the issue of whether most pornography is harmful.[214]

Dr. Judith Becker of Columbia University and a member of the commission, called attention to the fact that the word, *pornography*, was not defined in the commission's final report.[215] She also noted "a number of the commissioners wanted to discuss what was appropriate sexual behavior; the only appropriate sexual behavior would be that which occurs within a marriage and is procreative in nature. It was not the mandate of this commission to decide what the country should or should not be doing sexually."[216] On the issue of simple nudity, the commission expressed its concern about the impact of this "on children, on attitudes toward women, on the relationship between the sexes and on attitudes toward sex in general."[217]

The panel urged among other points that pornography and its censorship be targeted by state and federal prosecutors, that Congress enact laws that would make it unfair to hire actors and actresses for ex-rated films, that the interstate commerce laws be strengthened to combat pornography, and that obscene material on cable television and "Dial-a-Porn" telephone messages be banned. It also urged the formation of citizen groups whose responsibility it would be to monitor newsstands, videocassette stores, and other outlets allegedly displaying and selling obscene materials, and further, organize boycotts of the offending establishments.[218]

Two of the researchers whose work was cited extensively by the Attorney General's Commission on Pornography, Edward I. Donnerstein and Daniel G. Linz, have taken issue with several of the commission's contentions, charging that they simply cannot be supported by empirical evidence and, furthermore, that the commission did not fully understand certain fundamental assumptions in social science research on pornography.[219] The first point made is that violence, not pornography, is the most important problem confronting society today.[220] Although the commission found correctly the most dangerous form of pornography included violent themes, it assumes, without complete and accurate verification, "that images of violence have become more prevalent in pornography in recent years."[221] It also concludes that "increased aggressive behavior towards women is casually related, for an aggregate population, to increased sexual violence."[222] It has *not* been determined whether aggressive behavior, measured under *clinical* conditions, after exposure to violent pornographic films, has a cumulative effect or is merely temporary. A significant body of evidence suggests the effect is only temporary.[223]

While there is evidence that particular pornographic themes, specifically that women find forces or aggression a pleasurable quality, influence the male perceptions and attitudes regarding rape,[224] interpreting and drawing broad conclusions about measures of motivation and "likelihood to rape" is "tricky."[225] Thus, the commission's broadly sweeping conclusion that "substantial exposure to sexually violent material . . . bears a causal relationship to antisocial violence and, for some subgroups, possibly to unlawful acts of sexual violence," is flawed and not verifiable from present research and study.[226] The state of knowledge simply does not exist with certainty, and "it remains to be seen whether changes in attitudes about women and rape revealed in relatively small-scale tests have any applicability to rape and aggression in the real world."[227]

Donnerstein and Linz conclude that a number of studies suggest strongly "that violence against women need not occur in a pornographic or sexually explicit context to have a negative effect upon viewer attitudes and behavior . . . violent images, rather than sexual ones, are most responsible for people's attitudes about women and rape."[228]

Regrettably, the attorney general's commission did not seek to disentangle sexuality from violence.[229] Professor Frederick Shauer, who not only served on the attorney general's commission but was also the principal author of its final report, stated that "[t]here is no evidence that undifferentiated sexually explicit behavior causes violence."[230] He allowed that the report has been misinterpreted widely and *nothing* in it "urges regulation of obscene material that is not violent."[231]

Congressional Initiatives

While the cause of sexual abuse has been recognized as both complex and rooted within family relationships, the fact remains that actual sexual abuse of children is rising very significantly.[232] A direct correlation has been found to exist between pornography and child abuse.[233] A surgeon general of the United States has termed pornography "an accessory to the crime of child abuse."[234] Obviously, the sexual integrity of the nation's children must be guaranteed. Responding to this grave, national crisis, the Reagan Administration took bold action in November 1987 by transmitting the Child Protection and Obscenity Enforcement Act to the Congress and called for its "immediate consideration and enactment."[235]

Child pornography legislation has existed since passage in 1977 of the Protection of Children from Sexual Exploitation Act[236] as supplemented by the Child Protection Act of 1984.[237] Prior to 1986, these were the only two federal laws regulating child pornography. In that year Congress replaced these two legislative enactments with The Child Protection and Obscenity Enforcement Act,[238] which in turn was amended in 1988.[239] Interestingly, this amendment was prompted as a direct consequence of the conclusions drawn from the Report of The Attorney General's Commission on Pornography in 1987.[240]

Although the 1984 Child Protection Act allowed for increased prosecutions for the possession of child pornography, very few indictments were obtained—this because of the felt need to protect the tragic victims of the pornography.[241] Accordingly, the attorney general's commission recommended the adoption of new and more stringent laws.[242]

Even though in 1988 Congress amended the Child Protection and Obscenity Enforcement Act of 1986[243] to prohibit the exchange of information (e.g., notice or advertisement) regarding child pornography through computer networks, in practice this amendment has been found faulty in regulating effectively the outward transmission of this type of pornography.[244] Additionally, this amendment does not serve as a deterrent to individuals having an interest in child pornography, for it does not prohibit accessing computer networks.[245]

With the passage of the Communications Decency Act of 1996,[246] as a part of the Telecommunications Act,[247] the Congress stated its unequivocal purpose for acting here was to both deter and punish trafficking in obscenity, stalking, and harassment by means of a computer[248] and thereby tighten its overall regulation of obscene communications. By setting a maximum fine of $100,000 or imposing imprisonment for not more than two years for those who make, create, solicit, and initiate "the transmission of any comment, request, suggestion, proposal, image or other communication is obscene, lewd, lascivious, filthy, or indecent, with intent to annoy, abuse, thereafter, or harass another person"[249] or use interactive computers for this purpose with individuals under the age of eighteen,[250] the Congress sought to effect a balance between the needs of free speech with those of the government to set and regulate a standard of morality. Provision is also made within the Telecommunications Act to allow a cable television subscriber to request, without charge, a scrambling or blocking of the radio and video of each channel carrying obscene programming that he does not wish to receive.[251]

Whether the balance sought by the new telecommunications legislation has been achieved will, ultimately, be decided by the Supreme Court. A federal district court held in June 1996 that this aspirational legislative balance had not been met. More specifically, a three-judge panel ruled that the Internet, or the international computer network of both federal an nonfederal interoperable data, is entitled to First Amendment speech protections that apply to newspapers and magazines. In affirming obscenity and child pornography as unprotected speech and outlawed on the Internet as well as other media, the court nonetheless held that broad governmental attempts to limit the flow of indecent, offensive but constitutionally protected material to children who use the Internet, would place unacceptable restrictions on what adults can publish or see as well.[252]

In passing the Telecommunications Act of 1996,[253] Congress determined that the average American child is exposed to twenty-five hours of television each week, with some exposure levels reaching eleven hours each day; such levels of exposure mean that, on average, children are shown 8,000 murders and 100,000 acts of violence by the time they complete elementary school; and studies show conclusively the pervasiveness and casual treatment of sexual materials on television promote a higher tendency for violent and aggressive behavior later in their lives than children not so exposed.[254]

In a $1.5 million study funded by the National Cable Television Association, these congressional findings were underscored with an astonishing conclusion that a majority of programs on broadcast and cable television—57 percent of some 2,500 hours studied—contained some level of violence in their context.[255] Further, the study found that in 73 percent of the television programs studied, perpetrators of the violent acts on television went unpunished. It concluded that when violence is presented without punishment, viewers are more likely to learn the lesson that violence is indeed successful.[256]

In 1968, when public concern over the uneven quality of movie making forced Hollywood to create in the name of self-interested and preservation, the Motion Picture Association of America was established and it in turn developed a rating system to inform parents of those films deserving parental scrutiny. This was all done to prevent government censorship of movies.[257] In a similar effort to forestall, if again to prevent, censorship, the four leading television networks (ABC, CBS, NBC, and Fox) have agreed unilaterally to develop a voluntary rating system that would label all of the networks' entertainment programs according to sexual or violent content which became operational in 1997.[258]

The Telecommunications Act of 1996[259] was the direct impetus for the decision by the television industry to develop a rating system since, provisions within the act direct the industry to scramble or block sexually explicit adult programming in order to prevent children from viewing it.[260] Indeed, by 1998, all manufacturers of television sets must include a V-chip in new sets which will have the effect of automatically reading codes embedded in programs and, if activated, block those shows that viewers deem undesirable.[261] With additional demands from the White House for labeling sexually explicit and violent programs both in on-air advisories and in television program listings and advertisements,[262] the industry had a choice of either developing its own ratings system to thereby activate the V-chip or subjecting its total programming to a government-appointed panel to do the task of rating.[263]

An overlooked point about V-chips is that there is, at present, no standard chip design and–furthermore–the very real possibility that it will be many years after the 1998 date for installation of the chips before they even attain widespread use. The simple validity of this conclusion is seen when it is realized that at the current rate of about 200 million television sets sold each year in the United States, it would take more than twelve years to replace all of the (non-V-chip) sets now in use.[264] An additional factor militating against the effectiveness of the V-chip is the absence of any type of guarantee that people will actually utilize the chip's powers in the first place. This point is underscored when it is realized that two-thirds of 96 million American households have no children at all. Thus, for them, the remote control is more than adequate for regulating programming with there being no need for a technological filter.[265]

Disappointing Performance Record

Despite occasional successes,[266] the federal government is not curtailing traffic in obscenity effectively—with few convictions being sustained.[267]   Indeed, obscenity is being eclipsed by other issues such as violence in general, drug offenders, AIDS, gun control, abortion, and sexual abuse together with child prostitution.[268]   Pornography has continued to be a flourishing and profitable business, with estimations being that the adult X-rated video industry's rental and retail sales alone grew in 1993 to $1.6 billion—up from $992 million in 1989.[269] And, what is being seen, is that a wide proliferation of the total pornographic network has allowed the industry to expand beyond magazines and video to computer networks.[270]

CHILD PORNOGRAPHY AND THE INTERNET

The indoctrination of children to pornography is undertaken with the ultimate goal of luring them to engage in sexual activity.   This is accomplished by manipulating the child into believing that sexual conduct is acceptable because the children in pictures are engaged in it.[271]

The central dilemma presented by computer-generated child pornography is the extent to which the state can control, if not eliminate, such conduct. In other words, since this conduct is used as an aid in the sexual abuse of other children and, indeed, abuses the child through depiction of it as a sexual object, should not there be total censorship or federal preemption of the field?[272] Civil libertarians assert the underlying issue is whether the Internet is considered to be a print medium, as a newspaper, which thereby enjoys strong guarantees of protection against government interference, or whether it is to be classified as a broadcast medium, as is television, and is thus subject to control by the FCC.[273]

Since computer-generated child pornography is the creation of electronically generated pornographic images, the argument is put forward that such images, in actuality, do not exist. Thus, they do not exploit *real* children. Rather, what is seen is a pornographic picture and not a victim by any stretch of the imagination. Accordingly, the state has no compelling interest for regulating computer-generated child pornography.[274] Regardless of the argumentative posture taken, it must be understood that since typically underground networks are the only real sources for transmission of child pornography and, as such, they operate covertly, what is seen in practice, then, is that these networks are able to escape totally the full reach of the law.[275]

Computer Sex

Because of the obsessive American preoccupation with sex, the computer has become but yet another avenue for enjoying sex itself.[276] Interactive erotica, or "Net sex," has become quite popular[277] and yields a veritable sea of smut allowing its users to utilize material such as "sadomasochism, bestiability, vaginal and rectal fisting, eroticized urination, pedophilia, and ménages à trois."[278] Indeed, it has been estimated anywhere from 180,000 to 500,000 computer users drop in for "alternative sex" discussions on a monthly basis.[279] Chat lines are in fact a type of telephone, with the audio component being replaced by a computer screen.[280] Already, interactive videos on CD-ROM feature naked PENTHOUSE models and hard-core porn actresses who respond to commands from a keyboard. And, on the new horizon, is videophone sex complete with a CD called "cyborgasm" which allows one to listen to, with headphones, various sexual encounters and strap into virtual reality equipment for an imaginary sexual encounter.[281]

The central concern here again is that children will happen innocently upon all of this interactive erotica by accident. It should be remembered, however, that accidents just do not happen—especially when online blocks, and other sophisticated software, are available for parents who wish to exercise *their* responsibility to supervise *their* childrens use of the Internet and thereby seek to restrict access to areas inappropriate for them.[282] It is really that simple: parental supervision is the operative code.

CONCLUSIONS

There can be no definitive resolutions to the dilemmas that obscenity and pornography pose to the cultural, moral, and ethical fiber of the modern society, for, in a pluralistic nation such as ours, toleration of opposing views is the *sine qua non* of a vibrant democracy.[283] A right of moral independence must of necessity, however, guarantee a coordinate right of free expression.[284] If there is a justification for imposing restraints upon individual freedom, it is to be found only when restraint is undertaken to prevent injury to others or to the public good.[285] Under this position, acts, sexually explicit or pornographic, performed by consenting adults in private, should not be prohibited as criminal regardless of how some may view them as sinful or unvirtuous.[286]

Basic or central arguments made traditionally against legal enforcement, or even a working passive acceptance and consideration of moral standards, derive from the tendency of a liberal society to reduce questions of law and morals to the principles of liberty and equality. Thus, a society steeped in liberalism can hardly understand a moral-legal issue, except, perhaps, as a conflict of rights: either as a clash between individual claims of right or as one between the rights of the individual and those of the state. In such a liberal society, every individual is allowed to follow his own preferences to the extent of their compatibility with not only the rights of other individuals but also with their very social existence.[287] The overriding problem, however, is that the liberal society finds it increasingly difficult to evaluate preferences by any standards thought as a being in common with total societal standards. The conscience of society, then, must be the final arbiter when conflict arises. Consequently, where a society in a particular nation, "settles definitely into a secular, post-Christian view of life, the laws will inevitably change. But whilst the conscience of society is still in a state of frustration, the demands of liberalization should be contested, if only to pinpoint the moral issues, and make public opinion fully aware of the implications of the legal changes to which it is urged to consent."[288]

Thanks notably to a surprisingly aggressive Congress whose actions no doubt in passing the Federal Communications Decency Act of 1996 and the much broader Telecommunications Act itself were prompted by renewed public debate and awareness of the pervasiveness of obscenity and pornography in contemporary society, a new, enlightened structure for regulation has been framed. Having begun, this debate must not become unfocused or misdirected by mutant journalistic ploys of the popular liberal press.

Deregulation of any kind or manner of pornography should be evaluated cautiously because of the potential for misreading the symbolic effect of such action, for such specific deregulations of that, heretofore regulated, could well be perceived as an act of governmental condonation of the deregulated conduct.[289] "To take the affirmative step of deregulation would thus more likely be perceived as a governmental statement that the deregulated conduct is harmless . . . the burden of proof ought to be on those who would have society engage in a political symbolic deregulation in a way that it is on those who would have society initiate a potentially symbolic regulation."[290]

Even though there are laboratory studies that show violent pornography can influence aggression toward women,[291] the conclusiveness and projectability of these conclusions into nonstructured situations must be drawn carefully, especially since there is no conclusive proof that pornography has become more violent since the 1970s.[292] The very inconclusiveness of the clinical work in the field demands continued vigilance before definitive actions are undertaken one way or the other. The willingness of the U.S. Supreme Court to take judicial notice of the principle of secondary effects as applied to nude erotic dancing and thereby recognize prostitution, as well as sexual and associated crimes often flow from such entertainment, demonstrates a strong and protective *parens patriae* attitude by the Court and one which must be exercised with caution and not expanded unreasonably into other areas of communication and expression—and especially so with new technological developments on the information superhighway.

In the final analysis, no unequivocal, unyielding standard can be applied to efforts to determine, with dispositive clarity, when questioned materials, actions, pictures, and so on, are obscene or pornographic and the extent to which they should be censored or restricted—for standards of civility, sophistication, and tolerance simply vary from community to community. Our goal remains the same as it was state in 1964 in Chief Justice Earl Warren's dissenting opinion in

Jacobellis v. Ohio,[293] namely, to maintain a decent society and one in which individual rights may be expressed freely and consistent with the constitutional guarantees of the First and Fourteenth Amendments.[294] To this end, in rendering decisions regarding limitations or expansions on one side of this balancing equation, the Supreme Court must always endeavor to balance equitably conflicting social, ethical, moral, and political values and policies. If it allows too much weight to be given to alleged political or social dangers, of a real or imagined nature, these actions will have a chilling effect on the freedom of citizens to speak out on current issues. Contrariwise, when the Court appears to interpret the first amendment as offering cart'e blanche to the likes of writers, speakers, publishers, and so on, it will surely be met with the indignant outcries of those whose beliefs or values have been either attacked or ridiculed in the offending material. Nothing more should be expected within a pluralistic society than to have all ultimate actions be set within a framework of principled decision making and guided by the standard of reasonableness.

NOTES

1. Mano, *Good Sex!* PEOPLE Mag., April 15, 1985, at 109.

2. *See* Hubbard, *When Underwear Looks This Good, It's Gotta Be La Perla Lingere*, PEOPLE Mag., Feb. 1, 1988, at 71.

3. Britt, *Sex Sells, But We Don't Have to Buy*, WASH. POST, Sept., 8, 1996, at D1; *The Bum's Rush in Advertising*, TIME Mag., Dec. 1, 1980, at 95. *See generally* Hershman, *Was There Sex Before Calvin Klein?*, 53 WASH. & LEE L. REV. 929 (1996).

4. Shales, *Prime Time and The Play of All Flesh*, WASH. POST TV GUIDE, Nov. 11-17, 1979 at 3.

5. Clark, *Cableporn*, AM. FILM, Mar., 1982, at 57.

6. K. TURAN & S. ZITO, SINEMA (1974).

7. Leo, *Romantic Porn in the Boudoir: The VCR Revolution Produces X-rated Films for Women (Men)*, TIME Mag., Mar. 30, 1987, at 63.

8. Leo, *Stomping and Whomping Galore: Sadomasochism Comes Out of the Closet—Whips, Chains and All*, TIME Mag., May 4, 1981, at 73.

9. Lure, *Sex and Fashion*, N.Y. REV. OF BOOKS, Oct. 22, 1981, at 38.

10. J. HEIDENRY, WHAT WILD ECSTASY: THE RISE AND FALL OF THE SEXUAL REVOLUTION (1997); C. LASCH, THE CULTURE OF NARCISSISM (1979).

11. A. EDEL, ETHICAL JUDGMENT 93 (1955).

12. McCarthy, *Sex, Morals and the Teen-Ager of the '80's* WASH. POST, Oct. 26, 1980, at G5. *But see* Morrow, *Changing the Signals of Passion*, TIME Mag., Jan. 13, 1986, at 74.

13. Serrin, *Opponents of Flourishing Sex Industry Hindered by Its Open Public Acceptance*, N.Y. TIMES, Feb. 10, 1981, at B6.

14. *See* Currin & Showers, *Regulation of Pornography—The North Carolina Approach,* 21 WAKE FOREST L. REV. 263, 279 n. 4 (1986); Stachell, *The Big Business of Selling Smut,* PARADE Mag., Aug. 19, 1979, at 4.

15. *Cohen v. California,* 403 U.S. 15, 25 (1971). See also PORNOGRAPHY: PRIVATE RIGHT OR PUBLIC MENACE? (R. M. Baird & S. E. Rosenbaum, eds. 1991).

16. *See generally* W. KENDRICK, THE SECRET MUSEUM: PORNOGRAPHY IN MODERN CULTURE (1987).

17. Shapiro, *Introduction to the Issue: Some Dilemmas of Biotechnological Research,* 51 SO. CAL. L. REV. 987 (1978).

18. *Jacobellis v. Ohio,* 378 U.S. 184, 199 (1964) (Warren, C.J., dissenting).

19. Will, *Sex as Tabasco Sauce,* in THE MORNING AFTER: AMERICAN SUCCESSES AND EXCESSES 1981-86 at 20 (1986).

20. *A Porn Ban Fails in Maine,* NEWSWEEK, June 23, 1986, at 33.

21. *Id.*

22. Lucas, *Do We Still Care About Dirty Words?* INDIANAPOLIS STAR, Oct. 11, 1987, at H1.

23. *Koop Renounces Pornography,* WASH. POST, Sept. 12, 1986, at 17.

24. G. WILL, THE PURSUIT OF HAPPINESS AND OTHER SOBERING THOUGHTS 81 (1978).

25. Kimmel, *Pornography and Its Discontents,* PSYCHOLOGY TODAY, Feb. 1988, at 74. *See generally* A. SIMPSON, PORNOGRAPHY AND POLITICS (1983); A. DWORKIN, PORNOGRAPHY: MEN POSSESSING WOMEN (1981).

26. E. DONNERSTEIN ET AL., THE QUESTION OF PORNOGRAPHY: RESEARCH FINDINGS AND POLICY IMPLICATIONS 98 (1987).

27. W. HARTMAN ET AL., NUDIST SOCIETY 16 (1970). Today, in the fine tradition of the Greeks, Nude Olympics are staged each Winter at Princeton University and Purdue University where anywhere from twenty to one hundred fifty naked students run nude in and around libraries and dormitories. *Notebook,* CHRONICLE OF HIGHER EDUC., Feb. 11, 1987, at 31.

28. HARTMAN ET AL., *supra* note 27 at 18.

29. *Id.*

30. *Id.*

31. *Id.* at 19. *See* F. SCHAUER, THE LAW OF OBSCENITY 13 (1976).

32. HARTMAN ET AL., *supra* note 27 at 20.

33. *Id.*

34. *Id. See* SCHAUER, *supra* note 31. *See generally* J. LANGDON-DAVIES, THE FUTURE OF NAKEDNESS (1928).

The Comstock Act was a criminal statute designed for the suppression of trade in the circulation of obscene literature and articles for immoral use. Act of March 3, 1873, ch. 258, 17 Stat. 599 (1873). It was the precursor of modern legislation that makes mailing obscene or crime inciting matter a federal offense. 18 U.S.C. § 1461 (1976). *See also* 18 U.S.C. § 334 (1940).

35. HARTMAN ET AL., *supra* note 27 at 20.

36. *Id.*

37. *Id. See* E. SHAW & I. BOONE, THE BODY TABOO (1951). The body taboo is almost universal. *Id.* at 13.

38. HARTMAN ET AL., *supra* note 27 at 21 (1970).

39. *Id.*

40. *Id. See also* M. WEINBERG, SEX, MODESTY AND DEVIANTS 104 (1965).

41. *See* Fetherlin, *Nation's Nudists Seeing the Light*, WASH. POST, Sept. 18, 1977, at G4.

42. *Id.*

43. *Id.*

44. *Id. See* Yenckel, *Escapes: In the Buff,* WASH. POST, July 31, 1981, at B5; Hockstader, *Why Do People Want to Wear Wet, Slimy Bathing Suits?* WASH. POST, August 19, 1984, at B3.

45. *See* Zito, *The Cover Story: Commotion over the Nude Newsweek*, WASH. POST, June 4, 1982, at D1.

46. *Id.*

47. *Id. See generally* Press et al., *A Right to Pose in the Nude?*, NEWSWEEK, April 14, 1980, at 107.

48. Greenfield, *Portrait of a Lady*, WASH. POST, June 9, 1982, at A23.

49. *Id.*

50. *Id.*

51. *Id.* Mano, *supra* note 1 at 109. *See also* Leo, *supra* note 7 at 63.

52. Greenfield, *supra* note 48 (emphasis added).

53. Kornheiser, *Calendar Men: Men Can be Bimbos, Too, in an Era When Women No Longer Corner the Cheesecake Market*, INT'L HERALD TRIBUNE, Dec. 30, 1983, at 18.

One "proposal" for a resolution to the problem of erotica was presented by the Conference of the United Methodist Church which expressed the contention that erotica "can show persons in warm, caring, human and responsible relationships." Erotica is defined as "sexually explicit and arousing" material that does not "use coercion, inflict pain or use violence in any way." *Methodists Hold Debate on Erotica*, WASH. POST, Jan. 23, 1988, at G11. Blanket acceptance of this idea would surely resolve any and all problems with the issue itself!

54. Kornheiser, *supra* note 53.

55. Thomas, *The Naked Truth*, THE TELEGRAPH Mag., July 20, 1996, at 28.

56. *Id.*

57. *Id.*

58. *Id.* at 31.

See S. TISDALE, TALK DIRTY TO ME: AN INTIMATE PHILOSOPHY OF SEX (1995); F. BENNION, THE SEX CODE: MORALS FOR MODERNS, Ch. 4 (1991); R. J. STOLLER, PORN: MYTHS FOR THE TWENTIETH CENTURY (1991).

59. *Id.*

60. *Id.*

61. Thomas, *supra* note 55 at 30.

62. *Barnes v. Glen Theatre*, 501 U.S. 560, 115 L. Ed. 2d 504, 523, 524 (1991) (per Souter, J. concurring).

63. *Renton v. Playtime Theatres, Inc.*, 475 U.S. 41, (1986); *Young v. American Mini Theatres, Inc.*, 427 U.S. 50, 71 n.34 (1976).

64. *Supra* note 62 at 523.

65. *Id.*

66. *Id.* at 524.

See generally PORNOGRAPHY: WOMEN, VIOLENCE AND CIVIL LIBERTIES (C. Itzin, ed. 1992).

67. F. ILFELD & R. LAUER, SOCIAL NUDISM IN AMERICA 175 (1964).

68. C. WILLIAMS, THE PSYCHOLOGY OF NUDISM 33 (1941).

69. *Id.* "Clearly all nudity cannot be deemed obscene even as to minors." *Erznoznik v. Jacksonville*, 422 U.S. 205, 212 (1975) (per Powell, J.).

70. W. WELBY, NAKED AND UNASHAMED 41 (1934).

71. *Id.*

72. WILLIAMS, *supra* note 68 at 146 (emphasis added).

73. Stanmeyer, *Keeping the Constitutional Republic: Civic Virtue vs. Pornographic Attack,* 14 HASTINGS CONST. L.Q. 561 (1987).

74. *Id.* at 566.

75. *Id. See* THE FEDERALIST Nos. 10, 14, 18 & 55 (J. Madison) (E. Bourne, ed. 1937).

76. Stanmeyer, *supra* note 73 at 574.

77. *Id.*

The first recorded obscenity case in the United States was *Commonwealth v. Sharpless*, 2 Serg. & Rawle 91 (Pa. 1815), where a conviction was brought in against the defendant for exhibiting a painting for money that represented a man who was in an "obscene, imprudent and indecent posture with a woman." Stanmeyer, *supra* note 73 at 574 n.45. *But see* Reynolds, *Our Misplaced Reliance on Early Obscenity Cases,* 61 A.B.A.J. 220 (1975).

78. *See* 18 U.S.C. §§ 1461-1463 (1984).

79. Stanmeyer, *supra* note 73 at 574.

80. Reagan, *Politics and Morality Are Inseparable*, 1 NOTRE DAME J.L. ETHICS & PUB. POL'Y 7, 10 (1984).

81. Hyde, *Keeping God in the Closet: Some Thoughts on the Exorcism of Religious Values from Public Life*, 1 NOTRE DAME J.L. ETHICS & PUB. POL'Y 33, 43 (1984).

82. *Id.*

83. Marcin, *Ideological Pluralism and Government Regulation of Private Morality*, 7 CAP. U.L. REV. 621 (1978).

84. *Id.* at 625 (citing P. DEVLIN, THE ENFORCEMENT OF MORALS (1965)).

85. *Id.*

86. *Id.*

87. Stanmeyer, *supra* note 73 at 591.

88. *Id.*

89. *Id.* at 589.

90. *Id.* at 587.

91. *Id.*

92. Dworkin, *Is There a Right to Pornography?* 1 OXFORD J. LEGAL STUD. 177, 178 (1981).

93. *Id.*

94. *Id.*

95. *Id.* at 179.

96. *Id.*

97. *Id.*

98. *Id.* at 205.

99. *Id.*

100. *Id.* at 212.

101. *Id.*

102. S. MACEDO, THE NEW RIGHT v. THE CONSTITUTION 34 (1986).

103. *Id.*

104. *Id.* at 36.

105. *Id.* at 34.

106. Rehnquist, *The Notion of a Living Constitution,* 54 TEX L. REV. 693, 704 (1976). "There is no conceivable way in which I can logically demonstrate to you that the judgments of my conscience are superior to the judgments of your conscience and *vice versa.*" *Id.* at 704.

107. Posner, *The Meaning of Judicial Self-Restraint,* 59 IND. L.J. 1, 6 (1983).

108. MACEDO, *supra* note 102 at 35.

109. *Id.*

110. Scalia, *Morality, Pragmatism and the Legal Order,* 9 HARV. J.L. & PUB. POL'Y 123 (1986).

111. 367 U.S. 497, 545-46 (1961) (Harlan, J., dissenting). This exercise of the police power was reiterated in *Paris Adult Theatre I v. Slaton* (an obscenity case), where it was determined that "a legislature could legitimately act ... to protect the social interest in order and morality." 413 U.S. 49, 61 (1973) (quoting Roth v. United States, 354 U.S. 476, 485 (1957), quoting *Chaplinsky v. New Hampshire,* 315 U.S. 568, 572 (1942)).

112. *Bowers v. Hardwick,* 106 S. Ct. 2841 (1986). Here, a five member majority of the Court ruled that a Georgia statute criminalizing acts of sodomy was not unconstitutional and homosexuals therefore could not be granted a fundamental right to commit acts of sodomy in private with a consenting adult.

113. DONNERSTEIN ET AL., *supra* note 26 at 146.

114. *Id.* at 147.

115. *Id.*

116. *Id.*

117. 7 THE OXFORD ENGLISH DICTIONARY 26 (1970).

118. *Id.*

119. *Id.* at 1131. One commentator has defined pornography as "[t]he visual depiction of ultimate erotic acts, with erotic overtones portrayed in such a way to stimulate the psychology and imagination of the viewer, who vicariously engages in the same sex acts while beholding and thereby experiencing, through masturbatory fantasy, sexual pleasure." Stanmeyer, *supra* note 73 at 576.

120. 3 THE OXFORD ENGLISH DICTIONARY 246 (1969).

121. 7 THE OXFORD ENGLISH DICTIONARY 253 (1970).

It has been determined that nudity alone does not place otherwise protected material outside the mantle of the first amendment. *Schad v. Mt. Ephraim*, 452 U.S. 61 (1981).

122. I. KRISTOL, ON THE DEMOCRATIC IDEA IN AMERICA 35-36 (1969).

123. *Id.* at 40.

124. F. WERTHAM, SEDUCTION OF THE INNOCENT 90-91 (1954).

125. 161 U.S. 446 (1896).

126. DONNERSTEIN ET AL., *supra* note 26 at 148.

127. L.R. 3, Q.B., 360 (1868).

128. *Id.* at 370.

129. 354 U.S. 476 (1957).

130. G. WEAVER, HANDBOOK ON THE PROSECUTION OF OBSCENITY CASES 3 (1985).

131. *Roth,* 354 U.S. at 485. *Roth* specifically rejected that *Hicklin* test. *Id.* at 487.

132. *Id.* at 487 n.20.

In attempting to define prurience, the Court used such words as "[i]tching; longing; uneasy with desire . . . lascivious desire or thought. . . . A thing is obscene if, considered as a whole, its predominant appeal is to prurient interest, *i.e.,* a shameful or morbid interest in nudity, sex or excretion." *Id.*

The mere private possession of material considered obscene does not constitute a crime. *Stanley v. Georgia*, 394 U.S. 557, 568 (1969).

The Hawaii Supreme Court held on January 8, 1988, that a statute prohibiting the sale of pornography was invalid and that, without the state showing a compelling state interest, one's right of privacy includes not only a right to peruse pornography at home, but a correlative right to obtain such materials. *Hawaii v. Kam*, 748 P.2d 372 (Hawaii 1988).

133. WEAVER, *supra* note 130.

134. 383 U.S. 413 (1966).

The three elements necessary to establish that the questioned material was obscene were: (1) that its dominant theme, taken as a whole, appealed to a prurient interest in sex; (2) "the material is patently offensive because it affronts contemporary community standards relating to the description or representation of sexual matters; and (3) the material is utterly without redeeming social value." *Id.* at 418. *See* Mitchell, *The Naked Truth: Prurience Depends on the Body in Question,* WASH. POST, June, 9, 1982, at B1.

135. WEAVER, *supra* note 130.

136. *Miller v. California,* 413 U.S. 15, *reh'g denied,* 414 U.S. 881 (1973); *Paris Adult Theatre I v. Slaton,* 413 U.S. 49, *reh'g denied,* 414 U.S. 881 (1973); *Kaplan v. California,* 413 U.S. 115, *reh'g denied,* 414 U.S. 883 (1973).

137. 413 U.S. 15 (1973).

138. 383 U.S. 413 (1966).

139. *Miller,* 413 U.S. at 24. *See generally* Schauer, *Reflections on Contemporary Community Standards: The Perpetuation of an Irrelevant Concept in the Law on Obscenity,* 56 N.C. L. REV. 1 (1978); Bell, *Determining Community Standards,* 63 A.B.A.J. 1203 (1977).

In *Pope v. Illinois,* 107 S.Ct. 1918 (1987), writing for the majority, Justice White determined that in deciding whether sexually explicit material is legally obscene, the proper inquiry must assess the social value of the questioned material is legally obscene, from the standpoint of a "reasonable person", rather than applying community standards. *Id.* at 1921. More specifically, juries will be instructed to decide whether a reasonable person would find serious value in the challenged material. *Id.* at 1922.

140. *Memoirs,* 383 U.S. at 418.

141. *Miller,* 413 U.S. at 24.

142. *Memoirs,* 383 U.S. at 418.

143. *Miller,* 413 U.S. at 24.

144. *Id.* at 27.

145. *Id.* at 25.

146. *Id.*

In order to protect women more fully from the effects of pornography, a fourth prong has been suggested to the *Miller* test. Namely, does the questioned conduct "portray murder dismemberment, brutality, or violence in the context of obscene acts?" D. A. DOWNS, THE NEW POLITICS OF PORNOGRAPHY 195 (1990).

147. 413 U.S. 49, *reh'g denied,* 414 U.S. 881 (1973).

148. *Id.* at 69. *See* Comment, *Pennsylvania Obscenity Law: A Pornographer's Delight,* 41 U. PITT. L. REV. 251 (1980).

149. Currin & Showers, *supra* note 14 at 274. *See generally* O'Neil, *Federalism and Obscenity,* 9 U. TOLEDO L. REV. 731 (1978).

The Federal Communications Commission, acting in its role of enforcing federal laws which prohibit obscene programming, has ruled indecent programs must be channeled to time periods (e.g., safe harbors from midnight to 6 A.M.) when the risk that children will be in the audience is minimal. 18 U.S.C. §1464 (1988). Yet, 47 U.S.C. §315(a) (1988) prohibits a censoring of the content of a political candidate's material. *See* Mangan, *Aborting the Indecency Standard in Political*

Family Values and the New Society: Dilemmas of the 21st Century

Programming 1 COMMLAW CONSPECTUS 73 (1993); Farhi, Networks Ask What's News?, WASH. POST, April 22, 1996, at C1.

See generally I. HUNTER ET AL., ON PORNOGRAPHY: LITERATURE, SEXUALITY, AND OBSCENITY LAW (1993).

150. *Id.*

151. *F.C.C. v. Pacifica Foundation*, 438 U.S. 726, *reh'g denied,* 439 U.S. 883 (1978).

In shaping legal tests for obscenity and pornography, it has been suggested that the U.S. Supreme Court speaks of obscenity, although it is obvious that it has pornography in mind. DONNERSTEIN ET AL., *supra* note 26 at 47. "[T]he Court has primarily concerned itself with words, pictures, or the portrayals that cause the reader or viewer to become sexually aroused. The Court has not usually been concerned with what is obscene in the conventional sense–profanity, scatology, impolite language, objects that are disgusting to the senses, or nonsexual conduct that offends higher sensibilities." *Id.* at 147-48.

152. Pacifica Foundation, 438 U.S. at 747-51.

Chief Justice Warren, in his dissenting opinion in *Jacobellis v. Ohio*, 378 U.S. 184 (1964), acknowledged that he could not define "hard core pornography" without any greater clarity than terming it obscenity. *Id.* at 201 (Warren, C.J., dissenting). In determining whether the questioned materials are obscene, the use to which they are put–not just the words and pictures themselves–must be evaluated. *Id.*

See generally Henkin, *Morals and the Constitution: The Sin of Obscenity*, 63 COLUM L. REV. 391 (1963).

153. *Pacific Foundation,* 438 U.S. at 748-50.

154. *Id.* at 749. *See* Foltz et al., *Jazzing Up the Airwaves*, NEWSWEEK, Mar. 26, 1984, at 36.

The U.S. Court of Appeals for the Ninth Circuit held, in *Carlin Communications, Inc. v. Mountain States Telephone & Telegraph Co.*, that the First Amendment was violated when a telephone company expelled an "adult entertainment" message service from its 976 network after a threat of prosecution. Even with the ruling the court found no state action, and thus no violation of the first amendment with the telephone company's subsequent adoption of a policy banning all messages of this type from its 976 network. 827 F.2d 1291 (9th Cir. 1987).

More recently, it has been found that telephone users in the United States and in other countries seeking adult phone sex conversation are placing over $100 million dollars worth of business in calls to Guyana, the Netherlands Antilles, and Sao Tome Mills, *Money Flows Into Poor Countries on X-Rated Phone Lines,* WASH. POST, Sept. 23, 1996, at 1.

155. 458 U.S. 747 (1982).

156. *Id.* at 759-61.

157. *Id.* at 756-59, 759 n.10.

158. *See, e.g.,* M. GOLDSTEIN & H. KANT, PORNOGRAPHY AND SEXUAL DEVIANCE (1973).

159. *Id.* at 13.

160. *Id.*

161. A. KINSEY ET AL., SEXUAL BEHAVIOR IN THE HUMAN MALE (1948).

162. GOLDSTEIN & KANT, *supra* note 158 at 14.

163. *Id.*

164. *Id.*

165. *Id.*

166. *Id.*

167. *Id.* at 15.

168. *Id. See* Ramsey, *The Sexual Development of Boys,* 56 AM. J. PSYCHOLOGY 217 (1943).

169. GOLDSTEIN & KANT, *supra* note 158 at 15.

170. *Id.*

171. *Id.*

172. *Id.* at 17. *See* Levitt & Hinsley, *Some Factors in the Valances of Erotic Stimuli,* 3 J. SEX RESEARCH 63 (1967). *See also* Levitt, *Pornography: Some New Perspectives on an Old Problem,* 5 J. SEX RESEARCH 247 (1969).

173. GOLDSTEIN & KANT, *supra* note 158 at 16.

174. *Id.* at 17.

175. *Id.* at 21.

176. *Id.* at 22.

177. *Id.*

178. *Id.* at 21. Goldstein & Katz found no evidence in their studies to suggest erotica *per se* triggers anti-social sexual behavior. *Id.* at 138.

179. DONNERSTEIN ET AL., *supra* note 26 at 67.

180. *Id.* at 67, 68.

181. *Id.* at 71, 72. While it appears there is serious doubt about a direct relationship between nonviolent pornography and violent behavior, this does not preclude the possibility that exposure to this form of pornography has a detrimental effect on how men think about women. Perhaps exposure to pornography predisposes men to believe that women in general are open to a wide range of sexual activities including deviate forms of sexual activity such as rape. *Id.* at 73.

182. *Id.* at 174.

183. *See* Doughtery, *Parents vs. Rock,* PEOPLE Mag., Sept. 16, 1985, at 46.

184. *Id.*

185. Krauthammer, *X-Ratings for Rock? Censorship in the Guise of Consumer Protection,* WASH. POST, Sept. 20, 1985, at A.27. *See also* Attansio, *The Ratings: Defining a New Mortality,* WASH. POST, Nov. 25, 1984, at G1.

186. Will, *No One Blushes Anymore,* WASH. POST, Sept. 15, 1985, at D 7. *But see* Yardley, *Explicit Lyrics, Explicitly Society,* WASH. POST, Sept. 2, 1985, at C2; Harringtion *Rock with a Capital R and PG-13: The Debate over Steamy Lyrics Goes a Long Way Back,* WASH. POST, Sept. 15, 1985, at H1.

187. *Raunch'n'roll Radio Is Here to Stay,* U.S. NEWS & WORLD RPT., May 4, 1987, at 52.

188. *Id.*

189. *Id.*

190. *Id.*

191. *Id.*

192. Gladwell, *Pushing the Limits of Taste Is Nothing New in Pop Culture,* WASH. POST, June 11, 1995, at G1. *See also* R.H. BORK, SLOUCHING TOWARDS GOMORRAH: MODERN LIBERALISM AND AMERICAN DECLINE, Ch. 7 (1996).

193. *Id.*

194. *Id.*

195. Harrington, *The Song Remains the Same: Attacks on Music Industry Are Really Nothing New,* WASH. POST, June 7, 1995, at C7. *See also* Kurtz, *Bennett Renews Attack on Rap Lyrics: Record Firms Criticized for Spreading Cancer,* WASH. POST, May 30, 1996, at C1.

196. *Id.*

197. Lacayo, *Violent Reaction,* TIME Mag., June 12, 1995, at 25-29.

198. *Id.*

199. Powers, . . . *But Dole & Co. Are onto Something. The New Censorship: A Manifesto,* WASH. POST, July 11, 1995, at G1.

200. *Id.*

201. Gifford, *Movie Violations: Once Taboo, Rape Is Depicted, Often Graphically, in Today's Films,* WASH. POST, Feb. 11, 1996, at G5.

202. Valenti, *Lights! Camera! Rhetoric! Parents, Not Politicians, Have the Tools to Control TV and Movie Violence,* WASH. POST, Feb. 4, 1996, at C.

203. Powers, *supra* note 199.

204. *Id.*

See Raspberry, *Community, Heal Thyself,* WASH. POST, Mar. 18, 1996, at 17. *See generally* Thomas, Victims and Heroes in the Benevolent Society, 19 HARV. J. L. & PUB. POL'Y 671 (1996).

205. THE REPORT OF THE COMMISSION ON OBSCENITY AND PORNOGRAPHY [hereinafter PORNOGRAPHY COMMISSION REPORT] (1970).

206. D. SCOTT, PORNOGRAPHY—ITS EFFECT ON THE FAMILY, COMMUNITY AND CULTURE 1 (1985).

207. PORNOGRAPHY COMMISSION REPORT, *supra* note 205 at 53.

208. *Id.*

209. SCOTT, *supra* note 206.

210. Tofani, *Meese Names Pornography Panel,* WASH. POST, May 21, 1985, at A16.

211. *Id.*

212. *Id.*

213. Shenon, *Pornography in U.S. Linked to Violence*, N.Y. TIMES, May 14, 1986, at 1.

214. *Id.*

215. Kurtz, *The Pornography Panel's Controversial Last Days: Scientists Say Report Misrepresents Their Findings to Support Conclusion on Sex Violence*, WASH. POST, May 30, 1986, at 13.

216. *Id.*

217. *Id.*

218. *See generally* Grove, *Descent into the World of Porn*, WASH. POST, June 7, 1986, at D1. Buchwald, *Undercover Work on the Porn Patrol*, WASH. POST, July 17, 1986, at B1.

219. Donnerstein & Linz, *The Question of Pornography*, PSYCHOLOGY TODAY, Dec. 1986, at 56.

220. *Id.*

221. *Id.* at 57.

222. *Id.*

223. *Id.*

224. *Id.* at 57, 58.

225. *Id.* at 58. One-third of all reported sex offenses are acts of indecent exposure. J. MACDONALD, INDECENT EXPOSURE (1973).

226. Donnerstein & Linz, *supra* note 219 at 58.

227. *Id.*

228. *Id.* at 59.

229. *Id. See* Schauer, *Thinking About Causation—With Special Reference to Pornography*, 31 [MICH.] LAW QUAD. NOTES 24 (Winter 1987); Donnerstein, *Aggressive Erotica and Violence Against Women*, 39 J. PERSONALITY AND SOCIAL PSYCHOLOGY 269 (1980). *See generally* Cohen, *Pornography: The Causal Link*, WASH. POST, July 3, 1986, at A19.

230. *Experts Dispute Link Between Porn and Harm*, 16 THE [COLUMBIA] OBSERVER 4 (May, 1987).

231. *Id. See also* Schauer, *supra* note 229.

232. *Child Abuse Prevention and Treatment and Adoption Reform Act Amendments of 1983, Hearings Before the Subcommittee on Family and Human Services of the Committee on Labor and Human Resources*, 98th Cong., 1st Sess. 226-80 (1983) (statement of Gregory A. Loken, S. Staff Attorney, Covenant House).

233. Currin & Showers, *supra* note 14 at 275-77 nn.72-73. Over 80 percent of individuals who purchase child pornography will abuse children. *Id.* at 72. *See also* SCOTT, *supra* note 206 at 16-17; A. BURGESS, CHILD PORNOGRAPHY AND SEX RINGS (1984).

234. Kurtz, *Pornography Panel's Objectivity Disputed*, WASH. POST, Oct. 15, 1985 at A4.

235. MESSAGE FROM THE PRESIDENT OF THE UNITED STATES TRANSMITTING THE CHILD PROTECTION AND OBSCENITY ACT OF 1987, H.R. Doc. 1009-29, 100th Cong., 1st Sess. (1987) [hereinafter PRESIDENT'S MESSAGE]. For a detailed analysis of the Act, *see* Smith, *Nudity, Obscenity and Pornography: The Streetcars Named Lust and Desire,* 4 J. CONTEMP. HEALTH L. & POL'Y 155, 184-187 (1988).

The Pornography Victims Protection Act of 1987, was introduced by Senators Specter and McConnell on March 10, 1987, as S. 703 and referred to the Committee on the Judiciary. It imposed a civil penalty of $100,000 for those who caused, intimidated, or fraudulently induced an individual eighteen years or older to engage in any sexually explicit conduct for the purpose of producing any visual depiction of such conduct if the individual or individuals involved knew, or had reason to know, that the depiction would be transported in interstate or foreign commerce or mailed. This act was never enacted into legislation.

236. 18 U.S.C. §§ 2251-2253 (1979).

237. 18 U.S.C.A. §§ 2251-2255 (West Supp. 1985).

Congressional concern over interpretation of federal child pornography laws by the U.S. Department of Justice prompted a Sense of the Senate Resolution both clarifying and affirming the 1984 Child Protection Act. Thus, under the act, the term,*exhibition of genitals* is not limited to nude exhibitions or exhibitions in which the outline of those areas are discernible through clothing. Secondly, the Senate stated that the prohibitions in the act against depicting a minor engaged in sexually explicit conduct are violated if a person photographs a minor in such a way as to exhibit the child in a lascivious way—instead of requiring lascivious conduct by the child as submitted originally by the Justice Department. 139 CONG. RECORD S14974-03 (Remarks by Senator Grassley, Nov. 1993); 139 CONG. RECORD S15837-01 (Remarks by Senator Roth, Nov. 1993).

238. 18 U.S.C.A. §§ 2251-2254 (West Supp. 1986).

239. 18 U.S.C. §2251c(2)(b) *et. seq.* (1988).

240. *See* Scheller, *PC Peep Shows: Computers Privacy, and Child Pornography,* 27 J. MARSHALL L. REV. 989, 1008 at n.150 *passim* (1994).

See also Lynn, *Civil Rights' Ordinances and the Attorney General's Commission: New Development in Pornography Regulations,* 21 HARV. C.R.-C.L. L. REV. 27 (1986).

241. Scheller, *supra* note 240 at nn.154-55.

242. *Id.* at n.156.

243. 18 U.S.C. 2251c(2)(b) (1988).

244. Scheller, *supra* note 240 at 1009.

245. *Id.* at 1011.

See 18 U.S.C. §§1461, 1462, 1465 (1988) and 18 U.S.C. §§2251-2252 prohibiting the mailing of child pornography and other obscene material.

See also Naughton, *Is Cyberspace a Public Forum?,* GEO. L. J. 409 (1992) (highlighting the inability of law to keep pace with burgeoning computer technologies); Hilzenrath, *FBI Cites Basis for Targeting Online Child Pornographers,* WASH. POST, April 9, 1997, at A2.

246. 47 U.S.C. §223(a)(i, ii).

247. 47 U.S.C. §151 *et. seq.*

248. 47 U.S.C. §230(B)(5).

249. 47 U.S.C. §223(a) (i, ii).

250. 47 U.S.C. §223(d).

251. 47 U.S.C. §§503, 640, 641.

252. *American Civil Liberties Union v. Reno*, 924 F. Supp. 824 (E.D. Pa. 1996).

On appeal, the U.S. Supreme Court held on June 26, 1997, that the Communications Decency Act provisions regarding patently offensive displays of indecent transmissions were overbroad and vague and thus abridged the freedom of speech guarantees of the 1st Amendment. 117 S. Ct. 2329.

253. 47 U.S.C. §151. *et. seq*

254. 47 U.S.C. §551 (1996).

255. Farhi, *Study Finds Real Harm in TV*, WASH. POST, Feb. 6, 1996, at 1.

256. *Id.*

257. Harwood, *Morality at The Movies*, WASH. POST, June 23, 1995, at A23.

258. Farhi, *TV Industry Agrees on Rating System: Age-Based Formula is Similar to That Used for Movies*, WASH. POST, Dec. 3, 1996, at A1. *See also* Zoglin, *Rating Wars*, TIME Mag., Dec. 23, 1996; Farhi, *TV Ratings Agreement Reached: NBC Refuses to Join Deal for Stronger Advisories*, WASH. POST, July 10, 1997 at 1.

259. 47 U.S.C. §§330, 340, 640, 641 (1996).

260. *Id.*

261. *Id.*

262. Farhi, *Networks Consider Ratings System*, WASH. POST, Feb. 15, 1996, at 1.

263. *Id.*

264. Farhi, *The V-Chip Blip*, WASH. POST, Feb. 18, 1996, at 1.

265. *Id.*

See Comment, Second Best Solution: The First Amendment, Broadcast Indency, and The V-Chip, 91 NW. U.L. REV. 1190 (1997).

266. Thomas, *Postal Sting Changes 45 So Far in Child Pornography Probe: Videos Depict Children as Young as 7*, Official Say, WASH. POST, May 10, 1996, at A2.

267. *Despite U.S. Campaigns, A Boom in Pornography*, N.Y. TIMES, July 4, 1993, at 20.

See also McGee, *U.S. Crusade Against Pornography Tests the Limits of Fairness*, WASH. POST, Jan. 11, 1993, at 1.

268. *Id.*

269. *Id.*

270. *Id.*

271. Scheller, *supra* note 240 at 998.

272. *Id.* at 999.

273. *See* Sunstein, *The First Amendment in Cyberspace*, 104 YALE. L.J. 1757 (1995).

See American Civil Liberties Union v. Reno, supra note 252.

274. Scheller, *supra* note 240 at 999.

275. *Id.* at 996, 1012.

The Child Pornography Act of 1996, Public Law 104-208, deals specifically with computer-generated child pornography and imposes, upon conviction of transmitting it, a five-to-thirty-year prison term. Child pornography is defined as "actual or simulated sexual acts" as well as the "lascivious exhibition of the genitals or pubic area" of minors. This law outlaws—specifically—"any visual depiction, including any photograph, film, video image or picture that is or appears to be, of a minor engaging in actually explicit conduct."

See 18 U.S.C. §§2252A, 2256 *et. seq.* (1996).

276. P. ROBINSON & N. TOMOSAITIS, THE JOY OF CYBERSPACE: THE UNDERGROUND GUIDE TO ELECTRONIC EROTICA xvii (1993).

277. Levy, *No Place for Kids? A Parent's Guide to Sex on the Net*, NEWSWEEK, July 3, 1995, at 47.

278. *Id.*

279. *Id.*

See Rimm, *Marketing Pornography on the Information Superhighway*, 83 GEO. L. J. 1849 (1995). *But see* Comment, *Creating the Standards of a Global Community: Regulating Pornography on the Internet—An International Concern*, 10 TEMPLE INT'L & COMP. L. J. 467 (1996).

280. Servi, *Sexy F Seeks Hot M: A Mother's Tale*, NEWSWEEK, July 3, 1995, at 51.

281. Tierney, *Porn, the Low-Slung Engine of Progress*, N.Y. TIMES, Jan. 9, 1994, at 1.

282. Levy, *supra* note 277.

283. *See generally* Branit, *Reconciling Free Speech and Equality: What Justifies Censorship?*, 9 HARV. J.L. & PUB. POL'Y 429 (1986).

284. Dworkin, *Is There a Right to Pornography?* 1 OX. J. LEGAL STUD. 177 (1981).

285. M. ADLER, WE HOLD THESE TRUTHS 128 (1987).

286. *Id. See* Note, *Fornication, Cohabitation and the Constitution*, 77 MICH. L. REV. 252, 291 (1978). If it is assumed the existence of marriage is to serve as a means to facilitate emotional and sexual expressions of intimacy, intimacy becomes so fundamental "to individual liberty that it demands constitutional protection. Nothing is different about the psychological and emotional needs of unmarried couples which would justify denying them the same protection." *Id.*

287. Canavan, *Law and Society's Conscience*, 2 HUMAN LIFE REV. 1, 6 (1976).

288. *Id.* at 7.

289. Schauer, *supra* note 229.

290. *Id.* at 29.

291. DONNERSTEIN ET AL., *supra* note 26 at 67.

292. *Id.* at 91.

293. 378 U.S. 189, 199 (1964) (Warren, C.J., dissenting).

294. *Id.*

Dissolving the Family and Expanding Its Relevance

Chapter 8

Death

Even though theology and ethics are logically independent,[1] traditional moral attitudes regarding euthanasia are affected profoundly by theological ideas, three in particular: that God, alone, has total dominion and control over all human life; death is a form of punishment; and to kill innocent life places one's soul in jeopardy of eternal damnation.[2]

If a "right to die" is but merely a right to the inevitable,[3] the proper question to be raised is why the claim to the inevitable? And the answer lies, as has been seen, in a recognition of the vast technologies of medical science that make life almost endless.[4] Advanced medical devices that make respiration, cardiac massage, uterine curettage, intravenous feeding, and a limitless availability of antibiotics not only forestall death but also introduce untold confusion and lack of agreement in determining when in fact it occurs.[5]

Because a "good" death is now quite improbable for most, it is understandable that a majority of individuals when asked the manner in which death would be preferable reply that a death without warning (as with an accident) is their choice. The most common fear remains that of dying under protracted circumstances in a hospital, the *victim* of modern technological processes. Thus, according to present levels of conception, or misconception as the case may be, "the only way for a person to die in euthanasia is to be killed some how."[6]

For the bioethicist, the right to die with dignity is grounded in one basic principle: avoid human distress.[7] The right itself may be recognized as having three ethical parts that conduce to the whole: a right to have full information provided a patient by his physician regarding his medical problem—its origin and prognosis—in order that he may, in turn, give an informed consent to treatment or nontreatment as the case may be; a right to both "human company and care" that includes not only relief from pain but also the maintenance of a treating environment free of noxious stimuli; and, finally, a right to die unmolested by meddlesome procedures that would include a right to refuse this and other forms of treatment.[8] This composite interest in a right to die continues to be obscured and generally frustrated by the present use of the term *euthanasia*, in all its stated and more subtle definitional and practical applications.

EUTHANASIA

Euthanasia, as a term, concept, or attitude has been used under various and confusing circumstances to denote "any good death," "any assistance in helping dying patients in their dying (including the cessation of treatments)," and "only acting directly to kill the dying patient."[9] The intriguing fact emerging from any study of euthanasia, then, will be that it can mean "any good death" as well as a "morally outrageous death."[10]

Active euthanasia involves killing while passive euthanasia does not. One is not acceptable; the other is being tolerated and accepted more and more. But how can letting die be in some way preferable, from a moral standpoint, than helping die? If all other morally relevant factors—intention, motivation, outcome—are the same, why should there be a difference? In truth, the difference between killing and letting die has no moral significance. "In active euthanasia, the doctor initiates a course of events that lead to the patient's death. . . . In letting die, the agent stands back and lets nature take her sometimes cruel course."[11]

The traditional argument against adoption or acceptance of euthanasia is that a rational patient simply does not and cannot choose euthanasia.[12] If this were so, it would have to be maintained further that no autonomous and rational decision could ever be made by a patient to refuse a modality of treatment that was life sustaining.[13] Yet, this is not what the vast majority of active euthanasia opponents assert. Rather, they maintain that a patient can in fact make a rational choice to follow passive euthanasia but not active euthanasia.[14] The inconsistency is obvious. The crucial question that begs answering is whether a patient "can rationally choose an earlier death over a later one."[15] Accordingly, it is submitted that if one can make a rational choice to follow passive euthanasia, then he must also be entitled to make a rational choice to follow active euthanasia[16] or, as termed in this chapter, "enlightened self-determination."[17]

Beneficent Euthanasia

Beneficent euthanasia is defined simply as the painless inducement of a quick death.[18] The most common paradigm of it would include cases where an individual suffers from an irreversible condition such as disseminated carcinoma metastasis, has excruciating and incurable pain, is beyond reasonable medical doubt that death is imminent, is told of his condition and requests some means of "easy death" and aside from a desire to help such an individual, no other relevant conditions exist.[19]

The crux of the argument for beneficent euthanasia is found in what is termed a societal obligation "to treat members kindly"[20] consistent with a principle of beneficence.[21] Suffering should at all times be minimized and kind treatment maximized.[22] This position should be able to be advocated without fear of it being viewed in reality as another Nazi-type plan for extermination.[23] The fear that the use of euthanasia, however qualified, runs the risk of destroying the social fabric of society is unfounded.[24] Beneficent euthanasia's utilization is consistent totally with the basic human need for dignity or self-respect. It should not be viewed as a punishment but rather simply as a matter of meeting this basic need and, at the same time, executing the societal obligation or collective responsibility of treating all members of society kindly or with compassion.[25]

Perhaps at the heart of any discussion of euthanasia is whether such life-ending acts are cruel in and of themselves[26] and morally justified. As important, is a consideration of whether in point of fact the act of euthanasia is administered to a *person*.[27] For one to be recognized as a person, it is commonly regarded as necessary for him to have rational awareness.[28] But is a "betubed, sedated, aerated, glucosed, mechanically manipulated" individual one capable of being considered rationally aware?[29] Arguably, one simply is not a person under these conditions[30] and the individual who acts deliberately and with set purpose to relieve such suffering, incurably ill and extremely debilitated individuals should not be recognized as having committed an act of murder.[31] But, for this conclusion to have merit, some type of set criteria or characteristics for personhood must be acknowledged as either correct or acceptable,[32] or an incontrovertible definition of it agreed upon.[33] Sadly, it must be recognized that none of the criteria posited have achieved such a mark.[34] Yet, there is very wide agreement that when there is no "relational potential" or a capacity for love and engaging in interpersonal relations, owing to an absence of cerebral functioning, there can be no recognition of personhood.[35]

Blurred Definitions and a Posited Clarification

A good number of physicians and moral theologians use the term *euthanasia* only in connection with active euthanasia, preferring as such to refer to "passive euthanasia" as "the right to death with dignity."[36] The reality of the present situation is that many of the old, chronically ill, debilitated, or mentally impaired are *allowed* to die by withholding the aggressive medical treatment and available care as do young, mentally normal patients.[37]

Since little if any substance depends on what label is attached to these present actions under consideration, the debate about the distinctions becomes pointless.[38] Indeed, because of the blurring of distinctions between active and passive euthanasia, there is really no distinct difference between the two.[39]

If death is intentionally caused by doing something or withholding something, there is no morally significant distinction to be drawn between an active means to death and a passive means to death. Both are alike or intended means to death; and both the intention and the result are the same—the death of the patient. If one simply withholds treatment, it may take the patient longer to die, and he may suffer more than he would if more direct action were taken and a lethal injection given.[40]

In an effort to establish clarity of analysis, it has been suggested euthanasia be redefined as either the putting to death or the failure to prevent death in cases of terminal illness or injury.[41] The motives behind such an act would be to either relieve comatoseness, the effects of permanent suffering, anxiety or perhaps a perceived sense of burdensomeness.[42] Thus, as newly clarified, at least one other person would be seen as causing or helping to cause the death of a competent individual who desires death or, in the case of an incompetent, making a substituted decision regarded as in the individual's best interests to either cause death directly or to withdraw some mechanism or process that sustains life.[43]

Acts of Treatment Versus Omissions of Treatment

In classical Greece, medicine was given three roles: to alleviate the sufferings of the sick, lessen the violence of diseases that afflicted them, and not "treat those who are overmastered by their diseases, realizing that in such cases medicine was powerless."[44] Indeed, the most common duty of all Greco-Roman physicians was "to help, or least to do no harm."[45] It was a pure matter of discretion when a hopeless case was taken by a physician.[46] This prevailing sentiment of physicians in this period of civilization found strong precedent in Egyptian and Assyro-Babylonian medicine.[47] As a medical sentiment, in fact, it continued in vitality throughout the Middle Ages.[48] It is commonly thought that Francis Bacon writing in his *De augmentis scientairium*, in the late 16th and early 17th centuries, advanced the conclusion that medicine should seek to prolong life and expand longevity and the notion has grown in an exaggerated and misdirected manner since that time.[49]

So it is seen, then, that while a physician's so-called duty to prolong life *qua* life has no classical roots, the idea of "respect for life" does have a rich tradition of observance.[50] But to be remembered is the fact that even though physicians would not actively seek to terminate a life either by abortion or euthanasia, they were also *not* required to actively prolong life, itself.[51] While with the rise of Christianity, abortion, suicide, and euthanasia became sins, still the prolongation of life never did "become either a virtue or a duty."[52]

RELIGIOUS MORALITY OF ACTIONS

Pope John Paul II approved the *Declaration on Euthanasia* adopted by the

Sacred Congregation for the Doctrine of Faith on May 5, 1980, and in so doing advanced broad principles of humanistic care and treatment for the dying.[53] Acknowledging that one may seek to utilize advanced medical techniques of an experimental, and high-risk, nature in order to combat an illness, the declaration allows for the interruption of these processes when they render unsatisfactory results.[54] But before actions of this nature are allowed, the patient's "reasonable wishes" and those of his family, together with the advice of the attending physicians, must be considered.[55] Deferring to the physicians' expertise in matters of this nature, the Declaration allows that they "may in particular judge that the investment in instruments and personnel is *disproportionate to the results foreseen.*"[56] And that, further, they may conclude that, "the techniques applied impose on the patient strain or suffering *out of proportion* with the benefits which he or she may gain from such techniques."[57] What is seen here is a clear and unequivocable example of a cost versus benefit analysis which has been submitted as a proper standard of evaluation.

One may, of course, consistent with the declaration, "make do with the normal means that medicine can offer."[58] Thus, if such a course is followed, "one cannot impose on anyone the obligation to have recourse to a technique which is already in use but which *carries a risk or is burdensome.*"[59] A refusal of this type is not in any way to be regarded as an act equivalent to suicide but rather an acceptance of a human condition or desire to avoid the use of a modality of treatment "disproportionate to the results" or a wish to prevent excessive financial drains on the patient's family "or the community."[60] Again, the element of economic feasibility of treatment is set forth as a proper vector of force in ultimate decision making. The need to ration scarce medical resources so that they may be expended on those who have a real possibility of recovery is also impliedly recognized in the declaration.[61]

Evangelium Vitae

"The Gospel of Life," or *Evangelium Vitae*, was issued as Pope John Paul II's eleventh encyclical on March 30, 1995.[62] Here, for the first time, the Roman Catholic Church sets out a comprehensive moral rationale for its position on a wide range of issues. Of particular pertinence is the pope's position on euthanasia. Pope John Paul defines euthanasia as "an action or mission which of itself and by intervention causes death, with the purpose of eliminating all suffering."[63] While stating "euthanasia is a grave violation of the law of God"[64] and really, as with assisted suicide, "a false mercy,"[65] the pope nonetheless reaffirms Pope Pius XII's conclusion "that it is licit to relieve pain by narcotics even when the result is deceased consciousness and a shortening of life" if other means are not available.[66] He elaborated his own position and sought to distinguish aggressive medical treatment from euthanasia by underscoring the 1980 *Declaration on Euthanasia* which allows refusal of futile medical treatment which would serve no purpose other than prolong a "precarious and burdensome" activity.[67]

Civil laws which authorize either abortion or euthanasia cease to be morally binding because they are "crimes which no human law can claim to legitimize."[68] Thus, it is never licit to obey a law that permits abortion or euthanasia.[69] The contemporary posturing of ethical relativism (or the proportionalist approach of balancing) is rejected in favor of respect for objective and binding moral norms.[70] Again, the distinction between the need for aggressive treatment of medically hopeless and dying individuals, where proportionality is in fact utilized in determining when only palliative care should be given, and acts of euthanasia, where no ethical balancing should be condoned, must be made here and interpreted as such in light of the 1980 Declaration of Euthanasia. Previously, in his 1993 encyclical *Veritas Splendor*, "The Splendor of Truth," the pope underscored his conviction that the object of certain actions makes it intrinsically evil and that subjectivistic moral judgment cannot prevail over objective morality.[71]

ORDINARY VERSUS EXTRAORDINARY TREATMENT

The principles of ordinary versus extraordinary life-sustaining processes or treatments are relative not only as to time and locale but also in their application to specific cases. In essence, these concepts serve as basic value judgments that aid in reaching a determination whether a given modality of treatment presents an undue hardship on the at-risk patient or whether it provides hope for direct benefit. Thus, if too great a hardship would be imposed on the patient by following a particular medical or surgical course of treatment and no reasonable *hope of benefit* was to be derived therefrom, such actions would be viewed properly as extraordinary and not obligatory.[72] In practice, many physicians choose to equate "ordinary" with "usual," and "extraordinary" with "unusual" or "heroic" medical practice.[73] Once it has been decided to withhold "heroics," no rational process has been developed that facilitates decision making regarding what treatment should be pursued and what withheld. Indeed, sometimes half-treatments are initiated thereby allowing, for example, intravenous feeding but at a rate that will result in dehydration over time.[74] Such a gesture maintains the vital symbol of feeding that does not sustain the life of the patient over an extended period of time.[75] Although somewhat deceiving, it nonetheless serves as a type of artificial compromise for those wishing to respect the symbol yet at the same time act in accordance with patient's needs and, often, his present or previously expressed wishes.[76]

Determining whether medical or surgical treatment is either ordinary or extraordinary may be regarded as a quality of life statement. And, in reaching this statement, knowingly or unknowingly, the decision makers involved (legal, medical, ethical) utilize a substituted judgment to conclude whether—in and under similar circumstances to that which the patient *in extremis* exists—they would or would not wish to survive in such a physical and mental state. Obviously, decisions of this moment are made within a varied and yet complex vortex of highly charged emotions.[77]

If love or humanness is to be recognized ultimately as the binding force of life itself, it may be submitted that man should endeavor to seek to maximize a full response to life in a loving or humane manner. If this course is followed, suffering is minimized, over all social good advanced or maximized and value or utility in living achieved.[78] Thus, very simply stated, if an act when undertaken would cause more harm than good to or for the at-risk individual in question *and* to those associated closely with him, the act could be considered an unloving one. The central point to be understood is that, in cases of this nature, a basic cost-benefit analysis is almost always undertaken, be it on a conscious or unconscious level.[79]

On a case-by-case, or situational, basis with the standard of reasonableness as the linchpin—as opposed to an unyielding *a priori* ethic—health care providers should balance the gravity of the harm caused by extraordinary care, against the utility of the good that will result from such extraordinary actions. As such, the decision makers should be ever mindful of the ethical imperative to minimize human suffering at all levels when making ultimate decisions.[80] In reality, it is submitted that this mandated balancing test validates a cost-benefit analysis.[81] It is only after, however, recognizing that all life is sanctified by creation and is not only qualitative to the individual at peril as well as to mankind in general that inquiry may proceed to be made into whether the medically handicapped individual possesses a sustained ability to enjoy and fulfill loving, interpersonal relationships with others and whether the present or contemplated course of medical or surgical treatment maximizes that potential utility of life—assuming it exists—or, contrariwise, minimizes present suffering.[82]

Measures of an extraordinary nature undertaken for the specific purpose of prolonging a life of suffering should be recognized as not only unjust to the individual in distress but as an act of effrontery to the societal standard of decency and humanity.[83] The physician's primary responsibility is to relieve suffering when it occurs, not to seek the survival of a patient at all costs. Indeed, an overly aggressive modality of treatment for a terminally ill patient, regardless of age, should be recognized as a defilement of the very doctrine of *primum non nocere*. If therapy would be futile and to no end other than mere survival, it should not be administered.[84] Thus, the artificial feeding of a terminally ill patient in irreversible coma should be regarded as a *treatment* decision and not mandated except when benefits clearly outweigh burdens.[85]

Moralists suggest that three commonly accepted principles are at the center of the individual's—not his relatives, or the medical profession's—responsibility to preserve his life:

> *Per se* he is obliged to use the ordinary means of preserving his life. *Per se* he is not obliged to use extraordinary means, though the use of such means is permissible and generally commendable. *Per accidens*, however, he is obliged to use even extraordinary means, if the preservation of his life is required for some greater good such as his own spiritual welfare or the common good.[86]

Application of the principle of double effect, although recognized as an exception to these three controlling principles, is not extended to those cases regarded as *morally impossible*; thus the use of extraordinary means is not included within the principle, itself.[87]

The investment of economic and social resources in prolonging one's life where such actions constitute an inordinate drain on familial and societal resources and achieve little more than merely extending the dying process are not mandated morally under the ordinary-extraordinary principle.[88] Indeed, the very concept of ordinary means for preserving life has been defined as "all medicine, treatments, and operations, which offer a reasonable hope of benefit for the patient and which can be obtained and used without excessive expense, pain or other inconvenience."[89] Contrariwise, extraordinary or optional means of treatment are taken to be all those medicines, treatments, or surgeries that are incapable of being administered without excessive outlays of money or other inconveniences and, if in fact followed, would offer no reasonable hope of recovery or positive benefit.[90] The likelihood of success in undertaking the treatment is a valid consideration.[91] Accordingly, if for example a class of newborns for whom treatment would be so prohibitively costly and so unlikely of success could be identified, treatment would be excused.[92]

Evaluating Factors

A number of relative factors must be weighed in deciding whether to excuse a modality of treatment. As noted, the successfulness of the proposed treatment is a major factor for consideration, and, of course, there are degrees of success. While it is one matter to administer oxygen in order to alleviate a medical crisis for a patient, it is another matter to use that same oxygen to merely prolong a life for which recovery is negligible. Degrees of hope are a second factor to be evaluated when it concerns complete recovery. Thus, while in one case oxygen is administered to end a patient's bout with pneumonia and may and usually does offer a very high hope of complete recovery, in other cases the patient's physical condition may be so fragile that there is but an equally fragile hope of recovery from the medical crisis. The degrees of difficulty in obtaining and using ordinary means comprise the third set of factors; for some means are easy to obtain and use and are inexpensive, and others are much more difficult to obtain and to use.[93]

Intravenous feeding problems present a unique paradigm for study of the ordinary-extraordinary conundrum. For example, when a cancer patient in extreme pain has established a systemic toleration of any drug (meaning that dosages provide but brief relief from that recurring pain), the attending physician realizes the incurable prognosis of the disease. Because of a good heart, death will be drawn out, however, for several weeks. Remembering the one thing which will end the patient's suffering, the physician proceeds to cut off intravenous feeding. This done, the patient dies the next day.

The case involves the principle that an ordinary means of prolonging life and an extraordinary means are relative to the patient's physical condition. Intravenous feeding is an artificial means of prolonging life and therefore one may be more liberal in application of principle. Since this cancer patient is beyond all hope of recovery and suffering extreme pain, intravenous feeding should be considered an extraordinary means of prolonging life. The physician was justified in stopping the intravenous feeding."[94]

Further subtleties and ambiguities in the taxonomy of ordinary versus extraordinary care are seen dramatically in three landmark case opinions. In the case of *In re Dinnerstein* a Massachusetts court observed that its task was to discern the rather slight "distinction between those situations in which the withholding of extraordinary measures may be viewed as allowing the disease to take its natural course and those in which the same actions may be deemed to have been the cause of death."[95] In *Superintendent of Belchertown State School v. Saikewicz* it was held that no extraordinary means of prolonging life should be pursued when there is no hope that the patient will recover. "Recovery should not be defined simply as the ability to remain alive, it should mean life without intolerable suffering."[96] Finally, in *In re Quinlan*, the New Jersey Supreme Court opined, "One would have to think that the use of the same respirator or life support could be considered 'ordinary' in the context of the possible curable patient but 'extraordinary' in the context of the forced sustaining by cardio-respiratory processes of an *irreversibly doomed patient*."[97]

Circularity in Terminology

It has been suggested that both the terms, ordinary and extraordinary medical treatment, are "incurably circular until filled with concrete or descriptive meaning"[98] and that, furthermore, this language be abandoned in favor of a classification that merely recognizes "treatment medically indicated" for a nondying or salvageable person which would thus be expected to be helpful and "curative treatment not indicated (for the dying)."[99] Of course, the central weakness of this posture is that no objective criteria or concreteness is set forth with this classification itself that would enable a decision maker to act unerringly. No guiding or unyielding *a priori* standard is proffered—only a standard of situational reasonableness tied to the facts of each case. Perhaps, however, within this "weakness" is to be found the very strength of the suggestion: a straight recognition that no definitive position can be taken.

Another suggestion has been to ban the artificial distinctions between ordinary and extraordinary treatment and focus instead on whether, in a given case, medical treatment is "morally imperative" or merely "elective."[100] For a competent patient, a refusal of treatment would be accepted when he could present reasons relevant to this declining physical or mental health or to familial, social, economic, or religious concerns, that were valid to him and him alone.[101]   The incompetent patient is faced with the knowing reality that he is unable to make reasonable choices. Thus, the decision maker in this setting—spouse, parent, child, next of kin, guardian, or physician—may refuse treatment on morally acceptable grounds when such an action would seem "within the realm of reason to reasonable people."[102]

The question remains: What is the test of reasonableness?

> A reasonable person would find a refusal unreasonable (and thus treatment morally required) if the treatment is useful in treating a patient's condition (though not necessarily life-saving) and at the same time does not give rise to any significant patient-centered objections based on physical or mental burden; familial, social or economic concern; or religious belief.[103]

Both of these new classifications regarding ordinary-extraordinary treatment are inescapably tied to a standard of qualitative living—perceived as such by the at-risk patient, his family or supportive network, or health care decision maker. Does this not mean, then, that all ultimate decisions regarding treatment or nontreatment are essentially cost-benefit ones?

Suffice it to suggest at this juncture that ideally the concepts of ordinary and extraordinary means of treatment should be disregarded totally not only because of their imprecise terms of definition and application but also because they tend to support paternalism.[104]   While the standards of customary medical practice determine what ought to be done, both the disease entity together with the medical technologies needed to treat it displace the patient as the focus of concern. Indeed, the patient-person becomes subordinated totally to the patient-disease bearer.[105] What is demanded, then, is a simple recognition that no form of treatment is either obligatory or optional.   Rather, everything depends on the condition of the patient.[106]   Thus, the only reasonable standard of evaluation is to be found in considering the ratio of benefits and burdens of the treatment to the patient.   A competent patient should always make this determination himself.   For an incompetent patient, however, a proxy must use the previously expressed wishes or values of that patient when they are known or may be determined.[107]

DOUBLE EFFECT

The principle of indirect or double effect, one of the basic principles of Catholic medical ethics,[108] and one also intuited by many others not necessarily members of the Roman Church, is best understood by an understanding—or oftentimes but a vague feeling—that the administration of a potentially lethal narcotic that would relieve the intractable pain of a cancer patient is in some way different—morally—from a knowing act that would murder the same patient, justifying it on the grounds of acting mercifully.[109]   Stated otherwise:

The principle is intended to provide a halfway ground between a straightforward utilitarianism, which would simply consider the relative weights of the good and bad consequences of an action in order to make a moral judgment of it, and a variety of sterner moral positions, which would either deny the moral relevance of consequences to actions altogether or would judge immoral any action with bad consequences, no matter what other good consequences it had.[110]

The net result of recognizing and applying the principle of double effect is that certain actions *indirectly* producing certain evil consequences are justified, as long as four conditions are met: the action undertaken, independent of its effect, must not itself be inherently held to be morally evil; the evil effect must not be utilized as a means to produce the good effect; the evil effect is merely tolerated and not sincerely intended; and, finally, regardless of its evil consequences, there is a proportionate reason for undertaking the action.[111] Utilization of this principle provides the justification, for example, of removing a cancerous fetus-bearing uterus and the administration of pain-relieving narcotics that may, in turn, produce respiratory depression.[112] The principle's legitimacy has been attacked, alternatively, because it leads to discriminations that are wrongful by excusing acts (or thought to be killings, by some) it should not and forbidding other such acts it should allow.[113]

A principle of such ambivalence is open, obviously, to these and other logical deficiencies. But, it has been suggested that validation is recognized because of its "psychological validity."[114] A use-hypothetical attempts to bring into focus this point. Faced with a patient's intolerable pain and his pleas for relief that cannot be mitigated by lesser doses of nonlethal drugs, a physician chooses to administer a dose of an analgesic that will likely cause death. A crucial contrast is then undertaken between the attitude and the manner that the motive for relieving pain engenders compared with attitudes and manner pursued when a premeditated act to kill is pursued.[115] If there were a purpose to kill, would it be seen in the way a syringe would be grasped, the words which might be either spoken or withheld, the look in the eyes?

And would not the consequences of the difference be compounded almost geometrically at least for the physician as he killed one such patient after another? And what of the repercussions of the difference on the nurses and hospital attendants? How long would the quality and attitude of mercy survive death-intending conduct? The line between the civilized and savage in men is fine enough without jeopardizing it by euthanasia. History teaches the line is maintainable under the principle of double effect; it might well not be under a regime of direct intentional killing.[116]

Whether the lessons of history substantiate the alleged "psychological validity" of the principle and establish that it is efficacious and merits ready use and retention seem dubious at best. Rather than continue to enshrine an awkward concept, it should be replaced by the relatively simple and enduring standard of what is, under a given set of facts, *reasonable*. Guided or supported by the principle of triage and a consideration of what actions are in the best interests of the at-risk patient, a cost-benefit analysis should be undertaken in order to decide whether one modality of treatment or nontreatment should be pursued.[117] Thus, reasonable, humane and cost-effective actions should be both the procedure utilized and the goal sought here.

The intensive care unit found within the average hospital in the United States not only seeks to treat and to return patients suffering from serious injuries or acute disease to their original working or stabilized environments but also to serve as a sophisticated state-of-the-art hospice.[118] Even when there is no hope of recovery, studies have shown that approximately 19 percent of patients in intensive care units are nonetheless admitted and stay.[119] It would seem to be a reasonable and sensible idea for at-risk patients to decide not to be treated in an intensive care unit, this choice not being made necessarily with the idea of dying sooner but rather with the view in mind that access to family and friends will be more easily facilitated as well as family and social and economic resources conserved.[120]

Choices of this nature should not be confused or tied to the principle of double effect. Rather, when tragic choices are simply not between different chances of survival with different treatments but only between extending the process of suffering and death or shortening it, the principle has little pertinence or significance.[121] "Patients may very well sensibly decide to forego treatment or intensive care unit care so that they may in fact finally die and end their travail. They may directly will their deaths and thus within one strict interpretation of moral theory, passively commit suicide."[122]

Physicians in England are not allowed to initiate any actions that have, as their primary purpose, to cause a patient's death.[123] Accordingly, under the Suicide Act of 1961, if a physician were to endeavor to facilitate the request of a terminally ill patient for assistance in terminating his life, he would subject himself to criminal prosecution.[124] A physician is also, under this legislation, not allowed to honor suggestions from the family of a gravely ill patient to end the life of such a patient.[125] Yet, since one of the basic commitments of the medical profession is to ease pain, if acting to ease suffering a physician must introduce and follow a modality of treatment that may in fact hasten death, his actions are legally permissible so long as the understanding is maintained that the course of treatment is *only* for the relief of pain or associated distress.[126] This is a preeminently reasonable *modus operandi* for dealing with the double effect construct. Whether actions of this nature or constructions of the principle of double effect painlessly expedite death and thereby unwisely validate the traditional perception of passive euthanasia or (perhaps) passive suicide—more correctly termed "self-determination" in this chapter—and should accordingly be restricted or even forbidden socially and legally will be examined forthwith.

Legal Distinctions

The legal distinction between acts and omission is to be found in the determination of a legal duty and the distinction between action and inaction. Within the law of negligence is a deeply rooted distinction between misfeasance and nonfeasance or, in other words, between a state of active misconduct which brings a positive injury to others and passive interaction which is taken as a failure to take steps to protect them from harm. This distinction is validated by the fact that in misfeasance the defendant creates a new risk of harm to the plaintiff. Contrariwise, in nonfeasance, the defendant has not worsened his situation and has merely failed to benefit the plaintiff by interfering in his affairs.

> Liability for "misfeasance" . . . may extend to any person to whom harm may reasonably be anticipated as a result of the defendant's conduct, or perhaps even beyond; while for "nonfeasance" it is necessary to find some definite relation between the parties, of such a character that social duty justifies the imposition of a duty to act.[127]

It is argued, accordingly, that the distinction between assisting with the death of a patient and allowing him to die has a distinct parallel within the American legal system itself by the ways in which culpability is assigned for either "causing" or "permitting" harm to be inflicted upon others.[128] For, in those instances where an act can be found that caused a wrong or harm, once the agent who has brought about the harm is identified, liability is assessed.[129] Interestingly, with cases of omission, however, liability will not be imposed unless a "relationship" between the parties is established.[130]

The act of turning off an artificial respirator in use by a patient may be classified traditionally as either an act of commission or an act of omission.[131] Though a distinction may not be drawn easily here—because either action stems from the activity—the physician, if found to have committed an affirmative act of commission, may be held liable for murdering the patient.[132] Crucial to the determination of the nature of the action would be a characterization of whether the act itself caused life to be terminated or was more properly considered as an omission to render aid to sustain life, thus permitting it to end. The operative verbs here are "caused" and "permitting."[133] In "acting" or "causing," an act of intercession is made to terminate life; with acts of "omitting" or "permitting," a simple failure to intercede in a course of action to preserve life is recognized with the end result that death is permitted to occur.[134] In determining legally whether the act of turning off a hypothetical respirator is one of commission or omission, consideration must also be given to the very doctor-patient relationship (as opposed to a nonassociated one), patient reliance and reasonable expectation as well as the actual physical act of turning off the respirator itself and the circumstances surrounding it.[135]

It could be argued that the most crucial of all elements, motive, is the testing rod in aiding a determination of whether acts were those of commission or omission.[136] Accordingly, a deliberate act of killing—but one not done with a particularized motive or evil will—that is designed to allow the ending of life for a terminally ill patient and thus thereby relieve a life of suffering should not be classified as murder.[137] Inasmuch as no personal gain or good inures to the actor but rather to the recipient of the immediate action, this would be another reason not to recognize the act as murder.[138] Noble intentions, however, are not always exculpatory. For example, if one subscribed to the belief of metempsychosis and decided to hasten another along toward the road to ultimate perfection before he became either tempted or corrupted with moral guilt, this act would surely be held to murder.[139]

Under one line of philosophical reasoning, acquiescing to a request for murder made by one fully conscious, who for physical or psychological reasons finds life unbearable and finds no other act suitable to bring a resolution to the quandary, would not be an act of murder. Rather, it would be homicide. But, for a murder to be committed, there must be an infringement of rights. Here is seen but a simple and volitional release of the right to life.[140]

> If something is a right at all, then it can be given up; just as a gift, if it is a gift, can be renounced. Therefore, in cases where the quality of life has reached a certain subjective minimum, the individual has a right to give up that life, to request euthanasia. Consequently, in such cases euthanasia would be morally acceptable.[141]

Criminal Liability

For criminal liability to be imposed for not executing a duty owed, the leading American case holds that this duty must be "a legal duty, and not a mere moral obligation. It must be a duty imposed by law or by contract, and the omission to perform the duty must be the immediate and direct cause of death."[142] Since the relationship between physicians and patient is basically contractual, arising from the nature of an offer and acceptance, a physician has no obligation to treat all comers. Only when treatment is undertaken does the law impose a duty on him to continue the level of treatment, in the absence of a contrary understanding, so long as the individual case required.[143]

For the terminal patient desiring a swift, painless death, discharging the attending physician (in theory) terminates not only the physician's duty but also eliminates the primary basis for his criminal liability.[144] Therefore, the question of an imposition of criminal liability arises only in those cases where the physician has not been discharged or has failed to withdraw from a case with proper notice and thus, presumptively, the physician-patient relationship continues.[145] The physician may not seek a termination of this relationship by abandonment of the patient—for it is within this context that the possibility of criminal liability arises most generally.[146]

The history of the American case law of euthanasia presents an interesting record of a system that has prosecuted for the offense limitedly.[147] In fact, as early as 1916, the predominate view was that even when life is taken, with consent, in order to relieve either suffering or an "other greater calamity," and the resulting death is thus of meritorious character, such action would normally form the basis of a criminal prosecution.[148] Yet, both judges and juries are reluctant to act affirmatively here.[149]

A survey of American case law reveals some twelve cases involving active euthanasia, with only one having resulted in an actual conviction for murder. Three others were maintained for convictions for offenses less than murder. Seven of the other cases resulted in acquitals and one failed because no indictment was obtained.[150] In construing this same survey, one authority has noted that there were actually nine acquittals in all, with seven being allowed on the grounds of temporary insanity.[151] Observing that the standards for finding insanity are "tightening," he concluded that future acquittals of cases similar to these twelve may be more difficult to obtain.[152]

A CLEAR JUDICIAL POSTURE EMERGES WITH DELAYED EFFECT

On May 3, 1994, in a case of first impression in the federal court system, a district court judge in the state of Washington held that a state statute imposing criminal sanctions for physician-assisted suicide was violative of the Fourteenth Amendment's Due Process Clause as well as the Equal Protection Clause.[153] This holding will have enormous significance in validating what will be recognized undoubtedly within a few years as a constitutionally protected liberty interest in dying for terminally ill adults. I hold to this position even though, on March 9, 1995, the U.S. Court of Appeals for the Ninth Circuit, in a split two to one decision, reversed this case and in so doing acknowledged that while the right of privacy may encompass freedom from unwanted medical intervention, it did not include a right to have assistance from a second person. The dissent maintained, correctly, that the right of privacy and self-determination included a right to die with dignity.[154] I maintain this position will, over time and various appeals, carry the day.

This district court decision was based on two U.S. Supreme Court decisions[155]—one holding that a competent individual has a constitutionally protected liberty interest found within the Due Process Clause of the Constitution to refuse or withdraw unwanted medical treatment even if death results consequently[156] and the other reaffirming the right of an individual to make highly personal choices concerning marriage, procreation (here, abortion), and family.[157] The Washington court concluded mentally competent, terminally ill adults with no chance of recovery could make no more profoundly personal decision than to end their lives under such circumstances. In this regard, the court refused correctly to draw a distinction between refusing life-sustaining medical treatment and physician-assisted suicide by an uncoerced, mentally competent terminally ill patient.

Fortifying the constitutional merit of its position, the court concluded that since the state had enacted a Natural Death Act,[158] which recognizes a fundamental right of all citizens to control their own health care decisions (including decisions as such to withhold or withdraw life-sustaining treatment in instances of either terminal condition or conditions of permanent unconsciousness), to deny a comparable right to those similarly situated who do not need life support would be a denial of equal protection of the laws guaranteed by the Constitution.[159] Interestingly, when the full court of the Ninth Circuit reheard this case, it held on March 6, 1996, that the district court was correct in its original determination: namely, terminally ill patients have a due process liberty interest in hastening their own death and thus being assured of a dignified and humane death.[160] And, fortifying this position, the Second Circuit Court of Appeals held in *Quill v. Vacco* in 1996 that a competent, terminally ill patient has a right to hasten his death through the assistance of a physician, and, further, artificial distinctions between active and passive assisted suicide should not be determinative in respecting the ultimate decision to hasten death.[161]

A Growing State Consensus

At the state judicial level, there is a growing consensus that a legally protected right does exist for competent patients, or other surrogate decision makers acting on behalf of incompetents, to direct when life-sustaining treatment may be withheld or withdrawn together with an ethical commitment or recognition of a professional responsibility among health care providers to abide by and assist in whatever reasonable way to effect these medical directives.[162]

A Setback and a Recovery

A significant setback to this momentum was seen, however, by a 1995 ruling in a federal district court in Oregon, which held that a referendum statute, the Oregon Death with Dignity Act, allowing physicians to prescribe lethal doses of medication for competent terminally ill patients, was unconstitutional—this because it was determined to be a violation of the Equal Protection Clause of the Constitution's Fourteenth Amendment. More specifically, it was held that the referendum's classification or coverage of terminally ill citizens was not rationally related to the legitimate state interest in maintaining life and forestalling suicide.[163]

Fortunately, on February 27, 1997, a three-judge panel of the Ninth U.S. Circuit Court of Appeals decided unanimously that the challenges to the 1994 Oregon act were improper. The reasoning behind this determination was that since the challengers—a group of patients, physicians, and other caregivers who contended the act would allow sick people, and especially the depressed, to be pressured into suicide—had failed to prove they themselves faced any immediate threat of harm, under the law, they thus lacked standing to maintain an action.[164]

In June 1997 the Oregon State Legislature decided—for the first time in ninety years—to return an approval referendum for voter reconsideration.[165] Because of what was held to be defective scientific data supporting the original measure, the Oregon Death with Dignity Act was placed on the November ballot. And, the efforts to rescind it were rejected by sixty percent of the voters.[166]

A Final Clarification?

The Supreme Court of the United States held in late June 1997, in two companion cases,[167] that the Fourteenth Amendment's Due Process Clause is not violated by a Washington state statute which imposed a criminal penalty on anyone who knowingly "causes or aids another person to attempt suicide."[168] Also, in New York, it held that another statute—supported by a history of sound case law—which criminalizes assisted suicide yet permits individuals who are terminally ill and mentally competent to refuse life-sustaining medical treatments, is not violative of the Equal Protection Clause of the Federal Constitution.[169]

The outcome of these two decisions means, simply, that a unanimous High Court has determined that there is no federal fundamental right to commit suicide which would include a right to assistance in doing so. It remains for the individual states to determine the extent to which they will seek to resolve the thorny questions arising when citizens under medical treatment face the reality of impending death.[170] Some have speculated that the issue of whether assisted suicide is legal or illegal "has peaked" and that the new focus will be on how to provide better pain management in the end stages of life.[171] Others hold to the opinion that a new medico-legal debate will be structured around the use of specific medical practices such as the administration of potentially lethal doses of painkillers to terminally ill patients or those for whom palliative care brings no relief from suffering.[172] One point is certain: the extent of the rights of the terminally ill is yet to be charted and remained clouded in a penumbra.[173]

CLINICAL STANDARDS FOR ASSISTED SUICIDE

Although precise standards regarding the frequency of patients' requests of physicians for assisted suicide is unavailable, it is reported commonly that in the United States approximately six thousand deaths each day are thought to be in some way either planned or assisted indirectly. Within this latter classification would be actions that have the double effect of hastening death yet primarily relieve pain as well as those that either discontinue or fail to initiate potentially life-prolonging treatments.[174] Interestingly, some physicians in fact regard suicide as the last act in a continuum of care they can assist in providing hopelessly ill patients.[175]

Whenever thought, analysis, and final action are given over to the issue of physician-assisted suicide, all three should be focused on the strengthening of autonomy or self-determination for the incurably ill patient, thereby giving him greater control over death. All final plans of action should be directed toward effecting the implementation of a standard of compassion which recognizes that an individual's ultimate fate should—after all reasonably practicable alternatives have been exhausted—remain with the individual or, if allowed legally, with a previously designated surrogate decision maker.[176] In the final analysis, it is the physician's responsibility to create a medical environment which is promotive of a peaceful death.[177]

The Framework for Analysis

Assisted suicide, to be sure, is treatment of an extraordinary and irreversible nature. Before undertaken, certain clinical standards should be met. First, all types of palliative or comfort care should be discussed with the patient who is suffering with an incurable condition that is causing severe and unrelenting pain. When uncertainty exists regarding either the medical condition of the patient or his prognosis, it is wise to seek a second opinion or opinions that dispel uncertainties.[178]

The second step toward verification of a decision for assisted suicide requires the attending physician to assure himself that this ultimate request for an act of controlled death is simply not the result of faulty administration of comfort care. Thus, full discussion must be had with the patient before a decision to utilize death assistance is accepted—with it being understood fully that such actions should never be used "to circumvent the struggle to provide comprehensive care or find acceptable alternatives."[179] In this regard, as an outcome of this step, the third one recognizes that the physician ascertain that the patient's declaration of death preference be not only clear, serious, and unequivocal but also be given freely and seen as a choice to die instead of continuing life in a state of pain and suffering.[180]

The patient's capacity to understand the significance of his request for assisted suicide should be established as well—as this goes to the soundness of his judgment. When it is suspected that depression is distorting rational decision making or a reversible mental disorder is clouding rationality, psychiatric evaluation should be sought—again to establish beyond doubt the patient's comprehension of his decisions.[181]

The fifth clinical standard to be followed is met when an act of physician-assisted suicide is carried out within the context of a real doctor-patient relationship. In other words, ideally the physician has witnessed the progression of the patient's illness and, as important, his suffering as his primary physician. If no such preexisting relationship can be established, the physician must endeavor to know the patient personally so that a full understanding can be had of the reasons behind the request for health assistance.[182] Obviously, if the patient's personal physician cannot as a matter of conscience assist him in suicide, he should not be forced to perform the act. Yet, he should help in securing a transfer of care to a more receptive physician.[183]

To test not only the voluntariness and rationality of the patient's request but also the accuracy and the diagnosis and the prognosis as well as palliative care alternatives, as a sixth step, a consulting physician should be brought into the case. Additionally, he should review the supporting case materials and, furthermore, examine and interview the patient himself.[184]

Finally, all primary participants in the assisted suicide (i.e., patient, primary physician, and the consultant) must acknowledge, in writing, their consent to the procedure.

A physician-assisted suicide must neither invalidate insurance policies nor lead to an investigation by the medical examiner or an unwanted autopsy. The primary physician, the medical consultant and the family must be assured that if the conditions agreed on are satisfied in good faith, they will be free from criminal prosecution for having assisted the patient to die.[185]

A CONSTRUCTIVE PROPOSAL: REDEFINITION AND REEDUCATION

What is needed desperately in order to bring a contemporary sophistication—legal, medical, philosophical, ethical and moral—to the area of concern and investigation here is a strong definitional stance surrounding the terms *euthanasia* and *suicide*—quite simply, a reeducation. More precisely, what is proposed is a change in the essential taxonomy of euthanasia as a word, concept, principle, attitude, or legal action. Therefore, what has heretofore been recognized as acts of euthanasia of one form or other would be henceforth known as but acts of enlightened self-determination. Freed of the shackles of confusion and indecisiveness, actions undertaken within the context of an irreversible medical crisis or terminal illness[186] would be understood not as an act of autonomous rational suicide (or active euthanasia of oneself) or as a refusal of treatment but rather as merely an act of enlightened self-determination. For the incapacitated or incompetent individual, the action taken on his behalf by a surrogate decision maker would be viewed similarly and the actions of these decision makers judged on their *reasonableness* and *fairness* to the terminal patient and his immediate family or extended family (assuming one exists).

A New Attitude

This proposal would, in turn, begin to foster a new attitude toward death, one that would redefine the basic tasks of medicine as not only recognizing old age as an honorable estate but also viewing as unjust and inhumane to insist on an obligation being imposed on old people suffering from a terminal illness or otherwise severely incapacitated to be forced to live through a period of miserable decline and painful helplessness.[187] The competent decision maker, at whatever age, suffering from a severe debilitating (terminal) disease, as well as the incompetent who is similarly situated and further inconvenienced by infancy, mental incompetence or unconsciousness, would also be accorded the privilege of holding first-class citizenship. And, with this would come an inherent recognition of the fact that because of debilitation, the elderly suffer more than the comatose or the vegetative simply because they are conscious, or at least semiconscious, of their inescapable misery.[188] The coordinate result of this new attitude toward health care would be an unyielding recognition of the fact that a total right of personal autonomy is possessed by all.

Eliminating Confusion

Rational assisted suicide and all the varieties of euthanasia would no longer be considered. The major focus of all inquiry into actions previously classified as suicide or euthanasia would simply examine whether the individual in question, exercising his powers of rational thinking, exercised an act of enlightened self determination or autonomy. For the incompetent suffering from a similar terminal illness, the question to be answered would be: did the surrogate decision maker, acting with rationality and humaneness, and thereby within the best interests of the terminal patient, or employing the principle of substituted judgment for that individual, exercise an act of enlightened self-determination? Obviously, the health care providers, and when brought into this matter, the courts, would themselves act under the presumption an individual within these circumstances or his duly appointed surrogate decision maker acted properly. It is realized that this position is a large quantum leap in not only thinking and hoped-for action, but it is an eminently fair and reasonable contemporary approach to an age-old problem.

CONCLUSIONS

From a Judaeo-Christian theological perspective, the meaning, the substance, and, indeed, the consummation of life is tied inextricably to expressions of love: love of God and love of neighbor. It is through the love of others that God is recognized and loved. The meaning of life under this interpretation, then, is to be found in human relationships and the qualities of respect, concern, compassion, and justice that support such relationships.[189]

Social justice demands that each individual be given an opportunity to maximize his individual potential. Yet, a point is often reached where maintenance of an individual is in defiance of all concepts of basic humanitarianism and social justice. When an individual's condition is such that it represents a negation of any "truly human" qualities or relational potential, then the best form of treatment should be arguably no treatment at all.[190]

Life should not be viewed as an end in and of itself but rather as something that should be preserved so that other values can be fulfilled. It should be preserved when it holds a potentiality for human relationships. Although this standard does not admit of mathematical precision and must be applied with great humility and caution, it is nonetheless a beginning from which particular medical formulations may be developed.[191] In the final analysis, the penultimate norm for decision making must be that of love, simple kindness or mercy.[192]

NOTES

1. *See generally* M. KOHL, THE MORALITY OF KILLING (1974).

2. *Id.*

3. Kass, *Man's Right to Die*, 35 THE PHAROS 73, 74 (1972).

4. *Id.*

5. *Id. See also* M. BRAZIER, MEDICINE, PATIENTS AND THE LAW, 443-465 (2d ed. 1992).

6. Ladd, Introduction, in ETHICAL ISSUES RELATING TO DEATH at 4 (John Ladd, ed. 1979).

Machines have a tendency to de-personalize death and thus alleviate human responsibility for it. Annas, *Killing Machines*, 21 HASTINGS CENTER RPT. 33, 35 (1991).

7. KOHL, *supra* note 1 at 76.

8. *Id.* at 75, 76.

9. R.M. VEATCH, DEATH, DYING AND THE BIOLOGICAL REVOLUTION 77 (1976).

Positive euthanasia has been stated as doing something that ends life deliberately and is the form in which the issue of suicide is brought into question (as a voluntary or direct choice of death). The end goal of both direct or positive and indirect or negative euthanasia is precisely the same—the end of a patient's life and a release from pointless misery and dehumanizing loss of bodily functions. Fletcher, *In Defense of Suicide*, in SUICIDE AND EUTHANASIA: THE RIGHTS OF PERSONHOOD 38 at 47 (S.E. Wallace & A. Eser, eds. 1981).

10. VEATCH, *supra* note 9.

11. Kuhse, *The Case for Active Voluntary Euthanasia*, 14 L. MED. & HEALTH CARE 145, 147 (1986).

12. *Id.*

13. *Id.*

14. *Id.*

15. *Id.*

16. *Id.*

17. VEATCH, *supra* note 9 at 135.

18. KOHL, *supra* note 1 at 95.

19. *Id.* at 95-96.

20. *Id.* at 96.

21. *Id.* at 99.

22. *Id.*

23. *Id.* at 100.

24. EIKE-HENNER W. KLUGE, THE PRACTICE OF DEATH 149 (1975).

25. KOHL, *supra* note 1 at 103, 106.

26. *Id.* at 107.

National attention was drawn to the poignancy and humaneness of euthanasia when, in its January 8, 1988, issue, the American Medical Association printed an anonymous column titled, *It's over Debbie*, written by a physician who described the manner in which he deliberately injected a twenty-year-old woman suffering from ovarian cancer with an overdose of morphine, 259 J.A.M.A. 272 (1988). Subsequently, citing confidentiality and First Amendment issues, the American Medical Association refused to provide the Cook County State Attorney's request to provide a grand jury in Chicago with the name of the physician who authored the column. Specter, *AMA Won't Identify Mercy Killer*, WASH. POST, Feb. 17, 1988, at A3. The chief judge of the Cook County Court ruled later that no crime had been proved and dismissed a later grand jury subpoena demanding the physician author's identity. Wilkerson, *Judge Stalls Inquiry into a Mercy Killing Case*, N.Y. TIMES Mar. 19, 1988, at 6.

27. KLUGE, *supra* note 24 at 161.

28. *Id.*

29. *Id.*

The longest record for survival with nutrition from a feeding tube is 37 years. *Brophy v. New England Sinai Hospital Inc.*, 497 N.E.2d 626, 637 (Mass. 1986).

30. KLUGE, *supra* note 24 at 161.

31. *Id.* at 162.

32. *Id.*

33. *Id.* at 162.

34. *Id.*, Ch. 4, nn. 1-7.

35. McCormick, *To Save or Let Die: The Dilemma of Modern Medicine* in HOW BRAVE A NEW WORLD? at 339-49 (R.A. McCormick, ed. 1981).

36. Rachels, *Euthanasia, Killing and Letting Die* in ETHICAL ISSUES RELATING TO DEATH at Ch. 7, p. 148 (J. Ladd, ed. 1979).

See also, J. RACHELS, THE END OF LIFE (1986).

37. Applebaum & Klein, *Therefore Choose Death?*, 81 COMMENTARY 23, 27 (1986).

38. RACHELS, *supra* note 36.

For example, if someone were to see that an infant were drowning in a bathtub, would it make any difference whether an act of active or passive euthanasia were followed? It could be perceived "just as bad to let it drown as to push its head under water," for one act is as iniquitous as the other. Foot, *Euthanasia* in ETHICAL ISSUES RELATING TO DEATH *supra* note 36 at 29.

39. F. HARRON ET AL., HEALTH AND HUMAN VALUES 48 (1983).

40. *Id.*

See also Rachels, *Active and Passive Euthanasia*, 292 NEW ENG. J. MED. 78 (1975).

41. *Id.* at 42.

42. *Id.*

43. *Id.*

44. Amundsen, *The Physician's Obligation to Prolong Life: A Medical Duty Without Classical Roots*, 8 HASTINGS CENTER RPT. 23 (1978).

45. *Id.* at 27.

46. *Id.*

47. *Id.* at 25.

48. *Id.*

49. *Id.* at 27, 28.

50. *Id.* at 27.

51. *Id.*

52. *Id.*

53. President's Commission for the Study of Ethical Problems in Medicine and Biomedical and Behavioral Research, DECIDING TO FOREGO LIFE-SUSTAINING TREATMENT: ETHICAL, MEDICAL AND LEGAL ISSUES IN TREATMENT DECISIONS at 300-07 (1983).

See Hansen, *Doctors Assert Patient's Right to Die: Court Rules Man Can Keep Comatose Wife on Respirator Despite Hospital's Wishes*, 77 A.B.A.J. 26 (1991).

54. *Id.* at 305.

55. *Id.*

56. *Id.* (emphasis provided).

57. *Id.* (emphasis provided).

See Hansen, *Right to Die: A Consensus is Emerging with Assistance of Catholic Theologians*, NAT'L CATHOLIC RPTR, Dec. 11, 1987, at 1.

58. *Id.*

59. *Id.* (emphasis provided).

60. *Id.*

61. *See generally* Smith, *Triage: Endgame Realities*, 1 J. CONTEMP. HEALTH L. & POL'Y 143 (1985).

One prominent Jesuit theological, Fr. Edwin J. Healey, has implied that the maximum amount of money that could be expended on an ordinary course of treatment *before* it became extraordinary, was $2,000. Kelly, *The Duty of Using Artificial Means of Preserving Life*, 11 THEOLOGICAL STUDIES 203 at 206 n. 9 (citing Fr. Healey) (1950).

62. 24 ORIGINS 690-727 (CNS Documentary Service, April 6, 1995).

63. *Id.* at Ch. III., No. 65.

64. *Id.*

65. Ch. III., No. 66.

66. Ch. III., No. 65.

67. *Id.*

68. Ch. III., Nos. 72 & 73.

69. *Id.* at No. 73.

70. *Id.* at No. 70.

71. McCormick, *Veritas Splendor and Moral Theology*, 169 AMERICA 8 (Oct. 30, 1993).

72. R.A. McCORMICK, NOTES ON MORAL THEOLOGY, 1965 THROUGH 1980 at 565 (1981).

73. J.F. CHILDRESS, WHO SHOULD DECIDE: PATERNALISM IN HEALTH CARE 166 (1982).

74. Hilfiker, *Allowing the Debilitated to Die: Facing Our Ethical Choices*, 308 N. ENG. J. MED. 716 (1983).

75. Childress, *When is it Morally Justifiable to Discontinue Medical Nutrition and Hydration?* in BY NO EXTRAORDINARY MEANS at 81 (J. Lynn, ed. 1986).

76. *Id.*

77. Smith, *Quality of Life, Sanctity of Creation: Palliative or Apotheosis?*, 63 NEB. L. REV. 707, 734 (1984).

78. G.P. SMITH, II, GENETICS, ETHICS AND THE LAW 1-4 (1981). *See also* G.P. SMITH, II, THE NEW BIOLOGY, Ch. 8 (1989).

79. SMITH, *supra* note 77.

80. SMITH, *supra* note 78.

81. SMITH, *supra* note 77 at 738.

82. The ultimate morality of an action or inaction in cases of this nature being considered can never be evaluated properly without reference to the quality of life being extended by the heroic measures. Will, *When Homicide Is Noble*, in THE MORNING AFTER: AMERICAN SUCCESSES AND EXCESSES 1981-86 at 84, 85 (G.F. Will, ed. 1986).

83. SMITH, *supra* note 78 at 9.
A recent study of procedures followed by upstate New York hospitals found prolonged use of artificial ventilators to treat patients over eighty years of age in an intensive care unit is not cost-effective. Specifically, it was found that when the sum of a patient's age and the number of days on a respirator reached at least one hundred, the chances of survival were near zero. Thus, a ninety-year-old person on a respirator for ten days had a very minimal chance of survival. Cohen et al.,*Mechanical Ventilation for the Elderly Patient in Intensive Care: Incremental Changes and Benefits*, 269 J.A.M.A. 1025 (1993).

84. Beall, *Mercy for the Terminally Ill Cancer Patient*, 249 J.A.M.A. 2883 (1983).
See Schneiderman & Jecker, *Futility in Practice*, 153 ARCH. INTERN. MED. 437 (1993); Miles, *Medical Futility*, 20 L. MED. & HEALTH CARE 310 (1992).

85. 1982 A.M.A. JUDICIAL COUNCIL CURRENT OPINIONS, Am. Med. Assoc. 9-10 (1982); President's Commission for the Study of Ethical Problems in Medicine and Biomedical and Behavioral Research, *supra* note 53 at 288 (1983).
See Multi-Society Task Force on PVS, Medical Aspects of The Persistent Vegetative State, 330 NEW ENG. J. MED. 1499, 1592 (1994).

86. Kelly, *supra* note 61 at 203, 206.

87. *Id.* at 207.

88. H. TRISTRAM ENGELHARDT, JR., THE FOUNDATIONS OF BIOETHICS 307 (1986).

89. G.A. KELLY, MEDICO-MORAL PROBLEMS 129 (1958).

90. D. MAGUIRE, DEATH BY CHOICE 123 (1975).

Only when there is hope of health (*si sit spes salutis*) or where hope of recovery appeared (*ubi spes affulget convalescendi*) is treatment required. Futile treatments (*nemo ad inutile*) or treatments that only postponed death or blunted briefly the illness (*parum pro nihilo reputatur moralitier*) are not required to be undertaken. An obligation to accept treatment is defeated if the at-risk individual has an aversion to the particular form of treatment (*horror magnus*). ENGELHARDT, *supra* note 88 at 332, n. 122.

91. ENGELHARDT, *supra* note 88 at 225.

92. *Id.*

93. Kelly, *supra* note 86 at 214.

94. *Id.* at 210.

95. 380 N.E.2d 134, 137 n.7 (Mass. App. Ct. 1978).

96. 373 Mass. 728, 370 N.E.2d 417, 424 (1977) (emphasis provided). *See* Rosato, *The Ultimate Test of Autonomy: Should Minors Have a Right to Make Decisions Regarding Life-Sustaining Treatment?*, 49 RUTGERS L. REV. 1 (1996).

97. 70 N.J. 10, 335 A.2d 647, 668 *cert. denied* 429 U.S. 922 (1976) (emphasis provided).

In 1991 New Jersey became the first state to enact a statute recognizing a personal religious exemption or conscience clause which has the effect of requiring a physician to declare death upon the basis of cardio-respiratory criteria (or, the cessation of all circulatory and respiratory functions) rather than brain, or neurological death, in those cases where he knows or has reason to believe such action is consistent with a patient's religious belief. 26 N.J. REV. STAT. §§ 6A1-6A8 (1991 Supp.). See Olick, *Brain Death, Religious Freedom and Public Policy: New Jersey's Landmark Legislative Initiative*, 1 KENNEDY INST. ETHICS J. 275 (1991).

98. Ramsey, *Euthanasia and Dying Well Enough*, 44 LINACRE Q. 43 (1977).

99. *Id.*

See also Ramsey, *Prolonged Dying: Not Medically Indicated*, 6 HASTINGS CENTER RPT. 16 (1976).

100. VEATCH, *supra* note 9 at 110.

101. *Id.*

102. *Id.*

103. *Id.* at 112.

See McCormick, *supra* note 35 at Ch. 21.

104. CHILDRESS, *supra* note 73 at 166.

105. *Id.*

106. *Id.*

107. *Id.*

108. R.M. VEATCH, A THEORY OF MEDICAL ETHICS 37, 39 (1981).

109. *Id.* at 39.

110. Martin, *Suicide and Self-Sacrifice* in SUICIDE: THE PHILOSOPHICAL ISSUES 48 at 58 (M. P. Battin & D.J. Mayo eds. 1980).

111. VEATCH, *supra* note 109 at 39. *See* McCormick, *supra* note 35 at 412-29.

See also President's Commission *supra* note 53 at 80 n.10 (1983).

112. VEATCH, *supra* note 109 at 39.

113. *Id.* at 235.

Where treatment offered to extend life would be unreasonably burdensome or simply useless to a terminally ill patient, the principle would permit non treatment. *Id.* at 40.

114. Louisell, *Euthanasia and Biathanasia*, 22 CATH. UNIV. L. REV. 723, 742 (1973).

115. *Id.*

116. *Id.*

117. *See* Smith, *supra* note 61.

118. Engelhardt, *Suicide and the Cancer Patient*, 36 CA-A Cancer Journal for Clinicians 105, 108 (1986).

119. *Id.*

120. *Id.*

121. *Id.*

Interestingly, a recent study showed that many surviving elderly surviving heart attack victims do not receive potentially life saving treatments such as clot-busting drugs and blood thinners, and some are not even told to stop smoking. Ellerbeck, et al., *Quality of Care for Medical Patients with Acute Myocardial Infarction*, 273 J.A.M.A. 1509 (1995).

122. ENGELHARDT, *supra* note 118.

123. C. SAUNDERS & M. BAINES, LIVING WITH DYING: THE MANAGEMENT OF TERMINAL DISEASE 4 (1983).

124. *Id.*

125. *Id.*

126. *Id.*

The double effect principle was validated in the British case of *Rex v. Bodkin-Adams* (1957). Here, Dr. John Bodkin-Adams was acquitted of murder after having administered narcotics which apparently caused the death of his patient. The judge held (in this unreported case) that a physician who administers narcotics in order to relieve pain is not guilty of murder merely because the measures he takes incidentally shortens life. O. R. RUSSELL, FREEDOM TO DIE 255 (1977).

127. W.L. PROSSER, THE LAW OF TORTS § 56 at 373-74, (5th ed. 1984).

128. Fletcher, *Prolonging Life*, 42 WASH. L. REV. 909 (1967).

129. *Id.* at 1009-12.

130. *Id.*

131. *See* R.H. WILLIAMS, TO LIVE AND TO DIE: WHEN, WHY AND HOW (1973); Fletcher, *Legal Aspects of the Decision Not to Prolong Life*, 203 J.A.M.A. 65 (1968).

See also Angell, *The Case of Helga Wanglie: A New Kind of Right to Die Case*, 325 NEW ENG. J. MED. 511 (1991).

132. Comment, *The Right to Die*, 7 HOUSTON L. REV. 654, 659 (1970).

133. Fletcher, *supra* note 131.

134. *Id.*

135. Fletcher, *supra* note 128.

Truly, the bounds of moral judgment are strained to the point of collapse when an ultimate decision is sought as to whether switching off a respirator is an act of active euthanasia or merely passive euthanasia! Rachels, *Active and Passive Euthanasia*, 292 NEW ENG. J. MED. 78 (1975).

In a 1983 California case, *Barber v. Superior Court of Los Angeles County*, 147 Cal. App. 3d 1006, 195 Cal. Rptr. 484, the court recognized that there was a difference between killing and letting die and that actions by two doctors in turning off a respirator of a patient who was vegetative, with permission from the patient's wife, was not an act of killing.

136. KLUGE, *supra* note 24 at 171.

137. *Id.*

138. *Id.*

139. *Id.*

140. *Id.*

141. *Id.*

142. *People v. Beardsley*, 150 Mich. 206, 113 N.W. 1128, 1129 (1907).

143. Survey, *Euthanasia: Criminal, Tort, Constitutional and Legislative Considerations*, 48 NOTRE DAME L. REV. 1202, 1207 (1973).

144. *Id.* at 1208.

145. *Id.*

146. *Id.*

A new and novel tort action for *wrongful living* has been proposed recently. Under the proposal, the tort would be recognized as personal and hence redressed only by the individual whose right to die was compromised; or, if that individual should die subsequently, by his representative on a survival basis. If the interfering treatment is made and thereupon the patient lives, the interference with the right to die involves compensation for the living. Contrariwise, if the interfering treatment causes death earlier than non treatment, then there is a clear, casual connection between the interference and the loss: permanent death. Accordingly, wrongful death damages to the beneficiaries of the decedent would be appropriate; but damages could be calculated for that period of time by which the life was shortened by the treatment. Oddi, *The Tort of Interference with the Right to Die: The Wrongful Living Cause of Action*, 75 GEO. L.J. 625, 641 (1980).

See also Furrow, *Damage Remedies and Institutional Reform: The Right to Refuse Treatment*, 12 L. MED. & HEALTH CARE 152 (1982).

147. Survey, *supra* note 143 at 1213.

148. *Id.*

149. *Id.*

150. *Id.* at 1213 n.82.

151. VEATCH, *supra* note 9 at 79.

152. *Id.* *See generally* MacKinnon, *Euthanasia and Homicide*, 26 CRIM. L. Q. 483 (1984).

153. *Compassion in Dying, et al. v. Washington*, 850 F. Supp. 1454 (W.D. Wash. 1994).

See McCarthy, *Final Exits: Seattle Group Offers Terminal Patients Advice on Ways to Choose Suicide*, WASH. POST HEALTH MAG., Feb. 15, 1994, at 9.

154. *Compassion in Dying, et al., v. Washington*, 49 F.3d 586 (9th Cir. 1995).

155. *Cruzan v. Director, Missouri Department of Health*, 497 U.S. 261 (1990); *Planned Parenthood of Southeastern Pennsylvania v. Casey*, 114 S. Ct. 909 (1994).

156. *Cruzan, supra* note 155.

157. *Planned Parenthood of Southern Pennsylvania, supra* note 155.

158. REV. CODE WASH. § 70.122 *et. seq.* (1994).

159. *Compassion in Dying, supra* note 153 at 1468.

On August 2, 1995, the Ninth Circuit Court of Appeals decided to refer this case to an eleven-judge panel for a new hearing. N.Y.TIMES, Aug. 3, 1995, at A12.

160. 79 F.3d 790 (9th Cir. 1996).

161. 80 F.3d 716 (2d Cir. 1996).

On January 8, 1997, the U.S. Supreme Court heard a consolidated appeal of these two cases and determined in June that the Constitution did not recognize any so called fundamental right to have assistance in the act of suicide. *Infra* at notes 167-69.

162. Podgers, *Matters of Life and Death: Debate Grows over Euthanasia*, 78 A.B.A.J. 60, 63 (May 1992).

See, e.g., *McKay v. Bergstedt*, where the Supreme Court of Nevada acknowledged "the right to be free from pain at the time [a life support system] is disconnected is inseparable from his [a] right to refuse medical treatment." 801 P.2d 617, 631 (Nev. 1990); and *State v. McAffe*, 385 S.E.2d 651 (Ga. 1989) where the Georgia Supreme Court allowed a competent patient to remove a respirator and permitted a sedative to be administered to ease a resulting death.

See Fletcher, *The Courts and Euthanasia*, 15 L. MED. & HEALTH CARE 223 (1987-88) (arguing euthanasia should be decriminalized).

163. *Gary Lee v. State of Oregon*, 891 F. Supp. 1421, 1429 (D.Ore. 1995) (Sum. judg. granted).

In *People v. Kevorkian*, it was held by a divided Supreme Court of Michigan that Dr. Jack Kevorkian's patients did not enjoy a constitutionally protected right to obtain affirmative assistance from a physician in ending their lives. *People v. Kevorkian*, 527 N.W.2d 714, 724, 733 (Mich. 1994). *See also Hobbins v. Attorney Gen.*, 518 N.W.2d 487, 489 (Mich. Ct. App. 1994); Sunstein, *The Right to Die*, 106

YALE L. J. 1123 (1997).

But see Walsh, *Michigan Jury Acquits Kevorkian: Verdict Marks Third Victory for Doctor Who Assists Suicide*, WASH. POST, May 15, 1996, at A1; Walsh, *Kevorkian Critics Left with Dilemma: Legal System Failing to Halt Suicides*, WASH. POST, May 18, 1996, at A3.

164. *Lee v. State of Oregon*, 107 3d 1382 (9th Cir. 1997).

165. Claiborne, *Death with Dignity Measure May Make Oregon National Background,* WASH. POST, June 27, 1997, at A19; Egan, *Assisted Suicide Comes Full Circle to Oregon*, N.Y. TIMES, Oct. 26, 1997 at 1.

166. Claiborne & Edsall, *Affirmation of Oregon Suicide May Spur Movement*, WASH. POST, Nov. 6, 1997, at A19.

167. *Washington v. Glucksberg,* 117 S. Ct. 2258 (1997); *Vacco v. Quill,* 65 117 S. Ct. 2293 (1997).

168. *Washington v. Glucksberg, supra* not 167.

169. *Vacco v. Quill, supra* note 167.

170. Surro, *States to Become Forum for Fight over Assisted Suicide*, WASH. POST, June 27, 1997, at A19.

171. *Id.*

172. *Id.*

173. Goldstein, *Court's Decision on Help with Suicide Leaves Doctors in Gray Zone,* WASH. POST, June 27, 1997, at A18.

174. Quill et al., *Care of the Hopelessly Ill—Proposed Clinical Criteria for Physician-Assisted Suicide*, 327 NEW ENG. J. MED. 1380, 1381 (1992).

In a recent survey of intensive care nurses in the United States it was discovered that, acting on motives of compassion, almost one in five of the respondents hastened the deaths of terminally ill patients—sometimes even without the knowledge of attending physicians, the patients or their families. Asch, *The Role of Critical Care Nurses in Euthanasia and Assisted Suicide*, 334 NEW ENG. J. MED. 1374 (1996).

175. Wanzer et al., *The Physician's Responsibility Toward Hopelessly Ill Patients*, 320 NEW ENG. J. MED. 844, 849 (1989); Rhoden, *Litigating Life and Death*, 120 HARV. L. REV. 375, 442-443 (1988).

See Smith, *Utility and the Principle of Medical Futility: Safeguarding Autonomy and the Prohibition Against Cruel and Unusual Punishment*, 12 J. CONTEMP. HEALTH L. & POL'Y 1 (1995).

176. *Id.*

See also Brody, *Assisted Death—A Compassionate Response to a Medical Failure*, 320 NEW ENG. J. MED. 1384 (1989). *But see* Bernardi, *The Hidden Engines of the Suicide Rights Movement*, AMERICA at 14 (May 16, 1995).

177. Wanzer, *supra* note 175.

178. Quill et al., *supra* note 174.

179. *Id.* at 1382.

180. *Id.*

181. *Id.*

182. *Id.*

183. *Id.*

184. *Id.*

185. *Id.*

186. This term would be defined as "an illness in which, on the basis of the best available diagnostic criteria and in the light of available therapies, a reasonable estimation can be made prospectively and with a high probability that a person will die within a relatively short time." Bayer et al., *The Care of the Terminally Ill: Morality and Economics*, 309 NEW ENG. J. MED. 1490, 1491 (1983).

187. *See* Barrington, *Apologia for Suicide* in SUICIDE: THE PHILOSOPHICAL ISSUES at 90, 99, 100, *supra* note 110.

188. Conard, *Elder Choice*, 19 AM. J. L. & MED. 233, 234 (1993).

See Beauchamp, *The Jurisprudence of Physician-Assisted Death,* 29 IND. L. REV. 1173 (1986).

189. Smith, *supra* note 77 at 732.

190. *See* Smith, *supra* note 61 at 146. *See* McCormick, *supra* note 35 at 349.

191. Smith, *supra* note 61 at 149-50. McCormick, *supra* note 35 at 339-49.

192. *Id.*

See Smith, *Our Hearts Were Once Young and Gay: Health Care Rationing and the Elderly*, 7 U. FLA. J.L. & PUB. POL'Y 1 (1996); R.A. EPSTEIN, MORTAL PERIL: OUR INALIENABLE RIGHT TO HEALTH CARE? 283-312 (1997).

Chapter 9

Organ Harvesting: Salvaging a New Beginning

While the approximate total number of people on waiting lists for organs or tissue transplantation is 100,000[1] the number of organ donors has, from 1989 to 1991, stayed at approximately 4,000 in the United States.[2] Another study delineates the needs of Americans as follows: 15,000 could benefit from a heart transplant, 22,500 from a kidney transplant, and 5,000 each from a liver or pancreas transplant.[3] Interestingly, the most ready market source for harvesting, and thus meeting these needs in the United States, is to be seen in the automobile accident pool that yields approximately 60,000 cadavers each year with some 12,000 to 27,000 of them maintained sufficiently long enough after the accidents to die in hospitals.[4] At a minimum, these statistics suggest something along the lines of 12,000 hearts and livers and 24,000 kidneys are a potential market source for transplantation.[5]

MEETING MARKET DEMANDS

Whatever statistical profile is used, it can be seen easily that the demand for transplant organs clearly exceeds the supply.[6] The market base for obtaining organs becomes even more fragile and volatile when it is realized that the shortage of cadaveric organs is tied to the very suitability of the cadavers themselves. Thus, to be a suitable cadaveric candidate, the cadaver must have died as a result of either a cerebral hemorrhage or injury to the head and be maintained with respirator and ventilator assistance before its relatively healthy major organs are harvested.[7] The central task, then, is to design a scheme or develop a market mechanism that promotes greater opportunities for obtaining transplantable organs yet at the same time is not antithetical to present ethical values.[8]

Surely, as a society, Americans need to enter into a full dialogue regarding all approaches to saving lives and not dismiss any viable suggestion before it is debated fully (and even tested). This chapter initiates such a dialogue and demonstrates that as things stand at present altruistically induced organ donations at death are not as comprehensive a mechanism for providing a supply of transplantable organs as the demands of modern society require. New market strategies will have to be examined and eventually utilized if a premium is to continue to be placed on restoring health and sustaining life. At this state in the development of an agenda for a national debate, the payment of a standard death benefit as an inducement for organ donations appears to be the most attractive market mechanism to develop.

American Responses and Fears

A 1985 Gallup Poll found 75 percent of all Americans approved of organ donation and transplantation, yet only 27 percent expressed a willingness to donate their own organs in the event of their death, and of that percentage only 17 percent indicated they had signed organ donor cards to effect this commitment.[9] A more recent Gallup Poll in 1993 determined that while 85 percent of Americans now support organ donation, 42 percent acknowledge they have decided to donate their own organs.[10] These figures take on a greater relevance as market indicators of future organ sources when it is realized that approximately 80 percent of all Americans die without a will and thereby lose their opportunity to become donors.[11]

For those queried regarding their reluctance to become organ donors, three common reasons are given for this position: a central unwillingness to consider personal mortality,[12] aesthetic fears or religious beliefs forbidding dismemberment,[13] and an abiding fear that death will be hastened if previous consent to organ donation is given.[14] Meeting, and thereby seeking to resolve, these fears will take time and years of education. Even then, it will be extremely difficult to allay the fears that form the basis of these reasons for inaction.

THE COMMON LAW APPROACH

The common law, as interpreted in 1765 by Blackstone's COMMENTARIES, was clear: no one could have property rights in a human corpse.[15] Since the law of theft operated only to protect rights of property and ownership, a corpse was incapable of being stolen. Thus, body snatchers worked regularly to obtain cadavers for anatomists for subsequent use in medical schools. Interestingly, however, property rights could be held in coffins or shrouds and their theft was an imprisonable act.[16]

While stealing a corpse was a mere indecency, not a felony, consecrated burial grounds were protected and disruption of them carried a penalty as a misdemeanor. This was used as a basis by the common law judges to develop eventually new criminal laws prohibiting the disinternment of corpses without authority. At first, these new criminal offenses applied to body snatchers instead of to their customers. Executors and close family members could assert a right of burial but could still not assert ownership of a corpse. Accordingly, in cases where cadavers were discovered being used in anatomy or surgical dissection classes, there was no clear way of forcing their surrender unless they could be first identified (which, depending on the extent of the dissection, could be difficult) and then made the subject of a legal claim by the family or the descendent's executor. The only right possessed by the family was to have the body retrieved for burial and nothing more.[17]

In 1828, with parliamentary study being undertaken of this area, the courts seized the initiative and expanded the criminal law of body snatchers—as applied to cemeteries—to reach to the points of common delivery: the medical school anatomy classes.[18] And, in 1832, Parliament passed the Anatomy Act which destroyed the trade of body snatchers altogether by essentially introducing a strict licensing procedure on anatomy schools as well as on instructors and students themselves who wished to perform anatomical examinations. Government inspection, fines and imprisonment were set in place for violations of the act.[19]

CONTEMPORARY LEGISLATIVE INITIATIVES AND DISAPPOINTMENTS
Uniform Anatomical Gift Act

With the promulgation of the Uniform Anatomical Gift Act (UAGA) in 1968 and its subsequent adoption in some form by the fifty states and the District of Columbia in 1973,[20] a statutory right was conferred on all individuals allowing them, prior to death, to designate either their complete bodies or organs from them for donated transplants. When a descendant's wishes are not communicated prior to death, the act provides a right of disposition to the next of kin allowing him the right to decide whether to donate his relative's organs.[21] The UAGA was silent on the subject of sales.[22] Thus the common law position was largely controlling here and provided no one was acknowledged as having a definitive property interest or right in a human corpse.[23] This meant no one was granted any form of authority to enter into a sale or to make a gift of a cadaver or any of its parts.[24] It is important to note that this did not mean sales or gifts of this were illegal; rather, only contracts for sales or deeds of gifts were, at law, not enforceable.[25]

From 1968 to 1973 some five jurisdictions[26] prohibited the sale of human bodies and organs[27] yet permitted contingent sales to be made by decedents as well as sales by their next of kin.[28] With the promulgation, adoption and universal interpretation of UAGA, all state statutes permitting such sales—save one, Mississippi[29]—were abolished effectively.[30]

National Organ Transplant Act

To redirect national thinking from a purely voluntary behavior basis *vis-à-vis* organ donation, the UAGA was built on a principle of encouraged voluntarism.[31] To advance this principle, the whole process of consent was simplified. This was accomplished by the introduction of donor cards designed to allow individuals, carrying them as such, to indicate their consent to donate their organs upon death.[32] Wishing, if possible, to enhance the voluntary principle of altruism implicit in the UAGA for transplantable organs, yet facing the realities of the failure of UAGA's "encouraged voluntarism" to produce enough donors,[33] the U.S. Congress acted in 1984 by passing the National Organ Transplant Act (NOTA).[34] In addition to underwriting financial support for the development and maintenance of local nonprofit organ procurement organizations and additionally the National Organ Procurement and Transplantation Network to assist in matching organ donors with those needing transplants, the act criminalizes the intestate acquisition, receipt, or transfer of all transplant tissue (e.g., organs)—with the exception of blood.[35] Since the legislation is directed toward imposing a prohibition on sales affecting interstate commerce, some doubt has been raised about the validity of suppression of intrastate organ sales.[36] Interestingly, NOTA has been strengthened specifically on this issue of intrastate sales by the enactment of specific statutes prohibiting either the purchase or the sale of human organs.[37]

Again, in a national effort to both educate the public to the communal values associated with organ transplantation and thereby encourage and, hopefully, enhance opportunities for more organ harvesting, in 1986 a provision was added to the Omnibus Budget Reconciliation Act that was passed into law in 1987, mandating all Medicare-and-Medicaid- affiliated hospitals to establish "written protocols for the identification of potential organ donors."[38] This means that requests be made for organs and tissues whenever a death occurs in a hospital setting. Options to donate organs are to be presented in a discreet and sensitive manner to all families of potential donors enrolled as Medicare or Medicaid patients.[39]

Hospital compliance with required request provisions of the federal law or complementary state-enacted legislative schemes is very uneven, characterized in fact as poor to grudging in some states.[40] It is said that a number of physicians view the law here as an intrusion into their professional autonomy.[41] Still others are angered over perceived inequities in the distribution of the organs and tissues.[42] These attitudes translate into a lukewarm enthusiasm, if that, as the physicians seek to comply with required request   provisions[43] by phrasing their requests for permission to harvest the organs of a family member "in a way that encourages a positive response and does not impose distress on the survivors."[44]

With no set of rules designed to achieve this delicate balance, how can such a legal requirement as this be met?[45] As one organ transplant coordinator observed, "The consent rate when someone asks who does not want to ask, or does not know how to ask, is zero."[46] Thus, the reality of the situation is that unless negative incentives can be structured and then imposed on doctors or hospitals the net enforcement effect of required request laws will be viewed as little more than excessive hortatory language[47]—typical of so many congressional enactments.[48]

LIVING DONORS

Since World War II, in the United States live donors have been used as sources for organ and tissue transplantation running the gamut from blood and bone marrow to kidneys.[49] Interestingly, while no adult can be forced—without giving a mature, informed consent—to donate any organ, a minor, mental incompetent, or prisoner has traditionally not been accorded this option.[50] The case law in the United States, although lacking in any unified rationale, does evidence three bases for testing the validity of the application for a compulsory, nonconsensual donation.[51]

Under one test, the court inquires whether the donation would be in the best interests of the donor, with no relevance being given to any measure of sympathy for the proposed recipient of the family.[52] The second test is one of substituted judgment, where the court speculates how the minor (if mature or competent) would decide relative to the request to donate.[53] But this act of speculation is not flippant or inconsequential; rather, the court seeks to make a decision utilizing the same motive and considerations as would move the incompetent himself. In this regard, then, the test of substituted judgment does not deviate from adherence to the ethical principle of respect for persons. Indeed, it has been suggested that this very principle recognizes that one's welfare, rightly understood, may well depend on an act that helps others.[54] An absolutist approach to this principle of respect, however, would allow for no compromise of any nature.[55] The third test utilizes a judicial review of whatever parental decision has been made here, with the court accepting in principle the importance of the parental position yet, without accepting any correlative duty to the donor, weighing the entire family dilemma, making an ultimate decision based on achieving a balance of family interests.[56]

Ethical Concerns

Some argue ethically and morally that all intrafamilial donations should be prohibited simply because of the coercive forces operating within the family unit which, hypothetically, could justify the need for requiring an incompetent healthy sibling to make a forced organ donation to a competent, unhealthy brother or sister.[57] If such a scenario were in fact to be written, no destructive harm to the particular family unit would occur. Indeed, just the opposite would happen, for the unit would be preserved and strengthened by such a donation. At a minimum, the factors that constitute a valid consent should be defined with as much precision as possible, recognizing as such that there is an enormous factual difference between a family member authorizing tissue removal from the body of a deceased relative and, on the other hand, from a living relative.[58]

There are other ethical and social considerations raised regarding organ transplants from living donors. One simply finds such actions to be inherently immoral.[59] This idea builds on the belief that the general ethical principle that life should always be preserved and that one should never seek his own destruction nor endanger in any way his own life except as an expression of love for another.[60] Commerce in human body parts, it is maintained, also acts to restrict free will and individual autonomy. This, in turn, is buttressed by the view that in harming oneself by deliberately undergoing tissue removal, one may well indeed harm society by later becoming sick or enfeebled and thus a burden on it.[61] Abstract moral principles and concerns of this nature must give way to the realities and the needs of contemporary society[62] and not stand as roadblocks to the maintenance of actual life.

Utilitarian Reality

The counterutilitarian argument to these moral-ethical concerns states that any absolute prohibition on the use of organs from minors or incompetents is unjustified[63]—this in light of the fact that donations from such classes restore health and renew life to others, and they do this without jeopardizing or ending the lives of the donors. Where the risks from the donation to the minor, incompetent, or incarcerated prisoner are minimal or even if substantial—yet much less than the harm that would occur to an individual donee deprived of the benefits of sustained living—organ transplantations should be undertaken.[64]

ADDITIONAL SCHEMES AND PROCEDURES

Presently in the United States, the prevailing system for organ donation is one of presumed non consent; in other words, one is presumed "unwilling" to be an organ donor at death unless her or his family gives permission.[65] As noted, this scheme is failing to generate sufficient resources for transplantation; thus new approaches must be evaluated and then implemented.

Postmortem Examinations

One such approach was first proposed in 1968 and simply calls for compulsory postmortem examinations to determine the salvageability of cadaveric organs.[66] As such, autopsies would be done routinely, not, as now, performed only when requested by the decedent's family or as a consequence of violent death under suspicious circumstances. The postmortem examinations and autopsies would be carried out in all cases as long as they did not interfere with homicide investigations, and the dying person or his next of kin would be allowed to object to such procedures and give contra instructions thereby opting out.[67]

Right of First Refusal

A more contemporaneous suggestion has been to design and implement a system wherein persons who object to forced donations of this type could refuse to participate in a manner wholly consistent with individual patient and/or family sensitivities yet is both efficient and cost-effective and also meets the plethora of religious, ethical, and legal requirements of informed consent.[68] This suggestion, as engrafted on to the basic approach, is very sensitive and seeks to balance personal attitudes with the demands of a market society. Perhaps, in fact, the suggestion is too broad in its focus and seeks too wide an accommodation of personal interests. In any event, considerable more research must be undertaken to test its practical feasibility.[69]

Escheatage

A more expanded version of the compulsory postmortem examination and autopsy retrieval approach is seen in escheatage.[70] Although viewed as immoral by some authorities in the United States, as a system promoting recognition of the state's inherent right of ownership in the bodies of all its citizens unless otherwise specified by the citizen or its family,[71] escheatage is being utilized by some fourteen European countries as a means of combatting the shortage of donor organs.[72] In practice, the state simply delegates its ownership rights to licensed physicians who are thereby authorized to harvest and allocate salvageable organs to compatible donees.[73] Here is an example of utilitarianism at its highest order. Yet the practice has been analogized to both slavery and totalitarianism![74]

The social policy against escheatage in America is found rather simply in a recognition of the sacredness of the body in life and death and not regarding it as a form of collective personal property disposable at will by the state upon death. But, as dead bodies are recognized more and more as valuable sources of life, through the harvesting of their organs for the living, perhaps with time a definition of their status as property will of necessity be forced on all sophisticated societies in the world community.[75] Yet, even in countries where escheatage is in place, there is a natural reluctance among medical personnel to dismember their former patients' bodies whom they heretofore have worked to sustain life without an actual consent from next of kin; this, even though the state, through escheatage, has adopted a policy of presumed consent.[76] This attitude then, together with the high level of emotionalism rather than rationalism being exhibited on this issue in the United States, means that it is doubtful whether the system would have a real potential for successful adoption.

ADDITIONAL MECHANISMS
A Futures Market

Two other mechanisms are also available for consideration: the development of a futures market[77] and a standard death benefit payment.[78] The two central obstacles to implementation of these mechanisms are the need to (1) either repeal or amend present state and federal legislation that prohibits the sale or purchase of human organs[79] and (2) overcome the pervasive reluctance among physicians to seize the initiative at the appropriate moment and make timely inquiries regarding consent to undertake harvesting.[80] To resolve this second obstacle, it has been suggested that tort law be reshaped in such a way as to acknowledge a new standard of care with regards to a patient's body. Accordingly, should physicians fail to determine whether a patient has signified an organ sales contract, to preserve a cadaver for subsequent harvesting, or to inform the proper organ procurement agency of its status, liability would be imposed on the physicians to the estate of the deceased for the value of his organs.[81]

Under a futures market, an individual would enter into a prospective contingent sale of his own organs.[82] Proposed as such, a futures market would be only a small modification of the current system of contingent organ donation. Accordingly, individuals could be presented with an opportunity to execute a contract for the sale of their organs when they received a driver's license, bought insurance, answered a specific solicitation for organ donation through the mail, or, for that matter, stood on a street corner.[83] The main difference with this proposal from the present system would be that the seller-donor would be promised remuneration, primarily at death. Functioning along the lines of the National Organ Procurement and Transplantation Network, pertinent donor information, including any limitations imposed on which organs were harvestable, would be fed into a computer and accessed by telephone.[84]

Organ Sales Contracts

While payment at death for those organs harvested successfully would be the most efficient, two other payment systems would be available: under one, at the time of execution of the organ sales contract, a vendor could be paid a fee for all of his organs made available at death; or under another scheme, an executory contract could be entered into by both vendor and vendee, specifying that the vendor's estate or designated person would be paid a set fee for the cadaver whether or not upon examination at death the organs were determined harvestable.[85] Of central concern regarding the second scheme—payment at the time of contracting—would be the necessity to develop a monitoring system whereby individual sellers were not able to enter into multiple contracts for the sale of their body parts.[86] It has been suggested that the donor fee could be set at $5,000 for each major organ (e.g., liver, kidney, heart), with lower amounts for blood, skin bone marrow, corneas, and pituitary glands.[87] If, for example, married male donors could be educated to the fact that the contract for the sale of their organs at death had the effect of being a form of supplemental life insurance policy with a payoff as high as $30,000, it is thought many such men would sign on as donors.[88]

Death Benefit Payments

The final economic mechanism for obtaining organs for transplantation has been a standard death benefit payment of $1,000.[89] This would be paid by presently operating organ procurement organizations to the families of the organ donors; ideally it would not be viewed as coercive in any way but rather only motivational.[90] The amount and the source of the benefit would be controlled strictly by law thereby hopefully continuing the prohibition on bartering for organs.[91] Under this proposal, any organ obtained, regardless of whether the donor family accepted the death benefit payment, would enter the national organ allocation system where all donee-recipients are registered and treated alike and where allocations are made, in turn, on matching medical need and period of time waiting.[92]

Of course for this proposal to be adopted without any real or implied complications, as with the futures market itself, the illegality of such payments presently set forth in the NOTA and the Uniform Anatomical Gift Act of 1987 would have to be amended to allow administration of this one-time death benefit to a donor family.[93] Since these present laws allow reasonable payments to be made to those who participate in the actual harvesting of the human organs for transplantation (e.g., surgeons, hospital staff involved in donor care) why, it may be asked, should not a similar reasonable payment be allowed to the family members of the donor, who, next to the donor himself are the most important participants in the process of harvesting and transplantation.[94]

CLINICAL OPTIONS
The Pittsburgh Protocol

Brain-dead patients, termed "heart-beating cadaver donors" (HBCDs), exhibit no brain function, but their hearts are kept beating in order to maintain perfusion of their vital organs.[95] These donors are typically victims of automobile accidents or gunshot wounds to the head. Ironically, as the demand for transplantable organs increases, the pool of HBCDs are decreasing as a result of the implementation of strict automobile safety and gun control legislation.[96] As the availability of organs from HBCDs dwindles, physicians have begun to look to other groups for the needed organs.

In an attempt to satisfy the growing demand for donor organs, or at least contain the growing crisis, the University of Pittsburgh Medical Center approved a protocol which allows patients who would not otherwise qualify as HBCDs because they have some brain function, to nevertheless donate their organs if they or their surrogates so choose.[97] These patients, known as non-heart-beating cadaver donors (NHBCDs), are taken off life-support equipment at a predetermined time in an operating room.[98] The donors are declared dead at the "irreversible cessation of cardiopulmonary function," and after two minutes their organs are then immediately harvested.[99]

The protocol is applicable where the prospective donors cannot otherwise qualify as organ donors by the now traditional neurological criteria. These patients range from those who have full use of their mental faculties but suffer from various degenerative neurological or cardiopulmonary diseases that leave them respirator dependent to others who are terminally brain injured but nevertheless have sufficient neurological function to disqualify them as HBCD candidates.[100] After the patients or their surrogates (who are entrusted to act in the best interest of the patient) make known their desire to forego further life-sustaining treatment, and their desire to donate their organs, the attending physician may discuss the possibility of withdrawing treatment within the controlled environment of an operating room.[101] Two minutes after the heart stops beating, the patient is declared dead and the organs are harvested.[102] NHBCD organs acquired in this manner are without perfusion for only a short period of time. Warm ischemia time is greatly reduced, and the available evidence indicates that organs thus obtained are as viable as those from HBCDs.[103]

A fundamental question in determining whether the Pittsburgh protocol may be maintained as an ethical means of increasing the pool of organ donors is whether the patients or their surrogates knowingly submitted to the procedure. Was consent given as part of an informed decision-making process, or was it obtained through coercion or the withholding of necessary information?

The protocol provides numerous measures to ensure patient autonomy.[104] Foremost is that the physician cannot initiate discussion about the removal of life-sustaining equipment.[105] He may only discuss the steps outlined in the protocol after the patient manifests a desire to be free of artificial life support in conjunction with desire to become an organ donor.[106] Moreover, the protocol provides that decisions involving patient management are to be made prior to and separate from discussion of the procedure.[107]

The protocol mandates full disclosure of all information regarding the decision to forego artificial life support.[108] The physician must inform all involved parties regarding the procedures for removing life sustaining therapies and specifically the organ procurement process for NHBDs' acknowledge that organs will not be harvested until the patient is pronounced dead, and further advise the concerned parties that consent for the procedure itself may be withdrawn at any time.[109]

Furthermore, the Pittsburgh protocol minimizes the perception that patients may have been coerced in their decision by providing that the physician responsible for the withdrawal of life support cannot be involved in the harvesting or transplant procedure.[110] Similarly, physicians involved with the transplant procedure may not be involved in patient management prior to the death of the donor.[111] Finally, in addition to the conceptual separation of patient management from the transplant procedure, the protocol goes so far as to recommend the physical separation of the treating physician from the transplant team and that the transplant surgeon not be present in the operating room until after the patient is declared dead.[112] The personal interests of the physicians, as well as any institutional bias resulting from a perceived need to maintain a reputation or increase revenue, are thus effectively nullified.

The Loyola Protocol

Under a protocol approved by the Loyola University Medical Center, as well as several other hospitals, physicians are allowed, at death, to infuse the cadaver with a preservative fluid without obtaining consent from the family of the dead person. The fluid preserves the vital organs for an adequate period of time long enough to allow discussion with the family and formal consent for organ donation. Interestingly, to date, no organs obtained from this protocol have been actually transplanted. Rather, the protocol was designed to test the feasibility of harvesting under these specific circumstances and the manner in which families would respond.[113]

Criticism of both the Pittsburgh and Loyola protocols as "rationalized cannibalism" are nothing but appeals to unrestrained emotionalism and neglect totally the immense practical value of these rational and ethically balanced approaches to problem solving. These two protocols are not definitive solutions to a grave societal problem. Rather, they should be viewed as but prisms through which the complex issue of the procurement of organs for transplant may be analyzed further.[114]

ETHICAL, MORAL AND RELIGIOUS CONCERNS

As might be expected, various ethical, moral, and religious concerns have been raised to these market mechanisms designed to increase the supply of harvestable organs for purposes of transplantation.[115] Chief and foremost has been the financial vulnerability of the poor to being pressured into becoming "forced" donors, forced by their own circumstances and coerced by enticement of affluent buyers.[116] Other concerns are whether a commercial market would enhance opportunities for suicides and murders[117] and promote harvesting of the organs of anencephalic infants before actual death.[118] Those religious views and traditions that regard the body as a gift of God and man's rights in it as merely those of a steward with no correlative rights of ownership would include a prohibition on the sale of body parts and would thus be in direct conflict with these market mechanisms.[119]

These fears are understandable. However, while it is recognized that commercial profit making with nonrelated donors may have a tendency to promote an exploitation of those who are financially vulnerable, and may lead to progressive abuses and self-degradations, it is argued here that death payments benefits cannot be properly viewed as morally objectionable. This is simply because the verifiable benefits of sustained life that accrue to participating donees of noncommercial organ sales outweigh the moral fears or costs of using this mechanism as an inducement for stimulating the market for transplantable organs.[120]

Utilitarian Versus Egalitarian Allocative Standards

The search for rational and principled standards of apportionment of scarce resources is and will remain a vexatious problem for decades to come. Informal "rules of thumb" cannot be countenanced. Of course, one way to avoid totally the problem of distribution is to avoid using the scarce medical resource altogether. But this would mean certain death to the countless thousands of transplant hopefuls.

Both in the formation of the transplantation waiting list and the actual distribution of donated organs, there is, however, a consensus that the primary criterion operable at both stages should be medical: that is, medical need and probability of success. Intense debate focuses rather on whether these medical criteria should be defined broadly or narrowly (i.e., the relevance of factors such as age, lifestyle, and probability of success measured by a qualitative survival).[121] Rehabilitation or salvageability, consistent with basic principles of triage, is also of relevance.[122]

Since the law provides at present no uniformly agreed-upon principles that may be applied in order to regulate the allocation of scarce medical resources (e.g., cadaveric and human organs), current medical practice draws upon a structure for decision making evolved as such from a number of philosophical and ethical constructs. There are five utilitarian principles of application that are operative in the hierarchy of triage: the principles of medical success, immediate usefulness, conservation, parental role, and general social value.[123]

Decisional Operatives

Translated as such into decisional operatives, there emerges a recognition that priority of selection for use of a scarce medical resource should be accorded to those for whom treatment has the highest probability of medical success or would be most useful under the immediate circumstances, that is, to those candidates for use who require proportionally smaller amounts of particular resource or to those having the largest responsibilities to dependents or to those believed to have the greater actual or potential general social worth. The utilitarian goal is, simply stated, to achieve the highest possible amount of some good or resource. Thus, utilitarian principles are also commonly referred to as "good maximizing strategies."[124]

Egalitarian alternatives, on the contrary, seek either a basic maintenance or a restoration of equality for persons in need of a particular scarce resource. There are five basic principles utilized here: (1) the principle of saving no one; thus priority is given to no one because, simply, none should be saved if not all can be saved; (2) the principle of medical neediness under which priority is accorded to those determined to be the medically neediest; (3) the principle of general neediness which allows priority to be given to the most helpless or generally neediest; (4) the principle of queuing, where priority is given to those individuals who arrive first;

and (5) the principles of random selection, where priority of selection is given to those selected by pure chance.[125]

To the utilitarian, maximizing utility and hence what is diffusely referred to as the "general welfare" are both the primary ground and subject of all judgments. That which is required in order to maximize utility overall may thus infringe upon an individual's own entitlement of rights to particular goods. Accordingly, moral rights are either rejected generally or recognized as certainly not absolute.[126]

Philosophy and religion may well provide us all with the necessary balance and direction for life and allow us to develop an ethic for daily living and a faith as to the future. The basic challenge of modern medicine should be, simply, to seek, promote, and maintain a level of real—and, when the case may indicate, potential—achievement for its user-patients which allows for full and purposeful living. Indeed, man himself should seek to pursue decision-making responsibilities and exercise autonomy in a rational manner and guided by a spirit of humanism. He should seek, further, to minimize human suffering and maximize the social good. Defining the extent and application of the social good will vary obviously with each case.

CONCLUSIONS

Thus far, it has been seen that voluntary donations of cadaveric organs have been an ineffective means of tackling the crisis in organ transplantation, and the same is true of the required request provisions of the federal legislation in 1987. Under current federal and state legislative directives, sale of human organs is prohibited. Compulsory postmortem examinations and retrievals bear a close resemblance to recognizing a new collective property right by the government, through escheatage, in all the dead bodies of its citizens. Strong antigovernment sentiments against intrusiveness into issues of privacy and autonomy, when combined with equally strong moral, religious and ethical attitudes about the sacredness of the body, will preclude these two mechanisms from ever being adopted successfully in America.

The development of a futures market, although fraught with two major obstacles, as observed, nonetheless bears further study and testing. Perhaps the most attractive of all the suggested mechanisms is the standard death benefit—simply because of its noncommercial focus. But, as with the futures market option, present laws in the United States would surely have to be re-written or amended regarding present prohibitions against the sale of organs to make certain such one-time death benefit payments would be allowed. As well, harvesting physicians will have to be educated to the needs allowed. As well, harvesting physicians will have to be educated to the needs (or legal "rights") of their living patients to "prosper" from dead ones. Education on a massive scale in both public and private sectors is called for here.

Instead of trying to develop new and innovative approaches to organ retrieval, it has been suggested that more emphasis be placed on promoting voluntary, altruistic donations and ensuring the access to transplants is fair and the process for assisting transplant recipients to pay for their new organs is equitable. Indeed, the suggestion is even carried further urging public funding of transplants for the poor as well as establishing specific reimbursements policies for not only the costs of pretransplant evaluation, food, baby-sitters, travel, and housing for prospective patients but all economic assistance for those who are unable to work posttransplant.[127]

These are noble sentiments and set a broadly defined philosophical goal to total equality of opportunity. Yet these concerns are but one facet of the most central problem here: developing a reliable (market) mechanism for assuring a ready supply of cadaveric organs for ready transplantation. Once this mechanism is set, remedial problems can be tackled. Some type of informed consensus must soon be reached in any event that develops a new mechanism for retrieving organs if, that is, the preservation of human life is to be advanced and not paralyzed by social taboos. Stated otherwise, "If human lives are to be saved, the agony of hard choices cannot be avoided."[128] In the final analysis, then, a price—economic, social, legal, ethical, moral, or religious—*must* be set in determining the allocative process for organ retrieval and transplantation, and market mechanisms would appear to be the most functional and objective tool for achieving this. Forced altruism, nurtured as such through the pursuit of lofty educational goals, does not have a practical history for dealing with the problems of the day. Perhaps the words from the book of Deuteronomy provide both a contemporary and useful ethic to utilize here: "I have set before you life and death, blessing and curse; therefore choose life, that you and your descendants may live."[129]

NOTES

1. Rivers et al., *Organ and Tissue Procurement in Acute Care Settings: Principles and Practices*, 19 ANNALS EMERGENCY MED. 78 (1990).

2. Peters, *Life, or Death: The Issue of Payment in Cadaveric Organ Donation*, 265 J.A.M.A. 1302 (1991).

The United Network for Organ Sharing reported in 1996 that transplants increased by almost 50 percent from 1988 through 1994, when they totaled 18,270. Yet, organ donations increased by merely 37 percent (from 5,908 to 8,114) causing the number of patients on the waiting list to more than double. Consequently, in early February 1996 there were 44,000 patients on the waiting list. Interestingly, those who have received transplanted organs are surviving longer—with as many as 94.3 percent of them living three years with a transplanted kidney and 74.4 percent living three years with a transplanted heart. Auerbach, *infra* note 14.

3. Cohen, *Increasing the Supply of Transplant Organs: The Virtues of a Futures Market*, 58 GEO. WASH. UNIV. L. REV. 1 (1989). In all, some twenty-five body parts and fluids have been transplanted from cadavers to humans including parts of the inner ear, various glands, nerves, tendons, cartilage, and some. *Id.* at 3.

4. *Id.* at 5.

5. *Id.* Other figures suggest that each year some 29,999 harvestable cadavers are available. *Id.*

6. Hansman, *The Economics and Ethics of Markets for Human Organs*, 14 J. HEALTH, POLITICS, POL'Y & L. 57 (1989).

7. Cohen, *supra* note 3.

8. Hansman, *supra* note 6 at 58.

One potential market is to be found with animal transplants. In order to provide some necessary regulation for development of xenotransplantation, the Centers for Disease Control and Prevention of the National Institutes of Health issued proposed guidelines in September 1996. The guidelines seek to provide balance between the promise xenotransplantation and its potential perils and to prevent infection in transplantation. The guidelines cover a broad range of therapies from whole organ procedures—as with baboon heart transplants—to less-known treatments for diabetes using modified cells from cattle, pigs, and other animals. Draft Public Health Service, Guidelines on Infectious Disease, Issues in Xenotransplantation (Aug. 1996), Part IV, 61 Fed. Reg. 49920 (Sept. 23, 1996).

See generally Mark, *All Animals Are Equal, but Some Are Better Than Others: Patenting Transgenic Animals*, 7 J. CONTEMP. HEALTH L. & POL'Y 245 (1991).

9. D. MATHIEU, ORGAN SUBSTITUTION TECHNOLOGY 34 (1988).

10. Colburn, *Changing the Life-and-Death Rules for Transplants*, WASH. POST HEALTH, June 15, 1993, at 10.

11. Hoffmaster, *Freedom to Choose and Freedom to Lose: The Procurement of Cadaver Organs for Transplantation*, 17 TRANSPLANTATION PROC. 24, 29 (1985).

12. Caplin, *Commentary on Cohen*, 5 CLINICAL TRANSPLANTATION 467, 472 (1991); Caplin, *Problems in the Policies and Criteria Used to Allocate Organs for Transplantation in the United States*, 21 TRANSPLANTATION PROC. 338 (1989).

13. Naylor, *The Role of the Family in Cadaveric Organs Procurement*, 65 IND. U.L.J. 167 (1989).

14. Callender, *Organ Donation in the Black Population: Where Do We Go from Here?* 19 TRANSPLANTATION PROC. 36 (1987); Murray, *Morally Obligated to Make Gifts of Our Bodies?* 1 HEALTH MATRIX 19 (1991); Mannien & Evans, *Public Attitudes and Behavior Regarding Organ Donations*, 253 J.A.M.A. 311 (1985).

In February 1996 the U.S. Scientific Registry of Transplant Recipients and the Organ Procurement and Transplantation Registry reported the number of African-American donors increased 29 percent between 1988 and 1994, while donations by Hispanics increased 32 percent to 8.2 percent of all donations and Asians reached 1.8 percent. Auerbach, *Organ Donations by Minorities Rise*, WASH. POST HEALTH Mag., Feb. 27, 1996, at 7.

15. R. SCOTT, THE BODY AS PROPERTY, 6, 7 (1981).

16. *Id.*

17. *Id.* at 11.

18. *Id.* at 8.

19. *Id.* at 11, 12.

20. 8(a) UNIF. LAWS ANN. §§22-23 (Supp. 1991).

21. *Id.*

22. Stason, *The Uniform Anatomical Gift Act*, 23 BUS. LAWYER 919, 928 (1968).

23. Vestal, Jaber & Shoemaker, *Medico-legal Aspects of Tissue Transplantation*, 18 U. DETROIT L.J. 271 (1954); Calabresi, *Do We Own Our Bodies?* 1 HEALTH MATRIX 5 (1991).

24. *Id.*

25. *Id.*

26. Delaware, Hawaii, Oklahoma, Nevada, and New York. Cohen, *supra* note 3 at 7.

27. Hansman, *supra* note 6 at 59.

28. Cohen, *supra* note 3 at 7.

29. Mississippi still allows its citizens the right to sell their body parts to hospitals—with delivery to be effectuated after death. MISS. CODE ANN. § 41-39-9 (Supp. 1988).

30. Cohen, *supra* note 3 at 8.

31. Mehlman, *Presumed Consent to Organ Donation: A Re-evaluation*, 1 HEALTH MATRIX 31, 33 (1991).

32. *Id.* at 23.

33. *Id.*

34. 42 U.S. CODE §§273-274(c) (Supp. IV, 1986).

35. *Id. See* §273 note, §273(a), §274(b)(2). Violation of the act carries with it a fine of $50,000 or a five-year jail sentence or both. See §274(b)(2). The sale of blood, as a bodily substance, had had a ready market by hospitals and commercial blood banks for years. Dukeminier, *Supplying Organs for Transplantation*, 68 MICH. L. REV. 811, 847 (1970).

36. Hansman, *supra* note 6 at 59. Doubt has been expressed that intrastate sales would escape federal scrutiny. Cohen, *supra* note 3 at 8.

37. Scott, *Death unto Life: Anencephalic Infants as Organ Donors,* 74 VA. L. REV. 1527 (1988).

38. 42 U.S. Code §§ 273-274(c) (Supp. IV, 1986).

39. 42 U.S. Code §§ 1320(b)-8(a)(1)(A), 1302(b)-8(a)(1)(A)(ii) (Supp. IV, 1986).

40. Caplan & Welvang, *Are Required Request Laws Working? Altruism and the Procurement of Organs and Tissues*, 3 CLIN. TRANSPLANTATION 170 (1989); Colburn, *Organ Donations Hinge on Survivor's Consent*, WASH. POST HEALTH Mag., July 4, 1995, at 7.

41. Caplan & Welvang, *supra* note 40 at 170.

42. *Id.*

43. *Id.*

44. Cohen, *supra* note 3 at 22.

45. *Id.*

46. Caplan & Welvang, *supra* note 41.

47. Cohen, *supra* note 3 at 21.

48. Caplan, *Assume Nothing: The Current State of Cadaver Organs and Tissue Donation in the United States*, 1 J. TRANSPLANTATION COORDINATION 78 (1991).

49. SCOTT, *supra* note 15 at Ch. 5. W. WADLINGTON, J. WALTZ & R. DWORKIN, CASES AND MATERIALS ON LAW & MEDICINE 945-962 (1980).

50. SCOTT, *supra* note 15 at 121.

51. *See Little v. Little*, 574 S. W.2d 493 (Ct. App. Tex. 1979); *McFall v. Shimp*, (No. 78-17711, Equity), C.P. Allegheny County, Pa. (July 26, 1978); *Strunk v. Strunk*, 445 S.W.2d 145 (Ky. 1969).

52. SCOTT, *supra* note 15 at 116-20.

53. Robertson, *Organ Donations by Incompetents and the Substituted Judgment Doctrine*, 76 COLUM. L. REV. 48 (1976).

54. *Id.* at 71.

55. *Id.* at 51.

56. SCOTT, *supra* note 15 at 120-22.

57. *Id.* at 122. Interestingly, a father whose daughter is in need of a kidney may donate one of his kidneys–with no societal or legal retribution. Yet, if the daughter were in dire medical circumstances and in need of immediate surgery for which the father was unable to pay, by law, he would be penalized and considered a criminal if he sought to sell one of his kidneys in order to defray the costs of his daughter's illness. *See* Kinsley, *Take My Kidney, Please,* TIME Mag., Mar. 13, 1989, at 88.

58. *Id.* at 137.

59. *Id.* at 183.

60. *Id.*

61. *Id.* at 184.

62. Dukeminier, *supra* note 35 at 857-63.

63. Robertson, *supra* note 53 at 50.

64. *Id.* at 50-51.

65. Mehlman, *supra* note 31 at 31.

66. Sanders & Dukeminier, *A Proposal for Routine Salvaging of Cadaver Organs*, 279 NEW ENG. J. MED. 413 (1968).

67. Dukeminier, *supra* note 35 at 842 passim.

68. Mehlman, *supra* note 31 at 44-62, 66.

69. *Id.* at 66.

70. Cohen, *supra* note 3 at 15-21.

71. *Id.* The National Organ Transplant Task Force, in particular, inveighed against the immortality of the system.

72. Norrie, *Human Tissue Transplants: Legal Liability in Different Jurisdictions*, 34 INT'L & COMP. L. Q. 442, 460-461 (1985). The countries subscribing to this in 1985 were: Austria, the then Czechoslovakia, Denmark, Finland, Greece, Hungary, Italy, Norway, Poland, Spain, Sweden, Switzerland, and the then West Germany. *Id.* at 460-61.

After three years of debate, Japan passed new legislation which specifies that brain death will be recognized only for purposes of transplantation. Kageyama, *Japan Redefines Death to Assist in Transplants,* WASH. POST, June 18, 1997, at A20.

73. Cohen, *supra* note 3 at 15.

In 1992 the District of Columbia Council passed a law allowing a medical examiner to authorize open-heart surgery for the removal of heart valves from corpses without seeking permission from their families. Additionally, some fourteen states (together with the District of Columbia) allow removal of corneas from autopsied corpses without previous familial consent. Squires, *Transplant Tug-of-War: D.C. Official Objects to Law Allowing Heart-Valve Removal from Corpses*, WASH. POST HEALTH Mag., Nov. 23, 1993, at 7.

74. Cohen, *supra* note 3 at 16.

75. *Id.* at 17.

76. Cohen, *The Ethical Value of a Future Market in Cadaveric Organs* in ORGAN REPLACEMENT THERAPY: ETHICS, JUSTICE AND COMMERCE at 302 (W. Land & J. B. Dossetor eds. 1991).

77. Cohen, *supra* note 3 at 1; Hansman, *supra* note 6.

78. Peters, *Life or Death: The Issue of Payment in Cadaveric Organ Donation*, 265 J.A.M.A. 1302 (1991); Harvey, *Paying Organ Donors*, 16 J. MED. ETHICS 117 (1990). Another alternative to direct compensation for organs would be a promise of free medical care and assistance given to the organ donor for either a period of years or life for any or all subsequent diseases or disabilities arising from the removal of an organ. Dukeminier, *supra* note 35 at 848.

79. Hansman, *supra* note 6 at 59.

80. Cohen, *supra* note 76 at 308-09.

81. *Id.*

82. Cohen, *supra* note 3 at 32-33. Presently, two countries–Brazil and India–tolerate markets in body parts. Caplan & Welvang, *supra* note 40 at 170.

83. Cohen, *supra* note 3 at 33.

84. *Id.*

85. *Id.*

86. *Id.*

87. *Id.* at 35.

88. *Id.*

89. Peters, *supra* note 78.

Professor Gary S. Becker, a Nobel Laureate at the University of Chicago, has suggested that monetary inducements be made by the Federal government in order to obtain human organs, upon death, for transplantation. Becker, *How Uncle Sam*

Could Ease the Organ Shortage, BUSINESS WEEK, Jan. 20, 1997, at 18.

90. *Id.*

91. *Id.* at 1304.

92. *Id.* at 1303.

93. *Id.* at 1304.

94. *Id.*

95. Arnold & Younger, *Back to the Future: Obtaining Organs from Non-Heart-Beating Cadavers*, 3 KENNEDY INST. ETHICS J. 103 (1993).

The American Medical Association held in 1995 that anencephalic infants may be considered as potential organ donors even though their lives have not been terminated under the current definition of death—this, because they have never experienced consciousness and never will. Alternatively, ventilator assistance may be provided until a determination of death can be made in accordance with current medical standards. This new position is a shift from an earlier 1988 position holding that only after an anencephalic's death was it acceptable to remove organs. Council on Ethical and Judicial Affairs, American Medical Association, *The Use of Anencephalic Neonates as Organ Donors*, 273 J.A.M.A. 1614 (1995).

96. Colburn, *supra* note 10.

97. University of Pittsburgh Medical Center Policy and Procedure Manual reprinted in 3 KENNEDY INST. ETHICS J. App. A-1 (1993).

98. *Id.*

99. *Id.*

100. Younger & Arnold, *Ethical, Psychological and Public Policy Implications of Procuring Organs from Non-Heart-Beating Cadaver Donors*, 269 J.A.M.A. 2769, 2772 (1993).

101. DeVitta & Snyder, *Development of the University of Pittsburgh Medical Center Policy for the Care of Terminally Ill Patients Who May Become Organ Donors After Death Following the Removal of Life Support*, 3 KENNEDY INST. ETHICS J. 131 (1993).

102. *Id.* at 132.

103. Young & Arnold, *supra* note 100 at 2770.

104. DeVitta & Snyder, *supra* note 101.

105. *Id.*

106. *Id.*

107. *Id.*

108. University of Pittsburgh Medical Center Policy and Procedure Manual, *supra* note 97.

109. *Id.*

110. *See generally* Burdick, *Potential Conflicts of Interest Generated by the Use of Non-Heart-Beating Cadavers*, 3 KENNEDY INST. ETHICS J. 199 (1993).

111. *Id.*

112. *Id.*

113. *Supra* note 10.

See Weiss, *Demand for Organs Fosters Aggressive Collection Methods: In*

D.C. Consent Not Required before Transplant Preparation, WASH. POST, Nov. 24, 1997, at 1.

114. *Id.*

115. Childress, *Some Moral Connections Between Organ Procurement and Organ Distribution*, 3 J. CONTEMP. HEALTH L. & POL'Y 85 (1987).

See also R. A. EPSTEIN, MORTAL PERIL: OUR INALIENABLE RIGHT TO HEALTH CARE 281-82 (1997).

116. Harvey, *supra* note 78 at 117.

Moralisms (or assimilated moral and political rights) often act in a way to prohibit organ selling. Radin, *Market-Inalienability*, 100 HARV. L. REV. 1864 (1987).

117. Cohen, *supra* note 3 at 40-43.

118. Scott, *supra* note 15.

119. Caplan, *Commentary on Cohen, supra* note 12.

120. Harvey, *supra* note 78 at 118.

Some fear the slippery slope of commercializing organ sales will lead to personal discomfort, insult, degradation, or loss of value because bodily integrity will have become a fungible object. Radin, *supra* note 116 at 1881. Others are more positivistic and view the slope as leading to a totally free market economy where everything scarce and desired is ownable and saleable (or commodified). R. POSNER, ECONOMIC ANALYSIS OF LAW 29-33 (1977).

121. G. P. SMITH, II, THE NEW BIOLOGY: LAW, ETHICS AND BIOTECHNOLOGY (1989).

122. Smith, *Triage: Endgame Realities*, 1 J. CONTEMP. HEALTH L. & POL'Y 23 (1985).

The organization charged with coordinating transplant policy—the United Network for Organ Sharing—has determined that those with chronic liver disease induced, as such, by hepatitis or alcohol, no longer qualify for status one priority on waiting lists for transplants. U.S.A. TODAY, Nov. 15, 1996, at 1. *See also* Weiss, *Who Should Get Liver Transplants*, WASH. POST, Dec. 9, 1996 at 1; Weiss, *Group Proposes Rules to Revise Priorities for Organ Transplants,* WASH. POST, June 26, 1997, at A3.

123. *Id.* The three pivotal values that come into focus in any decisional process involving tragic choices are efficiency, honesty, and equal treatment—with most societies giving precedence to the conception of equality. G. CALABRESI & P. BOBBITT, TRAGIC CHOICES at 24-25 (1978).

124. SMITH, *supra* note 121. *See* Pellegrino, *Rationing Health Care: The Ethics of Gatekeeping*, 2 J. CONTEMP. HEALTH L & POL'Y 23 (1986).

125. SMITH, *supra* note 121 at Ch. 5.

126. *Id.*

127. Caplan, *Commentary on Cohen, supra* note 12.

See generally ORGAN AND TISSUE DONATION: ETHICAL, LEAL AND POLICY ISSUES (B. Spielman ed. 1996).

128. Dukeminier, *supra* note 35.

129. Deuteronomy 30:19.

Selected Bibliography

Annas, G. J. STANDARD OF CARE: THE LAW OF AMERICAN BIOETHICS, 1993.

Berger, P. L., and Neuhas, R. J. TO EMPOWER PEOPLE: FROM STATE TO CIVIL SOCIETY, 1996.

Besharov, D., ed. PROTECTING CHILDREN FROM ABUSE AND NEGLECT: POLICY AND PRACTICE, 1988.

Blankenhorn, D. FATHERLESS AMERICA: CONFRONTING OUR MOST URGENT SOCIAL PROBLEM, 1995.

Bork, R. H. SLOUCHING TOWARDS GOMORRAH: MODERN LIBERALISM AND AMERICAN DECLINE, 1996.

Childress, J. F. WHO SHOULD DECIDE? PATERNALISM IN HEALTH CARE, 1982.

Clark, H. J., Jr. THE LAW OF DOMESTIC RELATIONSHIPS IN THE UNITED STATES, 2d ed. 1988.

Coutois, C. HEALING THE INCEST WOUND, 1988.

Devlin, P. THE ENFORCEMENT OF MORALS, 1965.

Donnerstein, E.; Linz, D.; and Penrod, S. THE QUESTION OF PORNOGRAPHY: RESEARCH FINDINGS AND POLICY IMPLICATIONS, 1987.

Downs, D. A. THE NEW POLITICS OF PORNOGRAPHY, 1990.

Dworkin, A. PORNOGRAPHY: MEN POSSESSING WOMEN, 1981.

Epstein, R. A. MORTAL PERIL: OUR INALIENABLE RIGHT TO HEALTH CARE?, 1997.

Farrell, W. THE MYTH OF MALE POWER: WHY MEN ARE THE DISPOSABLE SEX, 1993.

Furrow, B. R.; Johnson, S. H.; Jost, T. S.; and Schwartz, R. L. HEALTH CARE AND ETHICS, 1991.

Glendon, M. A. THE TRANSFORMATION OF FAMILY LAW: STATE, LAW AND FAMILY IN THE UNITED STATES AND WESTERN EUROPE, 1989.

Hart, H.L.A. LAW, LIBERTY AND MORALITY, 1963.

Heindenry, J. WHAT WILD ECASTY: THE RISE AND FALL OF THE SEXUAL REVOLUTION, 1997.

Hernstein, R. J., and MURRAY, C. THE BELL CURVE: INTELLIGENCE AND CLASS STRUCTURE IN AMERICAN LIFE, 1994.

Hughes, R. CULTURE OF COMPLAINT: THE FRAYING OF AMERICA, 1993.

Selected Bibliography

Hunter, I.; Saunders, D., and Williams, D. ON PORNOGRAPHY: LITERATURE, SEXUALITY AND OBSCENITY, 1993.

Ilfeld, F. and Lauer, R. SOCIAL NUDISM IN AMERICA, 1964.

Itzkoff, S. W. THE DECLINE OF INTELLIGENCE IN AMERICA: A STRATEGY FOR NATIONAL RENEWAL, 1994.

Klein, E. R. FEMINISM UNDER FIRE, 1996.

Kmiec, D. W. CEASE FIRE ON THE FAMILY, 1995.

Mathieu, D. ORGAN SUBSTITUTION TECHNOLOGY, 1988.

Mackinnon, C. A. TOWARD A FEMINIST THEORY OF THE STATE, 1989.

O'Carroll, T. PAEDOPHILIA: THE RADICAL CASE, 1980.

Posner, R. A. ECONOMIC ANALYSIS OF LAW, 4th ed., 1992.

Posner, R. A. SEX AND REASON, 1992.

Posner, R. A. OVERCOMING LAW, 1995.

Ragone, H. SURROGATE MOTHERHOOD: CONCEPTION IN THE HEART, 1994.

Reed, R. POLITICALLY INCORRECT: THE EMERGING FAITH FACTOR IN AMERICAN POLITICS, 1994.

Robertson, J. A. CHILDREN OF CHOICE: FREEDOM AND THE NEW REPRODUCTIVE TECHNOLOGY, 1994.

Scott, R. THE BODY AS PROPERTY, 1981.

Smith, G. P., II. GENETICS, ETHICS AND THE LAW, 1982.

Smith, G. P., II. THE NEW BIOLOGY: LAW, ETHICS AND BIOTECHNOLOGY, 1989.

Smith, G. P., II. BIOETHICS AND THE LAW: MEDICAL, SOCIO-LEGAL AND PHILOSOPHICAL DIRECTIONS FOR A BRAVE NEW WORLD, 1993.

Smith, G. P., II. LEGAL AND HEALTHCARE ETHICS FOR THE ELDERLY, 1996.

Spielman, B., ed. ORGAN AND TISSUE DONATION: ETHICAL, LEGAL AND LEGAL AND POLICY ISSUES, 1996.

Sullivan, A. VIRTUALLY NORMAL: AN ARGUMENT ABOUT HOMOSEXUALITY, 1995.

Tooley, M. ABORTION AND INFANTICIDE, 1983.

Twitchell, J. FORBIDDEN PARTNERS: THE INCEST TABOO IN MODERN CULTURE, 1987.

Veatch, R. M. DEATH, DYING AND THE BIOLOGICAL REVOLUTION, 1976.

Index

About the Author

GEORGE P. SMITH II is Professor of Law at The Catholic University of America, Washington, D.C. He is both nationally and internationally known as a lecturer and is a widely published and recognized legal scholar in the field of law, science, and medicine. He is the author of many books, including *Bioethics and the Law* (1993) and *Legal and Healthcare Ethics for the Elderly* (1996).

ISBN 0-275-96221-0

90000>

EAN

9 780275 962210

HARDCOVER BAR CODE